DATE DUE

Bridging the Gap:
Literary Theory in the Classroom

LOCUST HILL LITERARY STUDIES
NO. 17

Locust Hill Literary Studies

Bridging the Gap:

Literary Theory in the Classroom

edited by

J.M.Q. Davies

LOCUST HILL PRESS
West Cornwall, CT
1994

Library of Congress Cataloging-in-Publication Data

Bridging the gap : literary theory in the classroom / edited by J.M.Q.
Davies.
    373p.   cm. — (Locust Hill literary studies ; no. 17)
    Includes bibliographical references and index.
    ISBN 0-933951-60-4 : $38.00
    1. Criticism--Study and teaching. I. Davies, J. M. Q.
II. Series.
PN61.B75 1994
801'.95'0711--dc20   94-17926
                                               CIP

Printed on acid-free, 250-year-life paper
Manufactured in the United States of America

Contents

Notes on Contributors

Larry Anderson is Assistant Professor at Louisiana State University in Shreveport, where he co-directs a National Writing Project site. Besides his interest in the teaching of literature and composition, he is also researching the phenomenon of incubation.

Simon Barker is Senior Lecturer in the Department of Language and Literature at King Alfred's College, Winchester. He was educated at the University of Stirling in Scotland and at the University of Wales College of Cardiff. Author of numerous articles and reviews on early modern culture, he is currently preparing an international collection of essays on Shakespeare and an edition of the Caroline play, *'Tis Pity She's a Whore*.

J.M.Q. Davies is Senior Lecturer in English at the Northern Territory University in Darwin. His publications include *Blake's Milton Designs: The Dynamics of Meaning* (1993), a translation, *German Tales of Fantasy, Horror and the Grotesque* (1987), and articles in theoretical contexts on Jane Austen, Bulgakov, Tieck, and Patrick White.

Richard Freadman is Professor of English at La Trobe University. His publications include *Literature, Criticism and the Universities* (1983), *Eliot, James and the Fictional Self: A Study in Character and Narration* (1986), *On Literary Theory and Philosophy: A Cross-Disciplinary Encounter* (1991; co-edited with Lloyd Reinhardt); and *Re-Thinking Theory: A Critique of Contemporary Literary Theory and an Alternative Account* (1992; co-authored with Suemas Miller).

Gerald Graff, long an advocate of educational reform in the humanities, is George M. Pullman Professor of English at the University of Chicago. His books include *Literature Against Itself* (1979), *Professing Literature: An Institutional History* (1987), and *Beyond the Culture Wars* (1992).

David Jasper is Director of the Centre for the Study of Literature and Theology and a Senior Lecturer in English Literature and Biblical Studies at Glasgow University. He is Editor of the journal *Literature and Theology* and General Editor of the Macmillan series *Studies in Literature and Religion*. His most recent book is *Rhetoric, Power and Community* (1992).

Stephen Knight is Professor of English at Simon de Montfort University, Leicester, and until recently held the Chair of Medieval Studies at the University of Melbourne. He is the author of *Arthurian Literature and Society* (1983), *Form and Ideology in Crime Fiction* (1980), and, in the ReReading Literature Series, *Geoffrey Chaucer* (1986).

Robert Mackie is a graduate in philosophy and education of the University of Sydney. He has taught there and at the Australian Studies Centre, University of London, and currently is Senior Lecturer in Education at the University of Newcastle. He is author of *Literacy and Revolution: the Pedagogy of Paulo Freire* (1981), and is presently researching critical legal studies and preparing a biography of the late Jack Lindsay.

Colin Martindale is Professor of Psychology at the University of Maine. His recent books include *The Clockwork Muse: The Predictability of Artistic Change* (1990), *Cognitive Psychology: A Neural-Network Approach* (1991), and an edited volume, *Psychological Approaches to the Study of Literary Narratives* (1988).

Robert J. Merrett, Professor of English at the University of Alberta and an Associate Dean of Arts, is serving a three-year term as President of the Canadian Society for Eighteenth Century Studies. The author of *Daniel Defoe's Moral and Rhetorical Ideas*, (1980), he is completing a second book on Defoe. Recent articles have appeared in *Eighteenth Century Fiction, Eighteenth Century Studies, Études anglaises, Mosaic*, and *Canadian Literature*.

Marea Mitchell is a graduate of the Universities of London and Sussex. Following appointments at Adelaide University and the University of Newcastle, she now lectures at Macquarie University, continuing her research into Marxist and feminist approaches to literary studies, as applied in particular to the *Book of Margery Kempe*.

Joycelyn Moody teaches courses in African American, nineteenth-century American, and women's literature at the University of

Washington. Her recent work explores the autobiographies of nineteenth-century women from a black feminist perspective.

Jeanne Moskal is Associate Professor of English at the University of North Carolina at Chapel Hill. She is the author of *Blake, Ethics, and Forgiveness* (1994). Her edition of Mary Shelley's travel books forms one volume in the 8-volume *Works of Mary Shelley* forthcoming from Pickering-Chatto in 1995. She is also writing a study of British women travel writers during the Napoleonic Wars.

D.G. Myers, Assistant Professor of English at Texas A&M University, has published criticism in *Commentary, New Criterion, Sewanee Review*, and elsewhere. Forthcoming work is to appear in the *Journal of the History of Ideas, South Carolina Review*, and William E. Cain's Garland critical volume on Gerald Graff.

Alan R. Roughley is Senior Lecturer in English and Communication Studies at the University of New England, Armidale. He is the author of *James Joyce and Critical Theory* (1991).

M.E. Roughley was born in the United States and educated in Canada and England. Her doctoral thesis was on Djuna Barnes's *Nightwood* as a "Freudian" and deconstructive text. She teaches literary theory, feminist theory, and twentieth-century literature in the Department of English and Communication Studies at the University of New England, and is currently at work on an edition of the work of Louisa Lawson.

Imre Salusinszky is Senior Lecturer in English at the University of Newcastle, Australia. He is the author of a book of interviews, *Criticism in Society* (1987), and co-author of *Writing in Australia* (1991). His study of the Australian writer Gerald Murnane was published by Oxford University Press in 1993.

Charles I. Schuster is Professor of English at the University of Wisconsin-Milwaukee. Most recently he has co-edited *Speculations: Readings in Culture, Identity, and Values* (1993) with William V. Van Pelt.

Helen Tiffin is Associate Professor of English at the University of Queensland. She is co-author of *The Empire Writes Back* (1989) and of *De-Colonising Fictions* (1993), and editor or co-editor of *South Pacific Stories* (1980). *After Europe: Critical Theory and Post-Colonial Writing* (1989), *Past the Last Post: Post-Colonialism and Post-Modernism* (1990), and *Re-Siting Queen's English: Text and Context in Post-Colonial Literatures* (1992).

Darren J. Tofts is Senior Lecturer in Literature at Swinburne University of Technology, Melbourne. He has published essays on Beckett criticism, popular culture, and literary theory. He is currently working on a comparative critical study of Francis Bacon and Samuel Beckett.

R. Rawdon Wilson, Professor of English at the University of Alberta, is the author of *In Palamedes' Shadow: Explorations in Play, Game, and Narrative Theory* (1990). He has published widely on literary theory, metafiction, narratology, postmodernism, and Canadian literature.

Preface

This collection attempts to explore some of the pedagogic problems and opportunities the advent of theory has created in the teaching of literature. About half of the essays are by contributors who would think of themselves perhaps primarily as theorists, and half by literary scholars who find themselves turning increasingly to theory to invigorate their teaching and research. But as the emphasis is mainly practical, the volume may have less to interest those who consider theory principally a research activity. The initial impetus was in part provided by Gerald Graff's reflection in the article included here that, although it "has always been assumed" that "graduate students are being trained to teach literature as well as research it," it is all too often an assumption "honored only in the breach." These essays tackle the problem of bridging the gap between innovation and tradition in different ways, focusing variously on method, individual paradigms, cross-disciplinary perspectives, the social context and the curriculum. The constraints of space and multiple authorship have meant that some important but more technical areas of theory have been slighted or mentioned only in passing, but as far as practicable an attempt has been made to cover a representative selection of the current theoretical approaches that lend themselves to effective classroom use.

Pedagogically effective theorizing of literary studies is of course vitally dependent on pitching things right at a given level, particularly where undergraduates are involved. A slightly unusual feature of this collection is that the contributors teach at different kinds of tertiary institutions not only in North America but in the United Kingdom and in Australia, where undergraduate education is of particular concern because most higher degrees are by dissertation only. Though theory is still not easy, one suspects it is being better taught than in earlier, more embattled days. The number of studies addressing the pedagogic side of theory is increasing, and works like Catherine Belsey's *Critical Practice* (1980) or Ian Saunders' *Open Texts, Partial Maps* (1993) negotiate the minefield with eloquence and ease. But if there is to be no turning back the clock, no ultimate evasion of the implications of theory for the classroom, there might be a case for giving the exchange of ideas on the practicalities of teaching theory a higher profile in the profession.

The essay by Gerald Graff first appeared in *New Literary History*, 21 (1990), pp. 817–39, and that by Imre Salusinszky in a special issue of *Meridian* entitled *Border Crossing: Studies in English and Other Disciplines*, ed. John Barnes, 10.2 (1991), pp. 108–16. Material from the second part of the essay by David Jasper appeared in an earlier form in an essay entitled "The Study of Literature and Theology: Five Years On," *Literature and Theology*, 6 (1992), pp. 1–10. Grateful acknowledgment is made to the editors concerned for permission to reprint.

Introduction

The process of osmosis, whereby ideas are or are not communicated to students, has always been a little mysterious. Stephen Leacock, writing about Oxford, was convinced it had to do with being smoked at in tutorials: "A well-smoked man speaks and writes English with a grace that can be acquired in no other way."[1] C.S. Lewis alarmed a student who had disparaged Arnold's *Sohrab and Rustum* by "brandishing an old regimental sword ... and shouting, 'The sword must settle this!'"[2] The creator of Rambo used to advise impecunious teaching assistants at the University of Iowa on the advantages of frequent costume changes to keep their students guessing—a unique combination of Core Lit and the catwalk. Whether or not the advent of theory has increased the amount of smoke and sabre-rattling in the classroom since those rambunctious halcyon days, its inherently interdisciplinary nature has certainly increased the number of hats the tertiary English teacher is being called upon to wear. Moreover, as Gerald Graff's essay in this volume reminds us, it has also created a generation gap which often makes it hard for colleagues to meet on common ground. Not everyone would accept K.K. Ruthven's implied verdict on traditional scholarship when he writes that, "faced by mounting evidence of one's own intellectual obsolescence, the options are either to retire gracefully or to become a student again."[3] But a traditionalist hesitating on the brink of the abyss might well feel daunted by the seemingly infinite regress of theory's specialized metalanguages and arguments. And if she gives ear to the siren voice of skepticism—invoking the Soviet collapse, or Foucault's selective scholarship, or Freud's low scientific rating, or the general question of the empirical persuasiveness of theory raised here by Colin Martindale—she might understandably be tempted to opt for Japanese or Russian studies as the fresher, more rewarding field.[4]

Yet to disparage theory as intellectually modish, or publication-driven, or empirically unsound, is to ignore what is surely its

real aggregate achievement, the opening up of new and often socially and intellectually liberating modes of perceiving, however
flawed or partial individual enterprises may appear in retrospect.
One might not agree that language precedes thought, but focusing
on the extent to which it shapes it has a defamiliarizing effect analogous to learning a foreign language.[5] Twenty years ago Propp's
work might have seemed less relevant to English than to Anthropology, and Jakobson's analyses of Blake or Baudelaire scarcely adequate alternatives to the best work in the New Critical tradition.[6]
Yet narratology, one product of such cross-fertilizations, has
evolved highly sensitive tools for literary analysis, which as R.
Rawdon Wilson's essay demonstrates are capable of revealing
subtleties in works a Leavisite might have perceived as trite. If
Marxism's solutions have been largely discredited, its legacy in
oppositional thought has been an enhanced awareness of the
workings of power and ideology in culture, the inherent inequities
of capitalism, and the destructive tendencies of cultural imperialism that is surely humanizing.[7] Read in this light, a poem like Jonson's "To Penshurst," discussed here by Robert Mackie and Marea
Mitchell, appears less idyllic than it might on a conventional historicist reading; and Shakespeare's *Henry V*, as Simon Barker intimates, acquires new significance in the context of Thatcherism and
the Falklands War. Equally, the pervasive influence of Freud's and
more recently Lacan's ideas on literature and criticism has less to
do with their scientific or professional standing than with the kind
of commonality of interest in the subliminal explored in studies
like Malcolm Bowie's *Freud, Proust and Lacan: Theory as Fiction*, and
to the suggestiveness of such unquantifiable notions as repression
and displacement for literary analysis.[8] Lacan's vision of the decentered, socially determined self quite strikingly resembles that implied in writers like Virginia Woolf, and can provide a helpful theoretical underpinning for the kind of exploration of different notions of the subject undertaken here by Alan Roughley.

It is true that the tendency in theory for ideas to migrate from
one intellectual context to another, and resurface in ingenious
novel combinations, can be disconcerting from an empiricist perspective. In her book on fantasy, Rosemary Jackson assimilates
Freud's ideas on the uncanny and Tsvetan Todorov's structuralist
analysis of fantasy in terms (resembling reception theory) of the
reader's hesitation between natural and supernatural explanations
of events, to a theory of fantasy centering on the return of the *political* repressed.[9] Catherine Belsey's work makes eclectic use of ideas

from Macherey, Bakhtin and deconstruction.[10] Such appropriations have not been universally applauded, and there is perhaps some justice to Frederick Crews's complaints against the critical practice of what he calls "Left Eclecticism," where the aim is not "primarily to show the work's character or governing idea. The goal is rather to subdue the work through aggressive demystification, ... scanning it for any encouraging signs of subversion, and then judging the result against an ideal of total freedom"—an ideal he traces back to the era of the Counterculture and the Vietnam War."[11] But while concepts may indeed become invalid when they migrate from one discipline or context to another—Social Darwinism and Nietzsche's *Übermensch* are notorious cases—feminist and post-colonial appropriation of notions such as hegemony and othering are scarcely in this category, and their goal is not total freedom but greater social justice.

Generally speaking, though, it seems increasingly hard to deny that theory—difficult, tendentious and jargon-ridden as it has often been in the process of evolving—has enriched our perception of literary texts and contexts and encouraged transgression of traditional subject boundaries in ways that have often proven illuminating. A single idea—Bakhtin's dialogism or his notion of "threshold" regions explored here by Charles I. Schuster—can lead to a complete reassessment of *Paradise Lost*, or reveal unsuspected connections between quite disparate texts. Derrida's subversion of the metaphysics of presence presents what David Jasper, whose interests straddle theology and literature, regards as a potentially invigorating challenge to the dogmatic slumbers of both disciplines. Post-colonial theory has the equally bracing effect of exposing the false universalism of Eurocentric ideologies, and as Helen Tiffin's essay demonstrates, challenges received notions of what in English should be regarded as a representative curriculum.

Arguably, however, theory is inherently not only an interdisciplinary but a research-oriented activity, and this compounds the ordinary mediatory problems of teaching literature at the tertiary level. The pace at which theory has become a highly specialized affair since the innovative phase of scholars like Harold Bloom and J. Hillis Miller, who started as traditionalists, began, has resulted in a mode of presentation among theorists in which stages in a given line of argument necessary to general comprehension are frequently elided. This might be good reason for responding to D.G. Myers' emphasis on theory as a mode of thinking by teaching it as a wholly new autonomous discipline closer to philosophy, and many teaching theory in virtual isolation will need little persuading of the advantages of this approach. On the other hand, such a move might tend to perpetuate the generation gap and further marginalize theory in the way Graff fears, and there are also drawbacks in the humanities (as against the natural sciences) to recruiting whole departments of like-minded people. Moreover, as Robert J. Merrett's essay using a text by Gay to interrogate New as well as Old Historicism, and Stephen Knight's use of leftist theory to illuminate medieval texts both illustrate, traditionalists of very diverse intellectual backgrounds are turning eclectically to theory to enrich and integrate their research and teaching. And as their ranks increase within more traditional departments, it becomes easier to envisage a cooperative *via media*, with a measure of informed cross-referencing between theorized and empirically-based courses, which does not disadvantage students in the ways deplored by Alan Roughley.

Because of the complexity of the issues, the pedagogic practicalities are often formidable, particularly at the undergraduate level. One fundamental perplex is how to navigate effectively between the Scylla of reductive simplification and the Charybdis of unassimilable elaboration. As Imre Salusinszky points out, it is quite possible to convey the principles of deconstruction to students who would not make much headway with Derrida's *Of Grammatology*. Larry Anderson shows that sensitive use of some of the principles of reader-response theory can be made to enhance the reading skills of quite unsophisticated students. And Darren J. Tofts makes Socratic use of the defamiliarizing effects of a metafictional text by Italo Calvino, to set his students theorizing themselves about the expectations and assumptions they bring to reading literature. Barthean semiotic analysis of movies, ads, and fashion is routinely undertaken—often replacing Shakespeare—in many secondary schools. The danger of simplifying things, of course, particularly with politicized readings, is that the New Critical virtues of close scrutiny of textual detail may be replaced by the kind of uncritical attitudinizing Crews complains about. Yet deployment of the Machereyan principle of reading a text for what it represses or omits to foreground feminist issues, and thus drawing on what students know, can be very effective in opening up critical discussion.[12]

Arguably, erring on the side of simplicity is the lesser evil at the undergraduate level, since technically demanding courses can be intimidating and leave the student with nothing. Simon Barker is from this point of view perhaps rightly critical of theory courses that proceed at breakneck speed through an "approach" a week, fragmenting or reducing theory to a tortuous academic exercise. But anthologies like those by David Lodge or Philip Rice and Patricia Waugh have their attractions, particularly for the non-aligned, since students have to wrestle *directly* with finite amounts of closely argued and often conceptually difficult material.[13] The team-taught approach to theory that Graff calls for clearly has immense potential, not only in avoiding the simplistic, but also in maintaining a pedagogic balance between *educere* and *indoctrinare*.

On the related question of how early to theorize undergraduates, many would agree with Knight that if this mode of thinking is to be assimilated gradualistically, the first year is the place to start. And as Richard Freadman and his colleagues demonstrate, it is quite possible to cover a lot of ground efficiently and non-coercively in a full-year introductory course. Of course there are difficulties with this proposition, too. I remember teaching a second-year course on modernist and postmodernist fiction to a group of bright, intellectually fashion-conscious University of Melbourne students who, having been very proficiently theorized in their first year, tended to look for confirmation of the theory and to be impatient of textual actualities that did not fit. Also, from a traditionalist point of view, both Knight's and Freadman's courses have been theorized at the expense of longer or more demanding texts, like *Middlemarch* or Chaucer's *Troilus*, and there is certainly much to be said for the Leavisite view that undergraduates should be encouraged to read widely and receptively—the more so as the classics are replaced in high schools by cultural and media studies. Appreciation of the niceties of New Historicism is contingent on a firm sense, based on solid reading, of traditional literary history.

The dilemma highlights the need for a *rapprochement* between the two cultures within many English departments, and a collaborative approach to the problems the advent of theory has created. Clearly a course like Freadman's, or the many one-off theory surveys required as prerequisites for honors programs in Australian universities, will remain cosmetic if the issues are not picked up later on. Equally clearly, theory has opened avenues for innovative teaching of traditional courses, and a rationale and methodologies for extending and reconceptualizing the traditional curriculum. Embracing liberalized notions of what constitutes a text, Jean Moskal defamiliarizes the Romantics by teaching them in the context of travel literature, feminism, and race relations. M.E. Roughley isolates principles in Freudian and Lacanian thought that can illuminate a good deal of post-Romantic literature of inwardness. And Joycelyn Moody and Helen Tiffin point to ways in which whole areas of literary activity, marginalized or excluded by hegemonic notions of a great tradition, might become the means of a radical revaluation of our cultural assumptions. No doubt, some are born theorists, some laboriously achieve it, and some of us have theory thrust upon us; but while at the cutting edge of theory Rambo tactics might be in order, in the pedagogic context there would seem some virtue in more student-centered discussion of our ideas and teaching difficulties in the dialogic, cooperative spirit Graff has urged.

Notes

1. Stephen Leacock, "Oxford As I See It," in *A Book of Essays*, ed. Robert Chambers and Carlyle King (New York: St. Martin's Press, 1963), p. 52.

2. See A.N. Wilson, *C.S. Lewis: A Biography* (London: Collins, 1990), p. 130.

3. K.K. Ruthven, ed., *Beyond the Disciplines: The New Humanities* (Canberra: Australian Academy of the Humanities, 1992), p. ix.

4. See J.G. Merquior, *Foucault* (London: Fotana/Collins, 1985), pp. 26–34; James Miller, *The Passion of Michel Foucault* (London: Harper Collins, 1993), pp. 105, 151; and Frederick Crews, *Skeptical Engagements* (New York: Oxford University Press, 1986), pp. 43–74.

5. See David Carroll, *The Subject in Question: The Languages of Theory and the Strategies of Fiction* (Chicago: University of Chicago Press, 1982), pp. 14–15 for an incisive account of the "theoretical break" represented by structuralism, whereby "the subject finds itself now within, not at the source of language," and "philosophy as such is no longer the explicit model for critical theory, for linguistics replaces it—at least on the surface." For a discussion of how Derrida distorts and draws false conclusions from Saussure's ideas on language, see John M. Ellis, *Against Deconstruction* (Princeton: Princeton University Press, 1989), pp. 18–66.

6. See Vladimr Propp, *Theory and History of Folklore*, ed. Anatoly Liberman (Minneapolis: University of Minnesota Press, 1984), which includes an essay by Claude Lévi-Strauss, "Structure and Form: Reflections on a Work by Vladimr Propp," acknowledging an influence Propp thought to be based on misunderstanding of his work. See also Roman Jakobson and Lévi-Strauss, "Charles Baudelaire's 'Les Chats,'" in Michael

Lane, ed., *Structuralism: A Reader* (London: Cape, 1970), pp. 202–21; and Jakobson, "On the Verbal Art of William Blake and Other Poet-Painters," *Linguistic Inquiry*, 1 (1970), pp. 3–23.

7. See Robin Blackburn, ed., *After the Fall: The Failure of Communism and the Future of Socialism* (New York: Verso, 1991).

8. Malcolm Bowie, *Freud, Proust and Lacan: Theory as Fiction* (Cambridge: Cambridge University Press, 1987), pp. 14–44.

9. Rosemary Jackson, *Fantasy: The Literature of Subversion* (London: Methuen, 1981).

10. See Catherine Belsey, *Critical Practice* (London: Methuen, 1980); and *John Milton: Language, Gender, Power* (Oxford: Blackwell, 1988).

11. Frederick Crews, *Skeptical Engagements* (New York: Oxford University Press, 1986), pp. 138–39.

12. Pierre Macherey, *A Theory of Literary Production*, trans. Geoffrey Wall (New York: Routledge, 1978), pp. 85–89. See Belsey, *Critical Practice*, pp. 109–17.

13. David Lodge, ed., *Twentieth Century Literary Criticism: A Reader* (London: Longman, 1972); and *Modern Criticism and Theory: A Reader* (London: Longman, 1988); and Philip Rice and Patricia Waugh, eds. *Modern Literary Theory: A Reader* (London: Arnold, 1989).

Part One

Issues and Cross-Disciplinary Insights

On the Teaching of Literary Theory

D.G. Myers

What does it mean to teach literary theory? Is it a matter of teaching *about* the historic alliance of schools and "isms" that, since the seventies, has collectively sought to refashion the study of literature in the image of "theory"? Is it to teach students instead how to *do* theory for themselves? Should literary theory take a political role? Or is it to be conceived (and hence to be taught) in another way altogether?

If the available materials are any indication, the most common approach is the taxonomical survey, with lessons or units on Saussurean linguistics, structuralist anthropology, *la nouvelle critique,* deconstruction, *Rezeptionsästhetik* and reader response, Marxist criticism, psychoanalysis, feminism, the New Historicism, etc.[1] Here theory is represented as theories, and what is imparted in the classroom are the propositional contents of various and differing bodies of doctrine. Students are instructed that language, meaning, and the self are socially constructed, that discourse is ideological, that *il n'y a pas de hors-texte,* that paradigms shift, that the author is dead. The ideas of literary theory, in short, are treated as accomplished facts, and such an approach has something to recommend it. It is a convenient way to organize a syllabus; it acknowledges and conveys the significance of theory as a historical movement; it is founded upon the sound educational precept that learning can take place only where there is something in particular to be learned. But pretty clearly, the teaching of literary theory as a set of facts is not the teaching of it as theory.

Although theorists like to speak of solving problems, and although their followers act upon occasion as if the achievement of recent theory has been to settle certain issues and close off certain inquiries, it is a betrayal of literary theory to teach it with this attitude, reducing theory to received ideas. On the one hand, the attitude is untheoretical. Humanists are abused for believing in the normative force of pre-existing standards when "post-modernist lit profs by definition recognize that 'literary standards'—literatures themselves—are socially constructed and therefore ideological."[2] But to talk so confidently of what is "therefore" the case is to insist without further argument that true statement p entails true statement q, and this is not (in Gilbert Ryle's words) a "theory-constituting sentence": such expressions belong not to players on the field of theory, but to spectators and cheerleaders.[3] If teachers really believe that theory has solved some of the traditional problems of criticism and interpretation, it would be dishonest of them not to drill students in the solutions, perhaps with the aid of mnemonic rhymes. But if literary theory means anything by definition it is that *all* verdicts about literature and literary standards—not only those of humanists—are open to interrogation. Otherwise the culture of humanism is merely being unseated by the culture of theory, and theory is misunderstood as the authoritative source of a new wisdom. The original hope that theory would offer defiance to just such a moral and literary education based on cultural authority is thwarted.

Most teachers would probably agree that genuine learning has not been attained with the ability to recite *that*-sentences ("Derrida says that ..." or "feminists assert that ..."). It also involves the knowledge of *how* to carry forward a specific inquiry for oneself. Is theory then a set of methods and probative techniques?

R.S. Crane once proposed such an approach, in which critical theories would be treated heuristically, "not as doctrines to be taught, but rather as more or less useful tools of our trade...."[4] Instead of boggling at the word *trade*, which suggests a bourgeois conception of teaching and critical activity, it might be worthwhile to consider this heuristic approach, while holding the question of its class consequences in abeyance. For it, too, is a favored approach to the teaching of literary theory, perhaps only slightly less common than the taxonomical survey. Here different theories are abridged and combined into a "strategy" for the interpretation of texts, a systematic interpretive technique which is "immensely rich in its critical potential" and which is destined to become "a basic part of the critic's repertory, likely to endure even the excesses of its current vogue."[5] There is something to recommend this approach, too: it produces results, in the form of readings. It gives teachers something to say about a text, which is the nagging worry in all classroom teaching of literature. And so it appeals to what J. Hillis Miller has described as the "impatience to get on with it, that is, not to get lost in the indefinite delay of methodological debates...."[6] As Miller observes, though, the impatience felt by so many teachers for "the impalpabilities of theoretical abstractions" explains much about the reaction against theory and the turn to history in recent literary study. And once again it should be clear that, whatever else it is, the heuristic approach—the use of theory in the production of readings—is not the teaching of literary theory as such.

It is the abandonment of theory. One reason for the ascendancy of theory in English studies has been the success of its attacks on established norms of interpretation. Deconstruction, for instance, has successfully called into question the New Criticism's presumption of unity, coherence, and pattern in the literary text. These are primarily significant, it is now apparent, methodologically—they are injunctions of what to look for in a text, revealing the *ways* that critics claim to know something rather than nailing the *truth* of their claims.[7] On this view, deconstruction is superior to interpretation. Since it places the methodological presumptions of interpretation under scrutiny, its own epistemic procedures are more advanced. Deconstruction is a reminder that literary inquiry is always already conditional; it is not itself the provision of a new, more "correct" set of conditions.[8] To study literary theory for the purpose of extracting from it a useful interpretive strategy, then, is to turn aside from the adventure of questioning and trace one's steps back to an earlier stage of unquestioned norms. It is to mistake theory for an ersatz, which Frederick Crews calls theoreticism.[9]

The larger trouble with both the taxonomical and heuristic approaches is that they subtly encourage a pedagogical regime of authoritarianism. To learn *about* theorists, even those as uncoercive as Bakhtin and Cixous, is to be instructed in their authority to propound a vision. And to be taught how to *do* a new method of literary interpretation is to acquiesce in the security of its findings, for that semester at least. Whether it is handled taxonomically (as schools of doctrine) or heuristically (as repertories of technique), where theory is conceived largely or exclusively as a body of materials—to be passed on in the shape in which it was received—the very structure of the transaction between teacher and student is one of supervision and correction, entailing authority and deference.[10] It may be that the exercise of authority is unavoidable or even necessary in the teaching of certain subjects. (Challenges to the validity of a technique or questions about the meaning of "life" in the immediate context would be out of place in a course on life-saving.) But theory is not such a subject.

A pedagogy of authoritarianism comes into office when theory is studied and taught on the grounds of its being the dominant genre of knowledge in literary study at present. A dominant genre lures those who would be better off (or at least happier) doing work in another field. And, bound to it not by a love of theorizing but by a sense of professional obligation, these experts on good scholarly "form" arrest theory in a condition of mere instrumentality, because it is no longer subject to investigation. Good teaching, by contrast, demands that questions remain open, because this is the spirit in which teachers approach the subject when they themselves are studying it; and if the question has been closed, if further challenges are unwelcome, students may respond to the teacher's commands, but not to the subject.[11] Students who have learned *about* theory may reproach those who unselfconsciously sustain traditional assumptions; students who know how to *do* a new mode of interpretation may be scornful of those who know only the old, discredited ways. But this is not evidence of theory's oppositional role. As the philosopher John Passmore observes, "Authoritarian systems of education very commonly produce pupils who are extremely critical, but only of those who do not fully adhere to the accepted beliefs, the accepted rules, the accepted modes of action...."[12]

It is sometimes said that if theory is to act in an oppositional role it must emphasize the relation between politics and cultural practices such as literary criticism and interpretation. And on this view, any approach to teaching is fundamentally flawed which relaxes into an uncritical pluralism. This is the radical objection to either a taxonomical or heuristic approach. The many-sidedness of recent theory, the reluctance to pass up any of its riches, may be just what attracts some teachers to the subject. But when it becomes the principle of organization behind a syllabus, such unselective craving merely "reproduces the political pluralism that conceals the relation of domination by representing the elements of power as sovereign, individual, and equal, each element operating within its own 'truth.'"[13] To a disinterested observer the field of theory may *look* as if it were divided pluralistically among many different schools and "isms," but an attitude of scholarly disinterestedness only serves the interests of the dominant cultural powers. It covers up the political conflict which is at the root of theoretical disagreements. It compares school to school, contrasts "ism" with "ism," rather than pitting theory *as a whole* against the entrenched interests of cultural production. Thus, the radical alternative to pluralism in the teaching of literary theory is a monistic one. Here theory is conceived to have but one goal, and anything else is a stopping short; it is "calculated to lead not just to theoretical interpretation, but to radical change."[14]

The radical approach draws its inspiration from Paulo Freire's *Pedagogy of the Oppressed* (1968). From this perspective—an openly Leninist one—the teaching of literary theory must empower students by showing them how to disclose the ideological conditions behind any cultural performance, and then leading them to repoliticize their newfound knowledge by placing it in the context of the class struggle. At a stroke this removes the barricade between theory and practice, between academic inquiry and political agitation, because "what universities pay us to do—teach—is our main political praxis."[15] Such an approach reattaches the knowledge of how to *do* theory to knowledge that theory is *about* something in particular. And aside from the fact that it promises a way for many teachers of literature and theory to salvage their political commitments, this is its greatest strength.

But there are objections to a radical monist approach; questions not about *how* it should be put into practice, but *if* it even can be. And perhaps these deserve a moment's thought. For the objections come from both the Right and the Left (or, rather, to adopt a less predetermined vocabulary, questions about radical monism are raised both by those who are sympathetic to it and those who are not). On one side is the argument that radical teachers are themselves a politically privileged elite whose position in the university (and the freedom to teach as they wish) is contingent upon the very distinction between academic and political activities which they claim in their teaching to subvert.[16] Either they fail to achieve what they claim, in which case the effect of their teaching is the conservative one of maintaining traditional distinctions; or they succeed in destroying the basis of academic freedom from outside interference, creating an opening for state reprisal. And this leads to the argument that, whatever its educational aims, radical teaching is ultimately of little consequence as political praxis when set against the massively greater powers of monopoly capital.[17] Politically speaking, radical teaching is either self-betraying or self-deluding.

The deeper objection to the political teaching of theory is not political, however, but theoretical. Radical teaching calls into question the ways in which cultural practices are traditionally represented—it makes them problematical—in order to substitute an account of the real relations between culture and politics, which are rooted in class. It should be fairly obvious, though, that such a procedure is only half-theoretical. Some notions are problematized (the special category of literature, individual authorship, the claim to social autonomy), but not others (class, real relations, social constructedness). Insofar as it is monist, then—insofar as it dedicates itself tirelessly to the goal of radical change—oppositional pedagogy passes beyond the stage of theory to a new understanding of culture, but this understanding may in turn be exceeded by further theorists who raise doubts about *its* assumptions. The very monism of radical teaching gives it the advantage over pluralistic approaches. Besides being easier to apply, a single mode of analysis verifies its results to at least that degree of corroboration which is provided by self-consistency and integration. But a claim of self-consistency is an invitation to interrogate it further. And where a mode of analysis has asserted its universality, it becomes itself the system of beliefs which must be deconstructed.

We are now in a position to begin saying what a genuine teaching of literary theory might be. For although we have found much to fault in the three approaches which are most commonly taken, there is something of value to be retrieved from each of them. The customary approaches to the teaching of theory, we might even say, all are based on genuine insight; but each of them misinterprets it. The taxonomical survey recognizes that literary theory is a substantial historical achievement which ought to be apportioned a share of every serious student's literary education. The heuristic method—applied theory, as it might be called—discerns that literary theory is something which must be actively engaged in, not passively learned about. Radical monism is a summons to remember always that the role of theory is to be oppositional. But each of these principles must be understood more adequately.

Theory is first of all a substantial historical achievement. Paul de Man explains:

> The advent of theory, the break that is now so often being deplored and that sets it aside from literary history and from literary criticism, occurs with the introduction of linguistic terminology in the metalanguage about literature.... Contemporary liter-

ary theory comes into its own in such events as the application of Saussurean linguistics to literary texts.[18]

Whatever this may be as a historical statement, when construed as a pedagogical imperative it is the *locus classicus* of a pedagogical mistake. The study of theory must contain a historical *that* which is predicated in such sentences as "Derrida has said that ..." or "feminists have asserted that...." And yet, whatever their historical consequences, theoretical statements are illocutionary, not perlocutionary acts. *In* arguing for *p* a theorist may achieve the unintended effect of convincing some literary critics to apply his or her conclusions in the interpretation of texts. But it is not *by* arguing for *p* that a theorist establishes the conclusiveness of these interpretations.

It is an error to distribute theoretical readings as if they were perlocutions which had had the consequence of establishing the veracity of certain ideas, altering the academic landscape forever. Such a manner of speech is not even native to theory, for one would never say "I establish that ..." or even "I apply that...." What is more, to conceive of theory's historical achievement as a paradigm shift which has radically transformed what counts as "literature," "criticism," and "interpretation" is to resign ourselves to the present impasse at which theory is either zealously embraced or scoffingly rejected. There is no third way, in which theory becomes an occasion neither for applause nor catcalls, but merely for reflection. In teaching and studying theory, then, perhaps we need to return from historical and institutional effects to the particular and sustained feat of intelligence which is performed within every theoretical utterance. Instead of taking up arms for or against it, we might just read and re-read theory. And without going any further, what this would require is a conception of theory's historical content, not as solutions to be committed to memory, but as problems to be reconsidered.

As Gerald Graff has pointed out, the recent history of literary theory has been a series of controversies over such questions as value, meaning, social function, and canonicity.[20] And if it is true that theory is something which must be engaged in—something a theorist and student of theory must *do*—it follows that studying theory means to re-engage in these controversies. But an established literary theory is not a methodology or paradigm or "strategy" that one puts on, in order to dress for academic success. It is an argument. It is an uncompromising reflective struggle to work out a vexing tangle in literary experience. Nor can a theoretical argument be directly applied, as if it were an ointment; it must be thought through, point by point and in detail; it must be inter-locked with, in a reflective struggle. Theoretical arguments are of-ten so difficult that merely to follow them is a rigorous undertak-ing. Only a fool would claim to understand everything in Derrida or Lotman or Ricoeur. To accept a theorist's argument *in toto* be-cause it is daring or stylish, or because others have hailed it as unanswerable, is to be neither a theorist nor a student of theory. "Read Foucault" is not a reply to an objectionable argument. To struggle with a literary theory is to entertain the possibility that it might contain defects. It is to scramble for counterarguments, to test the theory for logical soundness by submitting it to refutation. To do anything else is not really to know literary theory, but to remain ignorant of it.

It is sometimes said, though, that any literary criticism or in-terpretation "presupposes" a theory. From this angle of vision, a knowledge of theory has been acquired when the presuppositions have been reduced to reason. This would seem to imply that inter-pretive presuppositions may be written down in black and white, and revised where necessary. The study of theory would then seem to be a relatively simple matter of refining one's conceptual achievement. Now it is probably true that the study of theory can improve any critic's performance. But theory is not merely this performance reexpressed in different (and perhaps more abstract) terms. It is an effort to understand what the performer has not yet understood, because he or she has exchanged the effort to under-stand for the opportunity to perform. Thus, "theory" in the sense intended here cannot be "presupposed" by a critical or interpretive performance. It has not yet come into being. It is itself an achieve-ment, though of a different order. It is the controversial maneuver by which any solution that is proposed to a critical or interpretive problem is not applied to a fresh text but converted into a fresh problem; one which has no ready solution.

And this is the real regard in which theorists and teachers of theory are oppositional. They join with Anne Elliot in *Persuasion* "to oppose the too common idea"—the commonly mistaken idea—behind much literary thought. That is their driving motive, al-though it is a question of epistemic policy rather than preemptive conviction: literary criticism is usually wrong, and usually needs to be rethought. Especially since Barthes and Derrida and Foucault, the special role of theory has been to let the air out of critics' assur-ance that the terms and categories of their discipline refer to things which self-evidently exist. Literary theory is a demand for proof and further defense. Its advantage as a course of study, then, is that it introduces students into the rough-and-tumble of genuine inquiry, where the only sure way to go wrong is to decline to meet the challenge.

And for this reason, the best approach to the teaching of theory may be to presume that the texts which one includes in one's syllabus are in error. They are to be swallowed only if, upon consideration, they succeed in making their case. Theoretical texts cannot be taught as if the truth or falsehood of their contents were not in question, and to teach them as *prima facie* true is to foreclose the question. One has allegiances, of course, and it is absurd to pretend that these ought to (or can) be suppressed. Then perhaps it is smarter to assign one's antagonists. For if we are serious in believing that the role of theory is to oppose cultural authority, if we are sincere in our objective of putting self-evident certainties under interrogation, what better way than by leading our students to struggle against the authorities that we ourselves have placed in their hands? Surely the texts will withstand rough handling, and if nothing else the class sessions will be lively. Although this approach may not be for everyone, it should appeal to those of us who enjoy the contention of theory. As Montaigne once said,

> I could stand to be rudely jarred by my friends: "You're a fool, you're dreaming." I like to see people speak up bravely among gallant men, and to see the words go where the thought goes. We should strengthen and toughen our ears against this tenderness toward the ceremonious sound of words. I like a strong, manly fellowship and familiarity, a friendship that delights in the sharpness and vigor of its intercourse, as does love in bites and scratches that draw blood. It is not vigorous and generous enough if it is not quarrelsome, if it is civilized and artful, if it fears knocks and moves with constraint. *For there can be no discussion without contradiction.* [21]

Notes

1. Consider the plan of organization in, e.g., Terry Eagleton, *Literary Theory: An Introduction* (Minneapolis: University of Minnesota Press, 1983); Ann Jefferson and David Robey, eds., *Modern Literary Theory: A Comparative Introduction* (London: Batsford, 1986); Rick Rylance, ed., *Debating Texts: Twentieth-Century Literary Theory and Method* (Toronto: University of

Toronto Press, 1987); K.M. Newton, ed., *Twentieth-Century Literary Theory: A Reader* (Basingstoke: Macmillan, 1988); Vincent B. Leitch, *American Literary Criticism from the Thirties to the Eighties* (New York: Columbia University Press, 1988); David H. Richter, ed., *The Critical Tradition: Classical Texts and Contemporary Trends* (New York: St. Martin's Press, 1989); K.M. Newton, *Interpreting the Text: A Critical Introduction to the Theory and Practice of Literary Interpretation* (New York: St. Martin's Press, 1990); Stephen Bonnycastle, *In Search of Authority: An Introductory Guide to Literary Theory* (Peterborough: Broadview, 1991).

2. Patrick Brantlinger, "Eng Lit at Wayne State, at Indiana, at Harvard, at Sea," *Criticism,* 31 (1989), p. 336.

3. See Gilbert Ryle, "'If,' 'So,' and 'Because,'" *Collected Papers* (New York: Barnes & Noble, 1971), II. 234–49.

4. R.S. Crane, "Questions and Answers in the Teaching of Literary Texts,"*The Idea of the Humanities and Other Essays Critical and Historical* (Chicago: University of Chicago Press, 1967), II. 180.

5. Robert Scholes, *Textual Power: Literary Theory and the Teaching of English* (New Haven: Yale University Press, 1985), p. 4. Scholes is speaking of the binary oppositions in structuralism and their critique in deconstruction, which he pursues throughout his book to good effect.

6. J. Hillis Miller, "The Triumph of Theory, the Resistance to Reading, and the Question of the Material Base," *PMLA*, 102 (1987), p. 283.

7. See Nicholas Rescher, *Dialectics: A Controversy-Oriented Approach to the Theory of Knowledge* (Albany: State University of New York Press, 1977), pp. 37–41, esp. n. 23. Some of my terminology in this passage (and elsewhere in the essay) is plucked from Rescher.

8. See Joseph Margolis, "Deconstruction: A Cautionary Tale," *Journal of Aesthetic Education,* 20 (Winter 1986), pp. 91–94.

9. See Frederick Crews, *Skeptical Engagements* (New York: Oxford University Press, 1986), pp. 164–77. David H. Hirsch uses the same term to denote the widespread current preference for devising an abstract interpretive strategy to "knowing what a given poem (or poet) is saying," in *The Deconstruction of Literature: Criticism after Auschwitz* (Hanover: University Press of New England, 1991), pp. 23–68.

10. See Ian Hunter, "The Occasion of Criticism: Its Ethic and Pedagogy," *Poetics*, 17 (1988), pp. 185–205.

11. See Judith N. Shklar, "Why Teach Political Theory?" in *Teaching Literature: What Is Needed Now*, ed. James Engell and David Perkins, Harvard English Studies, 15 (Cambridge: Harvard University Press, 1988), pp. 151–60.

12. John Passmore, *The Philosophy of Teaching* (Cambridge: Harvard University Press, 1980), p. 170.

13. Mas'ud Zavarzadeh and Donald Morton, *Theory, (Post)Modernity, Opposition: An "Other" Introduction to Literary and Cultural Theory*, Post-ModernPositions 5 (Washington: Maisonneuve, 1991), p. 213.

14. Robert Con Davis, "A Manifesto for Oppositional Pedagogy: Freire, Bourdieu, Merod, and Graff," in *Reorientations: Critical Theories and Pedagogies*, ed. Bruce Henricksen and Thais E. Morgan (Urbana: University of Illinois Press, 1990), p. 263. For a critical inspection of the monistic impulse in teaching and study, see Kenneth R. Minogue, *The Concept of a University* (Berkeley: University of California Press, 1973), pp. 76ff.

15. Richard Ohmann, *Politics of Letters* (Middletown: Wesleyan University Press, 1987), p. 131.

16. See Edward Shils, "Academic Freedom and Academic Obligation," in *Sidney Hook, Philosopher of Democracy and Humanism*, ed. Paul Kurtz (Buffalo: Prometheus, 1983), p. 136.

17. See Richard A. Brosio, "Teaching and Learning for Democratic Empowerment: A Critical Evaluation," *Educational Theory*, 40 (1990), pp. 69–81.

18. Paul de Man, *The Resistance to Theory*, Theory and History of Literature 33 (Minneapolis: University of Minnesota Press, 1986), p. 8.

19. Gerald Graff, "Taking Cover in Coverage," *Profession*, 86 (1986), p. 44.

20. See Gerald Graff, "Other Voices, Other Rooms: Organizing and Teaching the Humanities Conflict," in this volume.

21. "Of the Art of Discussion," *The Complete Essays of Montaigne*, trans. Donald M. Frame (Stanford: Stanford University Press, 1958), p. 750. Montaigne's last sentence is lifted from Cicero.

Other Voices, Other Rooms:
Organizing and Teaching the
Humanities Conflict

Gerald Graff

In the Faculty lounge the other day, a dispute arose between a couple of my colleagues that typifies the warfare currently agitating the educational world. It began when our departmental Victorian specialist, an older male professor, complained that he had just come from teaching Matthew Arnold's "Dover Beach" and had been appalled to discover that the poem was virtually incomprehensible to his class. Here was yet another sorry illustration of the deplorably ill-prepared state of today's students. Why, can you believe it, said the older male professor (taking a page from the personal ads, let us call him OMP for short), my students were at a loss as to what to make of Arnold's famous concluding lines, which he proceeded to recite with slightly self-mocking grandiloquence:

> Ah, love, let us be true
> To one another! For the world, which seems
> To lie before us like a land of dreams,
> So various, so beautiful, so new,
> Hath really neither joy, nor love, nor light,
> Nor certitude, nor peace, nor help for pain;
> And we are here as on a darkling plain
> Swept with confused alarms of struggle and flight
> Where ignorant armies clash by night.

My other colleague, a young woman who has just recently joined our department (let us call her YFP), replied that she could appreciate the students' reaction. She recalled that she had been forced to study "Dover Beach" in high school and had consequently formed a dislike for poetry that it had taken her years to

15

overcome. Why teach "Dover Beach" anyway, YFP asked? No wonder so many of our students hate poetry when this is the way "poetry" is presented to them!

Furiously stirring his Coffee-mate, OMP replied that in *his* humble opinion—reactionary though he supposed it now was— "Dover Beach" was one of the great masterpieces of the Western tradition, a work that, until recently at least, every seriously educated person took for granted as part of the cultural heritage. YFP retorted that while that might be so, it was not altogether to the credit of the cultural heritage. Take those lines addressed to the woman by the speaker, she said: "Ah, love, let us be true / To one another ... ," and so on. In other words, protect and console me, my dear—as we know it's the function of your naturally more spiritual sex to do—from the "struggle and flight" of politics and history that we men have regrettably been assigned the unpleasant duty of dealing with. YFP added that she would have a hard time finding a better example of what feminists mean when they speak of the ideological construction of the feminine as by nature private and domestic and therefore justly disqualified from sharing male power. Here, however, she paused and corrected herself: "Actually," she said, "we *should* teach 'Dover Beach.' We should teach it as the arch example of phallocentric discourse that it is."

OMP responded that YFP seemed to be treating "Dover Beach" as if it were a piece of political propaganda rather than a work of art. To take Arnold's poem as if it were a species of "phallocentric discourse," whatever that is, misses the whole point of poetry, OMP said, which is, to rise above local and transitory problems by transmuting them into universal structures of language and image. Arnold's poem is no more about gender politics, declared OMP, than *Macbeth* is about the Stuart monarchical succession.

But *Macbeth is* about the Stuart monarchical succession, retorted YFP—as its original audience surely would have thought. It's about gender politics too—why else does Lady Macbeth need to "unsex" herself before she can participate in murdering Duncan? Not to mention all the business about men born of woman and from their mothers' womb untimely ripped. The fact is, Professor OMP, that what you presume to be the universal human experience in Arnold and Shakespeare is male experience presented as if it were universal. You don't need to notice the politics of sexuality because for you patriarchy is the normal state of affairs. You can afford to ignore the sexual politics of literature, or to "transmute" them, as you put it, onto a universal plane, but that's a luxury I don't enjoy....

Theory Has Broken Out

There are many possible ways to describe what happened here, but one of them would be to say that "theory" has broken out. What we have come to call "theory," I would suggest, is the kind of reflective, second-order discourse about practices that is generated when a consensus that was once taken for granted in a community breaks down. When this happens, assumptions that previously had been taken for granted as the "normal state of affairs"—in this case OMP's assumption that literature is above sexual politics—have to be explicitly formulated and argued about. What had formerly gone without saying now has to be *argued for*.

OMP would probably complain that this trend diverts attention from literature itself. But YFP could reply that literature itself was not being ignored in their debate but discussed in a new way. It was not that she and OMP stopped talking about poetry and started talking theory. It was rather that because their conflicting theoretical assumptions differed about how to talk about poetry, they had to talk about it in a way that foregrounded those theories. Not sharing the same assumptions about literature, criticism, and the aims of education, OMP and YFP could not discuss "Dover Beach" without being drawn into matters of theory—the very matters of theory, in fact, which have preoccupied the literary theorizing of the last several decades: the nature of literary value and meaning and its relation to questions of politics, canonicity, and pedagogy. But then, the very question of whether this kind of discussion should properly be called "talking about literature in a new way" or "abandoning literature for theory" is doubtless another of the questions that OMP and YFP would disagree about.

The recent prominence of theory, then, is the result of a climate of radical disagreement, and the complaint that theory is pervasive finally reduces to the complaint that literature and criticism have become too controversial. Yet the complaint only has the effect of generating more theory and more of the theoretical disagreement being deplored. Forced by the disagreement to articulate his principles, OMP, the traditional humanist, was "doing theory" just as much as was YFP, articulating assumptions that previously he could have taken as given. That opposition to theory is itself a theory is increasingly borne out today, as opposition to theory becomes an attitude one has to argue for, or at least explicitly assert, with the effect not of drawing the discussion back to "literature itself" but only of adding to the theory-talk.[1] For this reason, the belief that the theory trend is a mere passing fad is likely to be wishful thinking.

The question is who and what are hurt by this situation. Who and what are damaged by conflicts like the one in the faculty lounge? The obvious answer would seem to be "Dover Beach." But this answer raises the question of just how well "Dover Beach" was doing in college (and high school) literature classes before radical teachers like YFP came along. We need only look at the complaint by OMP that triggered the lounge-debate to be reminded that such classics have often inspired deep apathy in students even when taught in the most reverential fashion—perhaps especially when taught in that fashion.

Anyone who has studied the history of modern education will know that professorial complaints about student apathy and incomprehension in the face of the classics have been chronic since American education became a mass enterprise after the turn of the century, when humanists began to feel beleaguered by the philistine culture of vocationalism, fraternity-sorority life, and football.[2] If the problems seem to us to be more grave in the 1990s than they were in the 1920s, this may be only because the number of students available to be bored by works like "Dover Beach" is so much larger in the 1990s than it was in the 1920s. Long before academic feminism and Marxism, pressure to open the canon has stemmed from the recognition of students' problems with classics like "Dover Beach."

Considered in this light, one might argue that "Dover Beach" has little to lose from the debate between OMP and YFP and a good deal to gain. In an odd way, YFP is doing "Dover Beach" a favor: in treating Arnold's poem as a significant instance of ideological mystification, her critique does more to make the poem *a live issue* in the culture again than does the respectful treatment of traditionalist teachers like OMP, which, as he himself complains, fails to arouse his class.

But will "Dover Beach" survive in the course at all if the YFP's of the world have their way? The question is difficult to discuss in the atmosphere of hysterical exaggeration created by wildly misinformed journalistic reports, but its logic is not as clear-cut as it has been made out to be, for the question of what will be read and taught is not easily separable from the question of how and in what context it will be read and taught.[3] If YFP expects to alert students to the phallocentrism of "Dover Beach," she will have to assign the poem. Conversely, it is OMP whose interest is served by dropping the poem from the syllabus. For if teaching it is going to mean demystifying it, then taking it off the reading list would at least have the effect of damage control. Such speculation may be perverse, but it is far from obvious that an attitude of polite deference is more favorable to the survival of a classic like "Dover Beach" than an attitude of ideological interrogation. That survival may well depend on the extent to which "Dover Beach" remains interestingly pertinent to such challenging concerns as those raised by YFP.

What the debate between OMP and YFP really threatens is not "Dover Beach," I think, but OMP's conception of "Dover Beach" as a repository of universal values that transcend the circumstances of its creation and reception. Whereas this decontextualized concept of culture was once axiomatic in humanistic education, it has now become one theory among others, a proposition that has to be argued for rather than taken as given. What is threatened by the canon-controversy, in other words, is not the classics but their unquestioned status. But again, when the classics enjoyed that unquestioned status there is little evidence that it made them seem more compelling to students than they seem now. In short, from an educational point of view, the classics have less to fear from newfangled ideological hostility than from old-fashioned indifference.

I would argue that what is most unfortunate about the conflict between OMP and YFP is not *that* it is taking place but *where* it is taking place, behind the educational scenes where students cannot learn anything from it. What is really injurious to students' interests is not the conflict over culture but the fact that students are not more active participants in it. For the canon-conflict is not something that is taking place apart from culture, but is necessarily part of what we mean by "culture" in a multicultural society where controversy is increasingly not the exception but the rule. In a society increasingly being forced to come to terms with cultural difference nothing could be more practical than an education that treats cultural and ideological conflict as part of its object of study.

My thought as I watched OMP and YFP go back and forth in the faculty lounge was that if OMP's students could witness this debate they would be more likely to get worked up over "Dover Beach" than they are now. They might even find it easier to gain access to the poem, for the controversy over it might give them a context for reading it that they now do not possess.

Then again, it might not. The controversy would have to be presented in a way that avoids pedantry, obscurity, and technicality, and this is difficult to do. And even when it is done, many students will still have as much trouble seeing why they should take an interest in critical debates over "Dover Beach" as they do seeing why they should take an interest in "Dover Beach" itself. This may be less of a problem as the conflict over the canon becomes ever more urgent and public and its relation becomes clearer to issues whose importance everybody can recognize, like the politics of multiculturalism. But the alienation of students from academic culture often remains deep, and it may deepen further as the terms of that culture become more confusingly in dispute than in the past.

Here lies both the challenge and the difficulty of the newly contested situation of the humanities. As academic culture has become more democratic and plural in content, more engaged in the most challenging problems of the present, and more prone to political conflict, the humanities have become potentially more relevant to the lives of students than the relatively antiquarian and re-stricted humanities of a generation ago. Yet the very conflicts that betoken the humanities' increase in potential relevance also make them more confusing and hard to penetrate.

The issue here is one of institutional legibility: how do institutional discourses become readable to people not already initiated into them? To what extent does a loss of tacit consensus impair an institution's readability to outsiders? Unless steps are taken to counteract it, an increased degree and intensity of conflict within an intellectual institution figures to make it harder to make the institution's discourses intelligible to its constituencies. It is hard in any period to clarify something so complex as intellectual culture to people not already at home in it, and sometimes not sure they wish to be. It figures to be all the harder to clarify that culture when there is less and less philosophical common ground to fall back on. In the humanities today, that common ground has so diminished that the very question of what counts as a "clarification" is part of what is politically contested. My clarification may be your ideological obfuscation.

In such a situation, helping students gain access to academic discourse communities means clarifying conflicts like the one between OMP and YFP (and numerous others not so neatly polarized), even as what counts as true clarification remains itself open to debate. If the aim is to help students become interested participants in the present cultural conversation instead of puzzled and alienated spectators—or as passive recipients of a one-way transmission in which "our" culture trickles down to "them"—the aim should be to *organize* such conflicts of principle in the curriculum itself.

Just opening reading lists to noncanonical works—necessary as that step is—will not in itself solve the problem. Merely replacing "Dover Beach" with *The Color Purple* does not necessarily help the student who has difficulty with the intellectual vocabularies in which both those texts are discussed in the academic environment. What makes reading and interpretation difficult for many students is not the kind of text being read, whether canonical or noncanonical, highbrow or popular, but the heavily thematic and allegorical ways in which all texts irrespective of status level are discussed in the academic setting—the student phrase for it is "looking for 'hidden meaning.'" Academics are so accustomed to attributing certain kinds of abstract meanings to all phenomena, not just texts, that they easily forget that this activity does not seem natural or self-evidently justifiable to everyone. If the practice of looking for hidden meaning seems strange to you, it will seem no less strange to look for it in *The Color Purple* than in *Hamlet*.

This last point needs underscoring, because educational progressives have been too quick to blame student alienation from academic literacy on the elitist or conservative aspects of that literacy. But students can be as alienated from democratized forms of academic literacy as from conservative forms, and from permissive as well as restrictive classrooms. What alienates such students is academic literacy *as such*, with its unavoidably abstract and analytical ways of talking and writing, regardless of whether that literacy comes in traditional or populist forms.

Perhaps too much educational writing is done by people who either never experienced this alienation from academic literacy or who forgot what it was like once they overcame it. My own recollection of school days is that *not* reading the assignments felt to me and my classmates like a heroic gesture of resistance against the sterile intellectualism being forced on us. I suspect this attitude still persists even where the content of what is taught is politically unexceptionable. Overlaid on the disparity between "radical" and "conservative" culture is an older disparity between the discourses of "intellectuals" and "lay" people.

In the heat of today's antagonisms it is easy to get so caught up defending one or another proposed list of books to be taught that one forgets that for many students it is *the life of books* itself that is strange and alien, regardless of which side gets to draw up the list. One becomes so embroiled in the battle between traditionalist and revisionist views of culture that one forgets that for many students categories like "traditionalist," "revisionist," and "culture" itself are remote and mysterious, no matter which view is in charge.[4]

There is no question of occupying a neutral position here: in my view, the shift from the traditionalist to the revisionist view of culture is very much a change for the better. But from the vantage point of students who feel estranged from the intellectual life as such, revisionist culture can easily seem like the same old stuff in a new guise. To such students a Roland Barthes and an Allan Bloom would seem far more similar to one another than to people like themselves, their parents, and friends. In their eyes, a Barthes and a Bloom would be just a couple of intellectuals speaking a very different language from their own about problems they have a hard time regarding as problems. Though the intellectual distance separating an OMP from a YFP may look vast to us and to OMP and YFP themselves, to these students it would seem relatively insignificant. The very issues that make it possible for OMP and YFP to attack one another so vigorously constitute a bond that puts them in another world from most of their students.

To those who are not at home in it, intellectual discourse is like a foreign language—some of it literally is foreign language. The best way to learn a foreign language is to live in the country in which it is spoken. In theory, the classroom is the "country" that mediates between the foreign languages of intellectual culture (I have elsewhere termed them Intellectualspeak) and the students. But making the classroom into an effective intellectual community is an uphill battle as long as the classroom has no functional connection to the larger "country" of other classrooms and to the general intellectual life of the university, a situation that intensifies the dependency of students on their teachers.

If the curriculum represents itself to students as a set of disjunctive discourses, it will naturally be difficult for them to recognize it as a community at all, much less one that seems attractive to join. The problem is obviously compounded to the extent that joining the academic intellectual community threatens to estrange the student from the communities he already belongs to—church, family, peer group, job. On the other hand, one senses that many students are not resistant to joining the academic intellectual community, but find it forbidding and hard to penetrate. Granted, some students manage to make their own individual sense of the curriculum. It is the many who do not with whom I am concerned here.

In other words, we pay a steeper educational price today than in the past for a disjunctive curriculum in which students encounter each course as an isolated unit and therefore have trouble seeing its conversational relation to other courses and discourses. For as the conflicts inside and outside the academy become more antagonistic, the amount of perceptible carryover and translatability from one course to another is less and less likely to take care of itself. Courses that in principle speak to common or related concerns will not always appear to do so unless something is done to make the convergence explicit. In a radically dissensual climate, the ground rules will change confusingly without notice from one course to the next.

The new climate of ideological contention in the university seems to me a sign of democratic vitality rather than the symptom of "disarray," relativism, and declining standards that the critics on the Right take it to be. But the university *has* failed so far to make a focused curriculum out of its contentiousness. For this reason, I doubt that it is tapping its full potential for drawing students into its culture.

Pluralism at the End of Its Tether

Just how "democratic" the university has become can be questioned. Though the curriculum is significantly more pluralistic, multicultural, and culturally representative than it was a generation ago, the faculty and student body remain preponderantly white and middle class. As Henry Louis Gates observes, "it sometimes seems that blacks are doing better in the college curriculum than they are in the streets."[5] Yet as Gates acknowledges, it is not a negligible fact that today's curriculum, by comparison with that of only a generation ago, is strikingly more responsive to the pressures of the surrounding culture and its democratizing impulses. By contrast with the university of the 1950s, in which the content of the humanities was still a predominantly New England WASP culture, today's humanities take cultural difference far more seriously.

For this reason, I would argue that the primary weakness of the humanities curriculum (at least in the institutions that set the standard) is no longer its failure to embrace cultural and ideological difference, but its failure to take maximum educational advantage of the impressive range of difference that it now does embrace. The curriculum encompasses a far wider range of cultural differences than in the past but instead of engaging those differences it still tends to keep their components in noncommunicating courses and departments. As a result students are often unable to recognize difference *as* difference, since they experience its components only in separation.

To say this is not to dismiss academic pluralism, an immense progressive improvement over the exclusionary system of the nineteenth-century college, but to criticize the failure of pluralism to engage its own pluralities. Pluralism deserves credit for opening academic culture to previously unrepresented groups, methodologies, and viewpoints, and greatly expanding its ideological diversity. But it has done so by adding innovative and revisionary subjects and perspectives without asking that the challenges these innovations pose to traditional assumptions and methods be confronted and worked through.[6]

Thus when the New Criticism overcame the resistance of the older historical and philological scholarship and entered literature departments after World War II, it came to coexist peacefully with the traditional courses whose approaches it was challenging. As feminism and poststructuralism have today made their way into the department and the curriculum, they too coexist peacefully with the New Criticism and old historicism which they radically subvert. After a century of it, this system of growth by accretion and assimilation now seems so natural and normal that one in which differences were engaged in the curriculum itself seems virtually unthinkable. It takes an effort of defamiliarization to see something strange in the result— that the humanities have become the site of the most radical cultural transgression without ceasing to be a bastion of traditional values. It is this contradiction that explains how the humanities can be attacked at once from the Left for clinging to hidebound traditions and from the Right for welcoming revolutionary insurrection. Again, academic peaceful coexistence has its benefits (as it does in the global arena), especially when compared to the authoritarian system that preceded it. But the heavy intellectual costs of such a system are passed on to students, who are exposed to the ideological contradictions of the curriculum without enough help in making sense of them, or even in recognizing them as contradictions.

The problem has not gone unrecognized—witness the mounting chorus of recent complaints about academic "fragmentation" and "pluralistic disarray" and the "cafeteria-counter" or "garage sale" curriculum that gives students little help in connecting the disparate subjects and values the curriculum offers them. But the terms in which such complaints are framed are themselves inadequate, failing as they do to acknowledge the problem of ideological conflict.

In the liberal-pluralist rhetoric officially adopted by most universities today, the university is characterized as a scene of "diversity" without conflict. The iconography of the college catalog, with its juxtaposition of pastoral and technological imagery, represents the campus as a reconciler of contraries, where ivy and steel, the chapel and the laboratory, the garden and the machine need not clash. This effect is reinforced by the numbered department and course listings, which make it seem unexceptional that conflicting values and methods should coexist side by side. The university is conceived as a site of infinitely multiplying differences that never need to be confronted, since in the end they presumably conduce to commonly shared social goals. As long as the major fields are covered by departments and courses and as long as students cover a reasonable spread of those fields, questions about how these contents converge or conflict can be left to work themselves out on their own, or as each student may work them out by himself.

Conservatives mount an effective attack on the evasive and relativistic implications of this laissez-faire approach to the curriculum (the analogies with cafeterias and garage sales reflecting their patrician disdain for the vulgar marketplace). They point out with justice that it lets educators transfer the responsibility to students for deciding which knowledge is most worth having. But the only alternative proposed by conservatives for this evasion of responsibility is to reinstate a concept of tradition that also ignores or suppresses conflicts. Whereas the liberal appeal to diversity assumes that the clarification of ideological conflicts will work itself out through the free play of individual initiatives, the conservative attempt to reimpose an ideal of "our common culture" denies the very legitimacy of ideological conflicts, and blames their eruption on rabble-rousing Leftists, who are accused of "politicizing" a culture that is naturally above politics. Thus neither liberal-pluralist nor conservative approaches to the curriculum have a strategy for dealing with ideological conflict in education by making it a productive part of the curriculum.

In *Professing Literature,* my narrative of the history of academic literary studies in America traced the way successive attempts to break this pattern of routinized absorption and cooptation had each in turn been absorbed, routinized and coopted into the structure of conflict-free pluralism. The story traced a kind of institutional compulsion, in which repressed conflicts repeatedly return in the form of neurotic repetition: what initially emerges as a subversive innovation (modern language philology, old historicism, New Criticism) subsequently becomes the traditional humanism of a later period. I speculated at the end of the book that what endangers today's radical literary theories is not that they will be repressed but that they will be accepted and relegated to the margins where they will no longer need bother those they challenge. The new theories are ghettoized in the theory course while the other courses go on about their business as before (or they are quietly absorbed into the older forms of work where they spruce up a tired methodology). The picture still seems to me accurate, but it is only part of the story. Like other recent "cooptation" analyses, this one leaves out the extent to which a system can be altered in the very process of coopting innovations.[7]

For as the ideological conflicts within the university have become more open and acrimonious, the university's time-honored strategies of conflict-avoidance are ceasing to work as efficiently as they once did. As these conflicts become too fundamental to be papered over by the device of keeping opposing factions isolated in noncommunicating classrooms and departments, students, increasingly, can hardly help knowing there is trouble behind the scenes. Thus the war over the canon has already had a certain educative effect not planned by any curriculum committee, at least in leaking the news that the humanities are not the calm, uncontested terrain that they have pretended to be. The news is not merely leaked, of course, but openly taught in courses like women's studies, post-colonialism, cultural materialism, and other theory-conscious forms of study, and in the standard period and genre courses that increasingly bear their influence.

Even so, I believe it will take more than new courses (and new styles of individual pedagogy) to produce a curriculum that makes more than a small minority of students articulately aware of the controversies surrounding them and able to take an aggressive part in them. For the powerful vocabularies in which the controversies are fought out remain in the control of the faculty rather than the student body. And as long as it continues to be taught in a privatized space, even the best-taught course is limited in its power to help students gain control of those vocabularies.

I doubt the privatized classroom has ever been an effective structure, but at least it made consistent sense in the relatively consensual conditions that existed in the socially restricted academic culture of the past. That is, when academic culture was socially and intellectually homogeneous, it was reasonable to assume that common premises would be randomly repeated and reinforced over a span of courses, so that the latent conversations between different courses did not need to be programmatically actualized. In an institution in which everyone presumably speaks (or wants to learn) a version of the same master discourse, the random effect of their voices speaking it separately figures to produce enough redundancy to convey a coherent picture to students.

All accounts suggest that, at least since the demise of the old college, professors have not shared a master discourse (ruptures appeared immediately between scientists and humanists and professional and antiprofessional humanists), and the coherence of the academic humanities has never been apparent to more than a minority of students. Now that the academic humanities can no longer take for granted even the shaky consensus they once had, and now that it is no longer clear that such a consensus would even be desirable, it is all the less likely that an accessible picture of the humanities can emerge for students without an attempt to structure the latent connections between courses and discourses.

Thomas S. Kuhn observes in *The Structure of Scientific Revolutions* that at moments of crisis or paradigm shift in the sciences, "a law that cannot even be demonstrated to one group of scientists may ... seem intuitively obvious to another."[8] Imagine what happens in the mind of a student caught in the crossfire between several conflicting paradigms, each of which represents itself to him as "intuitively obvious" and uncontroversial. Kuhn's own book is a case in point, having been treated as holy writ by many literary theorists even as it has been ignored or disparaged by some scientists and philosophers of science. A student would be asking for trouble if she assumed that the assumptions about scientific truth and paradigm-change that she learned from her Kuhnian instructor carry over into other courses. In the same way, a student would be asking for trouble if she assumed that what counts as "literature" or "criticism" (or as good literature or genuine criticism) in a course taught by OMP carries over into a course taught by YFP. In OMP's class it may go without saying as uncontroversial that great literature is a repository of universal truths, while in YFP's it may go without saying as equally controversial that this view is pernicious, reactionary, and passé.

The problem is further intensified when a paradigm shift occurs so rapidly that a new set of truths attain the status of commonplaces in one discourse community before other communities have even heard of them. One now hears one's more advanced colleagues saying things like, "I'm getting so tired of hearing about 'hegemonic discourse.' And if I hear one more time that reality is 'socially constructed' I'll pass out." Since the theories that have become so self-evident as to be boring to these professors have never been encountered by most of their students, it would not be surprising if the professors did not explain the theories to their students but presupposed them as going without saying among those in the know. Since no student wants to be exposed as not in the know, he will naturally think twice before asking teachers for clarification.

We might be tempted to write off such behavior as a case of mere bad teaching, correctable by urging the instructors to be more sensitive to their students' difficulties. But as long as she teaches in isolation from her colleagues, even the most sensitive teacher cannot know how much of what she tells her students may be considered controversial by some of those colleagues. In teaching the history of criticism this year, I persistently had the suspicion that many of my colleagues would probably raise their eyebrows at about three-fourths of the picture of literary and cultural history I drew for my class, and probably for very different reasons. I had no way of knowing how much of the picture I drew might or might not jibe with the one my students were getting from other colleagues, but I would be amazed if there were not major discrepancies.

My students probably noticed discrepancies between my account and that of other teachers, but they were too polite to mention them. Rather than ask instructors to confront apparent contradictions among their views when these arise, shrewd students will usually decide that it is safer to put the matter out of mind and give each teacher what he or she "wants." A student in my criticism course last semester told of an earlier teacher who warned her class that she would not tolerate the word "problematize." This student happened to be concurrently taking another course in which it seemed clear that using words like "problematize" would be to his advantage. What did you do, my class asked? "What else could I do?" he said. "I avoided 'problematize' in one course and plugged it to death in the other."[9]

Note that the instructors in all these cases are protected by the closed nature of their classrooms, which makes it unnecessary (or even impossible) for them to confront the challenges to their assumptions that might be represented by other teachers. The students, on the other hand, having no such protection, become the battleground of the university's increasingly more violent ideological contradictions. They, too, naturally protect themselves by repressing the contradictions, as my student did with his judiciously selective use of "problematize." Taking a series of courses thus becomes a game of psyching out each instructor's paradigm, playing along with it for the duration of the semester, and then forgetting it as soon as possible after the final examination in order to make mental room for the next instructor's paradigm.

But why, it will be objected, could not any teacher represent the views of other teachers to their students? Surely if they are good teachers, OMP and YFP will each represent their dispute over "Dover Beach" to their classes—differently to be sure, but that is all to the better. Does not any good teacher already "teach the conflicts" by presenting students with opposing perspectives on controversial important issues? The flaw in such an objection should be obvious to anyone trained in literary studies over the last generation, where the crucial difference between didactic and dramatic forms of representation has been axiomatic. That is, seeing a conflict represented by one person is a very different experience from seeing it acted out in a community and still more different from taking part in that acting-out. There is a qualitative difference between having a conflict described to you in a particular register and participating in the actual clash of viewpoints.

The foregoing objection expresses the common habit of reducing educational problems to a matter of good or bad teaching. This reduction of education to teaching, which goes hand in hand with the glorification of the autonomous, self-contained course as the natural locus of education, fails to see that educational problems are systematic ones that involve not just individual teaching but the way that teaching is organized. Individual teaching is arguably the least promising place to start in transforming education, since it is the aspect of the system that is most subject to idiosyncrasies

of talent and inclination and thus the least amenable to being programmed.

Even the most radical theorists of socially transformative education make their objective the alteration of teacher and student
behavior in closed classrooms rather than the rethinking of the organization of instruction. The system is to be transformed by the
sum total of individual teachers employing alternative pedagogies
in closed classrooms. This tactic makes sense in a situation in
which the closed classroom is the only sphere in which transgression is possible or permissible, but its limits become clear if one reflects that the closed classroom model is rooted in the very bourgeois positivist individualism that these Leftist critics persistently
attack. We have no trouble seeing the *department* as an expression
of this positivist individualism, but the *course* appears as the alternative to it—the garden over against the machine—instead of an
expression of the same forces.

Toward a Dialogical Curriculum

Citing the work of Ira Schor, Paulo Freire, and Henry Giroux,
Dale M. Bauer has recently argued for the need "to foreground dialogics in the classroom."[10] Only a dialogical classroom, Bauer argues, can turn education into a place where questions of authority,
identification, and resistance are explored rather than repressed or
taken for granted. I agree with Bauer's argument, but I maintain
that its logic points to something larger than "the classroom" as the
locus of dialogue. I doubt whether "the classroom" can become
effectively dialogical as long as it is not itself in dialogue with
other classrooms.

What is the advantage of a dialogical structure over a monological one? Simply that in a dialogical curriculum, questions that
challenge or redefine the premises of the discussion would not
arise in one class only to be abruptly dropped in the next, as tends
to be the case now. Since such questions would have a chance to
become part of other conversations besides the one taking place in
the privacy of a single course, the more pertinent ones would figure to be sustained and reinforced. This is the case if only because
the inevitable inequalities of authority in the pedagogical situation
mean that questions like "So What?" "Who cares?" "Could you
clarify that?" "How is that point relevant?" and "Why are we going on about *this* issue to the exclusion of that one?" are more

likely to come from other faculty than from students, at least for the moment.

Granted, a dialogical curriculum would also risk inflicting new kinds of boredom and alienation on students. Instead of being turned off by a single instructor, students could now be turned off by a whole phalanx of instructors. And there is no doubt that a dull, pedantic faculty teaching collaboratively will produce no better result than a dull, pedantic faculty teaching separately. But even in this worst-case scenario, the outcome would not be worse than it can already be under the prevailing system. More to the point, for a generation, hiring and promotion committees have gone to increased expense and trouble to recruit faculties that are not only intellectually gifted and original, but far more representative of the diversity of culture than in the past. So it does not seem unreasonable to assume a faculty with a reasonable potential for intellectual liveliness. My proposition is that, assuming such a faculty, that faculty organized to teach dialogically is more likely to realize this potential than it is working in uncoordinated classrooms.

For the greater the degree of collective interaction, the more likelihood of generating and sustaining self-criticism of whatever is problematic in that interaction, including its lack of relevance to students' interests and needs. To put it another way, a faculty working dialogically figures to be self-correcting in a way that a faculty working in privatized courses is not. That is, given a faculty representative of the present diversity of academic culture, a dialogical curriculum figures to be more theoretically, historically, and politically self-aware than a privatized one. Instead of repressing its own history and politics, such a curriculum would tend to foreground its own history and politics and open it to theoretical debate.

By the same logic, a more collective organization of teaching would figure to foreground questions of political power that a privatized system tends to evoke only intermittently in periodic eruptions. Take the question debated by OMP and YFP about the legitimacy of seeing sexual politics in a poem like "Dover Beach," a central question by anybody's reckoning in the conflict over the humanities. Instead of a situation in which YFP takes it for granted in her course that it is self-evidently a crucial question while OMP takes it for granted in his that it is self-evidently out of order, the crucial debate over the politics of literature would have a chance to become and remain a common context of discussion. This outcome would not in itself redress the power inequalities that concern YFP, but it would at least enable those inequalities to become a theme of general discussion instead of one that erupts now and then only to be buried.

Since some groups and interests are inevitably excluded from any institutional conversation, the metaphor of "conversation" or "dialogue" is often justly criticized as an ideological mystification. But if some groups must be excluded or marginalized, an organization that foregrounds difference and conflict would promise to give the more arbitrary exclusions and marginalizations a better chance than they now have of coming to light and becoming an explicit theme of discussion. Conversation, then, becomes a less politically suspect trope the more the conversation thematizes its own exclusions. The interests of the disempowered tend to be jeopardized most by a privatized system, which offers no public sphere in which their situation can become generally visible.

For this very reason, of course, it will seem to be in OMP's interest to resist entering into dialogue with YFP. Why should the OMPs of the world agree to debate with the YFPs over such an issue as the canon, especially when what bothers the OMPs is that there should *be* a debate over the canon to begin with? Once OMP acknowledges that the canon is a *debate* rather than a self-evident embodiment of value, he has lost the culture war. Why should he lend the debate legitimacy?

For one thing, he may not have a choice. Hiding in his private classroom is not going to make the canon debate go away or cause the issues to become less controversial. OMP can try to deny YFP tenure, but he may not have the power to do so (evidently he could not prevent her from being hired, so he may not be able to prevent her from being promoted), and he may regard such tactics as professionally and morally repugnant. One might argue that it is in OMP's interest to fight for his cause in public where he may be able to persuade students to his view of things, whereas if he withdraws into the privacy of his classroom he figures to lose the war by attrition to his younger opponents. As for YFP, for different reasons it may be in her interest too to fight her battle in public, lest the victory of her faction result in yet another marginalized radical enclave in the university.

Some OMPs and YFPs may not see it this way, of course, and this is their right. Where it is possible, those of us who want to teach more collectively should go on without those who do not. It is not necessary to get one hundred percent faculty (or student) participation to increase the degree of intellectual community enough to have a significant impact on teaching and learning. Those who want to be left alone should be respected, but it does not follow that the university has to be run for their convenience.

Then, too, their proportions may be smaller now that a generation of teachers has entered the university for whom terms like "dialogical," "rhetoric," "interdisciplinary," "conversation," and "public sphere" pack a positive charge. This development is part of a larger transformation in the conception of knowledge and culture, one that shatters the old partnership which founded the modern university between the positivist idea of knowledge as a series of building blocks added to an ever-accumulating pyramid and the humanistic idea of culture as a fixed set of traditions. Knowledge and culture now look less like a unified package, capable of being formalized in a list of great books or cultural literacy facts, and more like a set of unruly and conflicted social practices. But though the shape of knowledge and culture has been transformed, departmental and curricular structure continues to express an earlier positivist-humanist paradigm, though one that most lay people and conservative academics still hold. This very conflict and the need to work through it demands a model of the curriculum that is neither a cafeteria counter nor a core, but something more like a conversation.

Several promising models are already at hand: in the new English major in "English and Textual Studies" at Syracuse and a comparable one at Carnegie Mellon; in interdisciplinary programs such as the one in Cultural Studies at the University of Pittsburgh that emphasize collective teaching and make use of metacourses in theory and methodology to give coherence to the variety of other courses in the curriculum; in integrated programs that have arisen on campuses off the prestige mainline like Evergreen State, Alverno College, Mount St. Mary's of Maryland, and the University of North Carolina at Greensboro; in the Ph.D. program in "English Studies" under development at Illinois State University, which actually takes seriously and makes part of its object of study what has always been assumed but honored only in the breach— that graduate students are being trained to teach literature as well as research it.

The rationale guiding the Syracuse major is worth quoting: the major attempts

> to distinguish between a traditional pluralism, in which there are many separate viewpoints and each exists without locating itself

in relation to opposing viewpoints, and a multiplicity of positions, each of which acknowledges a contestatory relation to
other positions. The purpose of a curriculum based on the latter
model is not to impose one way of knowing on everyone but to
make the differences between ways of knowing visible and to
foreground what is at stake in one way of knowing against another. The goal is to make students aware of how knowledge is
produced and how reading takes place and thus able to make
them capable of playing an active role in their society, enabling
them to intervene in the dominant discourses of their culture.[11]

This and other new programs, which need to be discussed at more
length than is possible here, should be studied seriously by curricular planners. But steps in the direction they point can be taken
right away without elaborate bureaucratic complications, and I
want to suggest one strategy (I have observed something like it
used successfully in an NEH-funded Freshman Seminar program
at the University of North Carolina at Greensboro entitled
"Teaching the Canon and the Conflicts"). This idea has the advantage of building on the courses that happen to be already scheduled in a department or college at a given moment, and of drawing
on a familiar format, the academic conference.

The idea is to *thematize the semester*. It works this way: a department or college (or a group of teachers in different departments or colleges) decides that in the coming semester some or all
of its courses will have a common theme. The theme should be one
that packs contemporary urgency but also has a history that can be
traced and opens out potentially into diverse lines of inquiry.
Sample themes could be, Interpretation Across the Disciplines; The
Crisis of Traditional Culture; Majority and Minority Cultures; The
Canon Controversy; The Politics of Representation; Contemporary
Art and Academic Scholarship; Social Constructionism and Its Discontents; The Arts in a Business Society. Disagreements will inevitably arise in choosing the theme, but since the theme can
change from year to year it should be possible to avoid the kind of
deadlock that results when it is assumed the aim must be to
formulate definitively the core subjects of a liberal education.

Having determined the theme, instructors (with interested
students) choose two or three common texts, which will help give
focus to the theme and provide a basis for common meetings of all
the courses involved. Two or three of these common meetings are
scheduled during the semester at a convenient hour. The common
meetings are modeled along the lines of the academic conferences

and symposia which so many faculty now find indispensable to our intellectual life, the premise being that if such conferences are so helpful in socializing faculty (and increasingly graduate students) into academic discourses and debates, then if suitably adapted they could perform the same function for undergraduates.

The multicourse symposia would concentrate on common issues across the courses raised by the common texts and on exemplary points of difference and convergence over them. Speakers (possibly an author of one of the texts) could be invited from outside to bring a further perspective to the discussion. It would be of crucial importance that students not remain in a passive relation to this symposium, but their roles could vary depending on degrees of initial aptitude and interest, ranging from writing papers about the conference, to presenting some of the papers and responses in it, to planning and organizing the program itself. The point would be not just to expose students passively to the interplay of diverse discourses, but to help them gain control of these discourses by experiencing them as part of the social practices of a community rather than in closed classrooms. If successful, the experiment might provide the basis for more ambitious changes, such as a required metacourse in "Contested Issues in the Humanities," or a revised major or interdisciplinary program.

Thematizing the semester figures to bring about a number of desirable things that now tend to be missing from day-to-day academic life. It would create the common sites of discussion that I have been arguing are necessary for the clarification of academic discourse communities, yet it would create those common discussion sites without the need for either a faculty consensus on first principles or a fixed canon or core curriculum.[12] For it would now be the differences of perspective themselves that would give the discussion its coherence and commonality without fixed subjects or texts. Since the common texts and issues would be revisable from semester to semester, conflicting interests would be satisfiable without the sacrifice of intellectual community that results from the "Let's Make a Deal" tradeoffs of the laissez-faire curriculum.

To follow the strategy outlined here would be to shift the terms of the recent curriculum debate, which has tended to be fixated on single components of the educational process rather than on the total system as students experience it. Attention would shift from isolated great books, cultural literacy facts, and subjects, and from isolated classrooms, to the special social practices in which books, facts and subjects are treated by academic communities. For finally what students study is not books, facts, and subjects, but the way an intellectual community at a given moment deals with these components. As long as students remain outsiders to that community, education is likely to remain an alienating process for the majority, regardless of what texts and subjects are studied.

I have operated on the premise that the best way to learn a foreign language is to live in the country in which it is spoken. Most students, like most Americans generally, do not speak the language of academic intellectual culture because they do not feel themselves part of the country in which the language is spoken. Those students experience that country through a curriculum that does not appear as a community at all, much less one they can imagine joining. So the curriculum obscures rather than clarifies the country of the academic intellectual community that it potentially represents and helps produce a normal environment whose most energizing features, its political and philosophical conflicts, are hidden from view. The country is not intrinsically impenetrable, but the way it is represented by the curriculum makes it *look* more impenetrable and less interesting than it has to be. If it is to represent the country in its real vitality, the curriculum needs to put its own philosophical differences at its center.

Notes

1. I have in mind such attacks as Robert Alter's *The Pleasures of Reading in an Ideological Age* (New York: Simon & Schuster, 1989) and the essays and reviews of Denis Donoghue, Roger Shattuck, and others, the effect of which is to provoke more of the metadiscourse about assumptions, values, and principles that these writers regret.

2. In *Professing Literature: An Institutional History* (Chicago: University of Chicago Press, 1987), I quote a number of statements by professors of this era on the absolute imperviousness of the contemporary college student to literary culture of any kind (pp. 104–18).

3. Of course one who has been following recent journalist reports would get the idea that the trendier English departments have virtually stopped assigning anything but rap songs and rock videos. The full story of how the issue has been reported would make an interesting chapter in the annals of disinformation.

For example, in a 1988 editorial in the *Chronicle of Higher Education*, Christopher Clausen, who is Head of the English Department at Pennsylvania State University and thus might have been expected to know better, offered to bet that Alice Walker's novel *The Color Purple* "is taught in more English courses today than all of Shakespeare's plays combined" ("It is Not Elitist to Place Major Literature at the Centre of the English Curriculum," *Chronicle of Higher Education*, Jan. 13, 1988, sec. A, p. 52). Perhaps Professor Clausen intended his remark as hyperbole—surely even at peak popularity *The Color Purple* has never been assigned with a third of the frequency of any of Shakespeare's major plays. In any case, before any money could be got down on Clausen's improbable wager, his remark was cited as sober truth by Secretary of Education William J. Bennett, in a widely reported address to the National Association of Independent Colleges and Universities. This was the address in which Bennett charged that a group of "trendy lightweights" was undermining the western cultural heritage. "The American public is losing faith in colleges and universities," the *Chronicle* reported Bennett as saying, "because faculty members are eliminating classic works from the curriculum and replacing them with 'nonsense' promoted by 'trendy lightweights.'" ("Bennett: Colleges' 'Trendy Lightweights' Replace Classics with Nonsense," *Chronicle of Higher Education*, Feb. 10, 1988, sec. A, p. 27).

The same week as Bennett's speech, Clausen's remark was cited once again as truth by David Brooks in another angry denunciation of canon-busting professors in the *Wall Street Journal* (Feb. 2, 1988). Brooks's article, entitled "From Western Lit to Westerns as Lit," conveyed the impression that at Duke University and elsewhere the teaching of popular Westerns by such writers as Louis L'Amour had virtually superseded Shakespeare and other major authors.

Only a month earlier, Jonathan Yardley had written in a piece in the *Washington Post* on "The Fall of Literary Standards" that "according to [current] vigilantes of the English departments, literary quality is irrelevant.... Makes you want to rush right back to college, doesn't it? To hell with Shakespeare and Milton, Emerson and Faulkner! Let's boogie! Let's take courses in the writers who really matter, the writers whom the WASPish old guard sneers at. Let's get relevant with courses on Gothic novels, bodice-ripper romances, westerns, detective stories—all of which, The [New York] Times advises us, 'are proliferating' in the English departments" (Jan. 11, 1988). Yardley did not identify the *Times* article, but by now the network of self-confirming falsehoods was so thick that it hardly mattered who was quoting whom. It was now common knowledge that the canon-busters were plotting, and perhaps had already achieved, nothing less than the liquidation of the classics. As Terry Teachout put it in the March 1988 issue of *Commentary*, it was the expressed objective of the revisionists "to erase the values of Western culture from the minds of the young by deliberately failing to introduce them to the history and literature in which those values are embodied" (p. 71).

It is of course true that the canonical classics now share time increasingly with the texts of popular culture and minority traditions. Yet the extent and pervasiveness of that displacement has been grossly exaggerated, as a Modern Language Association sampling of undergraduate English offerings has recently documented. (See Charles B. Harris, "The ADE Ad Hoc Committee on the English Curriculum: A Progress Report," *ADE Bulletin*, 85 [Winter 1986], pp. 26–31.)

4. Traditional humanists deny responsibility for this problem by blaming the impenetrability of academic culture on the "jargon" of their trendy opponents. They conveniently ignore the fact that to most people in our society the word "humanist" is no less a form of jargon than the word "deconstruction" or "problematize." This fact was brought home to me recently when, waiting with a group of scholars for a bus to the National Humanities Center in North Carolina, I heard a pager announce, "Will the group going to the National *Humanitarian* Centre please come to the baggage claim area."

For a typically smug attack on theory jargon, see Alter, *The Pleasures of Reading* (pp. 16ff). After quoting a specimen from an article on Kafka, Alter says that the perception it contains "has been stated not only more elegantly but also more instructively by critics who do not use this jargon of the new literary technocrats; that Kafka invents a mode of enigmatic fiction which taps an inchoate realm of the unconscious and defies conventional habits of interpretation" (p. 17). I asked my class what they thought of Alter's supposedly more eloquent and instructive version. "It's no better, is it?" they declared. To them, "… invents a mode of enigmatic fiction which taps an inchoate realm of the unconscious," etc., was indistinguishable from Alter's most barbaric cases of theory jargon.

5. Henry Louis Gates, Jr., "The Master's Pieces: On Canon Formation and the African-American Tradition," *South Atlantic Quarterly*, 89.1 (Winter 1990), p. 91.

6. Gary Waller has called this strategy the "park bench principle": "When a powerful newcomer shows up, everyone on the bench shuffles over just a little to make room for the latest arrival. Occasionally, if things get a little crowded, the one at the end falls off—Anglo Saxon, perhaps, or philology." (Gary Waller, "Powerful Silence: 'Theory' in the English Major," *ADE Bulletin*, 85 [Winter 1986], p. 33.)

7. For an analysis of the paradoxes of cooptation theories, see my "Cooptation," in *The New Historicism*, ed H. Aram Veeser (New York: Routledge, 1989), pp. 168–81.

8. Thomas S. Kuhn, *The Structure of Scientific Revolutions* (Chicago: University of Chicago Press, 1962).

9. One cannot overlook the possibility that my student got some benefit from trying out conflicting vocabularies without committing himself to any just yet. The question is how well he can try out those vocabularies if he never sees them engaging one another.

10. Dale M. Bauer, "The Other 'F' Word: The Feminist in the Class-room," *College English,* 52.4 (April 1990), p. 387.

11. The Syracuse curriculum is described in the Syracuse *English Newsletter* (from which I have quoted here); the Carnegie Mellon curriculum is described by Gary Waller in the article cited in n. 6; the Evergreen State model resembles the "Federated Learning Communities" developed by Patrick A. Hill in the late seventies at the State University of New York at Stony Brook; see Hill, "Medium and Message in General Education," *Liberal Education,* 67.2 (1981), pp. 129–45, and "Communities of Learners: Curriculum as the Infrastructure of Academic Communities," *Opposition to Core Curriculum: Alternative Models of Undergraduate Education,* ed. James W. Hall and Barbara L. Kelves (Westport, CT: Greenwood, 1982), pp. 108–34.

On course integration at Alverno, see *Teaching Critical Thinking in the Arts and Humanities,* ed. Lucy S. Cromwell (Milwaukee: Alverno College Productions, 1986), esp. Ch. 4 by James Roth.

In addition to the essay by Waller just mentioned and conversations with Waller and Steven Mailloux of Syracuse, my thinking has been influenced by the well-known work on "discourse communities" by composition and rhetoric specialists like Patricia Bizzell and David Bartholomae, work that has been in turn influenced by the theorizing on "interpretive communities" of Stanley Fish. The writings of Bakhtin, Rorty, Habermas, and Derrida provide various kinds of stimulus for the idea of a "dialogical curriculum."

12. Adapted to the lower schools, these principles need to be developed as an alternative to E.D. Hirsch's Cultural Literacy project, which in my view wrongly assumes that information can and should be acquired *before* a student enters an intellectual community. My assumption is that decontextualized lists or other inventories of facts are essentially unlearnable in themselves, and can never generate the incentive to learn them. Information is usefully acquired only through an interested engagement in a community's activities and purposes. We should proceed on the assumption that a curriculum structured as a viable intellectual community would itself provide the information necessary to enter the community's discussions, and would generate the incentive to learn that information.

Teaching Post-Colonial Literary Theory

Helen Tiffin

The resilience of humanities disciplines in the face of the increasing pragmatism of government-inspired agendas for university education is due to their being simultaneously conservative and radical. The humanities preserve and promulgate knowledge of the past while constantly examining and reevaluating the conceptual frames within which that knowledge was generated. Their dynamic is thus one of preservation and interrogation; of historical recuperation and epistemological exploration.

In recent years there has been a struggle (or accommodation) within English departments over two major issues: literary theory and its relationship to literature and literary texts; and the relationship between a canonized and deeply institutionalized "mainstream" British literature and other literatures in English. My focus in discussing these related schisms is on the teaching of literature and literary theory in universities outside Britain and the United States. My particular context is Australian, but the question of the teaching of post-colonial literary theory within post-colonized tertiary institutions does have some application to Canada, the Caribbean, India, New Zealand, and some African countries. Though the teaching of post-colonial literary theory is likely to stand in a different relationship to the discipline and the departments in Britain (and to a lesser degree the United States), I think that some of what I draw from my own experience still has applicability in English departments worldwide.

Teaching post-colonial literary theory has at least two purposes: to historicize and theorize literary teaching generally and English literature and post-colonial literatures in particular; and secondly, on the basis of such theorization and contextualization, to influence the ongoing processes of decolonization at their interface with contemporary forms of neo-colonialism, specifically those which are effected and maintained through representation. The teaching of post-colonial literatures and literary theory will not save the world, reverse historical injustices, or stop contemporary atrocities; it will not radically reconfigure inequalities or marginalizations. But through an understanding of the ways in which oppression operates and has operated in and through representation, we can hope to eventually educate our own populations in a greater critical and interrogative awareness of its processes. Understanding the force of representation in international capitalism will not provide a mechanism to halt its march, but an awareness of forms of oppression and the part played by representation may in the end lead to changed perspectives, and thus to altered priorities.

Literary Theory and the Post-Colonial Text

I want to begin this account not with the teaching of theory as it is usually understood, but with a post-colonial literary text, since literary texts, in spite of the recent turn to theory, remain the focus of most English department curricula. "Set texts" (outside theory courses themselves) are still predominantly novels, poetry collections, anthologies, and published dramatic works. Anyone planning to teach post-colonial theory in an English department, without teaching post-colonial *literary* texts is less likely to attract students whose former training and indeed proclivities (otherwise they might have chosen philosophy as their discipline) accord with a text-centered curriculum.

But secondly, there is a particular reason why any post-colonial literary theory course would prioritize the literary text. As Stephen Slemon and others have noted, "for most post-colonial literary critics, a return to—a grounding in—the post-colonial literary text itself comprises an absolutely crucial gesture within the politics of critical writing and the *sine qua non* of a literary critical engagement with the structures of neo-colonialist power."[1]

Thirdly, in spite of the unsettling theoretical climate which currently surrounds the literary text, literature remains focal in English departments not just through conservatism or inertia, but because of the sheer potency of literature itself, its psychological, emotive "footprint." Macaulay's 1835 *Minute*, which insisted that all funds appropriated to education in India be expended on English education alone, recognized the interpellative power of language-as-culture. Such education, Macaulay calculated, would produce a "native" civil service "Indian in blood and colour, but English in taste, in opinions, in morals, and in intellect."[2] And as Gauri Viswanathan has demonstrated from the 1852–53 British Parliamentary papers, literary education, and the British literary text were focal in this process.[3] Learning "by heart" the products of British culture would replace Christian teaching in the crucially emotion-centered aspects of imperialist interpellation. That such "colonization by consent" (to adapt Gramsci's term) was one of the most effective tools in the imperialist arsenal is attested by the persistence, well beyond political independence, of Anglo-canonical curricula in English departments throughout the post-colonized world. In the complex processes of *de*colonizing minds (and "hearts"), literature and literature departments have played—indeed still play—a major role.

As well as its metaphoric potency and its theoretical valency, the post-colonial literary text also offers a particularly appropriate "beginning" in that, in contemporary literary theoretical scholarship and teaching, Europe has recolonized the academy. That the philosophies of Lyotard, Althusser, Derrida, and Cixous are originally *Algerian* perceptions generated from a colonialist crucible has long been occluded by their cooption to the Parisian metropole. As the Nigerian writer Wole Soyinka has commented: "We ... have been blandly invited to submit ourselves to a second epoch of colonization—this time by a universal-humanoid abstraction defined and conducted by individuals whose theories and prescriptions are derived from the apprehension of *their* world and *their* history, *their* social neuroses and *their* value systems."[4] Soyinka, like Hayden White, thus finds that "The contours of criticism are unclear, its geography unspecified, and its topography therefore uncertain. As a form of intellectual practice, no field is more imperialistic."[5] Even though much of the dis/mantling of Anglo-canonical investiture has taken place under the auspices of contemporary post-structuralist theory, as many post-colonial writers and scholars have pointed out, post-structuralism's very latinate language evokes missionary education and colonialist subjectification, acting to silence Third World intellectuals and readers in their work as theorists through its interpellation of a subordinate subjectivity.[6] For all these reasons, the starting point for me in teaching post-colonial theory remains the literary text.

Erna Brodber's novel *Myal* (1988) is a profound meditation on colonialist education and potential modes of decolonization. Set in Jamaica, *Myal* has a complex plot, both strands of which are concerned with "spirit thievery" and the strategies whereby "illegal" and profoundly destructive representational capture and confinement might be undone.

The protagonist Ella O'Grady (whose mixed blood is itself metonymic of the effects of Anglo-education on Black Jamaicans, "divided," in Derek Walcott's terms "to the vein" by that "ambiguous gift" of the English language) is introduced as the reciter ("by heart") of a poem by Kipling.[7] Speaking as if she were of the imperial party (and not the subjectified colonials the poem represents), Ella enjoins the Jamaican primary school class to

> Take up the whiteman's burden
> Send forth the best ye breed
> Go bind your sons to exile
> To serve your captive's need
> To wait in heavy harness
> On filtered folk and wild
> Your new caught sullen peoples
> Half devil and half child.[8]

Symptomatically, Ella *lives* in the world of the English books she has been taught and has read (and the poems she recites), and not in her Jamaican Grove Town. As a teenager she is eventually taken to the United States where she meets Selwyn Langley, the man who will administer a cruel but vital lesson in representational aggression and imperialist interpellation. Eager to move from his family's patent medicine business to stage production and direction, he extracts and transforms Ella's Jamaican memories, "distilling" them into a classic "coon show." Langley, pleased with his production, triumphantly presents these grossly racist representations to Ella on opening night. Where Ella had not apparently been affected by British textual representations, Langley's (re)production of Jamaicans literally brings the dis/ease of imperialist stereotyping home. Ella begins to suffer from an apparently incurable abdominal swelling and is taken back to the Caribbean. She has as yet no way of analyzing the two forms of "spirit thievery" that have occurred and which Langley's "patent medicine" is powerless to cure. But back in Jamaica, Ella ("the little cat choked on foreign") is finally restored through the ministrations of Mass Cyrus and the processes of communal healing (Myalism).

Still, Ella's cure is not quite complete. For this to be effected she must return to the source of original infection, the school, and to the texts she was taught there. Ella has recovered sufficiently to become a teacher, and finds she is constrained by the primary syllabus to teach the stories of Mr. Joe's Farm. On this farm the animals are protected and well cared for, but they have no freedom or autonomy, no way of relating to the world except through the benevolent rule of Mr. Joe. A number of the animals decide to rebel and set off to make their own way in the outside world. One by one, however, they find they cannot fend for themselves, and like naughty children, they return, chastened, to Mr. Joe's forgivingly adult care and attention. Since this story is on the primary school syllabus, Ella is forced to teach it. She risks dismissal (and replacement by a compliant teacher) and/or disadvantages the children who will be examined on it if she refuses. So in conjunction with other members of the Grove Town community Ella adopts the following strategy: she will teach the text, but she will teach it against the grain, situating it historically and politically, critiquing and interrogating the parable of colonial obedience it was designed to inculcate. Ella, the once proud re/presenter of Kipling's poem, thus comes to not only interrogate the practices of a colonialist literary education, but to do so through the very texts which deliberately (and sometimes adventitiously) produce(d) obedient colonial subjects.

Myal is both an enjoyable novel and a theoretical text, one which offers a theory of post-colonized literary teaching which is inextricably interwoven with a politics of demystification of literary representation in what Sara Suleri has termed "context[s] of colonial exchange."[9] It thus insists on situating the text culturally, politically, and institutionally; *and* in terms of its imperial production and colonial consumption. It insists on the importance of texts—specifically literary texts—in sponsoring colonialist subjectification and creating obedient subjects who "consent" in their own colonization. And it suggests ways in which the same texts might be presented and taught differently so that their potency is harnessed to a project of de- rather than re-colonization. Moreover *Myal*, like many post-colonial novels, raises the issue of the fetishization of education and hence of the Anglo-canonical in colonized communities—even in those classes/groups who have not themselves had access to education. Most important of all, perhaps, *Myal* demonstrates the ways in which bodies are constituted, re-constructed, dis/eased through representation.

Teaching Against the Grain

Within colonial and post-colonial contexts, then, teaching a genuinely post-colonial theory does not mean to me simply a study of major essays and monographs by canonized post-colonial theorists (in the more narrow definitions of the term), though a study of their works is of course important. But it does seem to me that the crucial issues and debates in the area should first be seen to arise out of the literary texts themselves, and that commentary by post-colonial intellectuals such as Edward Said, Homi Bhabha, Stephen Slemon, Gayatri Spivak, Sara Suleri, or Kwame Anthony Appiah might *then* offer valuable intervention.

But teaching post-colonial literary theory also involves more than teaching the literary texts and relevant "theorists." It involves, for me, an approach which necessarily impacts on literary study generally and the current structures and ideologies of English departments as they are still generally organized. In the rest of this paper I will consider four ways in which post-colonial literary theory can be effectively introduced into the curriculum.

The first way is to offer courses which consider post-colonial texts themselves. Courses of this kind take many forms and may include works from settler-invader societies as well as those from colonies of invasion and occupation. (In English departments these tend to be from formerly Anglo-colonized cultures.) Not all literature from these areas is likely to be *counter*-colonial, but many teachers may choose to focus on texts which are. My definition of colonial/post-colonial is, however, a historically determined one, since I do not regard the term "colonialism" as synonymous with all forms of marginalization or oppression. I thus see these basic courses as inescapably grounded in the history of European colonialism. The contemporary *counter*-colonial texts which are studied in these courses are then as much a product of that history as they are of the pre-colonized indigenous or post-colonized creolized cultures which are frequently constructed as unequivocally oppositional to imported/imposed Anglo-European culture. Each specific "context of colonial exchange" will necessarily be different and hence, while a history of (British) colonization and its processes and institutions provides the connections between the different, formerly colonized societies, *the differences*, both in indigenous cultural base, history of conquest and colonization, creolization, landscape, climate, and so on are crucial. Similarly, differences in the kinds of colonialist institutions imposed or introduced at different times, and the very varying conditions of their reception will generate widely differing effects within both the colonialist and post-colonial paradigms which form the cultural basis for consideration of post- or counter-colonial texts.

Over the last twenty years "post-colonial" and generally counter-canonical courses of various kinds have multiplied within English departments. Yet this increasing pluralism has not displaced in any really significant way the emphasis on British literature; indeed in many cases the effect of apparently radical challenges to the canon has been, paradoxically, a re-enforcing of the status and fetishization of the Anglo-canonical. Any teaching of post-colonial literary theory in the academy is thus obliged to address the issue of literary teaching as a whole, of structural placement within departments and particularly the relationship between British literature and other literatures in English.

The intersection of post-colonialism and contemporary Euro-American literary theories, particularly those which might be broadly designated as "post-structuralist," becomes important here. For all its apparently radical critique and destabilizing implications, recent Euro-American post-structuralist theory has not disturbed the centrality of the English literary canon within the academy, but rather reinforced it. This has occurred, I think, for a number of reasons.

First, where post-colonial, Marxist, and Feminist theory had begun to destabilize the naturalized centrality of British literature courses (usually still being taught in New Critical mode), post-structuralist interventions facilitated new and revivifying ways of reading and teaching canonical works without disturbing their status in the academy. "The Body in Shakespeare" or "Shakespeare's Representations of Women" still fetishize the study of Shakespeare, without questioning *why* Shakespeare or Milton may still be accorded separate courses while all of Australian literature (or worse, Caribbean, Indian, and African) might be compressed into a similar time frame. Secondly, the fetishization of European theory itself as a sort of universal intelligence test within the discipline has reinstated Europe as originator of normative modes of thought, at the precise moment when post-colonial analysis was exposing its earlier techniques of appropriative ideational control in the colonial enterprise. Paradoxically, this new hegemony contradicts the very relativities and attention to difference which the theories imply. Ironically, too, it is the post-colonized cultures which have proved most susceptible to what Simon During has called "import rhetoric."[10] Thirdly, the attractions of contemporary literary theories, where they *are* associated with potentially radical challenges to an Anglo-core curriculum, have tended to isolate theoretical study from analysis of the literary text, leaving the literary ground in English departments to the English "core" texts while those students with more generally philosophical (rather than literary) inclinations do contemporary theory courses. And where literary texts are studied or used as illustrative material they tend to be Anglo-conservative: Shakespeare, Milton, the Romantics, George Eliot.

For all these reasons contemporary Euro-American literary theory, which should have been the Trojan Horse of Anglo-centered departments, has instead smuggled in a revivification of the English canon. In its frequent conjunction with post-colonial theory, and where—in the work of some theorists—it is inextricably interwoven with it, post-structuralism offers a great deal; but it can prove a dangerous travelling companion. A genuinely post-colonial literary theory needs to be wary of (while utilizing) this potential, aware of the dangers incurred in accepting such an "ambiguous gift." Thus the second part of a strategy of teaching post-colonial literary theory involves a consideration of and accommodation with other contemporary theories, and an interrogation not just of their contents, but their *effects* within post-colonial academies.

The third major consideration/strategy is, like the second, concerned with relationships and placement. Around this persisting (and sometimes newly invigorated) English core curriculum, "radical" courses of various kinds have recently proliferated. Though this proliferation has become increasingly subdued by economic constraints, it has nevertheless produced a number of contemporary English departments genuinely pluralist in their content, teaching methods, political and philosophical underpinnings. While this seems an ideal and harmonious arrangement, the result is frequently student confusion and/or cynicism. For all its benefits, such pluralism never forces staff or students to confront the crucial questions of what they teach and why they teach (or read) it (let alone how). Since a major issue for any post-colonial theory is current institutional placement and the history of colonialist education, the *relationship* between post-colonial courses and English canonical ones within an "English" department becomes a crucial theoretical and political issue.

Teaching *against the grain*, as it did in *Myal*, involves more than a study of post-colonial literary texts and theorists, or even the proliferation (where that has been possible) of post-colonial literature and theory courses in congenially pluralist academies. Inevitably it involves departments as institutional units, and it involves dialogue about educational and institutional history, curricula, and teaching methods.

Given current departmental structures and competition for resources in an atmosphere of financial stringency, such "dialogue" frequently becomes friction over issues of the English canon and its post-colonial interrogation, read as a threat of supplantation. Since this friction and competition is clearly undesirable, most departments will (not unreasonably) adopt the pluralist option. But even in the absence of department-wide dialogue, there are ways of opening up this discussion within the post-colonial courses themselves. A lesson in pedagogy and theory can again be elicited from *Myal*, indeed from many post-colonial novels and plays: English canonical literary works cannot simply be ignored, they must be directly challenged. In a very important sense, Ella O'Grady could not afford to ignore the story of Mr. Joe's farm. Teaching it was an essential part of her "cure" and that of her community.

This point can be illustrated through a particularly influential English novel, Daniel Defoe's *Robinson Crusoe*. Like William Shakespeare's *The Tempest* (or, later, Joseph Conrad's *Heart of Darkness*), *Robinson Crusoe* issues from a post-Renaissance complacency about the "natural" power relations between white and black as a master/servant, civilized/savage dominance. Subsequent use of such texts in both domestic and imperial educational systems reproject these relationships, not as historically relative and subject to critique, but as transparent attributes of a text for which universal validity and value are claimed on the basis of psychological realism, material specificity, formal innovativeness, and authorial magnanimity. Thus the racial power relationships become naturalized as a facet of a work whose significance is cast in absolute, not relative or historical, terms. That the iconic power of this endorsement stretches far beyond the boundaries of the classroom even today is easy to demonstrate.

If *Robinson Crusoe* has become an increasingly difficult text to persuade students at tertiary level to read in its entirety, in, say eighteenth-century English novel courses, it nevertheless remains a crucial text in western consciousness. I can recall, in the last year alone, three television commercials which depended for their impact on a basic knowledge of the Robinson Crusoe story. I recently asked a class of two hundred students whether they had read *Robinson Crusoe*. While only twenty remembered ever having done so, almost all could tell me at least three things about the text: that it was set on an island; that a white man was wrecked there; that he had and/or acquired a "black" or "native" servant called "Friday." Some could add that there was "something about cannibalism" and about a "parrot." All of those who "re-membered" the first three things were of course in no doubt as to the power relationship between Robinson Crusoe and Friday. Only those who had recently read the full account (about three people) were clear whether Friday was or was not the original "owner" of the island before the European "shipwreck." Of those who remembered cannibalism as a vague motif, none thought it attached to the hungry castaway (in spite of *Alive!* and two popular television commercials which deliberately attached it to whites for humorous effect). Unquestionably it was Friday who was associated with "cannibalism," even though, in the text, it is his (possible) rescue by Crusoe from this fate which renders him servant-for-life to the white man.

I use this purely anecdotal evidence to suggest two things—the persistence in post-colonized popular culture of the tropes of Anglo-canonical texts (and the violent hierarchies they sponsor and naturalize) and the importance therefore of continuing to teach them, and to teach them in their historical and cultural contexts. Released from these, as free-floating "popular" tropes, their power remains, and remains undiminished. Teaching post-colonial literary theory thus involves continuing to teach the Anglo-canonical, but teaching it, as Ella did *Mr. Joe's Farm*, against the grain.

There are, in my experience, two very useful ways of effecting this. The first involves courses structured around dialogue *between* post-colonial re-writings of Anglo-canonical texts and those texts themselves; the second involves teaching those canonical texts within British literature "mainstream" courses, but teaching them differently from the ways in which they have traditionally been taught.

The first strategy, that of bringing post-colonial texts into direct intertextual engagement with their British "pre-texts," can be organized for different university levels. Several years ago I introduced at advanced level (fourth-year honors) a course on the post-colonial rewriting of canonical texts. I structured the course in terms of historical eras, but for political reasons reversed the "pairs" of texts studied so that the post-colonial text was discussed before its British "pre-text." This helps to counter the persisting belief of some students/readers that an intertextual relationship between two works implies a dependent hierarchy; that, as one student put it, "*Wide Sargasso Sea* (1966) is plagiarized from *Jane Eyre*." And once students consider the post-colonial text as autonomous, raising issues of representation, power, colonial history, they can then better go back to the historical and cultural roots of these representations and power structures, seeing them as situated and culturally sponsored, rather than regarding a work like *The Tempest* as establishing some "universal norms" about "human" behavior on which, for instance, Lamming's *Water with Berries* (1973) can then be construed as offering a "merely local" West Indian comment.

The course begins with both settler-invader and colonies-of-occupation rewritings of Shakespeare's *Tempest*—George Lamming's *Water with Berries* (or *Natives of My Person* [1971]) and Randolph Stow's *Visitants* (1981). We then consider *The Tempest* in its own historical context, and the occasion and effects of its re-placement in Caribbean/Australian reading culture and curricula. We also consider the fetishization of "Shakespeare" as a popular cultural phenomenon in post-colonized societies. In a third session we then attempt to discuss the texts together, considering the ways in which *Water with Berries* and *Visitants* have interrogated not just the text of *The Tempest* (or, for later works, of *Robinson Crusoe*, *Jane Eyre*, or *Heart of Darkness*) but the whole of the discursive field within which such texts, produced out of European exploration, conquest and colonization, are situated in terms of their (re)production and consumption in contemporary post-colonial societies.

We then move to Samuel Selvon's *Moses Ascending* and J.M. Coetzee's *Foe* (1986), considering these contemporary works in their own cultural settings before returning to the roots of their intertextual relationship with *Robinson Crusoe* in the contexts of eighteenth-century European expansion, travel narratives, slavery, and the rise of scientific and anthropological epistemologies, those multiple modes of European "capture" of the rest of the globe. After considering *Jane Eyre* and *Wide Sargasso Sea* and various postcolonial rewritings of Joseph Conrad's *Heart of Darkness*, I conclude the course with a study of the Canadian writer Timothy Findley's *Not Wanted on the Voyage* (1984), which, as well as being a profoundly feminist text, offers one of the best analyses in literary form of strategies of colonialist domination and control through representation. Moreover, *Not Wanted on the Voyage* rewrites the Biblical *Genesis*, perhaps the most influential text of all in colonialist discourse.

The novels and plays are supplemented by a "theory" *Reader* and a reading list of relevant theoretical articles which students at fourth-year level can be expected to know. But again I find that discussion of the crucial theoretical issues for post-colonialism—intertextuality, agency, the body, gender, politics and theory, nationality, ethnicity, multiculturalism—arises in the first instance, out of the *textual* intersections on which the course itself is based.

The post-colonial Anglo-canonical "dialogue" provides a very useful honors course for students who have majored in post-colonialism *and* those whose concentration has been on the English canon. But it is possible to teach such a course at an earlier level where its placement may be more politically effective. Russell Mc-Dougall, then at the University of Adelaide, restructured the first-year course along similar lines. Since this course could not be solely controlled by him, compromises with other staff were necessary, and not all the intertextual relationships could focus on the counter-canonical. Not all staff who wished to have some input into English teaching at first-year level agreed with the intertextual framework either, and some refused to teach against the grain in this way. Nevertheless, as McDougall has noted, this could itself be made to work as part of the dialogue.

The second route to "dialogue" between a core English curriculum and its post-colonial "others" involves returning to the English core courses and orienting them rather differently. Last year John Frow and I began teaching an eighteenth-century course entitled "The Enlightenment and Its Contradictions." Refusing to collude in the fiction that eighteenth-century England existed independently of the rest of the world (eighteenth-century scholarship and criticism has long abandoned this fiction, but it is only very recently that the teaching of eighteenth-century literature has begun to follow suit), we structured it to address questions of gender, colonialism, modes of representation in terms of both the paradoxes inherent in Enlightenment philosophy itself, and those generated by the increasing contact between England (and Europe) and "its Others." In this course we consider, as well as Enlightenment philosophy and English domestic history, the representation of women, slavery, colonialism, travel, and science. We thus relate M.G. Lewis' *The Monk* to Revolutionary discourse and to representations of women; but we also study Lewis' Jamaican *Journal of a*

Residence Among the Negroes in the West Indies and Lady Nugent's *Journal.* We begin with *The Spectator* and *Robinson Crusoe,* concluding with the *Journals of Captain James Cook* and *Mansfield Park,* a text we read for, among many other things, its colonial inflections. We also study twentieth-century writing about the eighteenth century—extracts from Foucault's *Discipline and Punish,* Paul Carter's *The Road to Botany Bay,* Barbara Stafford's *Journey into Substance.* Such a course facilitates a critique of European colonization as it was developing, a critique which is based on historical knowledge and is not simply the product of an *a*-historical anti-colonialist reflex. Similarly, the Renaissance period and particularly the nineteenth century provide exciting material for geniune *post*-colonial reformulations (and revitalization) of the teaching of English literature.

The teaching of post-colonial literary theory at University level thus involves, for me, a multi-layered department-wide strategy. Primarily post-colonial texts should be made available to the students within their cultural and historical contexts. Such texts, within the context of post-imperial education, are *necessarily theoretical* in that, whether overtly counter-colonial or not, they inevitably offer a commentary on—a response to—that context of colonial exchange. Secondly, contemporary post-colonial "formal" theory and its relationship to contemporary Euro-American poststructuralist theory needs to be considered. Thirdly, a necessary dialogue between persisting Anglo-centered curricula and postcolonialism can be facilitated by courses with an intertextual basis, and by a post-colonized re-presentation of earlier periods of British literary history.

It is possible to conceive of a course in post-colonial literary theory which addresses the major issues such as agency, representation, intertextuality, the relationships between modernism, postmodernism, colonialism and post-colonialism, subject formation, and (to adopt Pecheux's term) "disidentification," without ever reading a literary text by a post-colonial writer. Such theory studied *in vacuo* will, I believe, prove ultimately forgettable and politically inefficacious. A novel such as Erna Brodber's *Myal,* by contrast, introduces and "discusses" most of those major theoretical issues I have noted above, but does so as the British colonizers did, by appealing to the imagination and the emotions as well as to the intellect.

Notes

1. Stephen Slemon and Helen Tiffin, eds., *After Europe: Critical Theory and Post-Colonial Writing* (Mundelstrup: Dangeroo Press, 1989), p. xvii. Writing specifically of Second-World (settler-colony literatures) in the context of anti-colonialist theories of resistance, Slemon notes that the

> internalization of the object of resistance in Second-World literatures, [the] internalization of the self/other binary of colonialist relations, explains why it has always been Second-World *literary* writing rather than Second-World *critical* writing which has occupied the vanguard of a Second-World post-colonial literary or critical *theory*. Literary writing is *about* internalised conflict, whereas critical writing—for most practitioners—is still grounded in the ideology of unitariness, and coherence, and specific argumentative drive ("Unsettling the Empire: Resistance Theory for the Second World," *World Literature Written in English*, 30.2 [1990], p. 39)

2. Thomas B. Macauley, "Indian Education: Minute of the 2nd February, 1935," in G.M. Young, ed., *Macaulay: Prose and Poetry* (London: Rupert Hart-Davis, 1952), p. 359.

3. Gauri Viswanathan, *Masks of Conquest: Literary Study and British Rule in India* (London: Faber, 1989) pp. 68–93 and passim.

4. Wole Soyinka, *Myth, Literature, and the African World* (Cambridge: Cambridge University Press, 1976), p. x.

5. Hayden White, *Tropics of Discourse: Essays in Cultural Criticism* (Baltimore: Johns Hopkins University Press, 1973), p. 281.

6. See Barbara Christian, "The Race for Theory," *Cultural Critique*, 6 (1987), pp. 51–63.

7. Derek Walcott "A Far Cry from Africa," in *Derek Walcott Collected Poems 1948–1984* (New York: Farrar, Straus and Giroux, 1986), p. 18.

8. Erna Brodber, *Myal* (London: New Beacon Press, 1988), p. 6.

9. Sara Suleri, *The Rhetoric of English India* (Chicago: University of Chicago Press, 1992), p. 2.

10. Simon During, "Postmodernism or Postcolonialism," *Landfall*, 19.3 (September 1985), p. 369.

Teaching Literature and Theology: A Lesson in Two Parts

David Jasper

I

Teaching literature and theology or religion is undoubtedly now on the agenda in colleges and universities, problematically so for academic institutions since it should not be claimed that such interdisciplinary concern constitutes a subject, and no one can properly be called an expert in this field. At best, perhaps, one might claim to be an *entrepreneur*. My own professional situation is uncomfortably, though creatively, suspended between two departments, one of English literature, the other of theology, between which one is tacitly expected to be an "expert" in both fields, or, at least, a biblical critic (lacking much of the "technical" skill required) who ventures into literary theory from time to time (and bothers biblical studies with the "wrong" sort of language). The discomfort one feels is, perhaps, the more surprising inasmuch as so many people, at least initially, appear to perceive the relationship between literature and theology as essentially simple, even natural, and a kind of new, palatable way of pursuing a theological interest. For example, in a little book much read some years ago entitled *The Passion of Man* (1980), David Anderson wrote that "the passion of man explored in tragic literature is the same passion as that appropriated by the Son of Man on Calvary, and that there is a comparability of meaning between the one and the other which may help us to gain a deeper understanding of the story of our redemption."[1] If the writer of these words had read George Steiner's *The Death of Tragedy* (1961), he might have perceived how extraordinarily dangerous his naïveté was in our post-holocaust world. More sophisticated than David Anderson, but, in my view, no less blind to the implications of European thought and culture in our own times, is Michael Edwards' *Towards a Christian Poetics* (1984), with its "steep perspective" on literature. My students, mainly postgraduates, and largely from North America and Britain, take their starting points variously from training in literature, theology or religious studies, and engage in seminar discussions which oblige them to revise their critical preconceptions in reading under the overarching scrutiny of contemporary cultural and political tendencies to dogmatism and suspicious of any disciplinary leanings to self-contained and merely "academic" claims.

In retrospect, though I have often used him in my own teaching as a fall guy, I have increasing respect for the insights of T.S. Eliot in his seminal 1935 essay "Religion and Literature," though I would no longer wish to stand by his "explicit ethical and theological standards."[2] Precisely because the essay is so problematic, I tend to open my seminar with it. Eliot recognizes the clear distinction between the two elements in his discussion, and most acutely in his perception of the literary nature of biblical texts. I now share with him a critical distaste for the phrase "the Bible as literature"— recently re-vivified by a book of that title by John B. Gabel and Charles B. Wheeler[3]—and agree with Eliot that "the Bible has had a *literary* influence upon English literature *not* because it has been considered as literature, but because it has been considered as the report of the Word of God. And the fact that men of letters now discuss it as 'literature' probably indicates the *end* of its 'literary' influence" (*Selected Essays*, p. 390).

Underlying Eliot's remark is the inevitable tension which exists between biblical critics and literary critics who have turned their attention to scripture—a tension born of far more than simply professional jealousy. It arises out of different understandings of textuality, the one driven by broadly theological or even spiritual motivation, the other, not surprisingly, a hydra-headed child of old New Criticism, with, as one of its early proponents put it, its frustation with "the mishmash of philology, biography, moral admonition, textual exegesis, social history, and sheer burbling" that largely makes up what goes for literary criticism in biblical studies.[4]

Literary-critical approaches to scripture have been largely iconoclastic. That is not to negate their value. Frank Kermode's *The Genesis of Secrecy* (1979) remains an important study, despite or perhaps because of its somewhat morose skepticism, and not least because it develops so challengingly the implications of the work of so devout a Christian biblical critic as Austin Farrer. More recently, the three books of the feminist critic Mieke Bal on the Old Testament have challenged the theological undergirding of mainstream biblical critics by a piercing literary analysis of the texts.[5] My experience in teaching suggests to me that such bravely "literary" studies have, as T.S. Eliot intimated, proved far more stimulating for students who measure them against the commentaries and face the difficult theological issues which result, rather than the more amiable work of people like Northrop Frye or Robert Alter—from the Christian and Jewish traditions respectively. Such critics seem to feel that they can keep a leaky ship afloat with new "literary" tools. My problem with Frye is that he is just not a very good *reader* of texts.

One scholar who combines in a spectacular manner solid New Testament scholarship with a sensitive appreciation of contemporary literary theory and criticism is Stephen D. Moore, in his book *Literary Criticism and the Gospels* (1989), which is significantly subtitled *The Theoretical Challenge*. New Testament scholarship, usually conducted from within the fold of theological or religious studies, is here challenged by the broad, many-sided sweep of literary criticism and theory. Moore—an erstwhile Cistercian monk who has since gone on to apply creative literary theory to a reading of the gospels in the rhetoric, and language (as well as techniques) of Derrida, Lacan, and Foucault—expresses his own experience succintly:

> Convinced now of the necessity of an iconoclastic moment in biblical studies (for myself, at any rate)—a revision, though not a religion, of foundational concepts such as Bible and exegesis ...— I feel a spring-like quickening of my intellectual *and* spiritual sap such as I have not felt since historical criticism's first rude accostation mated my quest for Reality ... with a questioning. "For to begin thinking such thoughts is to approach the boundaries of faith." (Kierkegaard)[6]

Iconoclastic we may have to be, but we should recognize with Stephen Moore that any program in literature and religion will be, at heart, a theological or even spiritual enquiry. The failure to perceive that has, I suggest, resulted in the initial confusion and ultimate failure of most North American programs in the field, although even there—in a university culture which is deeply suspicious of theology in general—there are signs of a theological return in interdisciplinary studies, as it were through the back door. Theological we are bound to be, but as that rare bird, a theologian who is also a good reader. That might be a good description of my long-

term pedagogic aim with my postgraduate students. For this reason, any course of study in literature and theology must face the
matter of hermeneutics head-on, for, as the father of modern
hermeneutics, or interpretation theory, Friedrich Schleiermacher,
maintained, his concern is with nothing other than the art of good
reading.

Students of literature and theology (indeed all students of theology) should, I maintain, have at least an acquaintance with the
development of hermeneutical theory since Schleiermacher
through thinkers like Dilthey, Husserl, Heidegger, Bultmann, and
Ricoeur. A tall order, you may say, but it can be done and can provide the background of self-reflective critical enquiry to encourage
reading across discipline boundaries—a difficult enough task. We
should, of course, bear in mind that Schleiermacher did not consider hermeneutics as a *theoretical* tool to sharpen our understanding of particular texts.[7] Rather, as understanding is the goal of
hermeneutics, so we should assume that in reading misunderstanding and not understanding usually occurs. To achieve proper
understanding, Schleiermacher does not presume to offer abstract
or theoretical programs. His practical approach to the subject—
now readily available in a translation of the handwritten
manuscripts on hermeneutics[8]—actually sets the tone for the modern tradition of hermeneutics, which lends itself to direct application to texts in literature and the biblical corpus.

As we have established the theological heart of our program,
and the necessity of attention to interpretation theory, we come to
appreciate also the necessary *philosophical* dimension of our task. It
has long been recognized that literary theory and theorists have
fractured the distinctions between disciplines in the arts and in the
history of ideas. Jürgen Habermas appends an excursus to his
chapter on Derrida in *The Philosophical Discourse of Modernity* (1985
trans.) which is devoted to "leveling the Genre Distinction between
Philosophy and Literature." Who owns critics like Derrida, or
Harold Bloom, or Paul de Man—philosophy, literature, or even
perhaps theology? In some ways, Schleiermacher is to blame for
the problem since not only did he demand a *universal* hermeneutic—the same for the Bible as for any other literature—but more
important still, he turned the discussion from the meaning of texts
to how understanding the meaning of texts is possible. Clearly he
was working in the critical spirit of Kant's philosophy. Equally
clearly he points forward to Heidegger, who transforms
hermeneutics into practical philosophy and speculative ontology.

More clearly still, Schleiermacher throws down the gauntlet to anyone struggling with the distinction between secular and sacred in textual interpretation.

Though I can do no more than hint at the theoretical and philosophical demands which must be made upon the student of literature and theology, I should not wish it to be thought that we may never therefore encourage any reading in literature itself! Literature, after all, still consists, at least in part, of poems, plays, novels, essays. And it is precisely these creative texts of literature which we must continuously introduce to the reflections of systematic theology and the textual exercises of biblical critics. If *intertextuality* is now a familiar enough term—and we are wise always to recall the basis of the worry which Andrew Marvell and Dr. Johnson expressed about *Paradise Lost* as an intertext of Genesis—we need to be reminded by Harold Bloom and others of the anxiety engendered in intrapoetic relationships. It is that uncomfortable imaginative space between texts that we must inhabit and reflect upon.

All this properly makes the business of literature and theology jumpy and skeptical. If we do take contemporary literary anxieties seriously, questioning language, reference, the status of the reader—the status of the author one dare hardly mention!—and if we recognize the philosophical traditions which we have inherited and lost from the enlightenment, what, then, are our prospects? Do we go forward, or scuttle back into pre-critical darkness?

I suggest that literary theory, and particularly in its shading into continental philosophy, is unavoidable for such a program of study. For one thing, it is remarkable how at its heart are emerging profoundly *theological* questions. Derrida, for example, spends many pages in one of his most significant essays of recent years, "How to Avoid Speaking Denials," explaining why he is not writing a "negative theology."[9] More loosely, critics as diverse as J. Hillis Miller and Wayne Booth have firmly put ethics back on the map of reading and interpretation. I would go so far as to say that almost every major critic writing today has recogized a theological—or an a-theological—undergirding to the venture.

Not least among these issues is that relating to the question of *textuality*, and it is remarkable how little theologians themselves have been prepared to pick this up, or biblical critics to recognize the centrality of it for their task. Geoffrey Hartman has recently published an essay entitled "The Struggle for the Text" in the collection edited by himself and Sanford Budick, *Midrash and Litera-*

ture (1986). What it is crucial for students to recognize is that the notion of a text, its textuality, and therefore processes of reading are very far from being stable. As Matthew Arnold put it long ago in *Culture and Anarchy* (1868), significantly quoted by Jacques Derrida at the head of his essay on Emmanuel Levinas, "Violence and Metaphysics" (1964)[10]:

> Hebraism and Hellenism,—between these two points of influence moves our world. At one time it feels more powerfully the attraction of one of them, at another time of the other; and it ought to be, though it never is, evenly and happily balanced between them.

I am increasingly persuaded that at the heart of these two influences are two distinct views of textuality—so that it is not surprising that within Western interpretation theory there is a confusion arising from its roots in Greek notions of textuality on the one hand, and Jewish notions of textuality on the other. Still the best place to introduce anyone to this difference is the first chapter of Erich Auerbach's *Mimeses* (1946), entitled "Odysseus' Scar," with its celebrated comparison between the Homeric text and the Genesis narrative of the Sacrifice of Isaac. This chapter's critical preeminence is noted by Geoffrey Hartman in the paper already referred to, "The Struggle for the Text," which draws our attention also to Roland Barthes' essay "The Struggle with the Angel" on Genesis 32, the episode of Jacob's wrestling.[11]

Barthes, like Auerbach, is profoundly interested in textuality— how a text is structured and how it is appropriated. Reflection of this kind is not notable among biblical scholars or theologians who work with a deep sense of the "givenness" of sacred text. But it is worth a pause for thought that so many contemporary literary theorists are Jewish, and self-consciously so: Derrida, Levinas, Bloom, Hartman, Alter, Fishbane.... The list is impressive. Susan Handelman has given us a fine study, *The Slayers of Moses* (1982), which is subtitled *The Emergence of Rabbinic Interpretation in Modern Literary Theory*.[12] My sense is that Rabbinic, midrashic notions of textuality, with their endless intertextual debates, their ceaseless textual escape from textuality (Edward Said has remarked that "Everything about Jesus ... resists textuality") respond immediately to our contemporary decentered, postmodern condition. Even though Kant had turned philosophical attention from the contents of knowledge to the conditions of the possibility of knowledge, nevertheless the liberal humanist tradition of Enlightenment thought continued to assume an essentially Hellenic notion of textuality—that meaning lay embedded in text like a jewel in rock, waiting for the critical instruments of the interpreter to reveal it to us.

Students of literature and theology must be enabled to turn a more acute and skeptical eye to texts which are inescapably presented to their attention, recognizing, as Werner Jeanrond has put it, text and interpretation as categories of theological thinking, and prepared to ask, with Stanley Fish, is there a text in this class?[13]

II

But now I want to offer more controversial, and, I trust, constructive, suggestions to the field of literature and theology. It seems to me not in the least surprising that the most lively and intellectually creative work in North American studies has tended to be among Jewish scholars who have been influenced by French poststructuralism and postmodernism. For I suggest that all too often the prevailing theological and critical religious consciousness has been fed by the German Protestant tradition which has not only sheltered it, philosophically and culturally, from the primarily French postmodernist critics, but has also structured an exclusively Christian attitude out of a dangerously anti-Semitic tendency. Here I acknowledge that I am on dangerous ground, but at the extreme of religio-political statements I refer you to Adorno and Horkheimer's classic chapter on the elements of anti-Semitism in *Dialectic of Enlightenment* (1944):

> The fanatical faith of the leader and his followers is no different from that for which men were once willing to submit to the stake; only the content has changed. But the hatred for all who do not share the faith remains. Anti-Semitism is all that the German Christians have retained of the religion of love.[14]

In an admittedly highly diluted form, the background of German Protestant systematic theology has sponsored the strictly "Christian" content of English religion—in T.S. Eliot par excellence with his intellectual background in British Hegelianism—and, via such theologians as Reinhold Niebuhr and Tillich, the significance in North America of a primarily Christian religious tradition in culture and society. (Eliot's clearly anti-semitic tendencies have been notoriously exposed in the recent biography by Peter Ackroyd.)

It is Jewish critics who have, in different ways, responded to the interdisciplinary challenge outside the Christian tradition, yet deeply conscious of a French, rather than a German, philosophical initiative which includes self-consciously Jewish thinkers like Levinas and Derrida who are, I would argue, the real critical inheritors of that brilliant, alternative and exiled European cultural tradition which includes intellectuals as diverse as Freud, Einstein, Buber, Kafka, and Schoenberg. Indeed, one American critic, Carl Rashke, has significantly argued that the fundamental failure of theological and religious reflection lies in its never experiencing an Einsteinian revolution towards a theory of relativity, in the way that quantum physics provides a new model of thinking for science. Defining his conditions for "quantum faith," Rashke suggests that

> ... the new quantum science, as opposed to its mechanistic elder brother, is always in quest of novel settings for generating information. Like the Navajo weavers who never joined the first and last stitches of their prodigious tapestries, leaving the pattern open-ended because of their "superstition" it would be an affront to the universe, the quantum theorist is unwilling to finalize either his presuppositions or his findings out of respect for the "uncertainty relations" that entwine and "conjugate" every variable.[15]

If most students of literature and theology or religion have, so far, preferred to lodge safely with the mechanistic elder brother of critical thought, the Jewish prodigals have been bolder and, perhaps, returned to speak more wisely of what Geoffrey Hartman, following Lacan, has described as the "scandal of theological survivals in even the most secular thinkers."[16]

Absorption in the text and textuality is a Rabbinic practice which Susan Handelman closely links with the philosophical assumptions of literary critics such as Barthes and Derrida, as opposed to the historical absorption of the German higher biblical criticism which is, she claims, "most unfaithful to the true nature of Rabbinic thinking,"[17] yet which informs the technical processes of almost all contemporary scriptural study and conservative literary criticism. For the Rabbis, the mesh and interweave of the text itself remains at the heart of their concerns as opposed to the Greek tendency to abstract from the text. Handelman describes contemporary absorption in textuality as an example of "inadvertent Rabbinic sensibility,"[18] which is, at the same time, profoundly, if unselfconsciously, theological through a sense of the divinity of the text. One identifies this in Derrida as an ethical dimension which is generally unadmitted. For Derrida prefers to stand outside the epistemological problems which beset the Western tradition—problems involving truth and reason—and responds (with Levinas) to the summons of Jewish writings with their emphasis placed, as Christopher Norris puts it, "upon *writing* as an endlessly productive signifying practice irreducible to some ultimate, self-evident truth."[19] For the profoundly anti-Platonic Derrida, nothing is beyond the reach of writing, and writing is never derivative.

The Jewish obsession with textuality escapes the "Greco-Christian ontotheological mode of thinking"[20] and is the clue, it seems to me, to that crucial, reflective literature and thought which has arisen as a consequence of the Jewish experience of the Holocaust or Shoah. Embarrassed in the inevitable wake of Nietzsche, Christian reflection and literature has, by and large, continued to engage in futile, traditional theodical exercises in attempts to extricate itself from the guilt of genocide. More in the spirit of midrash, however, the condemned Jew remains within his own text, explaining nothing, endlessly suffering yet transcending closure in what Derrida calls a "negative atheology"[21]—the textuality of experience itself more important than, yet guaranteeing, the absent divinity. Thus in the Divine himself is found the experience of exile, repetition, otherness, inconclusion.

What Derrida in particular has taught us is the endlessness of the text in difference and deferral, reminding us of the Rabbinic compulsion to articulacy within Judaism and the need always to write and be in dialogue with—or against—even a silent, absent God. Literature and death are never far apart, so that Jewish survivors like Paul Celan or Primo Levi seem doomed to suicide even as they (impossibly) write, dramatically proving Roland Barthes' contention that literature is already a posthumous affair which "shines with its maximum brilliance at the moment when it attempts to die."[22] But it is in "fictional" works like Elie Wiesel's *The Testament* (1981) that the point is made that in writing and language against death is constituted a people's memory and, perhaps, its theology. The very inconceivability of Auschwitz enables a Derrida to pursue his aporetic critical career, and indeed makes it vitally necessary. Thus, Derrida's analysis of Emmanuel Levinas in his essay "Violence and Metaphysics," is an apt summary of the trends of Rabbinic thought, fuelled by the recognition that Levinas himself writes a specifically post-Holocaust, French-Jewish philosophy and is a survivor of the camps whose absent God, obscuring his face in the smoke of the ovens, becomes for Levinas, paradoxically, the condition of Jewish belief.

So far, I contend, even today most practitioners of the interdisciplinary exercise of literature and theology or religion have failed to perceive the profound theological possibilities, through art, of the Derridean critique of ontology. Some Jewish scholars in the United States, like Susan Handelman, have begun seriously to work towards this perception, while in Britain, with its very different ecclesiastically constrained theological tradition, there has been maintained a deafening silence, despite its own increasing multicultural experience. (The recent controversy surrounding Salman Rushdie's *The Satanic Verses* has reminded us that the blasphemy laws in England only exist in respect to the doctrines and formularies of the established Church of England which actually only represents a small percentage of the population). But the artistic, critical and theological Jewish response to a particular socio-political experience of the twentieth century opens up, for me, not only the creative possibilities of French postmodernism in its various forms—Lacan, for example, energetically pursued post-structuralist readings of Freud—but also revives on a vast multi-disciplinary canvas, a profound European tradition which our theologians and scholars of religion have tended to ignore. Thus, for example, I am prepared to expand my literary/theological interests to a serious involvement with the later and deeply Jewish Schoenberg whose haunting composition *A Survivor from Warsaw*, Op. 46, for which he wrote both words (in English) and score, anticipates Barthes' sense of literature and death in the Narrator's words:

> I must have been unconscious. The next thing I knew was a soldier saying: "They are all dead," whereupon the sergeant ordered to do away with us.

From Schoenberg, in the spirit of midrash, I am led to his friend and intellectual correspondent, the Russian Orthodox artist Wassily Kandinsky whose essay of 1914, *Concerning the Spiritual in Art*, remains a cornerstone of interdisciplinary reflection. Abroad from his native Russia and in Munich in those dark days, Kandinsky wrote prophetically:

> When religion, science and morality are shaken, the two last by the strong hand of Nietzsche, and when the outer supports threaten to fall, man turns his gaze from externals in on to himself. Literature, music and art are the first and most sensitive spheres in which this spiritual revolution makes itself felt. They

reflect the dark picture of the present time and show the importance of what at first was only a little point of light noticed by
few and for the great majority non-existent. Perhaps they even
grow dark in their turn, but on the other hand they turn away
from the soulless life of the present towards those substances and
ideas which give free scope to the non-material strivings of the
soul.[23]

From Schoenberg and from Kandinsky we rediscover how the arts
encroach one upon another in the pursuit of "Stimmung," an impossible German word to translate, but perhaps best rendered as
the "essential spirit," which I would relate closely to the notion of
"trace" in the critical philosophy of Levinas and Derrida.

What I am arguing for is a much broader canvas both within
and outside the Christian tradition, and that the study of literature
and theology should learn to relocate itself not as another discipline *within* academia, but remain uncomfortably, without stability, lodged between an almost limitless range of creative and critical expressions of our condition religiously, socially, culturally,
and politically. Remaining distrustful of all, it must risk professional rejection by continuing to draw our attention to the awk-
ward encounters in our traditions between expressions of belief
and instances of violence or beauty beyond the pale.

As one instance I would draw your attention to another, more
recent, Munich artist outside the walls of German systematic theology. Patrick Süskind's novel *Perfume* was translated into English
in 1986, and immediately attained almost cult status. A disconcerting, postmodern text in the tradition of Gothic literature, it is the
story of a serial murderer whose themes and images continually
recall Christian theology, but violently disconnected from the ec-
clesiastic tradition which renders that theology the potential material for a narrative of salvation history. The sense of the scandal of
theological survival is strong throughout this book. Christ-forget-
ting and Christ-haunted, it both parodies and provocatively deconstructs the salvific, messianic career of Jesus of Nazareth,
through familiar (and too often unexplored) theological images
effecting what Nietzsche describes in *The Anti-Christ* as a
"revaluation of all values."

In an eighteenth-century France which is characterized by the
stench of humanity, Jean-Baptiste Grenouille lives, incarnate yet
without body odor. The opening pages of the book, set in the
stinking streets of Paris, reflect the infancy narratives of St.
Matthew and St. Luke in a horrendous parody of the Bethlehem

stable metamorphosed into a Parisian street market, where "beneath a swarm of flies and amid the offal and fish heads they discovered a newborn baby." The narrative is built around that most human quality, smell; and Grenouille, himself odorless, possesses a perfect sense of smell, eventually producing from the bodies of the virginal young women whom he has murdered, the supreme perfume, which is the essence of human perfection. Apprehended and convicted of the murders, Grenouille is finally brought to the scaffold. And then a miracle occurs. Doused in his perfume, the essence, in all its corruption, of pure, young life, he drives the crowd mad with desire, even from the scaffold: a true anti-Christ; a murderer yet beloved in his human perfection. We see the Bishop himself:

> for the first time in his life basking in religious rapture, for a miracle had occurred before their very eyes, the Lord God had personally stayed the executioner's hand by disclosing as an angel the very man who had for all the world appeared a murderer. Oh, that such a thing had happened, here in the eighteenth century. How great was the Lord![24]

Finally, another crowd, also driven mad by Grenouille's pure "human" odor, dismembers and devours him so that, half an hour later, "Jean-Baptiste Grenouille had disappeared utterly from the earth."

> ... to eat a human being? They would never, so they thought, have been capable of anything that horrible.... [Yet] they were uncommonly proud. For the first time they had done something out of Love.[25]

The whole scene is, of course, a eucharist—ironic, loving, salvific— a veritable agape. A body is broken and its flesh distributed out of love, but at the same time the action is one of "sparagmos"—violent and unreflective dismemberment, as at the Euripidean Bacchic revel. In Süskind's postmodern novel there is an unreconciled confusion of influences from the European tradition, soaking the clear theological and liturgical references with the blood of Hellenic violence and literal self-destruction. The theme is not unknown elsewhere in postmodern fiction, and I would refer you to the dismemberments, for example, in Thomas Pynchon's *Gravity's Rainbow* or Ian McEwan's *The Innocent*, each with its own sense of the scandal of theological survival. No longer comfortably resident in the moral traditions of the "Christian" West, this literature edgily links its familiar images with a more diverse, often pre-Christian,

tradition and mingles their significance in the confusion of our violent, deconstructed, apocalyptic culture. Increasingly, also, writers
like Rushdie, another exile to the "West," have forced us to contemplate as part of our society the ethical and aesthetic qualities of
what he has called our "mongrel" selves thrown onto the wide
stage of multi-religious, multi-cultural interaction. "Reading" on
the margins of such textuality, intertextually and with the theoreti-
cal/practical skepticism of interdisciplinarity, may lead back to a
revaluation of the great themes and images of Christian theology
and religious belief in a surreal exercise of mind and imagination.

This paper has been a lesson in two parts. In the first I was
concerned to work through some of the practical questions involved in teaching courses in literature and theology or religion.
The very title is a problem—do we call it "theology" or "religion,"
for the terms are different, and each word means something different depending on your location. I myself feel committed to the
theological enterprise, but there are those for whom "religion" is a
more helpful and meaningful term. Perhaps the tension should be
left unresolved. In terms of teaching method, with postgraduates I
tend to adopt a fairly unstructured seminar form, usually centered
upon various ways of reading a particular text or biblical passage,
encouraging students to search for bridges between discreet modes
of discourse, to *think* theoretically and to *think* theologically.

In the second part of the paper, I have allowed myself more
imaginative scope, to explore some of the fundamental issues and
questions underlying and driving this particular academic inter-
discipline and its place within scholarship and teaching. I have
long been of the opinion that to launch into my chosen interdisciplinary study is not to *replace* the careful and systematic activities
of either theology (in its many guises) or the practice and critical
study of literature, as such. But it is rather to become something of
a nuisance, ranging broadly between unlikely stations and drawing attention to unconventional connections. It may be that the cir-
cles become even wider, and the question will be asked, when will
you stop venturing into territories—music, art history, political
theory—in which you have no "professional" right to say anything
and in which the risk is high that you will make a fool of yourself?

But in my defense I declare that I believe very firmly that the
parallel tracks to date of literature and theology in Britain, and literature and religion in North America have, indeed by their very
differences, indicated a profoundly conservative anxiety to pre-

serve something in each tradition and culture which is already being swept away in a vast multi-cultural anxiety which, in our
shrinking world, has consigned us all to the same firing line on the
stage of world conflict in a violence which is economic, political,
military, and cultural. Kandinsky was quite right, and 1914 may
have been the significant year in more ways than one—standing at
the end of the nineteenth century's broad optimism and on the eve
of the first terrible conflagration of modern warfare. What that
calls for from us is a revisiting of Renaissance values in which
scholarship and reflection are not confined to the tunnel-vision of
the specialist, but allowed to range freely to explore the common
creative possibilities in all human endeavour, if necessary *sub-
specie aeternitate*. I readily admit that this is not so very far from the
notion of "counter-culture" which was somewhat naïvely articulated by Theodore Roszak in the 1960s, though critically and philosophically we have come a long way since then. Theology, it may
be, has never really accepted the need to take on board its own
version of the relativity theory. Biblical studies, immersed as they
are in still crucially important texts, cannot continue to pretend
that the literary-critical upheavals of the last twenty years have not
taken place, or that the whole post-Saussurean linguistic turn does
not spread ripples out across vast seas of human activity. Literary
study, finally, should not refuse the profound religious questions
to which theory is now introducing it. As scholars, teachers, and
students we need to be more faithful, more skeptical, more believing, more wary.

Notes

1. David Anderson, *The Passion of Man in Gospel and Literature* (Bible
Reading Fellowship, 1980), "Preface."

2. T.S. Eliot, *Selected Essays*, 3rd ed. (London: Faber, 1972), p. 388.

3. John B. Gabel and Charles B. Wheeler, *The Bible as Literature: An Introduction* (Oxford: Oxford University Press, 1986). The same title was
used earlier by T.R. Henn in a book published in 1970, which was more
widely read in its essentials in an essay in *Peake's Commentary on the Bible*,
eds. Matthew Black and H.H. Rowley (London: Routledge, 1962), pp. 8–23.

4. Monroe C. Beardsley, "Intentions and Interpretations: A Fallacy
Revived," in Michael J. Wreen and Donald M. Callen, eds., *The Aesthetic
Point of View* (Ithaca: Cornell University Press, 1982), p. 188.

5. Mieke Bal, *Lethal Love: Feminist Literary Readings of Biblical Love Stories* (Indiana Studies in Biblical Literature) (Bloomington: University of Indiana Press, 1987); *Death and Dissymetry: The Politics of Coherence in the Book of Judges* (Chicago Studies in the History of Judaism) (Chicago: University of Chicago Press, 1988); *Murder and Difference: Gender, Genre, and Scholarship on Sisera's Death* (Indiana Studies in Biblical Literature) (Bloomington: University of Indiana Press, 1988).

6. Stephen D. Moore, *Literary Criticism and the Gospels: The Theoretical Challenge* (New Haven: Yale University Press, 1989), pp. 176–77.

7. See David E. Klemm, *Hermeneutical Inquiry: Interpretation on Text* (Studies in Religion [American Academy of Religion], No. 43), *Vol. I: The Interpretation of Texts* (Alpharetta/Atlanta: Scholars Press, 1986), p. 56.

8. F.D.E. Schleiermacher, *Hermeneutics: The Handwritten Manuscripts*, ed. Heinz Kimmerle; trans. James Duke and Jack Forstmann (Atlanta: Scholars Press, 1986).

9. See Sanford Budick and Wolfgang Iser, eds., *Languages of the Unsayable: The Play of Negativity in Literature and Literary Theory* (Irvine Studies in the Humanities) (New York: Columbia University Press, 1989), pp. 3–70.

10. See Jacques Derrida, *Writing and Difference*, trans. Alan Bass (London: Routledge, 1981), pp. 79–153.

11. Roland Barthes, *Image Music Text*, trans. Stephen Heath (London, 1977), pp. 125–41.

12. Handelman has recently followed this with a further study, *Fragments of Redemption: Jewish Thought and Literary Theory in Benjamin, Scholem, and Levinas* (Bloomington: University of Indiana Press, 1991).

13. Werner G. Jeanrond, *Text and Interpretation as Categories of Theological Thinking* (New York/Dublin: Crossroad Continuum Publishing Group, 1988); Stanley Fish, *Is There a Text in This Class? The Authority of Interpretive Communities* (Cambridge: Harvard University Press, 1980).

14. Theodor Adorno and Max Horkheimer, *Dialectic of Enlightenment* (1944); Eng. trans., second ed. (London, 1986), p. 176.

15. Carl Rashke, *Theological Thinking: An Inquiry* (American Academy of Religion: Studies in Religion, No. 53) (Atlanta: Alpharetta/Atlanta: Scholars Press, 1988), pp. 50–51.

16. Geoffrey Hartman, *Psychoanalysis and the Question of the Text: Selected Papers from the English Institute, 1976–7* (Baltimore: Johns Hopkins University Press, 1978), p. 91.

17. Susan A. Handelman, *Slayers of Moses: The Emergence of Rabbinic Interpretation in Modern Literary Theory* (Albany: State University of New York, 1982), p. 228.

18. Ibid., p. 50.

19. Christopher Norris, *Derrida* (London: Harper Collins, 1987), p. 228.

20. Handelman, p. 168.

21. Quoted in Handelman, p 169.

22. Roland Barthes, *Writing Degree Zero* (1953), quoted in Susan Sontag, *Barthes: Selected Writings* (London: Harper Collins, 1983), p. viii.

23. Wassily Kandinsky, *Concerning the Spiritual in Art*, trans. M.T.H. Sadler (New York: Dover, 1977), p. 4.

24. Patrick Süskind, *Perfume*, trans. John E. Woods (Harmondsworth: Penguin, 1987), p. 246.

25. Ibid., p. 263.

Shouldn't These Theories Be Tested?

Colin Martindale

There is always some sort of theory in the classroom. Without an at least implicit theory, it would be unclear whether the point of the class was to eat the chairs or read some books. To what extent should explicit literary theories be introduced into undergraduate courses on literature? To what extent should such theories determine which works of literature are to be read? The obvious answer would seem to be that a theory should influence teaching to the extent that the theory is valid. The problem, then, is how to assess the validity of literary theories.

From a scientific perspective, a theory is an explicit and coherent set of hypotheses that provides a simple and cogent explanation of some set of phenomena. A theory must consist of hypotheses at least some of which are empirically testable. More important, a theory should be falsifiable. That is, there must exist hypotheses derived from the theory that, if shown to be false, would mean that the theory is incorrect. Considered in this light, it is not clear whether a lot of literary theories are theories at all. No one would argue that deconstructionism consists of anything even approaching an explicit and coherent set of hypotheses. Derrida's *De la grammatologie* strikes me as closer to delirium than to an even incoherent theory.[1] At the other end of the spectrum, orthodox psychoanalysis is quite explicit and coherent. However, since so much of it is untestable and unfalsifiable, it is closer to delusion than to a scientific theory.

The real problem, however, is not with the theories but with the theorists. In general, they don't know how to test their hypotheses. In literary studies, assertions are usually supported by producing examples and attempts at persuasion. If one is convinced, it is unclear whether this is because of the truth of the assertion or the rhetorical skill of the theorist. Almost any literary theory contains at least some hypotheses that could be tested in a scientific manner. It has always surprised me that most literary scholars have shown no interest in doing such tests. Several reasons come to mind. An obvious reason is that most literary theorists do not have the slightest idea as to how to conduct an experiment or analyze the results. They have not taken the relevant courses on—or learned on their own—experimental design and statistics. Why might this be? Of course, it is partially due to the curriculum in literary studies. Such courses are not required or even suggested. Another influence coming from the curriculum is its heavy emphasis on literary *criticism* (what does this specific test mean?) as opposed to general theory. A notable thing about books on literary theory is that their authors often lapse into being critics rather than theorists. That is, they lapse into explaining the meaning of this or that specific text.

The ideal literary theorist should be proposing a completely scientific theory. This is very seldom the case. Part of the reason is training, but I suspect that part has to do with personality and attitudes. Science aims to discover abstract, general laws. It is not concerned with individual cases or with essences. Consider an experimental psychologist interested in color vision. He or she has no interest at all in how *you* or *I* see colors. The goal is to find universal laws concerning how everyone in the world sees colors. One would assume that a disposition to think in abstraction draws a certain type of person toward science. On the other hand, consider a clinical psychologist. He or she is interested in understanding a specific individual patient. By "understanding" is often meant what Dilthey called *Verstehen*—somehow thinking oneself into the other person's mind.[2] To the experimental psychologist, this seems both boring and pointless. Such a vague "understanding" of patient X cannot possibly produce any general laws. Of course, the clinical psychologist also finds the abstractions discovered by the experimental psychologist to be boring. In short, some people are interested in abstractions, whereas others are interested in concrete and specific instances—this specific person or that specific person—or this specific text or that specific text.

Those drawn to literary studies tend to be more interested in specifics than in abstractions. Thus, the vast majority of scholarly publications about literature deal with one or only a couple of texts or authors. As such, literary scholars are likely to mean something very different than a scientist when they speak of "understanding" or "explanation." So long as they focus on individual texts, this causes few problems. Difficulties arise, though, when a general law is proposed. The theorist seems to think that the only way to establish the law is to give a bunch of examples.

A bunch of examples may be interesting. They may or may not be convincing. However, this is simply not the correct way to test a general hypothesis. Below, I give a few examples of how it seems to me that literary hypotheses should be tested and what implications such tests have for the classroom.

Let us consider the question of whether cross-media artistic styles exist. The centuries of bickering did nothing at all to settle this question. Lessing argued that cross-media styles cannot possibly exist.[3] More recently, Wylie Sypher quite unconvincingly argued that they do exist, whereas Morse Peckham very convincingly argued that they don't exist.[4] The current consensus is that they are a figment of some theorists' imaginations. This question should not be and cannot be settled by argumentation. It is an empirical question that can be answered by a couple of simple experiments. The way we approached it was as follows.[5] We selected representative examples of baroque, neoclassical, and romantic paintings, architectural façades, musical compositions, and poems. Artistically naïve people were confronted with a mélange of pictures, cassettes containing excerpts of music, and index cards on which the poetry was typed. They were simply told to group together the stimuli that were similar. To our surprise—we had undertaken the study to show that cross-media styles do not exist—people grouped together the three styles at far beyond chance levels. A few more studies using rating scales showed the same thing: people perceive the similarities of baroque, classical, and romantic works across media. For example, baroque poems are perceived as more similar to baroque music, painting, or architectures than to romantic or classical poems.

The problem with the notion of cross-media styles was not one of theory. It is a perfectly acceptable scientific hypothesis. The problem was that those arguing about the theory did not know how to test it, how to gather credible evidence for or against it. These results have some pedagogical implications. It would make sense to teach, say, romantic literature in conjunction with samples of romantic music and painting. Because people are already implicitly aware of cross-media similarities, one would assume that explicitly studying the same style in different media would be beneficial. Before there was concrete evidence for or against cross-media styles it would have been senseless to argue whether or not this approach would be a good or bad idea.

Let me give another example of a rather implausible literary theory that seems, after all, to be true. Gaston Bachelard put forth the hypothesis that there is a correlation in imagination between the four elements and the four temperaments.[6] Specifically, the connection is the one postulated by the ancient Greeks: fire / choleric, water / phlegmatic, air / sanguine, and earth / melancholic. In a quite unsystematic way, Bachelard used poetic quotations in support of this idea. Was Bachelard right? To find out, we had people sort cards containing words referring to the four elements and the four temperaments.[7] At levels far beyond chance, they sorted the cards in accord with Bachelard's hypothesis. Was he right about poets? We constructed lists of words referring to elements and temperaments. We used these lists to do a computerized content analysis of samples from twenty-one eminent French poets. At a statistically significant level, poets who used a lot of fire words also use a lot of choleric words, and so on.[8]

Bachelard's theory has been around since the 1940s. These results suggest that the theory would be one perspective that could be useful in teaching a course on nineteenth-century French literature. Though the names have been changed and the axes rotated, the four temperaments are almost universally accepted by scientific psychologists as the most basic dimensions along which human personality varies. If one wants to bring psychological theory into a course on literature, it is better to use the scientific version rather than to use an ad-hoc psychology made up by the instructor.

One concept from psychoanalysis is certainly of relevance to a course on nineteenth-century French literature—or to almost any historical course on any type of literature. Marcel Raymond, Wallace Fowlie, and others have tried to describe what happened to French poetry across the course of the nineteenth century.[9] They used psychologically indeterminate terms such as "descent into the self." Eventually, one is able to decipher that they must mean that poetic content moved from what Freud called a secondary process orientation (reality-oriented and logical) toward a primary process orientation (autistic and dreamlike).[10] This movement is very clear. As if they were even needed, I have produced numbers to show that the trend is a strong one.[11] I have elsewhere proposed a theory as to why this trend occurred.[12] The point is that organizing such a course so as to describe the trend in terms of the secondary process *versus* primary process dimension would make clear to students what the major movement was.

Literary theorists who agree on little else tend to assume that people do not agree very well with one another in their interpretations of literary texts. For deconstructionist theorists, such as J. Hillis Miller, disagreement is a natural consequence of texts' indeterminacy or lack of stable meaning.[13] For reader-reception theorists, such as Wolfgang Iser or Stanley Fish, lack of agreement is ascribed to the fact that the text is underdetermined.[14] The author leaves so much to be filled in, assumed, or guessed at by readers varying in their beliefs and assumptions that a variety of interpretations is likely. Some reader-response theorists assume so much misreading and disagreement that they explicitly argue against the study of actual readers. Thus, to avoid uncontrolled subjectivism, Iser focuses on the implied reader. Jonathan Culler argues strongly against studying actual readers because their responses would be too idiosyncratic.[15] Rather, he notes, there is enough of a spectrum of interpretive possibilities in published literary criticism.[16] How can literary scholars be so certain that people do not agree in their judgments of texts? Though some have theoretical expectations that lead them to expect no agreement, these expectations should not have blinded them to empirical evidence altogether. Consider how the person in the street or the critic in the armchair conducts his or her observations. Most of the evidence for disagreement comes from cases in which two people (the observer and someone else) disagree in their judgment on one text. This sort of observation does not tell us anything at all about agreement in general. One could argue that one tallies up a memory of such disagreements and reaches a conclusion on the basis of this tally. Because disagreements are more striking or interesting than agreements, there is evidence that they may be vastly over-represented in memory.[17] Of course, a theorist who is a professor may have a better sample. He or she will have a mental tally of a large number of students' interpretations of a large number of texts. Many of these interpretations will be silly or downright idiotic. The fact that they are silly may well lead one to overlook the fact that they are silly in the same way. A number of reader-reception theorists confuse the issues of correctness or validity and of agreement. If the question is whether people agree, it is nothing to the point whether they are correct or not.

Whether or not people disagree in their interpretations of literature is a perfectly straightforward empirical question. All one needs to do is present a group of texts to a group of people and elicit some sort of quantifiable judgments of the texts. If people do not agree, their judgments of the texts will be uncorrelated. This is the approach I.A. Richards took—or should have taken.[18] He had about one hundred people—mainly Cambridge honors students in literature—read and give their impression of thirteen poems of varying quality. Each person was asked to write an essay about each poem. This was an unfortunate approach, because—though it can be done—there is no easy way to quantify such open-ended responses. Rather than attempting to do so, Richards presented over a hundred pages of excerpts from the essays. The excerpts do seem supportive of his conclusion that he got "a hundred verdicts from a hundred readers." Thus, different readers find the same poem to have "not even the smallest attempt at metre" and "perfect meter." Another poem is "absolute tripe" and "really first-rate." However, these excerpts are extremely misleading.

Richards gives an appendix containing his estimate of the percentage of readers who were *favorable, non-committal,* and *unfavorable* to each poem. He did no statistics on these figures, but we certainly can. Had readers not agreed at all, the percentage for each of these three categories should be 33.3%. We can use—as Richards could have—the chi-square test to assess whether the percentages deviate from this figure. For ten of the poems, the probability of getting the figure that Richards did is less than 1 in 100 if subjects had really disagreed. For only three of the poems do the numbers suggest disagreement. Across all thirteen poems, the probability of getting as much agreement as Richards did—if subjects actually did *not* agree—is well less than 1 in 1000. Richards' percentages suggest that he might have been trying to force responses into either the favorable or unfavorable categories and underemphasizing the non-committal category. If we bring the latter together with one or the other of the first two categories, we still get significant agreement. In either case, the probability of getting this much agreement across all thirteen poems is well less than 1 in 1000. In short, Richards seems to have completely misinterpreted his data at least so far as favorability judgments are concerned. This is unfortunate. Because his general conclusion of lack of agreement is very well known among literary theorists, further empirical studies were probably not done because the case was considered closed.

In a recent and as yet unpublished study, I had thirty-two people rate the thirteen poems used by Richards on a set of forty 7-

point rating scales—e.g., Like-Dislike, Simple-Complex, Rhythmic-Not Rhythmic. Across all forty scales the mean correlation between any two raters was 0.19. The highest correlation was 0.40 for Happy-Sad, whereas the lowest was only 0.01 for Static-Dynamic. The probability of getting this much agreement by chance was less than 1 in 1000 for all but three of the rating scales. A correlation of 0 means no agreement, whereas a correlation of 1.00 means perfect agreement. Thus, there was moderate pair-wise agreement, but it was far from perfect. For this number to have any meaning, we have to compare it with how well people agree when making other sorts of ratings. The comparable correlation for ratings of manuscripts submitted to academic journals is 0 .27.[19] If a person and a friend rate a person's traits, some sample pair-wise correlations are 0.29 for ratings of extraversion, 0.08 for openness to experience, 0.07 for agreeableness, and 0.21 for conscientiousness.[20] Across one hundred more specific traits, the self-friend correlation is 0.27.[21] For example, the correlation for physical attractiveness is 0.37, but the correlation for "insight into own motives and behavior" is only 0.05.

Before social constructionists gleefully leap to the conclusion that people don't agree about anything at all, I should point out that agreement or reliability is not usually expressed in terms of pairwise correlations. The correlation between any two items on an intelligence test is about 0.20. However, the reliability of the test as a whole is around 0.90. That is, if people are given the test on two occasions, the correlation between the two IQ scores will be about 0.90. This is because the test is composed of many items. Thus, the composite score is very stable. The same is true when people rate poems or other people. Let us say that I got a second group of thirty-two people to rate the thirteen poems and correlated the mean ratings of my group with the mean ratings of the second group. From what is called the Spearman-Brown formula, we know that the *mean* ratings would correlate about 0.88.[22] Even though pairs of ratings may not agree terribly well, so long as they agree at all, the consensus of groups of people will show marked agreement.

Do people agree or disagree as to the meanings of poems? I would argue that the results suggest considerable agreement. Agreement or disagreement between two randomly chosen people is of no great interest. To put the question in perspective, consider the question of whether Americans think that America should intervene militarily in Bosnia. No one would try to answer this question by asking just two Americans. Obviously, one would take a representative poll and look at the aggregate data. By the same token, if we want to see what Americans think of a given poem, we would ask a bunch of them. Given this, it is the reliability of 0.88 rather than the pairwise agreement of 0.19 that is of interest. One study by me is not going to solve the issue. We need more empirical studies and less quasi-theoretical chit-chat. As things stand now, you should assume that your students will agree fairly well as to the meanings of poems. If you disagree with me, then you should do some studies rather than engaging in pointless argumentation or telling anecdotes.

Let us turn to the canon of great works of literature. Whether such a canon does exist or should exist has been treated on a theoretical level. Those who want to revise the canon argue that it is not stable across time and that it is not valid, in the sense that good texts have been unfairly excluded and bad texts have been unfairly included. Whether the canon is stable is an empirical rather than a theoretical question. One needs simply to measure, in whatever way, eminence across time and see how much it fluctuates. The general answer seems to be that eminence fluctuates, sometimes wildly, after one's death and then settles down to its "proper" level. Dean K. Simonton has shown this for musical composers, and Gerald Reitlinger has provided some figures for painters.[23]

The canon can be understood in two ways: First, what authors must be included in order to make sense of a given tradition. Second, what authors should be taught in the classroom. In the first sense—the historical canon—there is probably little honest disagreement. If we want to study the history of a poetic tradition, we would obviously want to emphasize those who had influence on their contemporaries and successors and neglect those who didn't. This may mean including some bad—or boring—poets and paying little attention to some poets who wrote some good poems. For example, to understand what happened in British poetry, we obviously cannot leave out Milton or Wordsworth. At least to me, their poetry is rather boring, but what comes after makes no sense unless we give them a prominent place in the canon. Since his work was not discovered until the twentieth century, Thomas Traherne—though an excellent poet—could be relegated to a footnote. Because of their contemporary influence, John Cleveland and Edward Benlowes are solidly in the canon of British poetry in spite of their current relative obscurity. What if we discover some women who wrote good poetry but had little influence or were ignored? I don't think anybody argues that we are going to find such women. Disputes center on how much prominence should be given to women whose works are already clearly in the historical canon.

As to the canon in the second sense—what works should be taught because of their intrinsic value—there is more controversy. Gates and others have recently made the less than startling "discovery" that it helps to be a dead white man to be included in this canon.[24] Of course, it helps even more if the white man was rich while living. Is there a conspiracy here? If one considers that writing "great" as opposed to popular literature is not financially remunerative, it is hardly a surprise that mainly those with the leisure and freedom to do so would write such stuff. The conspiracy theory cannot explain why the vast majority of texts by dead white men—rich or not—are *not* in the canon. Are works in the canon better than those not in it? Are so-called great works of literature better than other literature? I don't think anyone would seriously want to argue that all works of literature are of equal value. The argument seems to concern a reordering of degree of eminence.

It must be that eminence is based upon certain qualities in texts. It is a scientific maxim that if something exists, it exists in some quantity and that if something exists in some quantity, it can be measured. At least among eminent French poets, the most eminent produced poetry with a moderate degree of incongruity.[25] In an extensive study of European composers, Simonton found something similar.[26] Eminence is related in an inverted-U fashion to improbability of note-to-note transitional probabilities. One imagines that there are many other objective correlates of eminence, but the relevant studies have not been done. I am not arguing that we should construct the canon using statistical formulae, but just pointing out that there are objective differences between good and bad literature. Anyone who has read very much already knows that, though.

It might be that statistical formulae could be found to help set the canon right. I do not have the formulae, but have read some of the relevant works. Here are some surprising figures concerning the holdings of the library at the University of Maine, which I assume are fairly typical. The library has 290 volumes by or about Charles Dickens, 176 for Anthony Trollope, 113 for Jane Austen, and 38 for Emily Brontë. Of course, Dickens and Trollope wrote more, but this seems backwards. To my mind, Jane Austen is by far the best of these novelists. Either I am wrong, or she has been neglected. Here are some other numbers for contemporary writers: 88 volumes by or about John Dryden *versus* none at all for Katherine Philips; 93 for Jonathan Swift *versus* 2 for Anne Finch, Countess of Winchelsea; 60 for Swinburne *versus* 18 for Christina Rossetti. In these cases, the man was a better poet than the woman, but was he *that* much better? The differences are not altogether due to sexism: once one is famous, he becomes very famous. Thus, we get 1,094 volumes for Shakespeare vs. 81 for Marlowe. Note also that it helps to have lived a long time ago: thus, Marlowe comes up with more volumes than Swinburne. If we wanted to see if there were any sexual bias as to which writers were attended to, we would need to take account of nuisance variables such as that. We would also need objective measures of merit or quality. In short, we would have to do our statistics correctly. To do that, we should certainly have to know how to do statistics in the first place.

What gives me the right to dictate to literary theorists how they should test their theories before using them in the classroom? As soon as one accepts the argument that the proper subject matter of literary studies is not objective texts (black marks on a piece of paper) but texts as perceived and understood, then he or she has admitted that literary studies are a sub-discipline of the behavioral sciences. After all, perception and understanding are topics that fall under the domain of psychology, sociology, and anthropology. It seems foolhardy to study texts without taking into account the theories and methods of these disciplines. Even those who hold to the notion that the canon of great works, however defined, provides us with a set of universal truths about human nature would have to admit that this also sounds like psychology. In any event, I at least would certainly like to have an explicit list of these universal truths so that I could see by scientific means exactly how universal they really are. As for those who wish to do cultural studies, the latter already exist. They are called anthropology, sociology, and social psychology. These disciplines could most certainly be revitalized. However, one should learn from them as well as trying to re-invent them.

Notes

1. Jacques Derrida, *De la grammatologie* (Paris: Editions de Minuit, 1967).

2. Theodore Abel, "The Operation called 'Verstehen,'" *American Journal of Sociology*, 54 (1948), pp. 211–18.

3. Gotthold Ephraim Lessing, *Laocoön: An Essay on the Limits of Painting and Poetry* (1766; Indianapolis: Bobbs-Merrill, 1962).

4. Wylie Sypher, *Rococo to Cubism in Art and Literature* (New York: Vintage, 1960); Morse Peckham, *Man's Rage for Chaos* (Philadelphia: Chilton, 1965).

5. Nancy Hasenfus, Colin Martindale, and Dana Birnbaum, "Psychological Reality of Cross-Media Artistic Styles," *Journal of Experimental Psychology: Human Perception and Performance*, 9 (1983), pp. 841–63.

6. Gaston Bachelard, *The Psychoanalysis of Fire* (1938; Boston: Beacon, 1964); *Water and Dreams* (1942; Dallas: Pegasus, 1983); *L'Air et les songes* (Paris: Librairie José Corti, 1948); *La Terre et les rêveries de la volunté* (Paris: Librairie José Corti, 1948). Bachelard is so vague that one has to read the whole book to get his point.

7. Anne E. Martindale and Colin Martindale, "Metaphorical Equivalence of Elements and Temperaments," *Journal of Personality and Social Psychology* (1988), pp. 836–48.

8. Ibid.

9. Marcel Raymond, *De Baudelaire au surréalisme* (Paris: Librairie José Corti, 1940); Wallace Fowlie, *Climate of Violence: The French Literary Tradition from Baudelaire to the Present* (New York: Macmillan, 1967).

10. Sigmund Freud, *The Interpretation of Dreams* (1900; New York: Random House, 1938).

11. Colin Martindale, *The Clockwork Muse: The Predictability of Artistic Change* (New York: Basic Books, 1990), pp. 77–116.

12. Ibid. pp. 34–76.

13. J. Hillis Miller, "The Critic as Host," in Harold Bloom, ed., *Deconstruction and Criticism* (New York: Seaburg, 1979).

14. Wolfgang Iser, *The Implied Reader* (Baltimore: Johns Hopkins University Press, 1974); Stanley Fish, *Is There a Text in This Class?* (Cambridge: Harvard University Press, 1980).

15. Jonathan Culler, *Structuralist Poetics* (Ithaca: Cornell University Press, 1975).

16. Culler, *On Deconstruction* (Ithaca: Cornell University Press, 1982).

17. Paul Slovic, Baruch Fischhoff, and Sarah Lichtenstein, "Behavioral Decision Theory," *Annual Review of Psychology*, 28 (1976), pp. 1–39.

18. I.A. Richards, *Practical Criticism: A Study of Literary Judgment* (1929; New York: Harcourt Brace Jovanovich, n.d.).

19. Herbert W. March and Samuel Ball, "The Peer Review Process Used to Evaluate Manuscripts Submitted to Academic Journals: Inter-

judgmental Reliability," *Journal of Experimental Education*, 57 (1989), pp. 151–69.

20. David C. Funder and Kathryn M. Dobroth, "Differences Between Traits: Properties Associated with Interjudge Agreement," *Journal of Personality and Social Psychology*, 52 (1987), pp. 409–18.

21. Funder and C. Randall Colvin, "Friends and Strangers: Acquaintanceship, Agreement, and the Accuracy of Personality Judgment," *Journal of Personality and Social Psychology*, 55 (1988), pp. 149–58.

22. Chranbach, Lee J., *Essentials of Psychological Testing* (New York: Harper & Row, 1960), pp. 131, 142.

23. Dean K. Simonton, *Genius, Creativity, and Leadership: Historimetric Inquiries* (Cambridge: Harvard University Press, 1984), p. 19; Gerald Reitlinger, *The Economics of Taste: The Rise and Fall of the Picture Market, 1760–1960* (New York: Holt, Rinehart, & Winston, 1961). (The whole of Reitlinger's book is relevant.)

24. Henry Louis Gates, Jr., "Canon Confidential: A Sam Slade Caper," *New York Times Book Review*, March 25, 1990, pp. 1–2.

25. Martindale, *Romantic Progression: The Psychology of Literary History* (Washington, D.C.: Hemisphere, 1975), pp. 177–87.

26. Simonton, pp. 116–17.

Part Two
Paradigms Close Up

Threshold Texts and Essayistic Voices

Charles I. Schuster

Let us begin with a poem, in this case "Incident" by Countee Cullen:

> Once riding in old Baltimore,
>   Heart-filled, head-filled with glee,
> I saw a Baltimorean
>   Keep looking straight at me.
>
> Now I was eight and very small,
>   And he was no whit bigger,
> And so I smiled, but he poked out
>   His tongue, and called me, "Nigger."
>
> I saw the whole of Baltimore
>   From May until December;
> Of all the things that happened there
>   That's all that I remember.

There is much that could and should be said about this magnificent, immediately accessible short poem—its child-like tone, its use of nursery-rhyme meter, its powerful use of dramatization and understatement, the terrible surprise concealed in its middle stanza. The poem discovers hate and betrayal yet somehow maintains in the face of this discovery a formal innocence.

I think the preceding analysis partly explains the success of the poem, and why undergraduates usually respond to it, but there is more to it than this. Cullen works a particular kind of magic here. Let us focus on just his opening line: "Once riding in old Baltimore." That "once" sets the story in the past, even in the distant past. It evokes the phrase "once upon a time" and as a result casts a fairy-tale aura upon this poem, a feeling that we are listening to a storyteller who will provide us with a moral fable and a happy ending. As readers, we tend to relax; we know this will be a com-

forting tale of goodness rewarded and evil vanquished. The phrase
"old Baltimore" reinforces this impression of a setting shrouded in
story time, for it suggests a distant, historicized past. Each time I
read this poem and arrive at the participle "riding," I envision the
young Cullen travelling on horseback down a muddy, rutted road
somewhere in rustic Baltimore, an interpretation that makes it
easier for me to conceive of how the incident could take place—after all, considerable time is needed for the give and take of the interaction to occur, more time than an automobile would allow.
And this sense of time being slowed down, almost stopped, is central to the entire argument of the poem, for in the mind of the
speaker that entire trip "from May until December" is reduced to
one moment only. Time, the passage of events, the movement from
spring to winter, the weaving of actions and impressions that ac-
crued during eight months in Baltimore have evaporated; it has all
been concentrated into one scene. The use of the present participle
"riding" suggests this compression of a long trip into a single, for-
ever-unfolding moment. Students tend to find this impression all
the more disturbing once they reflect that the poem is indeed
timeless, that the experience it recounts and the hatred it describes
are as much the coin of the realm today as they were in "old Baltimore," that this event could just as easily occur in new Baltimore,
new New York, new Milwaukee, new anywhere in America.

Considerably more could be explored in this poem, but for my
purposes here let me offer a central argument, namely, that this
poem succeeds in large part because it contains a range of tensions
and conflicts which are represented formally, semantically, ideologically. Constructed in a nursery-rhyme meter of alternating
iambic tetrameter and trimeter, framed within the point of view of
a childlike innocence both destroyed and maintained, situated
within the doubled contexts of real world and faerie world / real
time and faerie time, "Incident" is a poem that invites a reading
and then resists it. Countee Cullen's poem is a contested space, a
microcosmic representation of the contending forces of prejudice
and acceptance within our society. I call such a contested space a
"threshold," and by it I mean a conflictual, tension-filled, ideologically complex textual object which invites students to engage in a
series of successive interpretations. Threshold texts both contain
and represent a world in flux; like many young people, they live
on contested boundaries; like society itself, they cannot be reduced
to one definition, one meaning, one idea.

This notion of the "threshold experience," which I find useful in teaching, is a concept I have drawn from the work of Mikhail Bakhtin. In his discussion of the distinctive qualities of Dostoyevsky, Bakhtin offers a brief analysis of what he calls the threshold, which is both an aspect of the plot and a metaphor for Dostoyevsky's artistic point of view. In his discussion of *Crime and Punishment*, for example, Bakhtin writes that Raskolnikov

> lives, in essence, on a threshold: his narrow room, a "coffin" ... opens directly onto the *landing of the staircase*, and he never locks his door, even when he goes out....
>
> The threshold, the foyer, the corridor, the landing, the stairway, its steps, doors opening onto the stairway, gates to front and back yards, and beyond these, the city: squares, streets, façades, taverns, dens, bridges, gutters. This is the space of the novel. And in fact absolutely nothing here ever loses touch with the threshold, there is no interior of drawing rooms, dining rooms, halls, studios, bedrooms where biographical life unfolds and where events take place in the novels of writers such as Turgenev, Tolstoy, and Goncharov.[1]

According to Bakhtin, Dostoyevsky situates his characters quite literally within contested spaces, ambiguous territories that represent shifting boundaries. To be fully inside a room or outside in an open field is to place oneself in a completely defined environment. By contrast, to station oneself neither on land nor at sea but on the shore of a body of water, which is for example where E.B. White situates "Once More to the Lake," is to place oneself in a threshold space.[2] If we apply Bakhtin's concept to the college environment, we might say that a classroom is a well-defined space; in it, an instructor is (we hope) in charge and students are to do as they are bidden. Contrastingly, a doorway, a hallway, a set of steps upon which students move up and down—these are more contested areas in which identities and authorities become confused. In such spaces, inversions can occur: instructor and students can change places, mock each other, assume masks of innocence and betrayal. Threshold spaces undermine conventional and accepted ways of thinking and acting; they destabilize life, making it ambiguous; they maintain the potential of eroding the earth beneath one's feet. I think it no accident that in "Once More to the Lake," E.B. White loses perspective, cannot determine at one point whether he is himself, his father, or his son. Life on the threshold is disorienting.

Bakhtin extends this concept of the threshold, arguing that Dostoyevsky's fascination with the world of gamblers, for example, is a threshold concern:

> People from various (hierarchal) positions in life, once crowded around the roulette table, are made equal by the rules of the game and in the face of fortune, chance. Their behavior at the roulette table in no way corresponds to the role they play in ordinary life. The atmosphere of gambling is an atmosphere of sudden and quick changes of fate, of instantaneous rises and falls, that is, of crownings/decrownings. The stake is similar to a crisis; a person feels himself on the threshold. And the time of gambling is a special time: here, too, a minute is equal to years.[3]

Bakhtin describes here several aspects of threshold experience: a confusion of hierarchical positions of power and influence, a masking of identities that allows the participants to play out unusual roles, a rapid and often continuous change in one's fortune and fate, a sense of crisis and dangerous change, a warped and dreamlike sense of time. Indeed, the entire experience may be compared to dream, to a perception of the world as neither real nor unreal but rather irreal, existing on the border between wakefulness and sleep.

Following Bakhtin's example, I would argue that it is not hard to locate a wide variety of threshold experiences, both in life and in art, with which students from all backgrounds can identify. That first moment of entering into a crowded room in which one is a relative stranger, feeling the dislocation that results when one's ethnicity clashes with mainstream culture and ideology, travelling through unfamiliar terrain, meeting a half-recognized stranger— these are at least potentially threshold experiences. Sometimes they are situated literally on a threshold, a doorway, a shore, a passage from one environment to another. Other times the threshold is presented as a conceptual understanding and makes itself felt through a conflictual viewpoint, an experience of the world that is torn with ambivalence and uncertainty.

The concept of the "threshold" might be said to be fundamental to all literature: that is, all literature is in some sense poised in the imagination, a translation from experience into art. Virtually all works of literature in some sense explore moments of decision and transition that can conceivably be characterized as liminal. But the meaning of threshold that I am employing here has two constitutive elements. First, in its interpretive significance, the threshold experience is unfinalizable. It cannot be resolved in a unitary manner; it cannot satisfactorily be explained through the articulation of a single position, a finalized statement of meaning. It is multiple, ambiguous, polysemous. In describing the catharsis that he finds in Dostoyevsky, for example, Bakhtin writes:

> *Nothing conclusive has yet taken place in the world, the ultimate word of the world and about the world has not yet been spoken, the world is open and free, everything is still in the future and will always be in the future.*[4]

Similarly for the threshold event, the ultimate word has not been written nor can it ever be. Its significance can never be limited; its interpretive parameters never completely demarcated. As Bakhtin observes in the fragmentary "Toward a Methodology for the human Sciences":

> There is neither a first nor a last word and there are no limits to the dialogic context.... Nothing is absolutely dead: every meaning will have its homecoming festival.[5]

Literary threshold experiences are situated within an ongoing dialogic unfolding which makes them continuously available to the hermeneutic impulse.

Second, the threshold experience is bound concretely and specifically into the temporal, yet it dissolves time. Through his study of chronotopes, Bakhtin elaborated on the fundamental time/space dimensions within language. In Bakhtin's terms chronotopes are

> the organizing centers for the fundamental narrative events of the novel. The chronotope is the place where the knots of narrative are tied and untied. It can be said without qualification that to them belongs the meaning that shapes narrative.[6]

The threshold too is a kind of time/space mode; it represents another way in which space and time shift their borders. Threshold experiences, after all, exist within specific settings; they can be described in terms of characters, locations, narrative frameworks, as is evident in the "Incident" which Cullen evokes. They are not abstract, but concrete and particular. Yet simultaneously such events look through time: they possess a temporal resonance which transcends the specific without engaging in the bathetic, the sentimental, or the cloyingly familiar. Thus threshold experiences reorganize story time by making it possible to experience it both within the moment and forever.

How can this concept illuminate students' reading of texts?
The range of pedagogically appropriate paradigms one might
choose from is fairly broad, but for illustration, I will apply the
concept to a few selected works by essayists. Actually, formalizing
terms such as "essay" or "fiction" becomes less useful in this discussion, since threshold texts often blur formal boundaries. Essays
become stories; prose concentrates into poetry; and the casual distinctions between fact and fiction lose their force. When writers
produce works that are conceived through multiple perspectives,
those writings often overflow boundaries. Although such excess
can be initially confusing, this quality of not being containable
within conventionalized definitions, of overflowing boundaries,
best describes what we mean by the "literary," a term which is itself being increasingly thrust into threshold status.

Jamaica Kincaid's work is a case in point. Kincaid is perhaps
best known for three works of fiction: a collection of stories entitled
At the Bottom of the River, the autobiographical novel *Annie John*,
and *Lucy*, a second collection of stories. But the first two works are
situated in Antigua, Kincaid's native land, and focus on characters
that look suspiciously like Kincaid, her mother, her father, and
other islanders. *Lucy* similarly explores the life of a West Indian
girl who, like Kincaid, comes to America and works as an *au pair*.
In fact, when Kincaid submitted *Annie John* to *The New Yorker*, it
was rejected in part because the magazine defined it as autobiography, while Kincaid insisted it was fiction. For Kincaid as writer,
the world of fact merges with the world of fiction. She has stated
that all her work is autobiographical and depicts her life experiences, but she has also said that

> the facts often are not as you would like them to be. You might
> like to have a cloudy day, and on the day the thing happens, it's a
> very sunny day, and to say that such a thing happened on a
> sunny day, the rhythm might be all wrong. So, it's better to write
> fiction, obviously.[7]

By claiming her work as fiction but writing from autobiographical
experiences, Kincaid can recreate her life as truth.

Kincaid's work is sculpted, rhythmic, poetic, overflowing with
emotion, dream-images, impressions of loss and desire. One of the
major themes of *Annie John*, for example, is the adolescent Annie's
sense of loss and betrayal as she discovers the emotional and sexual relationship between her mother and father which ultimately
orphans her. Here is a short excerpt describing her feelings:

My mother and I each soon grew two faces: one for my father and the rest of the world, and one for us when we found ourselves alone with each other. For my father and the world, we were politeness and kindness and love and laughter. I saw her with my old eyes, my eyes as a child, and she saw me with hers of that time. There was my mother scrubbing my back as in the old days, examining my body from limb to limb, making sure nothing unusual was taking place; there was my mother making me my favorite dessert, a blancmange—a reward for excelling at something that met with her approval.... And there I was also, letting the singsong of her voice, as it expressed love and concern, calm me into a lull; there I was fondling the strands of her thick black hair as she unravelled her braids for a daily brushing, burying my face in it and inhaling deeply, for it smelled of rose oil.... But no sooner were we alone, behind the fence, behind the closed door, than everything darkened. How to account for it I could not say. Something I could not name just came over us, and suddenly I had never loved anyone so or hated anyone so. But to say hate—what did I mean by that? Before, if I hated someone I simply wished the person dead, but I couldn't wish my mother dead. If my mother died, what would become of me? I couldn't imagine my life without her. Worse than that, if my mother died I would have to die, too, and even less than I could imagine my mother dead could I imagine myself dead.[8]

For Kincaid, life has no clear boundaries, which is perhaps part of her appeal for students. *Annie John* offers an account of an adolescent girl, trapped between childhood and adult life, who teeters on the edges of love, hate, deception, honesty. She wishes her mother dead although it is inconceivable to her that her mother would die. Kincaid, an Antiguan who lives in Vermont but chooses not to become an American citizen, is a quintessential threshold writer. Earlier in *Annie John*, Kincaid writes:

I was afraid of the dead, as was everyone I knew. We were afraid of the dead because we never could tell when they might show up again. Sometimes they showed up in a dream, but that wasn't so bad, because they usually only brought a warning, and in any case you wake up from a dream. But sometimes they would show up standing under a tree just as you were passing by.

Nor is this purely an imaginative conceit; Jamaica Kincaid has stated that there is a surreal quality about life in Antigua, that islanders there participate in the unfinalizability of life:

The thing about death in the place that I come from is that people behave as if it's another stage, and in every way. Even when the person doesn't in fact come back and haunt you, people behave about death as if it were a pageant. Your life is a pageant, and death is a pageant, so that I'll say to my mother, "So what happened to so and so?" and she'll say, "Oh you know, he died," and then following that, "and then he went to Canada."[9]

For Kincaid, conventional understanding of life and death blur with the mythic, the surreal, the phantasmagoric. Her works compel reading and re-reading because of their threshold qualities.

Another pedagogically useful writer who maintains a similar threshold stance is Richard Selzer. Selzer is a surgeon who writes, an agnostic who celebrates the mysteries of the eucharist, a Jew by birth but a Catholic mystic by inclination. Selzer characteristically poises his work on the border: he often depicts himself as standing in a doorway to a patient's room or ministering to those who hover between life and death as in "The Masked Marvel's Last Toehold" and "Four Appointments with the Discus Thrower." One of his most powerful essay narratives is "Imposter" in the volume entitled *Letters to a Young Doctor*. It is the story of a healer who finds his way to a remote region (a frontier) of northern Asia and who works medical miracles there, providing people relief "from their pain and cough, and for the repair of their wounds."[10] For three years he lives among them until a city inspector arrives and unmasks him as a medical imposter, an epileptic, a fugitive wanted for murder. Such imposture is, in my view, the very essence of threshold status: a nameless man called "N.," wearing a mask (as the surgeon is masked), living out a conflictual existence in a remote world situated between civilization and barbarism. The imposter, after performing one last life-giving operation, enters the forest at night and engages in one last reverie:

> He remembered the cobblestones of the square dancing about his feet. He remembered leaning over the trough, dipping out the secrets of the river and listening to the heavy drag of water far below. It had the solidity of ice. He remembered it streaming through his body until he himself was transparent and permeable, like a fish. He had felt then that he was in the process of becoming—exactly what he did not know, something between the golden sun and the dark river, something like the moon, a midmost thing that hides itself in the light of the day. Now [he] turned to lie face down, pressing his cheek into the wetness. The cool mud was a healing poultice. He had never known such a sense of well-being, so exultant a physical health.... Now [he] turned his head and pressed his face into the floor of the forest. Deeply he inhaled, drawing the mud in, feeling it slide at the

back of his throat. There was no pain, no choking, as though water were passing over the gills of a fish. Nothing but immense
and endless comfort, a sense of being reclaimed. No pain! But
this was the death of a righteous man. He had not earned it!
Pushing in, he filled his lungs with the benevolence.[11]

I think the ways that Selzer positions himself on the threshold are
obvious: life and death; horror and exultation; the soft mud—both
earth and water—which slides down his throat without pain or
choking, the sense the imposter has of being "something between
the golden sun and the dark river"—"a midmost thing." Selzer's
genius as a writer has much to do with his sensitive and evocative
exploration of those shifting boundaries. Immersed in science,
Selzer is equally an artist who poises himself and his writings on
the edge of the unknowable.

Similar threshold elements can be found in the work of Gretel
Ehrlich, particularly her lyrical collection of essays *The Solace of
Open Spaces*. At first, *Solace* reads as a collection of essays that
might be loosely categorized under the heading of "nature" or
"Wyoming," since in them Ehrlich describes various perceptions,
insights and experiences centering on her move to the northwest
corner of Wyoming. But the essays actually chronicle a pivotal turn
in her life, as she leaves the glitzy world of documentary film-mak-
ing in New York to enter Wyoming's bleak and beautiful landscape of rock, mountain, and wind. The book moreover chronicles
a Victorian death/life scenario: Ehrlich stays in Wyoming to recover from the death of her fiancé, succumbs to an emotional dor-
mancy that signals the death of her old self, and then rediscovers
herself by the means of the raw power and magnificence of the
land as well as the love of a rancher whom she marries. All this is
done through evocative, crystalline language that is rooted in the
actual but is rich in poetry and lyricism. In "Just Married," Ehrlich
offers a brief accounting of her husband, whom she met at a John
Wayne film festival in Cody, Wyoming; she closes that essay with
the following:

The seasons are a Jacob's ladder climbed by migrating elk and
deer. Our ranch is one of their resting places. If I was leery about
being an owner, a possessor of land, now I have to understand
the ways in which the place possesses me. Mowing hayfields
feels like mowing myself. I wake up mornings expecting to find
my hair shorn. The pastures bend into me; the water I ushered
over hard ground becomes one drink of grass. Later in the year,
feeding the bales of hay we've put up is a regurgitative act:

thrown down from a high stack on chill days they break open in
front of the horses like loaves of hot bread.[12]

The concept of the threshold is easily over-played. As I suggested earlier, virtually every literary text balances consciousness
versus unconsciousness, the possible against the inevitable. Even
so, the threshold is the exception rather than the rule for both writers and cultures. Moreover, many significant works of nonfiction,
fiction, poetry, and drama can be celebrated for the unequivocal
expression of meaning and point of view, for the ways they deny
threshold status altogether. In spite of all these caveats, I believe
that the threshold concept allows us to lay claim to some exciting
texts that invite students to situate themselves within that uneasy
territory known as "interpretation" or "the making of meaning for
oneself as a reader." In the Preface to *Borderlands: La Frontera*, Gloria Anzaldúa states:

> I am a border woman. I grew up between two cultures, the Mexi-
> can ... and the Anglo. I have been straddling that *tejas*-Mexican
> border, and others, all my life. It's not a comfortable territory to
> live in, this place of contradictions. Hatred, anger and exploita-
> tion are the prominent features of this landscape.[13]

In a book written in both English and Spanish, by a woman who is
both (and neither) American and Chicana, and who describes herself as a "lesbian of color" (p. 19), Anzaldúa explicitly delineates
the threshold state within which she finds herself:

> Alienated from her mother culture, "alien" in the dominant cul-
> ture, the woman of color does not feel safe within the inner life of
> her Self. Petrified, she can't respond, her face caught between *los
> intersticios*, the spaces between the different worlds she inhabits.[14]

"*Los intersticios*, the spaces between the different worlds she inhab-
its"—this is the dimension of the threshold that I have been trying
to articulate. It is a quality of writing that is not quantifiable, a perspective, a thing felt more than seen. Like Bakhtin's celebrated dialogic, it is not something that can be artificially made or injected
into a work of literature; it is bound into the vision of the artist, the
tension and resonance of the language.

Unlike Kincaid, Selzer, and Ehrlich, Anzaldúa draws explicit
attention to the borderland, to that liminal territory on which so
much artistry lives. And, similarly, it seems to me no accident that
Countee Cullen's haunting poem describes the speaker as someone
travelling, in an alien city, somewhere beyond the borders of
home.

Notes

1. Mikhail Bakhtin, *Problems in Dostoyevsky's Poetics*, trans. Caryl Emerson, intro. by Wayne C. Booth (Minneapolis: University of Minnesota Press, 1984), p. 170

2. E.B. White, *One Man's Meat* (New York: Harper, 1944), pp. 246–53.

3. Bakhtin, p. 71.

4. Bakhtin, p. 166.

5. Bakhtin, *Speech Genres and Other Late Essays*, trans. Vern W. McGee (Austin: University of Texas Press, 1986), p. 170.

6. Bakhtin, *The Dialogic Imagination*, ed. Michael Holquist, trans. Caryl Emerson and Michael Holquist (Austin: University of Texas Press, 1981), p. 250.

7. Jamaica Kincaid, Public Lecture, Conference on College Composition and Communication, March 16, 1989.

8. Kincaid, *Annie John* (New York: New American Library, 1985), pp. 87–88.

9. Kincaid, Public Lecture.

10. Richard Selzer, *Letters to a Young Doctor* (New York: Simon & Schuster, 1982), p. 179.

11. Selzer, pp. 193–94.

12. Gretel Ehrlich, *The Solace of Open Spaces* (New York: Viking, 1985), p. 90.

13. Gloria Anzaldúa, *Borderlands: La Frontera* (San Francisco: Aunt Lute Book Company, 1987), preface, n.p.

14. Anzaldúa, p. 20.

"Who on Earth Is George W.M. Reynolds?" Literature, Teaching, Politics[1]

Robert Mackie and Marea Mitchell

"The abandonment of the notion of ideology belongs with a more pervasive political faltering by whole sections of the erstwhile revolutionary left, which in the face of a capitalism temporarily on the offensive has beaten a steady, shamefaced retreat from such 'metaphysical' matters as class struggle and modes of production, revolutionary agency and the nature of the bourgeois state."

(Terry Eagleton)[2]

First Principles

Terry Eagleton's *Ideology: An Introduction* (1991) attacks, with characteristic wit, the blithe and fashionable use of terms like "new world order," "postmodernism," "postmarxism," and "postfeminism." The energy of the book is directed against the complacency of those who, in arguing for the redundancy of master narratives, support local analyses without reference to structural systems, or proclaim the neutrality of the objective intellectual. Eagleton disavows Richard Rorty's prescription for the intellectual as "ironist, practising a suitably cavalier, laid-back attitude to their own beliefs," identifying the inherent elitism of this position.[3]

A correlative and popular position is that master narratives and politically explicit schemes are no longer necessary because battles have been won. So Camille Paglia can state, with astonishing confidence, that "Capitalism, whatever its problems, remains the most efficient economic mechanism yet devised to bring the highest quality of life to the greatest number. Because I have studied the past, I know that, in America and under capitalism, I am the freest woman in history."[4]

Raymond Williams, Bertolt Brecht, and Walter Benjamin pointed out years ago the costs of capitalist systems, and the blindness involved when the elision between capitalism and civilisation is presumed as it is by Paglia.[5] Celebrations of better pollution controls or standards of living within America, without consideration of Bhopal and the Exxon Valdez, obscure the causal relations between "First" and "Third" world freedoms. A knowledge of history ought not to lead simply to a celebration of locally improved living conditions. Claims that we are now postmarxist or postfeminist can be seen only to occur within "a particular phase of advanced capitalism."[6] That inequalities exist between people within countries, and between countries is obvious; that wage slavery is the best system by which to live is still contentious, as Noam Chomsky has argued.[7] In the face of world-wide recessions millions are unemployed and real wages are declining.[8]

Crucial in attacking the golden age tendencies of postmodern philosophies are interrogating ideology and identifying the political interests of cultural practices. Teachers have specific responsibilities in the communication of culture, and in explaining the ways in which culture is imbricated in wider social systems, themselves partial and discriminatory. Analyses of "the plurality of relations between literature, teaching and politics"[9] then begin with the acknowledgment that "capitalist society 'is no solid crystal, but an organism capable of change, and constantly engaged in a process of change.'"[10] To promote a critical consciousness becomes an important part and purpose of teaching literature.

The essay that follows concentrates on the intersecting domains between the production, reception and transformation of texts. The position advocated derives from an awareness of the political implications of teaching literature within tertiary institutions. We endorse an approach which produces "modes of analysis appropriate to a society which is multicultural, subject to change, and the site of a range of resistances."[11] We argue for the continued relevance of Marxist literary theories in dialogue with other critical theories; for the maintenance of a specifically socialist space which recognizes the discourses of others such as feminism and postcolonialism; and for politically informed and aware teaching practices that are collaborative and transformative.

Literature and Culture

All the changes and shifts in literature or literary studies, all the "crises in English" of the past fifty years, have meant, for most of us now teaching and researching, that the field is utterly different from that in which we were formally trained. Even recently appointed academics may find themselves in the position, having themselves been taught about Virginia Woolf in a "Beowulf to Woolf" format, of now presenting her work in a feminist course.

Here there are complex issues about canonicity. Is it enough merely to discharge the canon of masculinist imperialist texts? Do teachers include more women writers on core courses, or construct feminism and literature courses? Do either of these necessarily change the nature or political effect of literary studies? Such issues demonstrate that teaching is an activity with political consequences. [12]

Eve Kosofsky Sedgwick points out that texts such as *Billy Budd* and *Dorian Gray* have appeared in traditional literature courses, "each differently canonical within a different national narrative.... As what they are taught, however, and as what canonised, comes so close to disciplining the reading permitted of each that even the contemporaneity of the two texts (*Dorian Gray* was published as a book the year *Billy Budd* was written) may startle." So the same texts "that mobilized and promulgated the most potent images and categories for ... the canon of homophobic mastery" become recuperable for antihomophobic inquiry and analyses. [13]

Political as well as pedagogical decisions determine whether to teach Woolf, which Woolf text to teach, and in what contexts. Woolf as modernist, along with Joseph Conrad and James Joyce; Woolf as feminist, along with Kate Chopin and Charlotte Perkins Gilman; Woolf as part of the Bloomsbury group, along with Leonard Woolf, T.S. Eliot, and E.M. Forster? The choice of context shapes the readings permitted, so that locating Woolf in a tradition of feminist, or woman-centered, writing discourages a broader social contextualizing. Very often Woolf appears to be distanced from her social and cultural milieu. Her role in the creation of a tradition of women's writing is currently emphasized at the expense of understanding the class implications of her writing. Locating Woolf in a feminist canon risks duplicating the great male literary tradition, for a differently constituted cultural elite.

Mulk Raj Anand provides a neat illustration of our point in his *Conversations in Bloomsbury* (1981). These affectionate, yet critical, essays show Anand recently "arrived in London after a brief jail-going in the Gandhi movement in the early twenties ... removed, suddenly, from the realities of the freedom struggle into the world of Bloomsbury where the pleasures of literature and art were considered ends in themselves."[14] Anand's affection for the Bloomsbury group is clear, as his contextualization of them demonstrates: "the talks evoke some of those lovable, liberal Englishmen and women, who compensated us for Rudyard Kipling's contempt for the 'lesser breeds,' with inspirations for free thinking" (p. 6).

"Tea and Empathy from Virginia Woolf" locates her in relation to *Orlando*, her experimental writing on the dissolution of sexual and gender barriers within one personality, or life history. It is interesting to note, however, that while Woolf's keen awareness of gender inequalities is well known, from Mulk Raj Anand's perspective the power relations are differently inflected by class, race, and gender.

> Shy and tentative, I entered the Woolfs' drawing room from the hallway, coming up from the Hogarth Press basement office, where I had been correcting some proofs. I had dared to send Virginia Woolf some part of the beginning of my confession called *Seven Summers*, and I was afraid of her verdict on my amateurish writing. I thought Leonard Woolf was following me, but, apparently, he had gone to "wash his hands" in the bathroom under the stairs.
>
> Virginia Woolf got up on hearing my footsteps and offered me the long fingers of her right hand, a gracious smile on her elegant clear-cut profile. She was dressed in a soothing grey longish frock, unlike most other short-dressed English women young and old.
>
> Inside me, there was a commotion about how I would make contact with her without her husband being there.... With the arrogance of a young Indian philosopher, who had begun to ask fundamental questions about how we know, what we know, and whether there is any reality at all, I hoped to communicate my hunches to her. And yet I hung my head down in deference to her dignified aloofness. (pp. 94–95)

From the outset, Anand's perception of himself in relation to the Woolfs is spatially mapped out as he ascends to the Woolfs' drawing room. Furthermore, his own status in relation to the Woolfs' is marked by his dependency on them. He corrects proofs for them, while he sees his own creative work as "amateurish writing." The verb "dared" expresses his awareness of the gap between his own efforts and the perceived professionalism of the published Woolfs. The power structures in this unequal relationship are clearly present in Anand's profession of fear at Virginia's "verdict." Virginia is posited as judge to Anand's defendant.

Anand's uneasiness is symbolized in finding himself temporarily alone, abandoned by Leonard's going "to 'wash his hands.'" The euphemism itself indicates a liberal, middle-class reluctance to refer to material, bodily functions directly. Alone, then, he encounters Virginia, and his description marks his sense of her superiority, that her graciousness embodies the manner she can literally afford to adopt. The clothes, demeanor, and style of Virginia indicate to Anand her class position, and her distance from the popular. "She was dressed in a soothing grey longish frock, unlike most other short-dressed English women."

Anand's uneasiness as to how to relate to Virginia without the comforting and legitimating presence of Leonard problematizes any simple notion of gender relations, of women as always oppressed. The awkwardness Anand experiences registers class, gender, and racial differences which present him as inferior, uncomfortable, uninformed, socially "other" to what is perceived as Virginia's contained, secure self and social identity, her "dignified aloofness." From the perspective of someone kicking against the traces of colonialism in its repressive mode, the ideological implications of the liberal "room of one's ownness" emerge quite clearly. Despite the fact that graciousness and patronage differ in tone and spirit from racism, it does not disguise the similarity in class relations from which both are born.

Anand's retrospective account of his encounter with Virginia Woolf broadens the issues concerning gender, race, and class operating in the 1920s and 1930s in England, from those directly articulated in Woolf's own writings. The anecdote also exemplifies the relations between literature and culture, situating literature as a "high" cultural form, promulgated by those who believe in art for art's sake, and who operate in a closed circle of friends publishing each other's work. Later in the same essay, Anand confesses to being influenced by George W.M. Reynolds, which receives the question "'Who on earth is George W.M. Reynolds?'" from Virginia, and the explanation "'He wrote serials during the late nineteenth century. He is mainly read by bored Englishmen in the tropics. Hardly ever mentioned here'" from Leonard (p. 96).[15] This example of Anand's self perceived "folly of low-browness" (p. 97) lays bare the hierarchies of reading and writing, the differentiations of access to literature, and the determination of how it is constituted. The intellectuals in Anand's book, at best, are well intentioned, never neutral, and their pretensions at objectivity shown to be hallmarks of their middle-class liberalism.

Recounting these experiences, Anand, recently released from prison for supporting Gandhi's drive for Indian independence and his campaign of civil disobedience, finds himself in the capital of liberal apologetics. The Bloomsbury he writes of can tolerate passive disobedience, while the political regime of which it is part perpetrates savage acts of violence like the massacre at Amritsar.

In Althusserian terms, Anand both encounters the repressive state apparatus, and in his *Conversations in Bloomsbury* documents the effects of the ideological state apparatus. The Woolfs, Eliot, and E.M. Forster are the manifestations of English high culture. They are its movers and shakers. His text, published long after the events took place, facilitates a return to "such 'metaphysical' matters as class struggle and modes of production, revolutionary agency and the nature of the bourgeois state."[16] Metaphysicality is denied through precise and revelatory descriptions of a highly formative period in English literary modernism.

Knowledge, Teaching and Practice

What ought to be clear quite often is not, while that which presents itself with self-evident clarity is often reductively deceptive. Knowledge and the practice of teaching are a case in point. It should be clear that teaching practices, especially in the field of literature, are informed by understandings of the object of knowledge, processes of knowledge acquisition, and how a knowledge of literature contributes to human self-awareness. All too often, though, literary education involves, to rephrase Fish and Derrida, sustaining the illusions that there is a text in this class and that outside of the text there is nothing.

A pedagogical emphasis on the text, the whole text and nothing but the text affirms the professionalized narrowing of literary education while alluding to the growth and sophistication of criticism. At the dawn of the twentieth century literature occupied a wider, less institutionalized, terrain. Literateurs, mostly men of course, could, via *The London Mercury*, or the Literary Supplement to *The Times,* or even in the more august *Criterion* of T.S. Eliot, establish and sustain, rebut and refute, literary claims and contentions. Yet, as Jeremy Hawthorn maintains in his valuable introduction, *Unlocking the Text* (1987), literature today "is inescapably connected with education, both at school, college and university level. One might cynically suggest that whereas people read books, students study literature. The narrowing-down of the meaning of the term 'literature' is intimately related to the growing stress placed on a literary *education* by European and North American societies."[17]

The development of specialist and technically complex critical practices has had the crucial effect of interpellating an elite discourse of criticism between both reader and text, and even author and text. Not only does such an interpellation implicitly devalue the experience of an informed common reader, but it also establishes fertile ground for critical disputation ("new critics" versus "deconstructionists") to take on a seeming life of its own. Such developments are, as Hawthorn suggests, a result of literary studies being connected with higher education.

This connection has epistemological consequences as well. As Hawthorn points out, "a common problem in all knowledge concerns the extent to which our observations disturb, destroy or create what it is that we are studying. With literature and criticism this problem is particularly acute: their study today is inescapably centered in academic departments of literature, but these same departments are influential in defining what we see as literature; how such literature is to be studied, and even, in a more limited way, how it is to be written" (p. 7). This suggests, among other things, that the content of our literary knowledge derives directly from the political struggles within institutions over course inclusions and exclusions. Bearing in mind the variability of departmental politics within and between institutions, literary courses typically represent an uneasy compromise between established canonical texts and "marginal" writing like detective fiction, women's writing, or gay literature. While such compromises are often justified in neo-Panglossian terms as offering the best there is in a less than best of all possible worlds, what is often striking is how literary marginality seeks acceptance by establishing its own hierarchy of authorial worth. So, for example, in detective fiction, Conan Doyle, Hammett, and Chandler might be in, while Christie, Simenon, and Corris might be out.

Whatever the specific focus of a course, we would argue, with Hawthorn, that the emphasis be on "the literary process" rather than on "literature." This draws attention away from "literature as a 'thing', the text as an object commanding attention." Our concern with process entails as well a commitment to the ways of knowing in preference to squabbles over content.

Jeremy Hawthorn illustrates the point diagrammatically:

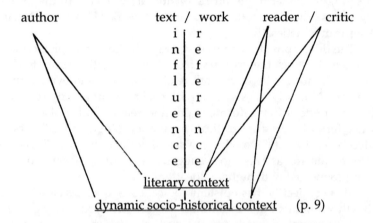

Depicting the literary process in this way encourages student and teacher to view the relations between author, text, reader, and so on as shifting or moving whilst "incorporated in, and mediated through, a relatively stable written text" (p. 9). Moreover, with regard to the production of such texts in particular, our approach foregrounds the fluidity of authorial practices in their literary and social contexts. If, as we suggest, the classroom and research task for student and teacher lies in an examination of the production, reception and transformation of texts, then the model of literary process posed above has the advantage of including what is often excluded. Under intentionalist, essentialist, or formalist renderings of literary endeavor more generally, it is common to find one or more elements of the literary process suppressed or excluded.

By contrast, an approach via the literary process neither forecloses critical outcomes nor predetermines appreciation. Counter-canonical and pluralist, it relates literature to wider fields, thereby expanding understanding and knowledge. With that said, we should not be unaware that the approach advocated is controversial. Many teachers and students would object that the ends of literature are not clearly stated, and point to the infusion of literature into sociology. Apart from failing to specify precisely what is "literary" in the process, such critics also claim that literary texts, in our view, are socially derived epiphenomena rather than original and individual results of purposive creative practices. To these objections we would simply reply that investigation is preferable to stipulation, while skepticism is healthier than dogmatism.

The institutional sites of literary education consist, as indicated earlier, in a series of uneasy compromises. Upon closer examination we can find in such sites examples of teaching practices which, while rhetorically aligned to pluralist outcomes, in fact sustain a largely uncritical acquiescence. As with formal education generally, there is within literary pedagogy a hierarchy of teachers— professors and tutors—who have widely disproportionate power and authority in the teaching process. Additional hierarchies can be found in courses—honors and first year—and texts—core and elective. Within these complex relationships what emerges most distinctively is the symbiosis between canonical content and stipulative teaching.

What is striking from an educational viewpoint is the deferential student response—cautious, self-preserving, almost reverential. Ironically, such outcomes are more likely where the teacher of literature is inspirational, exhilarating, witty, compassionate, and incisive. While few would discard the beneficial contribution such personal qualities can bring to the classroom, their intended positive consequence is undercut by the structural asymmetry of teacher and taught. There are, to use Pierre Bourdieu's phrase, vastly unequal "cultural capitals" operating in this educational exchange.[18] A realistic student can do well with the epistemology of received convention regarding texts, and better by deploying a personal demeanor congenial to the hidden curriculum of institutional literary education. By chancing little and absorbing much, the literature student is gradually inducted into a world dominated by approved allocations of sensibility. This should remind us that just as there are no innocent readings of a text, neither are there innocent practices in teaching. Properly regarded, teaching is an ensemble of practices—narrative, interrogative, evaluative— charged with political choice and consequence. Education, then, can be seen as comprising structurally unequal political exchanges.

It is an important part of literary educational practice not to reproduce this dominance/deferral asymmetry. The insistence that it is insufficient to read a novel of Virginia Woolf's, or "To Penshurst," in splendid isolation has implications for course construction. A generative reading list indicating starting points for student investigation serves to empower learners in their own inquiries. Class discussion on "To Penshurst" and Raymond Williams, which we suggest later, then occurs within a mutually agreed framework. The teacher enables and facilitates investigation beyond the classroom discussion, for essay work, for example, without predetermining its areas or its outcomes.

With regard to literary education, its present task and challenge could be described as one of developing integrative pedagogical practices where the literary process becomes central to the English curriculum. Put another way, this challenge involves resolving the dominative dependency of teachers and students—establishing for the latter a genuine realm of agency rather than the subordinate expectation of compliance. In short, teacher and taught have before them equally the task of developing about literature a critical, rather than naïve, consciousness. At minimum this will encourage inter-disciplinary contributions as literature is returned to its social and political context. It will also demand a reshaping of classroom interactions from formalist pontifications meekly accepted, into considered fallibilities critically adjudged.

The Politics of Literary Education: "To Penshurst"

Our point at the end of the last section can be illustrated by considering Raymond Williams' treatment of "To Penshurst" by Ben Jonson. Williams' discussion can be found in *The Country and the City* (1975), pp. 33–47. Jonson's 102-line poem, published in 1616, readily available in anthologies of verse, or in Jonson's works, can be set for class discussion. The poem makes clear, through the form it takes, its own position in relation to literary conventions and literary tradition. It is one of a group recognizable as country house poems. As the birthplace of Philip Sidney (1554), Penshurst is invoked as a means of linking Jonson himself with the aristocratic producers of culture. The poem can thus be located in terms of the author's own life and work. The relations between Sidney the courtier, scholar, soldier, and Jonson the bricklayer, soldier, actor can be investigated in terms of the poem's genesis, and its negotiation of English literary production in the early seventeenth century.

The formal properties of the poem might be discussed in relation to the project of the poem: praise of the estate which comes to symbolize everything valuable in England, both nature and culture. The deliberately archaic language, classical references, and formal tone ("thou/thy") might be addressed with reference to the declared subject of the poem. The ways in which the poem directly speaks to an estate/house as if it were capable of responding or hearing might raise further questions about the project of the poem. If the "argument" is one of praise for ways of living or a type of culture expressed by the values and aspects of a particular family, then we might ask who the audience of the poem was— given that it was not Penshurst itself! Here issues concerning technological change could be raised: how has the reproducibility of this poem, in collections, as part of Jonson's *œuvre*, in books of Sidney's works, in historical surveys of verse, and so on, affected possible interpretations? How does the context of the poem's reproduction affect its meanings? How would the poem have first appeared? To whom was it addressed, and how does this affect responses to the poem?

In this connection, particular lines provide direct discussion of the hierarchical structure of English society.

> And though thy walls be of the country stone,
> They are rear'd with no man's ruin, no man's groan,
> There's none, that dwell about them, wish them down;
> But all come in, the farmer, and the clown:
> And no one empty-handed, to salute
> Thy lord, and lady, though they have no suit
> (45–50)

Here class relations are presented as reciprocal and harmonious. The "clown" and farmer are posited as bringing gifts to the lord and lady, without wanting anything in return, and with no sense of envy at their inferior position. Though country stones have been used to build the house, no one, the poem says, is resentful. At this point it is worth returning to the likely early audiences for the poem. The likelihood of farmer and clown reading or hearing the poem, and being in a position to substantiate or refute the image of their supposed acquiescence must be debatable.

The meanings of the poem might be acknowledged to be less stable, if the socio-historical context of the poem is considered. Williams makes the material reality of Penshurst's construction quite clear: "It is not easy to forget that Sidney's *Arcadia*, which gives a continuing title to English neo-pastoral, was written in a park which had been made by enclosing a whole village and evicting the tenants."[19] How then do we relate Williams' historical account of Penshurst to Jonson's account of walls "rear'd with no man's ruin, no man's groan"? (46). Furthermore, what are the relations of production expressed in the poem? Nature seems everywhere abundant and generous: woods

> To crown thy open table, [do] provide
> The purpled pheasant, with the speckled side:
> The painted patrich lies in every field,
> And, for thy messe, is willing to be kill'd.
> (27–30)

As Williams points out, "To Penshurst," like other country house poems, creates "what can be seen as a natural bounty and then a willing charity ... achieved by a simple extraction of the existence of labourer. The actual men and women who rear the animals and drive them to the house and kill them and prepare them for meat; who trap the pheasants and partridges and catch the fish; who plant and manure and prune and harvest the fruit trees: these are not present; their work is all done for them by a natural order" (p. 45).

Their appearance is as reassuringly generous and undemanding faithful retainers. This effacement of the laborers, of work, is a direct denial of the materiality of production in the seventeenth century. We might then begin to re-question the purposes of the poem, given the social status of its likely audiences. Given that there had been riots over the forced enclosures of public lands, that a feudal economic system was giving place to mercantilism and population shifts to the cities, "To Penshurst" begins to seem less a contemporary reflection and more of a nostalgic reverie. In this context the anxiety of the poem emerges. By declaring the peasants to be friendly and undemanding, the specter of their non-complicity is raised. The effacement of the laborers, the denial of their importance in placing food on the table and in the lord's mouth, calls attention to the necessity of their cooperation and existence.

That the moment when one position is being firmly and confidently declared is precisely the moment at which the fearful, the excluded, can be heard to whisper is nowhere clearer than at the heart of bourgeois capitalism—the maintenance of property. So the epitome of Penshurst's bounty, saved until near the end as the poem's crowning glory, is the lady:

> These, Penshurst, are thy praise, and yet not all.
> Thy lady's noble, fruitful, chaste withall.

> His children thy great lord may call his own:
> A fortune, in this age, but rarely known.
> (89–92)

Central to Penshurst's continuation, yet marginal both to the poem and insignificant in her own right, the lady, like the laborers, is site of both congratulation and extreme anxiety. Should the lady withdraw her honor, refuse to be contained within monogamous marriage, should the laborers refuse their labor, then the walls of Penshurst would come tumbling down. The contradiction that the poem embodies—bounty without labor—suggests that "To Penshurst" functions as much as a fantasy of ideal relations as a realistic account of a seventeenth-century country estate.

The concept of ideology, as both Terry Eagleton and John B. Thompson have very recently argued, is one which facilitates analysis and the development of critical consciousness.[20] Drawing on Marx's *The Eighteenth Brumaire of Louis Bonaparte,* Thompson formulates a definition of ideology "as a system of representations which serve to sustain existing relations of class domination by orienting individuals towards the past rather than the future, or towards images and ideals which conceal class relations and detract from the collective pursuit of social change" (p. 41). Such a concept seems to us very productive in providing a starting point for the consideration of such literary texts as Ben Jonson's "To Penshurst."

When considered in the full range of relationships suggested by Hawthorn, the educational possibilities of the poem, or of the serials of George W.M. Reynolds, are expanded beyond the ones that the texts explicitly invoke. What might then be called a cultural materialist approach to literature encourages the consideration of the many relations in which a text is involved, and the processes by which textual meaning is produced. This is achieved without abandoning the text to relativism and the free play of subjectless signifiers.

These issues are important because, as Bourdieu, Eagleton, Williams, Althusser, Thompson, and many others have argued, as teachers within tertiary institutions we are all "concerned in part with the ascription and renewal of symbolic value."[21] The development of a critical consciousness, in both teachers and students, is then, we believe, crucial both in analyzing the political implications of that symbolic value, and in transforming it towards more egalitarian ends.

Notes

1. The subtitle of this essay refers to a journal of the same name, *Literature, Teaching, Politics*, produced in the 1980s by radical British academics.

2. Terry Eagleton, *Ideology: An Introduction* (London and New York: Verso, 1991).

3. Eagleton, p. 11.

4. Camille Paglia, "Junk Bonds and Corporate Raiders: Academe in the Hour of the Wolf," *Arion*, 3rd ed., 1.2. (1991), pp. 210–11. For a criticism of Paglia's position in relation to contemporary discourses on sexuality see Marea Mitchell, "Vision, Politics and Eros: Four Recent Essays on Criticism and Sexuality," *Southern Review*, 25.1 (1992), pp. 107–15.

5. "'Civilization' had produced not only wealth, order, and refinement, but as part of the same process poverty, disorder, and degradation," Raymond Williams, *Marxism and Literature* (Oxford: Oxford University Press, 1977), p. 18; "The mansion of culture is built on dogshit," Bertolt Brecht quoted in Lee Patterson, *Negotiating the Past: The Historical Understanding of Medieval Literature* (Madison: University of Wisconsin Press, 1987), p. 46; "There is no document of civilization which is not at the same time a document of barbarism," Walter Benjamin, "Paris, Capital of the Nineteenth Century," *Reflections*, ed. Peter Demetz, trans. Edmund Jephcott (New York: Schocken Books, 1986), p. 158.

6. Eagleton, p. 220.

7. Noam Chomsky in the film "Manufacturing Consent," concerning issues raised in the book *Manufacturing Consent*, by Edward S. Herman and Noam Chomsky (New York: Pantheon Books, 1988).

8. See, for example, Andrew Glyn, "The Costs of Stability: The Advanced Capitalist Countries in the 1980s," *New Left Review*, 195, September/October 1975, pp. 71–95.

9. *Literature, Teaching, Politics*, 1 (1982), p. 1.

10. Boris Kagarlitsky, *The Dialectic of Change*, trans. Rick Simon (London: Verso, 1990), p. 9, quoting Karl Marx, *Capital*, Vol. 1 (London: Penguin, 1976), p. 93.

11. *Literature, Teaching, Politics* 1 (1982), p. 2.

12. See Paul Smith, "The Political Responsibility of the Teaching of Literatures," *College Literature*, double issue: *The Politics of Teaching Literature*, 17.2/3 (1990), p. 81.

13. Eve Kosofsky Sedgwick, *Epistemology of the Closet* (Berkeley and Los Angeles: University of California Press, 1990), p. 49.

14. Mulk Raj Anand, *Conversations in Bloomsbury* (New Delhi: Arnold-Heinemann, 1981), p. 5.

15. Edward Said discusses the construction of English Studies and canonicity in relation to colonialism in *Culture and Imperialism* (London: Chatto & Windus, 1993), p. 48.

16. Eagleton, p. xii.

17. Jeremy Hawthorn, *Unlocking the Text* (London: Arnold, 1987), p. 7. This section follows Hawthorn closely.

18. Pierre Bourdieu and Jean-Claude Passeron, *Reproduction in Education, Society and Culture*, trans. R. Nice (London: Sage Publications, 1977), pp. 71–106.

19. Williams, *The Country and the City* (London: Granada, 1973), p. 33.

20. Eagleton, op.cit.; John B. Thompson, *Ideology and Modern Culture* (Oxford: Polity Press, 1992).

21. Thompson, p. 161.

Narratology: What We Read When We Read Raymond Carver's "So Much Water So Close to Home"

R. Rawdon Wilson

Narrative pervades all aspects of human life. Everything can be told as a story; everyone may wish to tell his/her own story. A six-teenth-century English writer, Sir Philip Sidney, remarks that sto-ries have the power to keep children from play and old men from the chimney-corner. What gives narratology its special dimension as a teaching tool is that it opens up the wide variety of ways in which stories can be told. Almost anything, sticks and clay, smoke and air, can be used as the means for telling a story. Drama and film, as well as puppet shows, opera, and ballet, are essentially narrative in that they are means for expressing stories. Comic strips, like Renaissance frescos, are narrative in terms of their structure, their treatment of time, and their final product which will be a fictional world, in some degree of completeness, that can be perceived and understood. Furthermore, many narratives are told in media that make them unclear. Television advertisements, for example, often tell highly slanted stories about the goodness and benefits of a commercial product in brief, elliptical forms that force the viewer to draw out implications, to make use of previ-ously funded experience, to interpret a rapid succession of images, to spring to conclusions (perhaps not actually justified by the story's content), and to keep open the story's line well after the fi-nal words or image. Narrative always relies upon the reader's or viewer's power to infer.

Stories told through the medium of television for the purposes of advertising indicate several important points about narrative: narratives may be brief, even fragmentary; they may move rapidly and discontinuously (like a montage of film images); they may try to influence the way they are read and understood in order to push a specific point (the pitch in advertising, the moral in traditional fables); yet despite these elliptical modes of presentation they are understood. Narratives are everywhere in human life; understanding how they have the effects that they do constitutes one of the important tasks of coming to grips with (any)one's personal lifeworld. The first step in teaching about narratives should be to point out their ubiquity; the second, their diversity.

Subsequent steps in teaching from a standpoint of narrative theory may involve pointing out the elliptical modes of telling. This should not pose much conceptual difficulty to a media-oriented generation of students. Students are usually familiar with a variety of narrative modes. Narratively, films are often as varied and as complex as novels. A Woody Allen film, for example, may be as reflexive and as playful in its narrative techniques as *Tristram Shandy* or *Pale Fire*. Opening up the subject to a discussion of narrative diversity in the students' own culture enables one to introduce two of narratology's fundamental precepts: (1) that there is an important (and heuristic) distinction between *what* is being told (the "story") and *how* a narrative is told (its "discourse"); (2) that a story (the what) may be told over and over in many different ways and in a great variety of media. For narratologists a "story" does not mean a source, an originary tale, an archetype, or anything that might be discovered outside the narrative being discussed. The story, a heuristic fiction, maps the writer's achievement: the distance travelled between the created discourse and its simplest conceivable structure. Narratologists do not assume that a writer must have had the story "in mind" prior to creating a narrative discourse. They *do* assume that storytellers have had some knowledge of the ways of telling, the techniques (or conventions) that allow a discourse to be created, and generally a familiarity with what one narratologist calls the "available repertory of artistic procedures and textual models."[1]

Narratology downplays a critical interest in questions of content ("themes"). The representative content of narratives, whether historical events and persons or imaginative constructions of what might have been or might still be, is less interesting than are the ways in which narratives have been constructed. The way(s) in which a narrative is *told* constitute the central focus. Nonetheless, as a way of getting into a discussion, it is often useful to initiate some conversation about content. This tends to involve students more actively than would a direct analysis of a narrative's formal features (the "artistic repertory," for instance). One can fruitfully begin with questions that concern the moral properties of a narrative's fictional world. In teaching Raymond Carver's "So Much Water So Close to Home," although the most interesting narratological questions concern time-shifts, voice, and character, there are good openings for discussion in the relationship between the male and the female character, in the wide array of gender-specific actions and expressions, and in the two characters' motivations which may seem to be either sincere, loathing arising out of love, or mechanically gendered responses.[2] "So Much Water So Close to Home" has the advantage for a classroom situation that it can prompt vigorous discussion about a large number of issues that are not themselves parts of the narrative's formal disposition, but aspects of the fictional world that the students must imagine. It is also possible to discuss the applicability of different theoretical perspectives before turning to a systematic narratological analysis. One might begin with some discussion of how the world of the narrative would seem from a feminist perspective or from that of culture theory. Questions about the woman's hemmed-in and subordinate position, about the man's attitude towards his wife, about male homosocial bonding (whether recreation or ritual), and about the presence of male violence in the fictional world, all serve to initiate discussion. However, none of these paths into the narrative is directly narratological.

Narratologists are interested in such matters as: (1) the time-scheme of a narrative (in contrast to the supposed chronological time of the "story"); (2) the nature of the voice telling the story; the distinction between that voice and the experience of the narrative's main character(s); (3) the potential of embedding (one narrative within another); (4) the creation of characters; (5) the creation of fictional worlds; (6) the collaboration of the reader in the creation of fictional entities, both characters and worlds. These are among the problems, inseparable from narrative experience, always available and always important, that narratologists take up in the analysis of specific texts. To the objection that these are "merely" formal issues, a continuation of the "rhetoric of fiction" under a new name, that obscure more important socio-cultural considerations, narratologists answer that more than one approach to fiction is possible, that these can be carried out in mutually supportive ways, and that the analysis of a text's formal features is never "merely" that, but an indispensable step in understanding. If a student cannot see *how* a story has been told, *how* a narrative has been written, then s/he will probably miss both the writer's creativity and the way in which themes are introduced and interrelated.

Carver's "So Much Water So Close to Home" typifies the kind of narrative problems that interest narratologists. It is also a story that contemporary students are likely to find immediately absorbing, since the setting and conflicts are familiar and the language both simple and ordinary. (This is one reason why students usually remember their initial theme-focussed reading vividly, when they are asked to assess what they have gained, or lost, in the process of becoming narratologically sophisticated readers.) Carver's narrative tells a story of marital disharmony and alienation (familiar territory in Carver's fiction), in which a female narrator implies accusations of male indifference, insensitivity and perhaps criminal behavior. The initial step in a narratological analysis is to infer the story from the narrative in order to determine the narrative departures. One can get students to appreciate the difference between the story and the narrative by asking them to summarize, and what they come up with might well look something like this:

> Four men go fishing in a remote mountain river. They find the body of a young woman floating in the water. When their fishing trip is over they report the body to the police. The wife of one of the men is upset at their insensitivity in waiting to report the body. She begins to sympathize with the dead woman. Her antagonism to her husband grows. They feel mutually alienated. The wife seems to accuse the man of complicity in the crime.

This should bring two things home to them: (1) that this story exists nowhere outside the narrative from which it has been inferred; (2) that it is not *interesting* in narrative terms and bears little similarity to Carver's short fiction in any of the respects that readers take seriously. Yet its very difference from Carver's narrative should help them to appreciate his craft.

A logical convention with which to begin analysis is Carver's manipulation of narrative time. "So Much Water So Close to Home" begins at the breakfast table the morning after the men have returned from fishing. The trip to the Naches river, discovering the young woman's body, the fishing camp and what the men did there, calling the police and returning home are all supplied in the narrator's voice after the narrative has begun. Later the narrator (Claire, the wife of one of the men) steps outside the immediate content of the story being told to narrate her childhood ("There was a girl who had a mother and father ... who moved as if in a dream through grade school and high school and then, in a year or two, into secretarial school" (p. 223), the couple's courtship and marriage. Students immediately perceive that Carver's narrative is expanded by this retrospective narration even as its chronology is broken. As a matter of course narratives perturb chronological order. One important convention of the classical epic, for instance, is to begin *in medias res*, at a high point in the action and then provide the necessary background information in the form of a long speech, or exposition. Such analogies can make for a more general discussion of how the perturbation of chronological order can work in either direction, looking backwards, analeptically, or forwards, proleptically.

Narrative time can disorder chronology in two further respects: duration and frequency. Duration refers to the amount of time that elapses *during* the narration of a series of story-events. It is obvious that what takes place in a story may be told at less or greater length. Carver's narrator, for example, narrates both the fishing trip and her personal history before her marriage in a terse, summary manner. The reader will infer that the fishing trip, which is said to have lasted more than one day and to have involved a long drive and a five-mile hike, must have taken longer than the relatively brief account that the narrator gives. In other narratives, the time of the story might well be expanded, or stretched, or even made to equal the time of narration or the sequence of narrative events themselves (this last possibility occurs, if ever, only during dialogue). Perhaps the most striking difference between the duration of story-events and their narrative telling occurs in ellipsis when "discourse halts, though time continues to pass in the story."[3] Much of what must be imagined as having happened during the fishing trip falls into ellipsis during Claire's narration. Neither the drive to the Naches river nor the hike into the fishing hole, though indicated, are narrated. A similar ellipsis occurs, even more unmistakably in Claire's narration of her girlhood and, within the boundaries of the narrative, of her own drive over the mountains to attend the dead girl's funeral.

Frequency refers to the relationship between the number of times a particular incident "appears in a story and the number of times it is narrated (or mentioned) in the text."[4] Something that happens many times in a story may be narrated an equal number of times; however, something that occurs only once may be narrated many times while something that occurs many times may be narrated only once. The third possibility, "iterative" narrative, in which one incident in the narrative stands for many similar incidents in the story indicates what is a very common narrative convention. In "So Much Water So Close to Home," iterative narrative occurs in many places. For example, when Claire describes (in her personal reconstruction of that experience) what the men did in the fishing camp while the young woman floated in the water nearby, she refers once to many things, such as cooking fish, drinking whisky, playing cards or telling "coarse stories" that must have happened more than once; later, when she recounts how she took their son to her mother-in-law's, she observes that the older woman "has a way of looking at me without saying anything" (p. 219), an unmistakable instance of iterative frequency. Like perturbations in temporal order and duration, frequency indicates the writer's attitude to the story and its potential for becoming a narrative. The primary reason for beginning with the problem of narrative time is to demonstrate to students that a narrative is distinct from its *story* and that conscious thinking must have gone into its writing. They will appreciate seeing that narrative time reflects the writer's sense of how best to tell a certain story.

The next logical step in teaching a narrative should be to introduce the concept of "voice" for analysis. The creation of a distinctive narrative voice constitutes one of the most obvious transformations of story. This occurs strikingly in Carver's narrative. The narrator, Claire, recounts the incidents of the fishing trip and the events that immediately followed (newspaper stories, angry telephone calls, the discovery of the dead woman's identity) so that the narrative is wholly her reconstruction. *All* narratives possess narrative voices, even when this is not obvious.[5] There is an evident distinction between third-person, neutral (seeming) narratives and those, such as Carver's "So Much Water So Close to Home," in which a first-person narrator clearly distorts, through ignorance, malignity, or madness, the content of the story it is telling. A mad narrator, distorting the story-events, necessarily lacks "authenticity." Nonetheless, readers will normally infer from the narrator's distortions an account that makes sense and holds together. Narratives are symbolic constructs, open to analysis and eventual understanding, and do not become more or less so according to the person of the narrative voice.

From the opening paragraph, Carver's narrator casts her husband as a distant, unsympathetic being, now alienated from her by irreconcilable differences. "Something has come between us though he would like me to believe otherwise" (p. 213). That something is the knowledge that her husband continued to fish while the dead woman floated nearby in the river. Her feelings quickly become evident. She resents her husband's indifference and, as she thinks, callousness in allowing the woman to remain in the water while he fished. She begins to associate with him a general sense of oppressiveness and insensitivity. She remembers that he made love to her upon returning from the trip, without mentioning the dead woman, and experiences revulsion: "I looked at his hands, the broad fingers, knuckles covered with hair, moving, lighting a cigarette now, fingers that had moved over me, into me last night" (p. 218). Claire easily believes the worst concerning her husband (whether or not he deserves the harshness of the narrator's judgments is left to the reader to infer), even associating him with the crime. In the final sentence of the narrative, she exclaims, "For God's sake, Stuart, she was only a child" (p. 237). Claire seems to project upon her husband feelings funded in memory, that she has for all men. At one point in her narrative, she remembers some brothers who had killed a girl whom she knew in high school, cut off her head and threw her into a river (p. 220). Stuart becomes a target for her generalized resentment and, focussed by his supposed insensitivity in the matter of allowing the woman to continue floating, androphobia. Various comments that she makes and, in particular, her long drive over a mountain range to attend the woman's funeral indicate her increasing sympathy with the dead woman and alienation from her husband. The reader can take the narrator's account as authentic, but it is also possible to read through the voice to another version in which the husband, though easily baffled and not particularly thoughtful with regard to the implications of his actions, may be seen as well-meaning, certainly innocent of an actual crime, and genuinely caring towards his wife. Close reading requires the reader continuously to re-evaluate the narrative voice.

Voice can be a slippery category. Students are often helped to understand it if they are asked, as a move in classroom discussion, to invent a voice, or to imagine how they might tell a story differently in order to create different effects. In studying Carver's "So Much Water So Close to Home," it also helps to ask them to think of other untrustworthy narrators, even to invent one themselves. Generalizing the problem of voice in this way also has the advantage of making them rethink the narrative in terms of the larger theoretical positions which they have adopted, or which they may generally assume in reading. For example, a feminist perspective in reading may make Claire appear to be entirely trustworthy in her narration (since these things do happen, and men do often act in the callous manner that Claire perceives). It is also important to get students to see that the concept of voice is wider than the notion of point-of-view. Much of what is called point-of-view refers to the experience of characters, not the narrator. Hence it is important to distinguish between a voice and the characters who appear in the story the voice tells. Voice answers the question, "Who speaks?" However, the question, "Who sees?" often points to the experience of a character. Point-of-view, except when the narrator narrates its own experience and makes itself into the narrative's perceiving character, generally refers to what is true of a character, not a narrator. Taking a term from film criticism, the relation between the narrator's voice and a character may be called "focalization." It describes the "angle of vision through which the story is filtered in the text, and it is verbally formulated by the narrator."[6] In "So Much Water So Close to Home" two kinds of focalization occur. First, the first-person narrator focalizes her own experience. As in all first-person narratives, Claire creates herself as a character. Second, the other characters, primarily the husband, Stuart, are focalized as characters that experience the same events as the narrator. This creates a double perspective. The narrator recounts her own experience, but also that of the other characters who either see the same events or they see her. Stuart, of course, though existing only in her voice, sees both the events and her. One can easily make this distinction clear to students by asking them to invent another narrative, or think more about the one they have already created to illustrate voice, in which there is at least one character who perceives something and comments upon it.

From the standpoint of narratology, characters are always the product of conventions (the "available repertory of artistic procedures and textual models") and never transcriptions from life. Contextual considerations, such as "real life" models from the author's biography or socio-historical types, are not of primary relevance to narratologists, though their empirical discoverability would not be denied. The self-characterizing narrator in Carver's fiction identifies herself initially by a social role, a wife and homemaker, and slowly allows the reader to see that she possesses feelings, both positive and negative. Ultimately, the reader may see that her antagonism towards her husband is no more rational than her identification with the dead woman. Her sense that her husband has been, somehow, complicit in the murder reveals itself late

in the narrative, adding a more definite layer of psychological im-
balance or neurosis. Each time that she reports having refused her
husband's sexual overtures, it is possible to read through her account to see her husband's baffled affection. Her character develops through a sequence of indirect psychological revelations. Her
husband's character, focalized in her voice, develops through an
inverse process. He is first seen eating: "My husband eats with
good appetite but he seems tired, edgy. He chews slowly ... He
wipes his mouth on the napkin" (p. 213). The narrator's observations concerning her husband are initially mostly physical and include bodily traits. Like the narrator, he eventually receives a
proper name, always an important (if not necessary) convention of
characterization.

One might ask students to discuss Stuart's vulgarity. It will
lead to questions of how vulgarity is understood generally and
what it may indicate about the speaker. Eventually, the students
should understand that the husband's coarseness and inarticulate
attempts at reconciliation mask rather more attractive feelings than
those the narrator attributes to him. The process of characterization
may be analyzed as a number of conventions that are layed one
upon another. Stuart's vulgarity is one layer (diction and sociolect),
but his continuing desire for Claire is another.[7] However, a narratologist would not assume that the increasing complexity discovered through the analysis of conventions constitutes increasing coherence. Literary characters are not persons.

The problem of fictional worlds is similar to that of character.
In both cases the literary text provides semantic indices, rather like
intellectual clues, that the reader transforms into a meaningful
simulation of human life. Like a character, a fictional world can be
experienced through reading as compelling, even overwhelming.
For narratologists, a fictional world emerges gradually through
reading. The interaction of text and imagination creates a fictional
world. Like character, a fictional world should be considered as an
alternative state of affairs that, given the text's presuppositions,
could be the case. Imagination, one philosopher observes, posits
"non-actual states of affairs, it enables us to consider what alternative states of affairs *could* be the case."[8] However, narratologists
have not been, for the most part, interested in investigating theories of reading; they have been content to assume the imaginative
transformation of the text without confronting what the process
involves. The complexity of a fictional world, again like that of a
character, reflects the diversity of the conventions rather than the

quantity of detail employed. Indeed, the sheer quantity of detail, the number of descriptive adjectives used to develop either a character or a world (for example), might well cause blockage, creating an "opacity to inference."[9] However, *diversity* in the kinds of conventions used will, on the contrary, lead to the experience of a complex fictional world in which distinct agential domains, possessing different, even antagonistic, presuppositions, interact and overlap. The world of a short story may prove to be more internally complex than that of a novel or an epic. Students will easily see this point if they are simply asked to think of the number and kinds of actions that take place in a fictional world. They should see that spatial extension and lapse of time do not themselves make a fictional world complex, but the presence of different kinds of action does.

Carver's "So Much Water So Close to Home" presents a fictional world that is narratively complex. Although it is relatively circumscribed in its place (rivers and mountains surround the unnamed town; no character travels more than a hundred miles from home) and contains few characters, the range of human feelings and actions is quite extensive. Characters experience feelings of affection, empathy, love, and many kinds of desire (for sex, community, and understanding); they also feel dislike, revulsion, and hatred. In the background of the narrative, characters commit rape and murder; in the foreground, they feel both passionate identification with, and apathy towards, victims. Claire's emotional closeness to the events verges upon madness, but Stuart's emotional remoteness *might* suggest complicity. Characters, yearning for both the past and the future, reach out to one another and strike each other back. On a first reading, it may seem that male characters are apathetic, but capable of violence; women, passionate, but easily victimized. However, this initial reaction misses Carver's suggestions that ambiguity surrounds human feelings and that intentions can never be directly known. A reader may infer that Stuart does feel love as well as desire for his wife, even though, in his frustration, he occasionally speaks to her with appalling violence:

> And then I am lifted up and then falling. I sit on the floor looking up at him and my neck hurts and my skirt is over my knees. He leans down and says, "You go to hell then, do you hear, bitch? I hope your cunt drops off before I touch it again." He sobs once and I realize he can't help it, he can't help himself either. I feel a rush of pity for him as he heads for the living room. (p. 236)

The reader must actively infer whether to feel pity for Stuart's (male) violence or for his frustration. During her drive over the mountains to the young woman's funeral, Claire is followed by a man in a pick-up truck. When she drives off the road to wait, he turns around, comes back and knocks on the window of her car which she has rolled up. Evidently, she fears that he may be violent, perhaps a rapist, but more likely, given the narrative situation, he is only worried about her and would like to help. Nonetheless, she asserts that he "looks at my breasts and legs" and that his eyes "linger on my legs" (pp. 232–33). Both the intention of the one character and the accuracy of the other's account are uncertain.

The fictional world of "So Much Water So Close to Home" is divided into two distinct narrative domains. The male characters inhabit one domain; the female, the other. The boundaries between them, despite their apparent clarity, are quite indistinct. The question whether the male characters are essentially violent or merely inarticulate hangs suspended, unanswered, at the narrative's close. Carver creates a double world with uncertain interaction across its borders: a world built upon feelings and perceptions, not upon geography or descriptions. Students can usually see that the fictional world is divided, though they may have trouble recognizing that Carver gives both domains, the male and the female, validity. One can cross this difficulty rather easily, however, by asking students to retell the narrative from the perspective of the character whose gender they other. A young man retelling the narrative wholly from within Claire's experience will see how dangerous and irrational male violence may seem; a young woman, rethinking the world from within Stuart's perceptions, will see how unfair judgments based upon gender stereotypes may be.

Like other analytic approaches to fiction that find it necessary to make many precise distinctions, narratology may occasionally seem to founder upon a difficult, even bristling terminology. However, the technical terms do point to useful distinctions and do help to isolate distinct elements in both the text and in the reading process. A technical terminology may be the price students of literature must pay for clarity. In any case, narratology provides a path to the understanding of narrative that can be followed and, indeed, improved as one moves forward. There would not appear to be any necessary final point in the search for lucidity and precision. Since narrative, in all media, does pervade human life and does have a huge role in living (since people will always need to tell their own stories and to understand those of others), narratology calls attention to an extremely important dimension of human interactions within culture. All members of a human culture will possess many narrative skills, but narratology makes this knowledge explicit. The stories one tells, in any situation, in whatever medium, are so fundamental to life and culture that a set of analytic procedures to increase one's understanding and command of narrative should prove to be rather like discovering a new means to explore reality itself. In asking students to read narratives more closely, one is also showing them how to deal more fully with their own lifeworlds.

Notes

1. Uri Margolin, "Narrative and Indexicality: A Tentative Framework," *Journal of Literary Semantics*, 67 (1983), p. 181.

2. Raymond Carver, "So Much Water So Close to Home," in *Where I'm Calling From: New and Selected Stories* (New York: Random House-Vintage, 1989), pp. 213–37.

3. Seymour Chatman, *Story and Discourse: Narrative Structures in Fiction and Film* (Ithaca: Cornell University Press, 1978), p. 70.

4. Shlomith Rimmon-Kenan, *Narrative Fiction: Contemporary Poetics* (London: Methuen, 1983), p. 56.

5. It is important to distinguish between the act of narrating itself and the situation of the narrative. The term "narration" can be used to indicate the activity of the voice in narrating. Narration involves questions of style, specific conventions, all the choices that any narrator must make in speaking, and point of view (slant or bias). The phrase "narrating instance" can be used to designate the socio-psychological situation from which the narrative is told. It entails questions of subjectivity, such as motivation and bias, and the interdynamics between the narrator and its audience.

6. Rimmon-Kenan, p. 43. See also Gerard Genette, *Narrative Discourse: An Essay in Method*, trans. Jane E. Lewin (Ithaca: Cornell University Press, 1980), pp. 185–91.

7. Genette remarks provocatively of Proust that his characters become "down through the pages more and more indefinable, ungraspable, 'creatures in flight.'" (p. 185).

8. Doreen Maitre, *Literature and Possible Worlds* (London: Middlesex Polytechnic Press, 1983), p. 119. The theoretical analysis of possible and

fictional worlds is extensive. See R. Rawdon Wilson, *In Palamedes' Shadow: Explorations in Play, Game and Narrative Theory* (Boston: Northeastern University Press, 1990), pp. 167–208. See also Thomas Pavel, *Fictional Worlds* (Cambridge, MA: Harvard University Press, 1986). Both Wilson and Pavel provide bibliographies of works dealing with fictional world theory.

9. Pavel, pp. 94–95. See also Wilson, pp. 195–96.

Part Three

Re-Presenting the Canon

"By Any Other Name": Theoretical Issues in the Teaching of Nineteenth-Century Black Women's Autobiography

Joycelyn Moody

"Holding down, as it were, several spaces at once marks the dilemma of African-American culture, of a people, of individual ones of us, and out of it our practice of criticism, teaching, and writing arises. We are called upon, then, to articulate the spaces of contradiction."

(Hortense Spillers)[1]

"Nineteenth-Century Black Women's Autobiographies" is an upper-division literature course I developed primarily for English majors. In 1991 I introduced this course at a small private liberal arts college in Michigan. I had eleven students, only one of whom was a man. After our end-of-the-quarter dinner, this young man and I stood in my doorway saying goodbye. He was solemnly thanking me for the instruction I'd given him in the course, nodding gravely into my eyes. "I never thought much about the colored people before," he said. "I never realized how important the colored people have been in our country."

Almost exactly a year later, at the end of my second teaching of this course, this time at a large research university, I stood on the threshold of my office, shaking hands and saying goodbye to one of only two men who had been in my class of thirty-five. As he earnestly thanked me for the course, he also unwittingly echoed my former student: "I'm so glad you exposed me to a part of American History that had been totally black to me before. Thank you so much!"

I remember feeling overwhelmed each time, stunned by the amount of work those remarks revealed I had yet to do. I remember wanting, trying to feel elation. After all, these expressions of gratitude marked the momentary attainment of a personal and professional goal: as my career evolved, without conscious reflection, I had made my primary activist-academic mission the education of whites from an African American canon. But closing the door on these two young white men, I felt only defeat. What had I been doing wrong all quarter that they should be so oblivious to the impact of their racist and egocentric words? How could they feel so entitled to (mis)name a people, to engage the very colonization we had deplored together for ten weeks? Both times I felt profoundly violated in my own space, and wished vehemently that I had been on the other side of the threshold so that when *I* walked away from *him*, the man's offending words would have lingered with him, not me. Yet even as I feared myself doomed to relive these events, I rushed to record them so that I would not forget.

My students' comments clarify for me that my work, however vital, is inadequate. Of course, the autobiographies of former slavewomen and of free-born black women ought to be taught because they are both historically significant and aesthetically beautiful. Besides, rare, neglected texts are currently *en vogue* as *litterateurs* reconstitute the American literary canon. However, as an African American feminist scholar, I have come to realize that my teaching functions as more than an act of sharing what I judge to be beautiful; it also serves important social and political needs. As Audre Lorde properly asserts in her essay "Poetry Is Not a Luxury": "It [i.e., poetry, teaching, any manifestation of 'the distilled creative experience'] forms the quality of light within which we predicate our hopes and dreams toward survival and change, first made into language, then into idea, then into more tangible action."[2] For at its most basic level, my teaching of the narratives of African American women of the Civil War era connects their lives to mine as a black woman in postmodern America. But no matter how earnestly one accepts one's tasks, or even how well one teaches, it is vain to presume that an academic quarter or semester could dismantle twenty-odd years of racist and sexist indoctrination that often impedes mainstream undergraduate students' comprehension of black women's complex lives (even when students are themselves black and/or female). In the face of such difficult work, despite my race and cultures and my expertise, I sometimes feel myself on alien terrain, treading on quicksand.

In casual conversations and professional consultations with other educators also engaged in curriculum reformation (and we are many in these days of pervasive political correctness and canon revision), I have found that we have abiding anxieties about the students we face, about our own capabilities. Among black literary scholars, the persistent fears may be expressed as: How do I teach the literature as something other than "my story," thereby denying to students who are not African American access to the texts? How do I distinguish the peculiar conventions of the African American literary tradition from those that are assimilated from other literary traditions, without seeming to disparage or to privilege either set of conventions? How do I avoid the ironic circle tracing the tauto-logical movement from metaphysical Blackness to corporeal black-ness, as Henry Louis Gates cautions in "Preface to Blackness"?[3]

Non-black professors have expressed to me similar concerns, perhaps the most urgent being that their anxiety about what they perceive as their lack of cultural authority may induce a lack of professional authority. This leads them to posit expertise in their black students (of which there are likely only one or two). When this happens, what the professor rationalizes as an anti-racist strat-egy of demystification or empowerment of blacks, the black stu-dent, elevated to race representative, rightly experiences as isola-tion or tokenism. These professors fear an inability to censure their own and their students' white liberal guilt, to foster an environ-ment free of racist intolerance, yet safe for the expression of gen-uine feelings. They want to know how to honor the primacy of dis-tinctive conventions of the black literary tradition and not do as Robert Stepto argues: "attempt to become amateur historians and social scientists in their pursuit of [African American] literature long before they actually get down to the business of teaching lit-erary art."[4]

It is these kinds of pedagogical issues that I address in this es-say by detailing how I teach the *Memoir of Old Elizabeth,* a dictated autobiography of a 97-year-old former bondswoman who became an itinerant minister and educator. The *Memoir* chronicles Eliza-beth's struggle to respond to her call by God to preach in the face of resistance to her ministry by patriarchal clergymen, both black and white. I teach Elizabeth's brief narrative because it is beautiful, complex, and evocative; moreover, it also illuminates many of the theoretical issues inherent in (the teaching of) the various tradi-tions of nineteenth-century/African American/slave/women's literature. Thus, it may be adapted to the syllabi of numerous humanities courses.

Whatever the course for which the text is selected, but especially for "Nineteenth-Century Black Women's Autobiographies," my goals for teaching the *Memoir of Old Elizabeth* might be defined as:

* to expose students to a nineteenth-century African American woman's account of her life;

* to revise students' misconception that all nineteenth-century African American women were (always, only) slaves;

* to correct students' misconception that nineteenth-century black women were uneducated and illiterate, and therefore unintelligent and uninformed;

* to introduce students to the different social, political, and economic issues and concerns African Americans faced before and after the Civil War, as defined by those within the culture;

* to introduce students to the literary conventions of the slave narrative;[5]

* to introduce students to the literary conventions of the spiritual narrative;[6]

* to engage students in discussions about black women's agency and narrative authority, particularly as they are complicated, and often compromised, by compulsory dependence on amanuenses for the transcription of their story.

A final goal ensues from my conception of theory, which coalesces with that definitively expressed by Johnnella E. Butler and John C. Walter in their landmark anthology, *Transforming the Curriculum: Ethnic Studies and Women's Studies*. They write:

> To us, theory is the essential understanding of just what we are doing, given a specific task, and the identification of what our efforts entail. In order to correct the insidious distortions of the liberal arts curriculum, with its severely flawed understandings of U.S. people of color and white women as well as its distorted self-worth of white cultures, ethnicities, and males, we must begin by recognizing that race, ethnicity, gender, and class form the basis of our societal human identities and that they are basic categories of analysis as well as of existence in the world we have concocted.[7]

Consequently, I set an additional goal: to equip students with the skills they need in order

* to interrogate the conditions of black women's lives across America in the nineteenth century;

* to analyze the similarities and differences in the experiences of free-born black women and African American women born and/or sold into slavery, acknowledging that, as one former slavewoman wrote, "... the slave woman ought not to be judged by the same standards as others"[8];

* to analyze the similarities and differences in the experiences of nineteenth-century African American women and their black male counterparts, especially as these inter-relationships are affected by patriarchal norms and values;

* to analyze the similarities and differences in the life conditions of nineteenth-century African American women and their white female counterparts, especially as these inter-relationships are affected by the Cult of True Womanhood[9];

* to identify the points at which these analyses intersect with other kinds of inquiries students are making in courses in other disciplines.

I begin "Nineteenth-Century Black Women's Autobiographies" with two two-hour class periods on the *Memoir of Old Elizabeth*, more time than that spent on any other narrative, even though the 19-page *Memoir* is considerably shorter than other required texts. In doing so, I want students to realize from the outset that the autobiographies we will study are intricate and multifarious. In my first teaching of it at Michigan, only five of the eleven juniors and seniors were English majors. A year later, the course was cross-listed as an upper-division elective for English and Women's Studies majors. In each instance, some students had read no nineteenth-century American literature; for most, their experience with texts of the period had been limited to cursory high school readings of *The Scarlet Letter*, *Billy Budd*, and maybe one or two of Poe's short stories. A few had read Frederick Douglass' 1845 *Narrative*, but even among the Women's Studies students, most had never considered or been introduced to the idea of *any* black women writing before Alice Walker. Indeed, when I mention my work to new associates, invariably I am asked, "What are your sources?" and "Do you have to travel far to do your research?" When I report that since 1988 the narratives have been published as textbooks, my new acquaintances express surprise that "there are enough of them to constitute binding in a single volume." (It seems pointless to note that the 30-volume Schomburg Library of Nineteenth-Century Black Women Writers includes over 20 full-length autobiographies.) Generally, too, both scholars and students, as well as persons outside the Academy, envision an Aunt Jemima when I speak of nineteenth-century women of African descent. For most Americans, all such women were slaves, were mammies; none were free- and/or Northern-born. So, I begin the course with the *Memoir of Old Elizabeth* because its emphasis is scarcely on the former slavewoman's life in servitude; the text might more precisely be identified as a spiritual autobiography because it narrates Elizabeth's life as a woman of God. Situating the *Memoir* in more than one literary genre enables me to begin to debunk what is perhaps the most prevailing myth about nineteenth-century African American women: that they were all always and only slaves.

The initial publication date of the *Memoir of Old Elizabeth*, 1863, also makes it a constructive starting point for the course. Because of its publication in the third year of the five-year Civil War, and in the same year as the Emancipation Proclamation (though it makes no allusion to that momentous document), it succinctly illuminates some of the features scholars have recently assigned to antebellum and postbellum autobiographies by nineteenth-century blacks. The remaining narratives we study are arranged chronologically, allowing Elizabeth's story at the outset to introduce students to the differing concerns of black Americans before and after the War. Moreover, students further recognize the complexity of this brief text when they see how it characterizes more than one set of sociopolitical values and rhetorical conventions.

The *Memoir of Old Elizabeth* is a dictated text, thus divergent from the majority of the remaining texts we read, all of which, with only one exception, are self-authored autobiographies. So, with the *Memoir* the class begins grappling with compelling questions about authorship and rhetorical selfhood as constructs that persist throughout the course. The inquiry is designed partly to dispel students' erroneous notion that the slaveocracy's ban on black literacy meant in actuality that no black person could read or write during the nineteenth century. This is a construct held by many Americans who believe there is a rampant disproportionate illiteracy among African Americans of the present century, derived from the restrictions on literacy of the past century. In fact, the two phenomena have radically different origins. As Johnnella E. Butler has observed about literacy and the American slave past, "... learning to read and count was closely connected to the slaves perceiving fully their human condition and to the Christian misuse of the Bible to justify slavery, and led, if not directly to revolt, to an intense desire for freedom."[10] In addition, students need to distinguish clearly between literacy and intellect. Near the end of the discussion of the *Memoir*, the class will explore the possibility that Elizabeth's actual voice subverts that of the amanuensis through whom she speaks, that the text is, in other words, double voiced, and that Elizabeth's utilization of two rhetorical strategies, heteroglossia and signifying, complicates some of the assertions her amanuensis attributes to her. To prepare students for this eventual reading, a great deal of groundwork must be done.

We begin our discussions of the *Memoir* by scrutinizing the title page, an activity most students have never fully engaged. They are surprised at how much this title page divulges. Besides announcing the genre and subject, the complete title, *Memoir of Old Elizabeth, A Colored Woman*, insinuates Elizabeth's former slave status through the adjective "old" and the lack of a surname; its use of "woman," in place of "lady," intimates her class. Ironically, any significance readers might attach to these designations is negated by the epigraph from Galatians that follows them: "There is neither Jew nor Greek, there is neither bond nor free, there is neither male nor female, for ye are all one in Christ Jesus."[11] This verse paradoxically denotes that who and what Elizabeth is (as identified in the title) is inconsequential with regard to her salvation, thus marking the text it prefaces as a spiritual narrative. For the epigraph tacitly extends a call to conversion to readers of the *Memoir* even before they enter the narrative proper. The title page further states that the text was printed by "Collins" at Philadelphia in 1863; the site of publication assumes significance later, when the narrator commends Quakers for their piety.[12] Furthermore, the information offers yet another, and in this case familiar, paradox: the (former) Southern slavewoman Elizabeth's memoir is published in a Northern city.

As we discuss the title page, I find that students attend most to the title itself; this allows me to contextualize the *Memoir* within the African (American) literary tradition, and to comment briefly on the importance of naming and self-designation, of identity and authority within the tradition, especially in the New World where the slaveocracy retained the power to declare who and what one was. Furthermore, if Elizabeth's title page indicates that her story has been appropriated by her amanuensis, and thus that her inability (or disinclination? or unwillingness?) to inscribe her narrative impedes her participation in the "one vast genealogical poem" that is African American literature, then Elizabeth's use of signification in the penultimate paragraph of the *Memoir* empowers her to (un)name herself as she is denominated on the title page.[13]

After we have thoroughly analyzed the title page, we spend some time on the disclaimer, a convention of nineteenth-century literature, especially autobiographies and novels, that generally transforms natural and/or fictional discourse into fictive discourse. The students who have read other literature of the period recall similar disclaimers, other prefaces designed to create credibility and to establish verisimilitude: the very title of Poe's "Manuscript Found in a Bottle" and his preface to *The Narrative of Arthur Gordon Pym*, "signed" by Pym himself; Hawthorne's "The Custom House," which he labels an "Introductory to *The Scarlet Letter*." We observe about the *Memoir* that its preface is unsigned: nothing explicit in the document betrays the amanuensis by race or ethnicity, religious creed (though clearly sympathetic to Quakerism), gender, or class (though apparently sufficient to secure the publication of the pamphlet). While the interlocutor confesses to having tampered with Elizabeth's words to some extent, it emphatically denies having altered her intentions. The single sentence preface reads: "In the following Narrative of 'OLD ELIZABETH,' which was taken mainly from her own lips in her 97th year, her simple language has been adhered to as strictly as was consistent with perspicuity and propriety."[14]

In its failure to name the amanuensis, this disclaimer differs sharply from those that generally preface nineteenth-century autobiographies by African Americans, especially the narratives of former slaves. As James Olney has cogently established, prefaces signed by prominent whites were among the extra-textual literary paraphernalia that might be appended to a black autobiography to affirm both the actual existence of the black author and the integrity and veracity of his or her narrative.[15] Given the extensive list of kinds of authenticating apparati that Olney asserts were used by white editors to validate black texts (including one or more letters from reputable, enfranchised leaders, a facsimile of the black author's portrait and/or signature, and the titular tag "Written by Herself"), it seems odd that the *Memoir of Old Elizabeth* would be without any of them. Instead, at the end of the period during which slave narrators were most prolific and most widely read (1845–1865), the *Memoir* features the one apparatus most likely to render it suspect: an unsigned disclaimer acknowledging its revisions of the black subject's words. In class discussions, we locate this act of faith in the conversion narrative tradition: it signifies that both author and amanuensis want readers to disregard the mortals who speak for God, to attend to God, who speaks through them. I go a step further and propose that the absence of a signature exposes both the race and the gender of the amanuensis: she is a white woman who, by enabling Elizabeth to speak through her about God, herself speaks through Elizabeth against the patriarchal forces in her life that render "unchaste" the promulgation, under her own name, of her own experiences of religious conversion and religious oppression as an attempt to usurp and to critique masculine privilege and power.

The hypothesis that the amanuensis is white and female allows for the discussion of feminist issues in the *Memoir*, particularly of relations between African American and white (Quaker) women of the era and of the Cult of True Womanhood. I am continually surprised to discover that while none of my students is *ever* willing to introduce the hypothesis, without exception *all* of them are eager to embrace it. About this time, chiefly because we are to spend the next three weeks studying women's conversion narratives, I introduce two of the earliest women spiritual autobiographers, Margery Kempe, whose fifteenth-century male-transcribed *Book* is regarded as the first autobiography written in English, and Julian of Norwich, a visionary (as was Elizabeth) whose fourteenth-century *Book of Showings* describes her religious divinations of both God the Father and *God the Mother*. Citing these early writers, who are women but not black, expands the various literary traditions in which African American women autobiographers participate. As students ponder the effect of Kempe's male scribe on her feminist narrative, I urge them to consider, too, Carolyn Heilbrun's contention about the implications of holy women bowing to a male god: "Occasionally women have put God or Christ in the place of a man; the results are the same: one's own desires and quests are always secondary."[16] The students generally brood over Heilbrun's statement, regarding it as more ominous when women worshippers represent a race that has been enslaved by Christianity and Christians.

The recognition that nineteenth-century African American women's lives were conspicuously more complex and complicated than those of white women marks a turning point in our discussions. Heilbrun's statement throws into palpable relief the *Memoir*'s understated descriptions of assaults that Elizabeth endured as a slave. For example, when the amanuensis reconstructs a beating of eight-year-old Elizabeth by an overseer for having walked more than twenty miles to see her mother, s/he effectively deflates the horror of the event by representing it in lyrical language: "He gave me some stripes of which I carried the marks for weeks."[17] If they have glossed over the violence insinuated in this recollection, students clearly perceive the multiple layers of subjugation that Elizabeth suffered when they contemplate Heilbrun's statement. For the first time in the quarter, the class collectively exhibits the profound grief, "that complex bundle of hostility, sorrow, denial, bargaining, and other feelings that can manifest itself in many forms," that Thomas Trynza and Martin Abbott address in their astute study "Grieving in the Ethnic Literature Classroom."[18]

To save students from a threatening morass, I strive to transform emotion into analysis: we look closely at the text for sources of woman power and Elizabeth's ingenuity. In addition, for the remainder of the time on the *Memoir*, we note the numerous narrative details contained in the text that clarify the vanity of severing feminist concerns from racial ones:

* the violent separation of slave families, particularly of mothers from their daughters;

* the slave girl's challenge to the established authority imaged in the overseer and slaveholder;

* the black woman's challenge to racist ideology and praxis;

* the impediments to the black woman's quest for personal autonomy;

* the black woman's (fearlessness in the face of her) challenge to established religious patriarchy and hegemony;

* the black woman's desire for religious, political, and social sisterhood, composed primarily of black women of her own ethnic community;

* the black woman's capacity to act to fulfill educational and moral needs she perceives within the black community.

As we discuss ways that gender intersects with race and class in the narrative details of the *Memoir*, students observe that major issues of racial significance in the black woman's life are consistently cursorily treated. For example, recalling my earlier assertions about the interrelationship between literacy and freedom, they are stunned that the disclosure in the *Memoir* of Elizabeth's manumission is limited to this scant paragraph: "Some years from this time I was sold to a Presbyterian for a term of years, as he did not think it right to hold slaves for life. Having served him faithfully my time out, he gave me my liberty, which was about the thirtieth year of my age."[19] The failure of the *Memoir* to elaborate upon Elizabeth's freedom from slavery quite plausibly derives from the conventional spiritual narrative's strict refusal to inscribe any personal element that might challenge the religious conversion as the most significant experience in the narrator's life. However, students tend to read the paucity of detail about Elizabeth's manumission as the amanuensis's blatant disregard for the most significant experience in a slave's life.

The observation that the text is reticent with regard to race matters opens out to a discussion of the *Memoir* as a double-voiced narrative.[20] I borrow the theoretical term *heteroglossia* from Mae G. Henderson's invaluable essay, "Speaking in Tongues: Dialogics, Dialectics, and the Black Woman Writer's Literary Tradition," in which Henderson defines heteroglossia as "the ability to speak in the multiple languages of public discourse.... heteroglossia connotes public, differentiated, social, mediated, dialogic discourse."[21] With this term, the class analyzes the rhetorical tensions of the penultimate paragraph of the *Memoir*. The most teasing ambiguity punctuates the paragraph:

> I established a school for coloured orphans, having always felt the great importance of the religious and moral *agri*culture [sic] of children, and the great need of it, especially amongst the coloured people. Having white teachers, I met with much encouragement.[22]

The phrasing of the final assertion would suggest that the amanuensis, transcribing Elizabeth's story out of his/her own sense of *noblesse oblige*, cannot discern the insinuated parallel between white teachers and black school children, and white amanuenses and black autobiographers (if one is correct in reading the amanuensis as white). Ironically, however, the various incidents in the *Memoir* that describe Elizabeth's brave confrontation with hegemonic forces ascertain that *she* would not miss the ambiguity of the assertion, that she would rather be fully aware of the manifold advantages blacks could accrue by manipulating (within) a racist society. Read from a perspective that privileges Henderson's use of heteroglossia, then, the relevant sentence signifies (on) the interlocutor's naïveté, and evidences the narrator's dexterous use of hegemonic discourse. This reading subverts the denotation of *literacy*, and shifts the power to manipulate discourse from the amanuensis to Elizabeth. Consequently, the first week of "Nineteenth-Century Black Women's Autobiographies" can close the unit on the *Memoir* with students' grief momentarily stayed. As we conclude, the class rejoices in the triumph of genuine intelligence over presumed "illiteracy." And at least one student wishes aloud, "We should all be so skillful at age 97."

Coda

In the early stages of writing this essay, I described to a colleague the shape that I planned it to take. I explained that I would begin with the two unsettling remarks of the young male students, to illustrate that racism and resistance run deep, whatever one's efforts, that one course is insufficient to alter belief systems long internalized. At that point my friend, a gay Latino, observed that the anecdotes also expose my need as an African American scholar for the men's affirmation. So what, he wanted to know, if two white male students didn't "get it"? Why do their comments continue to haunt me?

Reflecting on my colleague's questions, I came to realize that my recollections of the two students' remarks were entangled with anxieties I had about composing an essay for a volume to be entitled *Literary Theory in the Classroom*: both derived from my awareness of ways I subvert "theory" as pedagogical praxis, ways I resist it as academic chauvinism. But before writing this essay, I had not articulated the degree to which I have come to insist, with Angelika Bammer, on interrogating the usages of theoretical discourses like those engaged by poststructuralists and deconstructionists:

> When are we using language that is difficult? Are we using it because it is appropriate to the complexity of our analysis? Can we make complexity accessible in order to permit communication with others who can learn from us and from whom we can learn? In other words, when is our language a means of exchange, and when is it a tool of domination?[23]

The teaching of texts like the *Memoir of Old Elizabeth* is inherently theoretical and obviously revisionary. The incorporation of even one text like it—like Elizabeth herself: nonconformist, uncon-ventional, unacknowledged—opens out the canon and the curricu-lum in thrilling, unexpected ways. In light of the paucity of texts that thematize and theorize about nineteenth-century African American women's autobiographies, their inclusion in diverse canons is revolutionary, even vital. However, when we insist on the application of labels created by contemporary theorists (who are predominantly white and male) to mark the narratives of unen-franchised, poor, black women, we risk misnaming that female ex-perience. Yet as Elizabeth's heteroglossic skill demonstrates, nine-teenth-century African American women autobiographers were adept at naming themselves and their experiences, even under threat of excommunication and imprisonment. Her amanuensis notwithstanding, one hears Elizabeth's proud self-proclamation in her literary daughters, fictional and historical: "She stand up. My name Mary Agnes, she say."[24]

Notes

1. Hortense Spillers, "Response [to 'Boundaries: Or Distant Relations and Close Kin,' by Deborah E. McDowell]," *Afro-American Literary Study in the 1990s*, ed. Houston A. Baker, Jr., and Patricia Redmond (Chicago: Uni-versity of Chicago Press, 1989), p. 72.

2. Audre Lorde, "Poetry Is Not a Luxury," *Sister Outsider* (Trumans-burg, NY: Crossing Press, 1984), p. 37.

3. Henry Louis Gates, Jr., "Preface to Blackness: Text and Pretext," *Afro-American Literature: The Reconstruction of Instruction*, ed. Dexter Fisher and Robert B. Stepto (New York: Modern Language Association, 1979), p. 48.

4. Robert B. Stepto, "Teaching Afro-American Literature: Survey or Tradition—The Reconstruction of Instruction," *Afro-American Literature*, p. 9.

5. For background, two essential texts are William L. Andrews' semi-nal study *To Tell a Free Story: The First Century of Afro-American Autobiogra-phy, 1760–1865* (Urbana: University of Illinois Press, 1986) and Joanne Braxton's *Black Women Writing Autobiography: A Tradition Within a Tradition* (Philadelphia: Temple University Press, 1989). Especially valuable as preparation to praxis is Erlene Stetson's "Studying Slavery: Some Literary and Pedagogical Considerations on the Black Female Slave," *All the Women Are White, All the Blacks Are Men, But Some of Us Are Brave: Black*

Women's Studies, ed. Gloria T. Hull, et al. (Old Westbury: Feminist Press, 1982), pp. 61–84.

6. For background, two essential texts are the revised edition of Daniel Shea's *Spiritual Autobiography in America* (Madison: University of Wisconsin Press, 1988) and Patricia Caldwell's *The Puritan Conversion Narrative: The Beginnings of American Expression* (Cambridge: Cambridge University Press, 1983).

7. Johnnella E. Butler and John C. Walter, "Praxis and the Prospect of Curriculum Transformation," *Transforming the Curriculum: Ethnic Studies and Women's Studies* (Albany: State University of New York Press, 1991), pp. 325–30.

8. Harriet A. Jacobs, *Incidents in the Life of a Slave Girl, Written by Herself*, 1861, ed. Jean Fagan Yellin (Cambridge: Harvard University Press, 1987), p. 56.

9. The most thorough discussion of this phenomenon remains Barbara Welter's *Dimity Convictions: American Women in the Nineteenth Century* (Athens: Ohio State University Press, 1976).

10. Johnnella E. Butler, "Introduction," *Transforming the Curriculum: Ethnic Studies and Women's Studies*, p. 5. For a fuller discussion of the interconnections of literacy and liberty, see Stepto's "Teaching Afro-American Literature," which argues that "The Afro-American pregeneric myth is the quest for freedom *and* literacy" (*Afro-American Literature*, pp. 8–24). See also Joycelyn Moody, "Ripping Away the Veil of Slavery: Literacy, Communal Love, and Self-Esteem in Three Slave Women's Narratives," *Black American Literature Forum*, 24 (1990), pp. 633–48.

11. Gal. 3:25.

12. The *Memoir* was reprinted at Philadelphia in 1889, this time by the Tract Association of Friends, the name of which suggests a Quaker organization. The title of the post-Emancipation edition of Elizabeth's autobiography overtly identifies the text as a conversion narrative, diminishing the possibility of its being (mis)taken for a slave narrative: *Elizabeth, A Coloured Minister of the Gospel*.

13. Kimberly W. Benston, "I Yam What I Yam: The Topos of (Un)Naming in Afro-American Literature," *Black Literature and Literary Theory*, ed. Henry Louis Gates, Jr. (New York: Methuen, 1984), p. 152.

14. "*Memoir of Old Elizabeth*," *Six Women's Slave Narratives*, ed. William L. Andrews (New York: Oxford University Press, 1988).

15. James Olney, "'I Was Born': The Slave Narratives, Their Status as Autobiography and as Literature," *The Slave's Narrative*, ed. Charles T. Davis and Henry Louis Gates, Jr. (New York: Oxford University Press, 1986), 148–75.

16. Carolyn Heilbrun, *Writing a Woman's Life* (New York: Norton, 1988), p. 21.

17. *Memoir*, p. 8.

18. Thomas Trynza and Martin Abbott, "Grieving in the Ethnic Literature Classroom," *College Literature*, 18.3 (Oct. 1991), pp. 1-14.

19. *Memoir*, p. 8.

20. For thorough discussion of the black literary tradition as "double voiced," see Henry Louis Gates, Jr., *The Signifying Monkey: A Theory of African-American Literary Criticism* (New York: Oxford University Press, 1988).

21. Mae G. Henderson, "Speaking in Tongues: Dialogics, Dialectics, and the Black Woman Writer's Literary Tradition," *Changing Our Own Words: Essays on Criticism, Theory, and Writing by Black Women*, ed. Cheryl A. Wall (New Brunswick: Rutgers University Press, 1989), p. 22.

22. *Memoir*, p. 19.

23. Angelika Bammer, "Mastery," *(En)Gendering Knowledge: Feminists in Academe*, ed. Joan E. Hartman and Ellen Messer-Davidow (Knoxville: University of Tennessee Press, 1991), pp. 253–54. I am indebted to my colleague Vicki Ekanger for pointing me to Bammer's scholarship.

24. Alice Walker, *The Color Purple* (New York: Washington Square Press, 1982), p. 95.

Travel Writing, Women of Color, and the Undergraduate Romantics Course

Jeanne Moskal

As I teach British Romantic literature to undergraduates, one of my major concerns is to question its self-representations, along the general lines suggested by Jerome J. McGann's *The Romantic Ideology*, and its representations of gender, race, and ethnicity.[1] I introduce some questions informed by present-day theory, trying to balance them with a historical sense of period and with the demands of an institutionalized English major which expects the students to know the canonical texts by the six major male poets. In particular, the suggestions for teaching British Romanticism here presented arise from my interest in travel writing during the period. Numerous travel books were written during this time; moreover, travel provides one of the fundamental metaphors of the canonical literature, pervading the corpus from the epic poems of the period (*Childe Harold's Pilgrimage* and *The Prelude*) through the middle length (*The Rime of the Ancient Mariner*) to the familiar Keats and Shelley sonnets which begin "Much have I travelled in the realms of gold," and "I met a traveller from an antique land." In foregrounding the context of travel writing, the theoretical problem of alterity arises in repeated, overlapping, and contradictory ways: questions of race and ethnicity arise in the British representation of other nations and races, issues of gender arise in the representation by male writers of a feminized landscape. In a sense I teach British Romantic texts *as* travel literature, that is, as employing constructions of autonomy and freedom, self and other, which are shaped by race, nationality, and gender. In the discussion that follows, I shall briefly outline the overlapping representations of alterity in the otherness of race and the otherness of gender in various figures of women of color who come up in British Romantic texts. My teaching approach here uses an early strand of feminist criticism, the "images of women" approach, doing so in the belief that simply noticing the images of women of color in Romanticism alerts the students to questions of racism, colonialism, and sexism, and can lead the interested student into more theoretical considerations of "otherness" from de Beauvoir to Lacan.

At the beginning of the semester, I lecture about travel writing with a general eye to foregrounding British involvements in other nations and on other continents, emphasizing material which Romantic poems usually occlude or mystify. My general approach to using travel literature in this way is informed by Mary Louise Pratt's *Imperial Eyes: Travel Writing and Transculturation*, which argues that "travel books by Europeans about non-European parts of the world went (and go) about creating the 'domestic subject' of Euroimperialism" by positing a unified "rest of the world" against which it differentiated itself.[2] Pratt implicates several influential travel writers of the British Romantic period, including Mungo Park, James Bruce, and John Gabriel Steadman, in the project of colonialism. She argues that even travel books which did not explicitly advocate commercial exploitation of the non-European lands contributed to the ethos of conquest by presenting those lands as available for the gaze and use of the lettered European male. While Pratt focuses on travel books about Africa and the Americas, her generalization holds true, *mutatis mutandis*, of British writing about "the Orient," in which, as Edward W. Said has demonstrated, the Occident projects its own desires and fears onto "the Orient," which functions as "Europe's collective day-dream of the Orient."[3] Politically, Orientalism depends on silencing the actual Orient, creating a blank screen onto which the projection is made, so that "the Orientalist, poet or scholar, makes the Orient speak" (p. 20). Part of this silencing, as Martin Bernal points out, consists in consolidating, under the monolithic category "Oriental," the heterogenous populations of Asia and Africa.[4] I mention these thematic concerns to my students without giving much detail about the present-day scholars who have raised these issues, though I find that undergraduate students are intrigued by the information that scholars contest such matters. I tell them more if they are interested.

In class discussions I use Said's description of Orientalism to illuminate Romantic treatment of Jews, Turks, and Greeks. The acquisition of the Elgin Marbles and the Greek war of independence

from the Turks served as grist for the mill as Orientalists adjusted
their accounts of which races belonged to the Oriental monolith.
They still cast Turkey and its Ottoman Empire as the exotic,
despotic Orient. But the Philhellenic movement among Germans
and Britons increasingly cast contemporary Greeks as racially Caucasian in order to underwrite their view of ancient Greece as the
fountainhead of white European culture, seeing the war as, in
Bernal's words, a struggle between "European youthful vigour
and Asiatic and African decadence, corruption, and cruelty."[5] To
be sure, romantic Hellenism has other components besides racial
ones, as Marilyn Gaull reveals: Greek "primitive" poetics could
displace Latinate Neoclassicism, and Greek antiquity, conceived as
the fountainhead of European culture, could compensate for the
relative brevity of English history.[6] Orientalists rebuilt the monolith by including Jews as part of "the Orient" and thus "other." As
biblical scholars rejected the divine inspiration of the Bible, they
saw it as humanly made literature, the product of its culture, a culture alien to the European. I use Byron's *Hebrew Melodies* to illustrate this Orientalization of Jews by playing the original music by
Isaac Nathan, a composer who publicly proclaimed his Jewish heritage. The music provides a change of medium which makes the
period more vivid for several of the students. In employing musical motifs borrowed from Jewish chants and in promoting his
work as culturally "Hebrew" (analogous with Thomas Moore's
"Irish Melodies"), Nathan resisted the tendency of Jews to assimilate into the dominant culture, choosing instead a stance of otherness. Byron cultivated the sense of scandal which collaboration
with Nathan brought him. Working on the assumption that travel
writings frame and reproduce constructions of race (particularly in
regard to abolitionism and the slave trade) and of ethnicity
(particularly in regard to Hellenism and Orientalism), I summarize
contemporary travel books which figure in these issues, such as
John Gabriel Steadman's *Narrative of a Five Years' Expedition Against
the Revolted Negroes of Surinam*, which functioned as a major document in the abolitionist movement. Showing Blake's illustrations to
this work helps the students to realize the powerful issues involved.

   Gender, too, pervades the practices of travelling and travel
writing. The almost ubiquitous pattern in Western culture has been
that men travel and women stay home, associating men with mobility and exteriority, women with place and interiority, as Eric J.
Leed has demonstrated in *The Mind of the Traveler*. Leed writes:

"during a long and significant period of human history, a period of the growth of patriarchal civilizations, travel was thought to demonstrate a particularly male character, antithetical to a femininity rooted in place."[7] Within the Romantic œuvre, one of the best examples of this association of women with place and immobility—the corollary of men's freedom to travel—is Wollstonecraft's unfinished novel, *Maria, or the Wrongs of Woman*, which recounts the wrongs undergone by a young wife and mother, Maria Venables. Imprisoned by her husband, separated from her child, she denounces the English legal system for the difficulty of obtaining a divorce and the failure to guarantee married women's separate property. In a passionate outburst, Maria gives voice to the disenfranchisement of women: "the laws of her country—if women have a country—afford her no protection or redress from the oppressor."[8] Much of the pathos of this cry comes from Maria's own situation in the novel: utterly static, imprisoned in an asylum, she is both rooted in place and divorced from her country. Wollstonecraft implies that the cultural association of women with place can be felt by woman as imprisonment and as exclusion. Some semesters I develop this theme by including a Gothic novel, and in this context Ann Radcliffe's *The Mysteries of Udolpho* works as well as *Maria*, though some students protest *Udolpho*'s length. Indeed, Jane Austen's supposed refutation of Radcliffe in *Northanger Abbey* ("Dear Miss Morland.... Remember the country and the age in which we live. Remember that we are English, that we are Christians") makes that novel a good choice for raising these issues.[9] In my experience, *Northanger Abbey* appeals to students more than *Maria* or *Udolpho*.

In taking canonical works by Blake, I stress in lectures that the abolitionist movement provided some respite from the projection of largely negative otherness onto Africans, a negative projection which both preceded and followed the Romantic period. Abolitionism achieved large successes, Britain ceasing its participation in the slave trade in 1807 and abolishing slavery in the entire Empire in 1833. One must concede that abolitionism succeeded partly because of economic considerations: since it lost its major slave-holding colony, America, Britain could claim the higher moral ground over America in advocating abolition, as Eric Williams opines.[10] Concurrently with the change in public opinion, most British writers embraced the anti-slavery cause, producing an idealized other rather than a degraded one by presenting Africans as noble savages who should not be merely the occasion of British colonization and trade, a tendency described by Dorothy Hammond and Alta Jablow.[11] Racial science, during these decades, underwrote the public sympathy for Africans by promulgating the monogenetic theory that all races descended from a common ancestor. Their consensus shifted at about mid-century to the polygenetic theory of diverse racial origins and a hierarchy of races, a theory suited to imperialism, according to Nancy Stepan.[12] Blake exemplifies this idealizing tendency in "The Little Black Boy," in which the religion taught by the black boy's mother appeals to the reader far more than the paternal God of "little English boy" (E 9), suggesting a high degree of enlightenment in indigenous African religion and civilization.[13] Thus travel writing and the literature derived from it promulgated both positive and negative stereotypes—the other could be degraded and weak or ideal and powerful.

With this background, we discuss Blake's *Visions of the Daughters of Albion* which draws on and (perhaps) challenges sterotypes of race and gender and is illuminated by its sources in travel writing. *Visions* portrays a woman of color, a character named Oothoon who resembles the sexually liberated Wollstonecraft and who bears attributes of both female African slaves and Native American women as depicted in the literature and illustrations of Blake's time. The plot of *Visions* is relatively straightforward: Oothoon, newly awakened to her sexuality, seeks her lover Theotormon; on the way, Bromion the slavemaster rapes her; Theotormon blames Oothoon despite her eloquent laments. As a class we pause over Oothoon's eloquent speech on sexual freedom. How does Oothoon's racial identity serve her advocacy of sexual freedom? Does Blake himself practice the widely-recognized tendency to project sexual availability onto persons of color?

We begin with a preliminary question: Is Oothoon European, African, or native American? Blake suggests she is European when Oothoon calls her own limbs "snowy," though this word could refer to the "purity" she seeks to prove to Theotormon. Blake suggests she is African in relying on some conventions of abolitionist literature, which the students learned about in my lecture on Steadman's *Narrative*: Steadman recounts the rape of a virgin slave and her being branded as Bromion rapes and brands Oothoon; and Bromion, in valuing Oothoon's pregnancy, echoes the slavemaster's higher estimation of the value of a pregnant slave.[14] And perhaps Blake suggests that Oothoon is Native American as well: he calls her "the soft soul of America," and in one picture she resembles the American Indian woman Blake engraved for Steadman,

with "loose black hair, sad mouth, and angular limbs."[15] The repeated references to abolitionist literature, however, suggest that
the African racial identity is the most fully articulated. Once these
matters of plot and character have been clarified in class discussion, we can ask whether Blake is criticizing his culture's projection
of sexual licentiousness onto the woman of color—or reproducing
it.

At least three positions are possible and students disagree.
First, Oothoon autonomously advocates sexual desire in a way that
"real" women would. Second, Oothoon's advocacy for sexuality is
not autonomous, but a projection of what men would like to hear:
Bromion, Theotormon, and Blake himself. Third, Oothoon's advocacy for sexuality is not autonomous, reflecting instead the projections of Bromion and Theotormon, a projection *exposed* by Blake.
Students can readily observe that Bromion and Theotormon represent two faces of the sexually repressed male, Bromion the rapist
and Theotormon the prude; there is less agreement over whether
Oothoon forms part of one larger personality with her two inter-
locutors.[16]

The first position relies on the similarity between Oothoon and
Wollstonecraft in their fearless expression of sexual desire. In this
reading, Oothoon is autonomous, her prophetic advocacy of sexual
freedom opposing the repressive ethic personified in Bromion,
who calls Oothoon "Bromions harlot," and Theotormon, who
"severely smiles" when Oothoon cries for Theotormon's eagles to
"prey upon her flesh" (E 46). By insisting that Bromion and
Theotormon, rapist and prude, share common premises in con-
demning Oothoon, Blake demonstrates his sympathy with Wollstonecraft's ideological position. Further, one might say, Oothoon's
advocacy of sexual freedom signifies her autonomy, despite its
limited realization, as it would for a white woman in the situation
described by Wollstonecraft, a woman educated to be pure. Her
autonomy might be inferred from the final plate, where she flies
freely like the figure-head of a ship, borne by the clouds which had
formerly served as her bed of torment.[17]

The evidence for the second position, that Blake participates in
the common patriarchal projection of promiscuity onto the woman
of color, consists in his portrayal of rape and of sexual jealousy.
Undeniably, Blake attributes sexual pleasure to Oothoon's experience of rape, echoing the male fantasy that women really want to
be raped. Oothoon's ability to rise above sexual jealousy invites a
similar suspicion: Oothoon offers to trap girls with whom

Theotormon will copulate "bliss on bliss" (E 50), herself a voyeur. Oothoon declares

> But silken nets and traps of adamant will Oothoon spread,
> And catch for thee girls of mild silver, or of furious gold;
> I'll lie beside thee on a bank & view their wanton play
> In lovely copulation bliss on bliss with Theotormon:
> Red as the rosy morning, lustful as the first born beam,
> Oothoon shall view his dear delight, nor e'er with jealous cloud
> Come in the heaven of generous love; nor selfish blightings bring.
>
> (E 50)

Her offer to trap girls for him, in the absence of an analogous search for multiple lovers for herself, does tend to invite the response of one critic, Brenda S. Webster, that "[g]enerosity is all on one side: hers."[18] In overcoming sexual jealousy Oothoon allows herself to be used, approximating the projected ideal of a complaisant wife. (It could also suggest Oothoon is bisexual and/or voyeuristic.)

The third position, that Blake portrays Oothoon as a projection, and criticizes that projection, has some merit. If Blake deliberately depicts Oothoon as a part of the same personality as Bromion and Theotormon, then in effect he acknowledges her status as a cypher, upon which men project their fears and desires. Blake suggests this view in the frontispiece.[19] All three figures are naked and paralyzed, Bromion manacled, his arms restraining Oothoon, who kneels before the brooding Theotormon. Blake masses the rocks, clouds, and sun to suggest a human face in the sky, with Bromion, Oothoon, and Theotormon grouped at the jaw, neck, and base of the skull. Here Blake, as he does so often, works from the premise that his female characters, tellingly called "emanations," do not represent human women, but the view of nature held by a male character.[20]

Yet some images and typographical forms suggest that Blake is not complicit in this projection, that he sees "Oothoon" as merely a projection of the male characters. For example, Oothoon's obsession with reflecting Theotormon suggests that "Oothoon" is really a "reflection" and not at all really there.[21] Or again, there is the typography of Oothoon's name with all its o's that look like zeros and so are empty cyphers—a term Wollstonecraft uses in the *Vindication*—upon which we can project our own readings. By calling herself "Oothoon" not "I," she emphasizes her status as object not subject. The most compelling evidence that Blake resists the projection is the crucial passage quoted above, in which Oothoon of-

fers to catch girls for Theotormon. When we recognize the abolitionist background of Blake's work it is unmistakable that Oothoon
offers to enslave others. Blake begins *Visions* with "Enslaved"
(E 45), and the poem ends with the prospect of others becoming
enslaved. It would seem then that Blake finds fault with Oothoon
for envisioning a resolution in which she makes herself over in the
image of Bromion. Claiming that she is promoting "free love" (see
E 50), she acts like the violent Bromion, trapping the girls of silver
and gold just as Bromion trapped her. Thus free love is anything
but free. When Oothoon plans to spread "silken nets and traps of
adamant" to "catch for thee girls of mild silver, or of furious gold"
(E 50), she "frees" herself by trapping others. Blake would no
doubt see the contradictions in this resolution, at least in the context of race and slavery, if not in the context of gender and sexual
freedom.

I foreground these issues again when we discuss Coleridge's
"Kubla Khan," which envisions a woman whose race is ambiguous, the "damsel with a dulcimer," the "Abyssinian maid."[22] The
ambiguity here is curious: Coleridge's contemporaries used
"Abyssinia" to avoid the racial blackness associated with
"Ethiopia," as Bernal observes, yet Coleridge knew of the Ethiopi-
ans' color from reading James Bruce's *Travels to Discover the Source
of the Nile* (1790), as John Livingston Lowes notes—another use of
travel literature which I emphasize, though in Coleridge's case
travel literature gets a lot of attention in our sessions on *The Rime of
the Ancient Mariner*.[23] In either case, Coleridge evokes the exotic
connotations of Orientalism in this final section of "Kubla Khan."
The crucial result of the Abyssinian maid replacing Kubla, the Oriental despot, is the feminization of the Orient, a feminization
which tames Oriental power to make it available for the poet-
speaker.

In portraying Kubla's paradise, Coleridge practices the Orientalization of the Jews begun by the biblical scholars of his time. He
too creates a monolithic Orient by compounding Jewish elements
(my students easily recognize the biblical allusions) with references to China, Africa, and America. Specifically, Alph the sacred
river resembles the Nile as described by Bruce, and the pleasure
domes resemble a paradisal reward promised to his followers by
an Islamic leader. Jewish, African, and Islamic elements all meet in
this Oriental idyll.[24]

Creator and master of this paradise, Kubla exemplifies masculine Oriental power and imaginative power, creating his dome, as

numerous critics have observed, by a godlike decree. In Kubla Coleridge again synthesizes Oriental sources, combining Purchas's Cublai of Tartary (Mongolia) and also Prester Chan (or John), whom traditions variously located in India and Abyssinia.[25] In Kubla the Orient seems powerful, attractive, creative, as he is the benevolent version of the Oriental despot. Coleridge presents such power as appropriate for a male, while elsewhere, as Carl Woodring has shown, Coleridge wrote in horror about the "Oriental despotism" of a woman, Catherine the Great.[26] Thus, Kubla, the personification of the other under only one sign, the Oriental, retains his attractiveness and creativity, though the double other of an Oriental woman despot poses a threat.

When Coleridge does introduce the double other, the Abyssinian maid, she, like Kubla, possesses creativity but not power. Her creativity is carefully gendered, associated with the dulcimer, an instrument which contemporary literature contrasted with the masculine lyre of Apollo, declaring the dulcimer "of feminine character, weak and delicate, and from its great acuteness, and the smallness of its strings tending to dissolve and enervate."[27] The poet's surmise about reviving the Abyssinian maid's song is notoriously ambivalent, the poet implying that he can appropriate it while acknowledging that the community would exorcise him as if he were a demon.[28] Yet his implication that he does have the power indicates that this personification of the Orient, the Abyssinian maid, possesses a creativity which is available for him, unlike the divine creativity of Kubla. Unlike Kubla, she personifies an Orient which invites the Occident to speak for her. Schematically, then, Coleridge presents as attractive the figure of Kubla, the other only by race, who combines creative and political power; he recoils from Catherine the Great, the other by race and gender, finding her political power a threat; the Abyssinian maid, the other by race and gender, is not a threat but an opportunity, because she possesses only creative power, not political. Through the Abyssinian maid, the woman of color, Coleridge can in surmise assimilate back to the self the quality of creativity originally projected onto the Orient in the figure of Kubla.

A further occasion for the class to examine the threat of female Oriental despotism arises in Byron's *Don Juan* in the figures of Haidée the idealized Greek and Gulbeyaz the Turkish Sultana.[29] After the severely compromised society of Seville (a thinly disguised Regency England inhabited by Juan's mother, Donna Inez, a thinly disguised Lady Byron), Haidée's Greek island seems a

perfect idyll. Clearly a projection of Byron's desires, Haidée restores Juan to health, loves Juan completely, and asks for no commitments. She provides the dichotomously-conceived alternative
to Donna Inez and Donna Julia, who, as Peter J. Manning observes,
form one complex, as she unwittingly brings about Juan's affair
with Julia as Inez seeks to degrade Julia in her husband's eyes.[30]

Byron's projection of all a man could desire onto Haidée
makes sense in the light of his own Philhellenism, at its peak when
he wrote Canto the Second in 1819–20, immediately before the
outbreak of the Greek War of Independence. In general, throughout the passages in which he idealizes her, Haidée seems to be
racially Caucasian, as the Philhellenes presented the contemporary
Greeks. Byron mentions early on that she had some Moorish
ancestry, but postpones spelling out any sinister implications of
her belonging to another race. For most of Canto the Second, Byron
personifies what appears to be a natural, honest form of love in
Haidée, the benevolent mother, protector, and language teacher.
She gives Juan what Anne K. Mellor describes as a "symbiotic experience [which] unites them not only with each other but with the
landscape as well."[31]

With the onset of Canto the Third, however, Haidée the undemanding Greek begins to shade into Haidée the Oriental lady,
having acquired somewhat more power than before. Now, thinking her father Lambro dead, Haidée inherits his money and property, leaving behind the role of Lambro's potential victim which
she shared with Juan. Moreover, in Canto the Third, she begins to
assume the roles of wife and mother which confer power over
Juan. By the time of the party Juan is publicly acknowledged as
Haidée's consort, a marked difference from their earlier love which
neither gave nor asked vows. Moreover, as consort, Juan is
Haidée's inferior. And Haidée has in the meantime conceived a
child, as Byron tells us after her death, so that in retrospect we
know she is a mother throughout the party which celebrates her
coming into her inheritance. This hint of maternity reinforces her
connection to the threatening figures of Inez and Julia. Therefore,
Byron signals the danger inherent in Haidée's assumption of the
threatening roles of wife and mother by recasting Haidée, the
Greek ingenue on whom he had projected the fulfillment of his desires, as Haidée the Oriental noblewoman and hostess, a shade
away from the female usurpation of power signaled in Gulbeyaz.
This hint of Haidée's threat, however, quickly dissolves into elegy
upon her death. By elegizing Haidée and her child, Byron can

merge Haidée back into the lost, idealized Greece commemorated and lamented previously in the lyric "The Isles of Greece" (pp. 509–12); the loss of Haidée brings about the total ruin of Lambro's civilization.

Having put Haidée behind him as just another "scrape" (p. 427), Juan soon confronts another woman of color, the Sultana Gulbeyaz, who more fully articulates Byron's alignment of Oriental despotism with female sexual tyranny. Juan has been sold as a slave, bought by a servant of the sultana to be her lover, and disguised as a girl so the sultana can hide him in her husband's harem. "Juanna" is introduced into the court, and when the sultana has the customary private audience with the new "girl," she despotically demands his sexual services with the imperious question, "Christian, canst thou love?" (p. 577). When Juan refuses, Gulbeyaz bursts into tears, a properly feminine response which begins to evoke Juan's affection. Any possible tenderness is interrupted by the sultan, who upon returning, expresses his desire for "Juanna."

Byron treats the theme of female Oriental despotism quite differently with Gulbeyaz than with Haidée. He has much less invested in Gulbeyaz and can afford to mock her, since she does not evoke maternal projections. His mockery proceeds by placing her sexual demands in a world where numerous conventions of gender have been violated, most consistently in the extended incident of Juan's cross-dressing, analyzed by Susan J. Wolfson.[32] His mockery proceeds further in showing Gulbeyaz's inability to enforce Juan's compliance with her demands, and in the quick return, with the sultan, of the sexual status quo. This woman of color, Gulbeyaz, functions as a caricature of his fears of woman's desire, a caricature which he can mock. The most telling component of his fears seems to be the maternal power Haidée began to have—a tendency borne out in a later female Oriental despot who practices sexual tyranny, Catherine the Great, who like Gulbeyaz uses men as toys and who, unlike Gulbeyaz, has no husband to reign her in. The Oriental woman in *Don Juan*, then, signifies Byron's projected desires when, like the early Haidée, she has no power; powerful, like Gulbeyaz, Catherine, and the late Haidée, she evokes some of Byron's deepest fears. Most semesters I have time to teach only the first two cantos of *Don Juan*, so I fill in the information about Gulbeyaz and cross-dressing by lecture—a tactic which makes some students wish we would stick with *Don Juan* longer.

The woman of color, in a similar pattern, signifies the greatest hopes and deepest fears in Mary Shelley's *Frankenstein*, probably the most frequently taught text outside the six male poets' works.[33] On the one side, Shelley presents the idealized Safie, variously called Turk and Arab, who provides a model of independence and autonomy in escaping her father to join her lover Felix and his family, the De Laceys. On the other side, Shelley presents the unfinished female companion to Frankenstein's creature, the Eve of Frankenstein's new race. Shelley herself participates in projecting ideal desires onto Safie, yet she gains a certain distance from Frankenstein's projection of his fears about female power and sexuality onto the female creature.

Safie exemplifies feminine independence and autonomy. Her story appears in the male creature's account of his extended incubation in watching the De Lacey family. Safie had escaped her father's tyranny, a private Oriental despotism, in planning to marry her off to the highest bidder. Safie, as her mother counselled, "aspire[s] to higher powers of intellect, and an independence of spirit, forbidden to the female followers of Mahomet" (p. 119). She exhibits exemplary sensibility: early in her stay, while reading Volney's *Ruins of Empire*, she weeps for the original inhabitants of America. Mellor rightly concludes that Safie represents an "alternative to the rigidly patriarchal construction of gender and the family."[34] Paradoxically, however, Safie's independence is tamed once she leaves the Orient for Europe. Safie's daring escape was justified only by the extremes of the "Islamic oppression" she defied, but neither Elizabeth Lavenza nor Agatha De Lacey have so despotic a foe to defy. Moreover, because she has rejoined Felix and received his protection, the novel implies that Safie will never again have occasion for such displays of independence. Safie's gradual assimilation to the status of European woman is suggested by the failure of her compassion for other races, previously seen in her response to Volney, when the male creature reveals himself. She rushes out of the room along with Agatha. More significantly, Safie learns the De Laceys' language, French, rather than teaching them her language, Arabic, and her ways of independence. Safie's race provides the occasion for her great heroism yet also precludes others from following her example. Thus Safie may only exercise power against her own culture, a culture alien to the English culture, but she must submit, like a "good woman," to the De Laceys' Western European culture.

While Shelley may unconsciously project her ideal onto the one woman of color, Safie, she clearly exposes the mechanism of projection in Frankenstein's treatment of the other woman of color, the unfinished female companion. Throughout the novel, Shelley frequently draws on racial metaphors to define the difference in kind between humans and Frankenstein's creatures. For example, the male creature calls himself the Adam of a new race, and employs the rhetoric of slaveholders in making his demand for a female of Frankenstein, calling himself the master and Frankenstein the slave. In the case of the female creature, the word *race* occurs when Frankenstein expresses his fears that the female creature will give birth to "a race of devils" (p. 163); he recounts that destroying the female creature restores him to "a race of human beings like [him]self" (p. 167).

Two elements in Shelley's presentation of the female creature prove telling: the Scottish setting for her construction and her association with Frankenstein's best friend, Henry Clerval. The Scottish setting for the female creature's construction and murder suggests Shelley's own sympathy for her. It occurs in "some obscure nook in the northern highlands of Scotland" (p. 156), a locale Shelley associates with her own childhood in the introduction. "[M]y habitual residence was on the blank and dreary northern shores of the Tay near Dundee," she writes. "Blank and dreary on retrospection I call them; they were not so to me then. They were the aerie of freedom and the pleasant region where unheeded I could commune with the *creatures* of my fancy" (p. 223; emphasis added). Shelley's own "creatures of fancy" met a fate like Frankenstein's female creature, for she kept these creatures entirely private, sharing different products of her imagination.

In Chapters 19 through 22, Frankenstein and his best friend Henry Clerval travel to Britain, Frankenstein to construct the female monster and Clerval to study. Clerval's motives reveal his link with domination of other races. Frankenstein recounts:

> [Clerval's] design was to visit India, in the belief that he had in his knowledge of its various languages, and in the views he had taken of its society, the means of materially assisting the progress of European colonization and trade. In Britain only could he further the execution of this plan.... I now also began to collect the materials necessary for my new creation. (p. 253)

Clerval's education in Oriental languages would enable him to assist "the progress of European colonization and trade"—an aspiration "more entrepreneurial than missionary."[35] In the light of the themes of the course, Clerval seems to participate in British domination over the Orient in a way parallel to Frankenstein's assertion of his domination over the female by destroying the female creature. However, from Shelley's point of view, a consistently xenophobic one, Clerval's benevolence in assisting progress is probably meant as a contrast with Frankenstein's malevolence in destroying his creature. Ironically, of course, in pursuing the "execution" of his plan, Clerval falls victim to his own execution by the creature.

By constructing the plot around the parallel deaths of Clerval, what Frankenstein most values, and the female creature, what Frankenstein most fears, Shelley exposes Frankenstein's failure to perceive accurately due to his own projections. We have seen his shortsightedness before in perceiving the male creature as abhorrent, neglecting his sensibility and eloquence. His most startling blind spot, of course, is failing to recognize the threat to Elizabeth in the monster's promise, "I will be with you on your wedding night" (p. 166). Similarly, Frankenstein views the potential relation between the male and female creatures as a riot of monstrous sexuality and breeding, fearing their offspring will overrun the earth and that the female will exert sexual tyranny over human men. Frankenstein fears her will, her desires, her strength, her reproductive ability—in short, Mellor concludes, female sexuality as such.[36] He misses entirely the possibility that the male and female will be simple companions and friends, and his blindness towards friendship takes disastrous form in the death of his own friend, Clerval. Thus Shelley suggests the distortion inherent in his projection of exclusively bestial sexuality onto his creatures to the exclusion of companionate love.

Though Shelley criticizes Frankenstein's projections resulting from the femaleness of the female creature, it is less clear that she would object to the racial component in Frankenstein's fears of the female creature. In addition to her devaluation of Safie's Islamic culture in *Frankenstein*, Shelley's travelogue *History of a Six-Weeks' Tour*, written just before *Frankenstein*, reveals a xenophobic streak, and she may well have shared her culture's tendency to project excessive and deviant sexuality onto the female of another race.[37] That tendency is clear from the exhibition in London in 1810 of Sarah Bartman, "the Hottentot Venus." The memory of the scandal was revived at the time of *Frankenstein's* composition in 1816, for Bartman's autopsy was written up twice by different medical experts, once in 1816 and again in 1817. These medical reports stress Bartman's buttocks and genitalia, taking them as a sign of the lasciviousness of the African races.[38]

Near the semester's end, we examine the disturbing pattern in these texts' treatments of the woman of color: the imposition of silence, the appropriation of her voice. This pattern obtains not only when the woman of color embodies the culture's deepest fears, as in the case of Frankenstein's aborted female creature or the sultana Gulbeyaz reduced to tears. Surprisingly it obtains as well when the woman of color receives the projection of high hopes and desires. Oothoon, Blake's passionate advocate of passion, ends the poem with repeated wails and sighs: "Thus every morning wails Oothoon ... The Daughters of Albion hear her woes, & eccho back her sighs" (E51). Coleridge's Abyssinian maid sings an exquisite song which has fallen silent, unless perhaps the (male) poet revives it. Byron has eliminated Haidée before she can give birth to her child, one undeniable product of women's creativity, and one which would impede Juan's ranging among other women. And even Safie, Shelley's idealized autonomous Turk, abandons her native Arabic for French.

More generally, I locate these discussions of women of color in individual texts with a semester-long emphasis on gender and travel. I introduce the course with lectures on aesthetics and on Romantic travel practices. In addition to the gendering of mobility and place which pervades most historical periods, the Romantic period had its own particular gendered categories of landscape aesthetics in the triad of the sublime, the beautiful, and the picturesque, categories that evoke the otherness of women's bodies. Edmund Burke's *A Philosophical Enquiry into the Origin of Our Ideas of the Sublime and the Beautiful*, first published in 1757 and remaining influential for decades, defines the conventions of sublimity and beauty along gendered lines.[39] As he moves toward defining beauty in terms of smallness and gradual variation, Burke writes:

> Observe that part of a beautiful woman where she is perhaps the most beautiful, about the neck and breasts; the smoothness; the softness; the easy and insensible swell; the variety of the surface, which is never for the smallest space the same; the deceitful maze, through which the unsteady eye slides giddily, without knowing where to fix, or whither it is carried.
>
> (p. 115)

To the natural sublime, by contrast, he ascribes properties associated with masculinity, such as strength and vastness, all of which he reads as manifestations of power. "I know of nothing sublime which is not some modification of power," he writes (p. 64). To this pair of terms, "picturesque" was added by William Gilpin and Uvedale Price, the latter claiming that the picturesque reconciles sublimity and beauty. So the landscape aesthetics of travel litera- ture enforce the passivity, surface beauty, and deceit associated with women, allowing men to "conquer" the feminine landscape, or what Annette Kolodny calls "the lay of the land."[40]

The actual experience of travel by Britons on the Continent was one that was shaped by gendered conventions, most notably, that the normative traveller is a privileged, educated gentleman. This tradition originated in the custom known as the Grand Tour, a more or less standardized trip from England through the major cities of France, Italy, and Switzerland, with variations introduced because of the Napoleonic Wars. The Grand Tour had in the eigh- teenth century served as the capstone of an English gentleman's education, and in the habit of the tour, the experience of Mont Blanc was taken to be the culminating event. This earlier version of the Grand Tour as practiced by the well-to-do often lasted two years or more, and almost always the young man was accompa- nied by a "bearleader" or tutor, providing a buffer period between the academic education and the gentleman's assumption of his adult duties (often the father was, at the time of the son's Tour, perfectly able to discharge those duties himself and not at all ready to be superseded). In the last decade of the eighteenth century and the early part of the nineteenth, the Grand Tour became increas- ingly available to other travellers besides those in this privileged group, though the experience retained the traditional association with aristocracy and with coming of age because of its historical function. It is true that throughout the period women travelled in- creasingly to the Continent, almost always in the company of their husbands or families, as the journals of the time attest. Some con- temporary writers about travel express the fear that foreign travel will allow a woman too much sexual freedom, while it was true that the young men who made the Grand Tour frequently used it as an occasion for sexual exploration—a use many families ac- cepted as long as the son did not bring home a foreign wife! In- deed, a contemporary travel book provides an intriguing gloss on Wordsworth and *The Prelude:* "I should prefer a French woman for a mistress, but an Englishwoman for a wife."[41]

Against the backdrop of the conventional gendering of sublim- ity and beauty and of characterizing travel as masculine, the travel books of Wollstonecraft and Mary Shelley demonstrate the

(European) woman writer's struggle to find a voice.[42] In teaching Wollstonecraft's *Letters from Norway*, I emphasize Wollstonecraft's revision of Burke's categories.[43] Wollstonecraft, a mother travelling with her year-old daughter through Scandinavia, for the most part accepts the association of females with beauty and of men with sublimity. But to her descriptions of sublime and beautiful landscapes, she adds the generative categories of sterility and fertility, linking sublimity with sterility and beauty with fertility. For example, she judges the picturesque bay dominated by the sublime rocks as "*sterile* with its forbidding rocks" (VI.245); she concludes that Swedish men who are seldom visited by women lack "the curiosity to *fructify* the faint glimmerings of mind" (p. 245). Often in later letters she laments the bareness and barrenness of the ocean, a frequently cited occasion of the sublime.[44] The ocean is sterile, an "unvaried immensity of water, surrounded by *barrenness*" (p. 265); and "a boundless *waste* of water" (p. 295). In a late example, a description of the road to Gothenburg finds the Swedish farms a welcome relief from the sterility of the rocks:

> The rocks, it is true, were unusually rugged and dreary, yet as the road runs for a considerable way by the side of a fine river, with extended pastures on the other side, the image of sterility was not the predominant object. (p. 315)

The sublime prospects are not only barren, unable to give life to others, but at times they are themselves dead, skeletal. To her, a sublime ocean scene and its rocks "seemed *the bones of the world* waiting to be clothed with everything necessary to give life and beauty. Still it was sublime" (p. 262). Sublimity lacks the requisite beauty and life; moreover it suggests "the bones of the world," an "abode of desolation" where "the sports or prattling of children was neither seen nor heard" (p. 262). Despite the summer weather, "the current of life seemed congealed at the source" (p. 262). Her daughter Fanny, and children, and life itself depend on values excluded from the masculine, Burkean sublime. Wollstonecraft clearly delights in her traveller's freedom from gendered roles. At the outset, in Letter I, she proudly relates: "At supper my host told me bluntly that I was a woman of observation, for I asked him *men's questions*" (p. 248; Wollstonecraft's emphasis). Yet as the *Letters* continue, she subordinates her pride in asking men's questions to the identity she will present throughout the travelogue, the identity of "a woman of observation" (p. 245). The generative categories of fertility and sterility, of course, serve to distinguish mothers in particular from women as a group. By foregrounding these categories, then, she presents herself simultaneously as observer and as mother, in contrast to the convention of the male observer. Moreover, by attributing fertility to nature (implicitly, Mother Nature), she makes explicit the grounds of her authority as observer, namely, the property of fertility she shares with nature. Rather than appropriating and conquering nature, she finds kinship with it.

Travel literature, and the gendering of the sublime and the beautiful, provide the occasion for the tentative discovery of voice by Mary Shelley as well. *History of a Six-Weeks' Tour* reveals some of the anxiety a young woman might feel on approaching the climax of the gentleman's Grand Tour, the sublime Mont Blanc. The travelogue includes four letters, two by Mary to her half-sister Fanny Imlay (the same person who, as a child, accompanied their mother Mary Wollstonecraft to Scandinavia) and two by Shelley to Thomas Love Peacock, and concludes with Shelley's lyric "Mont Blanc." (This lyric was published for the first time in the 1817 edition of *History of a Six-Weeks' Tour*.) Since there is no inexpensive text of this travel book I lecture on the pertinent passages.

When Mary Shelley does describe Mont Blanc in the next paragraph, she characterizes it as feminized, "queen of all," and picturesque. She writes:

> To what a different scene are we now arrived! To the warm sunshine, and to the humming of sun-loving insects. From the windows of our hotel we see the lovely lake, blue as the heavens which it reflects, and sparkling with golden beams. The opposite shore is sloping, and covered with vines, which however, do not so early in the season add to the beauty of the prospect. Gentleman's seats are scattered over these banks, behind which rise the various ridges of black mountains, and towering far above, in the midst of its snowy Alps, the majestic Mont Blanc, highest and queen of all. Such is the view reflected by the lake; it is a bright summer scene without any of that sacred solitude and deep seclusion that delighted us at Lucerne. (pp. 94–95)

The description of Mont Blanc in this latter section of the travelogue reveals considerable overcoming of the conventional association at Mont Blanc with the masculine sublime, a general issue discussed by Fred V. Randel.[45] The most evident of these of course is the epithet "queen," but Mary Shelley substantiates this new characterization of Mont Blanc by suggesting that, rather than being an isolated peak, it is the member of a community "in the midst of its snowy Alps," however much Mont Blanc may tower above the rest of her sisters. Nonetheless, the restrictions of gender in actual historical practice emerge in the text, as Mary Shelley describes the "Gentleman's seats" which are scattered on the bank, suggesting her awareness that the trip to Mont Blanc remains a mark of masculine privilege. The most significant of these aesthetic gestures is the final deprecation, "Such is the view reflected by the lake." This turn of phrase and thought indicates that the previous description of this queenly Mont Blanc was actually a description of its reflection in the water—a gesture which softens the rebellion of Mary Shelley's elopement, the usurping of the masculine privilege of travel, by refusing to describe the *Ding an sich*. Moreover, the gesture defers to the authority of Percy Shelley, whose lyric "Mont Blanc" has pride of place at the end of the volume, daring to describe directly the prospect Mary described indirectly.

In addition to illustrating the difficulties of women writers finding a voice, even British women in a British culture, these final two examples, Wollstonecraft's *Letters from Norway* and Mary Shelley's *History of a Six-Weeks' Tour*, serve a final pedagogical and theoretical purpose—to problematize the boundaries between canonical and noncanonical, aesthetic and functional literature.

Notes

1. Jerome J. McGann, *The Romantic Ideology* (Chicago: University of Chicago Press, 1983).

2. Mary Louise Pratt, *Imperial Eyes: Travel Writing and Transculturation* (New York: Routledge, 1992), pp. 4–5.

3. Edward W. Said, *Orientalism* (New York: Random House, 1978), pp. 42, 52.

4. Martin Bernal, *Black Athena: The Afroasian Roots of Classical Civilization* (London: Free Association Press, 1987), p. 206.

5. Bernal, p. 291.

6. Marilyn Gaull, *English Romanticism: The Human Context* (New York: Norton, 1988).

7. Eric J. Leed, *The Mind of the Traveler: From Gilgamesh to Global Tourism* (New York: Harper Collins, 1991), p. 116.

8. Mary Wollstonecraft, *Maria, or the Wrongs of Woman*, p. 149 in Marilyn Butler and Janet Todd, eds., *The Works of Mary Wollstonecraft*

(London: Pickering and Chatto, 1980), I.75–184. Suitable editions for classroom use include Moira Ferguson's (New York: Norton, 1975) and Gary Kelly's (New York: Oxford University Press, 1975); the latter includes *Mary, A Fiction,* as well.

9. Jane Austen, *Northanger Abbey* (Harmondsworth: Penguin, 1972), p. 199.

10. Eric Williams, *Capitalism and Slavery* (Chapel Hill: University of North Carolina Press, 1944).

11. Dorothy Hammond and Alta Jablow, *The Africa That Never Was: Four Centuries of British Writing about Africa* (New York: Twayne, 1970), pp. 24–27.

12. Nancy Stepan, *The Idea of Race in Science: Great Britain 1800–1900* (Hamden: Archon Books, 1982), pp. 1–19.

13. David V. Erdman, ed., *The Complete Poetry and Prose of William Blake,* rev. ed., commentary by Harold Bloom (New York: Doubleday Anchor, 1982)—abbreviated in the text as E.

14. See Erdman, *Blake: Prophet Against Empire,* 3rd ed. (Princeton: Princeton University Press, 1977), pp. 230–33.

15. Erdman, p. 239.

16. Important discussions of *Visions of the Daughters of Albion* include those by Erdman in *Prophet,* pp. 226–42 and *The Illuminated Blake* (New York: Doubleday Anchor, 1974), pp. 125–36; Susan Fox, "The Female as Metaphor in William Blake's Poetry," *Critical Inquiry,* 3 (1977), pp. 507–19; Susan Fox, Alicia Ostriker, and Anne K. Mellor, "Blake's Portrayal of Women," *Blake: An Illustrated Quarterly,* 16:3 (1982–1983), pp. 148–55; Alicia Ostriker, "Desire Gratified and Ungratified: William Blake and Sexuality," *Blake: An Illustrated Quarterly,* 16:3 (1982–83), pp. 156–65; and Nelson Hilton, "An Original Story," in Hilton and Thomas A. Vogler, eds., *Unnam'd Forms: Blake and Textuality* (Berkeley: University of California Press, 1986), pp. 69–104. For more complete discussion and bibliography of *Visions,* see Jeanne Moskal, *Blake, Ethics, and Forgiveness* (Tuscaloosa: University of Alabama Press, 1994).

17. See Erdman, *The Illuminated Blake* (New York: Doubleday Anchor, 1974), pp. 135–36.

18. Brenda S. Webster, "Blake, Women and Sexuality," in Dan Miller, *et al.,* eds., *Critical Paths: Blake and the Argument of Method* (Durham: Duke University Press, 1987), pp. 204–24.

19. Erdman, *The Illuminated Blake,* pp. 125–26.

20. See Northrop Frye, *Fearful Symmetry: A Study of William Blake,* 2nd ed. (Princeton: Princeton University Press, 1969), p. 73.

21. Hilton, pp. 69–104.

22. See Coleridge, *Poems and Prose,* ed. Kathleen Raine (1957; rpt. New York: Penguin, 1985), p. 89, l. 36.

23. Bernal, p. 243; John Livingston Lowes, *The Road to Xanadu: A Study in the Ways of the Imagination* (1927; rpt. Princeton: Princeton University Press, 1982), p. 344. For various views on the Abyssinian maid's race, see John Beer, *Coleridge the Visionary* (London: Chatto & Windus, 1959), pp. 263–67; Norman Fruman, *Coleridge, the Damaged Angel* (New York: George Braziller, 1971), pp. 399–400; and Robert F. Fleissner, "'Kubla Khan' as an Integrationist Poem," *Negro American Literature Forum,* 8 (1974), pp. 254–56. For Coleridge's sympathy with abolitionism, see J.R. Ebbatson, "Coleridge's Mariner and the Rights of Man," *Studies in Romanticism,* 11 (1972), pp. 171–206.

24. See Lowes, pp. 312–77, 244, and 329–30.

25. See Elinor S. Shatter, *"Kubla Khan" and the Fall of Jerusalem* (Cambridge: Cambridge University Press, 1975), p. 83.

26. Carl Woodring, "Coleridge and the Khan," *Essays in Criticism,* 10 (1959), pp. 361–68.

27. Beer, p. 253.

28. See Mellor, *English Romantic Irony* (Cambridge: Harvard University Press, 1978), p. 157.

29. See *Byron,* ed. Jerome J. McGann (Oxford: Oxford University Press, 1986).

30. Peter J. Manning, *Byron and His Fiction* (Detroit: Wayne State University Press, 1978), p. 183.

31. Mellor, p. 73.

32. Susan J. Wolfson, "'Their She Condition': Cross-Dressing and the Politics of Gender," *English Literary History,* 54 (1987), pp. 585–617.

33. See Mary Wollstonecraft Shelley, *Frankenstein; or, the Modern Prometheus* (the 1818 Text), ed. James Rieger (Chicago: University of Chicago Press, 1982). My reading of *Frankenstein* draws from Mellor, *Mary Shelley: Her Life, Her Fiction, Her Monsters* (New York: Routledge, 1989); Mary Poovey, *The Proper Lady and the Woman Writer: Ideology as Style in the Works of Mary Wollstonecraft, Jane Austen, and Mary Shelley* (Chicago: University of Chicago Press, 1984); and Gayatri Spivak, "Three Women's Texts," in Henry Louis Gates, ed., *"Race," Writing, and Difference* (Chicago: University of Chicago Press, 1986), pp. 262–80.

34. Mellor, p. 118.

35. Spivak, p. 275.

36. Mellor, p. 120.

37. P.B. Shelley and Mary Wollstonecraft Shelley, *History of a Six-Weeks' Tour* (1817; rpt. with rev. intro. by Jonathan Wordsworth, New York: Woodstock, 1991).

38. See Sander L. Gilman, "Black Bodies, White Bodies: Toward an Iconography of Female Sexuality in Late Nineteenth Century Art, Medicine, and Literature," in Gates, p. 232.

39. Edmund Burke, *A Philosophical Enquiry into the Origin of Our Ideas on the Sublime and the Beautiful*, ed. James T. Boulton (Notre Dame: University of Notre Dame Press, 1958).

40. Annette Kolodny, *The Lay of the Land: Metaphor as Experience and History in American Life & Letters* (Chapel Hill: University of North Carolina Press, 1975).

41. J.C. Villiers, quoted in Constantia Maxwell, *The English Traveller in France, 1698–1815* (Cambridge: Cambridge University Press, 1929), p. 144.

42. Until recently, teachers have lacked a convenient anthology of British Romanticism that includes women writers. This lack is being remedied by two new comprehensive Romanticism anthologies: Jerome J. McGann's *New Oxford Book of Romantic Period Verse* (New York: Oxford University Press, 1993) and Anne K. Mellor and Richard E. Matlak's *British Literature, 1780–1830* (forthcoming 1995). New anthologies focusing on Romantic women poets include: Jennifer Breen, ed., *Women Romantic Poets, 1785–1832* (London: Dent, 1992); Andrew Ashfield, ed., *Women Romantic Poets, 1770–1838* (Manchester: Manchester University Press, 1994); and Paula R. Feldman, ed., *British Romantic Poetry by Women, 1770–1840* (Hanover: University Press of New England, forthcoming 1994).

43. Wollstonecraft, *Letters from Norway*, in Butler and Todd, VI, pp. 237–348.

44. See Burke, p. 57.

45. Fred V. Randel, "Frankenstein, Feminism and the Intertextuality of Mountains," *Studies in Romanticism*, 24 (1985), pp. 515–32.

Deconstruction in the Classroom:
Jane Austen's *Persuasion*

Imre Salusinszky

Matthew Arnold has had his revenge at last. Following the hegemony of a variety of linguistic and structural formalisms through
most of the last half-century—New Criticism, Fryean archetypalism, structuralism, then deconstruction—the Arnoldian appropriation of literature to the cause of *improvement* is back in full
swing.

With a difference, of course. Arnold, like his moralizing successors Eliot and Leavis, felt that the improving possibilities in a
literary education depended on students being taught how to distinguish good literature from bad, wholesome from degenerate,
mature from juvenile. The teaching of literature was thus the teaching of the power of discrimination. For Arnold's contemporary
successors, however, the trick—and the moral payload—is in
showing up the badness inhering in *literature as a whole*. When we
have come to see the whole of literary tradition spread out before
us as a history of bad faith; when we have freed ourselves at last
from the beguilements of an "aesthetic sphere"—then we shall be
saved. Many feminist critics now seem less interested in rescuing
forgotten women writers for the canon than in showing how much
the very *idea* of a literary canon is gender-based; Marxists of the
Eagleton variety present the whole of the aesthetic domain as an
ideology designed to obscure an historical truth; and the New (or
Foucauldian) Historicists see literature as a site—perhaps the pre-
eminent site—for the metaphysical legitimation of contingent social power.

What unites these three critical attitudes is their view of the
whole of literature as an ideology that must be seen through in order for our political consciences to be clear—and publicly visible.

Is there, though, a single name we could use to describe the recent
hegemony of these three divergent attitudes? I think there is—and
what name could it be but the "New Moralism"?

It is clear that an important figure in the transition from
Arnoldian to New Moralism, influential in all its three strands, has
been Bertolt Brecht. Brecht is perhaps the first sophisticated theorist since Plato to draw attention to the moral weakness of the
West's entire aesthetic history. He is the first seriously to argue
that Western literature's commitment to emotional depth and
characterological investigation is a flaw, and should be got rid of,
so that the audience may remain distant, objective, and receptive to
historical commentary. While it is worth noting the success that
Brecht's own efforts in this mode have achieved, it is worth noting
too that that success has been limited to the Western *middle* class. It
would seem that those whose experience of work is mainly one of
drudgery and exploitation remain less embarrassed than the bour-
geoisie about cordoning off an "aesthetic sphere" for escape—and
for entertainment.

Every critical movement, like every literary movement, needs
symbolically to murder its predecessor. In the case of the New
Moralism, the predecessor was deconstruction, and the New
Moralism's critique of deconstruction (Lentricchia's *After the New
Criticism* was an early example) has involved allying it with the old
New Criticism of the forties and fifties: to the New Moralism, de-
construction is little more than New Criticism with a French ac-
cent.[1]

This reading of deconstruction clearly has a great deal of force.
Deconstruction does have an affinity with the methods of the New
Criticism, an affinity that arises out of their shared preference for
"close reading." The problem, though, is to decide the extent to
which a claim that deconstruction is "nothing but the New Criticism writ large" actually invalidates deconstruction. Normally, the
argument of the New Moralists here is that deconstruction is in-
fected with the same bourgeois ideology as the New Criticism: an
ideology that sequesters art away from the productive world and
into a self-contained enclave—a "textuality" enclave where, finally,
no choices can be made between competing possibilities of meaning.

This, too, has some force, but I would argue that one place, at
least, where the method of close reading bolsters, rather than undermines, deconstruction's value is the classroom. This is hardly a
surprise, given that the New Criticism itself was (or so the argu-

ment goes) a response to the dramatic expansion in the American and British universities that took place after the Second World War, and to the fact that the new students coming into the system then—many of them returned soldiers—were educationally underdone. New Criticism, which required nothing but you, the text, the night, the music, and a few students whose natural language was English, quite simply *worked* as a pedagogy, in the most basic pragmatic/institutional terms: it succeeded in graduating students in the field of English Literature.

As another close reading method, it is in the classroom that deconstruction has least to fear from the New Critical affiliations claimed for it by the New Moralists. Oddly, New Criticism worked as a pedagogy precisely because it *had* no pedagogy—in terms of any kind of an elaborated program or curriculum (here, once again, the affinity with deconstruction is obvious). In New Criticism there was no body of knowledge that had to be gained prior to reading the poem: the poem *was* knowledge, albeit knowledge of a special (paradoxical, ambiguous) kind. Literary history, which once again would have drawn upon an educational background restricted to the well-schooled (that is, to the socially privileged), was seldom mentioned. That is why it was no longer even necessary to teach literature in chronological sequence. Indeed many of us educated in Australian universities, where a Leavis-compromised New Criticism reigned until quite recently, experienced literary tradition in reverse (a charmingly skewed tradition that begins with the earliest known poet, T.S. Eliot, and stretches forward to his contemporary descendants, Chaucer and Shakespeare).

So the strength of both New Criticism and deconstruction, in terms of theory in the classroom, is that they *bring* no theory to the classroom. It is true that, at times, the New Critics waded ankle-deep into the murkily dialectical waters of denotation and connotation, poetic language and "steno" language, paraphrase and paradox, meaning and intention, and so on, but all of this could be dispensed with in the classroom. An extreme instance of this is *Seven Types of Ambiguity*, which has no theory to it at all, and which in this sense is possibly the first example of literary deconstruction.[2] *Seven Types* (and Empson points out that even the "seven" is arbitrary) quite simply presents the reader with undecideable crux after undecideable crux, difference after difference: it has none of the eagerness of a Cleanth Brooks, say, or a Richard Blackmur, for resolving these differences into overarching, life-affirmative interpretations.

There was no really important "theory" attaching to the New Criticism of Brooks or Ransom or Wimsatt, except for the single theoretical tenet that could be extracted from whatever poem was being close-read: that poetic language is distinctive in being able to preserve multiple meanings by uniting them into new wholes. Similar to this, in deconstruction, is the notorious reluctance of Jacques Derrida to reduce whatever it is that *he* is saying to a set of digestible theorems. And if there is a central theoretical tenet in literary deconstruction, it too can be extracted from whatever poem is under study: that poetic language is distinctive, but only by showing in a particularly clear way that multiple meanings are in permanent tension, and are never united into new wholes. There is no "theory" of deconstruction in the sense that Northrop Frye, or Claude Lévi-Strauss, or the Chicago Aristotelians, had a theory. Deconstruction, as Derrida and his followers have constantly stressed, is not properly a theory at all, but a way of reading. It is true that deconstruction has a much more impressive extra-literary armory than the New Criticism had. However, while the *Grammatology* and its siblings are surely indispensable in informing a teacher's understanding and practice of deconstruction, these books are *not* necessary background reading for the students who are being taught to read deconstructively: such teaching can work perfectly well with students who would hardly get past the title page of the *Grammatology*.[3]

It is sometimes hard to see why deconstruction, with its distrust of the whole metaphysical tradition, got lumped in with "theory" in the first place. Perhaps it was deconstruction's origins in philosophy, or else simply that British literary critics of the seventies tended to label anything difficult as "theory." Neither New Criticism nor deconstruction are theories. They are activities (not activities to be encouraged, perhaps, but activities nevertheless); and activities, which by definition give you something to do, tend to work better in the tutorial than theories.

I don't want to deny for a single moment that feminist or Marxist or, in particular, New Historicist ways of thinking about literature have an important place in undergraduate teaching, especially since I exploit them every day. But that place seems to me to be most suitably the lecture theatre. I am making the practical sort of suggestion that, in the tutorial room, a close-reading method like deconstruction is particularly appropriate. This suggests a story of happy coexistence between the New Moralism and deconstruction; in fact, as I will show later, the relationship remains unavoidably dialectical.

I have conceded to the New Moralists that deconstruction and New Criticism are allied around their joint preference for close reading, but we need to stop and ask just what "close reading" means. It is a term commonly used to describe what New Criticism does to poems, particularly in the classroom, and I suppose that by it we mean slow, patient, detailed reading; reading that is alive to every resonance, suggestion, connotation and nuance in the words of the text being read. In that case, it is clear that the early deconstructors were close readers, too: at times, Paul de Man seemed almost to disappear *into* the texts he was reading; and I remember a class of Geoffrey Hartman's where he contrasted what he was teaching to the speed reading courses being offered in the newspapers—"slow reading," he said, was what he was about.

And yet it is hard to see in just what an alternative to close reading would consist. Wouldn't *every* critic like to think that she or he were paying scrupulous attention to each and every linguistic resonance in the text? What critical school has ever promoted hasty, careless and superficial reading? Close reading, in fact, occupies a motherhood position in critical method. Even Marxists are forced to valorize it, since if they are not going to do close reading they might as well go and work in History departments—and it is more amusing to read Dickens than Macaulay (though only just). The only notable example of a serious alternative to close reading is Northrop Frye's suggestion, in *Anatomy of Criticism*, that we need to "stand back" at a metaphoric distance from a work of literature in order to be able to "see" its archetypal organization and meaning (which Frye, following Aristotle, calls its *dianoia*).[4] But even Frye was careful to say that the close reading stage had to be passed through before this higher relation to the text could be assumed. Frye, the first powerful opponent the New Criticism ever had, always argued that the New Criticism was incomplete, not incorrect, and thus executed towards the New Criticism the variety of misreading that Harold Bloom calls "tessera."[5]

This probably helps us to get at just what made New Critical close reading special, given that critics of every persuasion would deny that what they practiced was cursory reading. New Critical close reading, like deconstructive close reading, is not so much close as *exclusive*: both of these modes of reading assume that a reading of the text, *and of the text alone*, can yield an interpretation of the text. In the New Criticism, this exclusive concentration on the text is indicated by the progressive whittling away of all external considerations, which are one after the other classified as "fallacies." The deconstructive equivalent is the idea that no *context* is ever sufficient to explain a text: there is something in every text, some writing trick, that pulls it away from any context that threatens saturation.

In contrast to exclusive-reading methodologies, New Moralist interpretations always correlate or subjugate the literary text to some other text: reports of the East India Company, medical accounts of exorcism and hermaphroditism, popular literature, newspaper articles, and so on. By this activity, the text's own principal pretension—that it stands as a free and independent creation—is undermined. New Criticism and deconstruction, on the other hand, accede to the text's own first fiction about itself—but in different ways, and with very different ends.

New Criticism, for all its sensitivity to irony, did tend to reconcile intra-textual differences into affirmative meanings. Brooks, for example, in *The Well-Wrought Urn*, sets up the central paradox in Wordsworth's "It is a beauteous evening"—which is that the unschooled girl worships more deeply than the Romantic poet—only in order to resolve it: unlike the poet, the girl worships unconsciously, and worships *all* of nature *all* the time.[6] So the paradox is a perpetual fall-guy. Deconstruction, on the other hand, refuses to resolve difference, or what it calls *différance* (the tendency of any binary opposition to reproduce itself to infinity within each of its original constituent terms), and hence shows up the instability and undecideability that haunts all of the text's attempts to mean anything at all. (This undecideability doesn't somehow "invalidate" meaning: it is the condition of possibility for meaning to occur.) So a deconstructor reading Wordsworth's poem might be much more interested in subverting the poem's oppositions (conscious/unconscious, schooled/instinctive) than in reconciling them. And while for the New Critics the reconciliation affect is a result of the poem's being a symptom of poetic language, for the deconstructors the instability affect is a result of the poem's being a symptom of writing.

Perhaps we could say that, on a scale of hermeneutic suspicion, deconstruction is poised somewhere between New Criticism and New Moralism. Deconstruction, along with New Criticism, submits to the text's fiction about being an independent creation, but *not* to the text's fiction about having securely established its own categories and distinctions and oppositions—its "meanings."

Of course, a universal textual instability may finally be as much of a fiction as the fiction of stable, achieved meaning: like people with red hair, it's amazing how much textual instability you find when you're looking for it. By concentrating on textual instability, on radical paradox, deconstruction—as a North American literary practice—may simply be the manifestation of the radical irony inherent in, but never fully acknowledged by, the New Criticism.

But deconstruction's particular kind of close reading is precisely what places it in a relentlessly dialectical relationship with that triple-headed monster, the New Moralism. That which the text can least sustain—when it is seen as a symptom of the writing condition and hence as marked everywhere by *différance*—is its own ideological burden: its attempts to render certain practices, beliefs, or codes "natural." So it is the text's very "failure" which, in a bizarre way, guarantees its success, if by success is meant some sort of freedom from stringent historical determination.

The text (and here I am talking about literature up to the Modernist period) wants to be outside history by naturalizing its own categories, in order that its truths shall be seen as universals. This desire of the text is easily demystified using any of the three strands of the New Moralism. *Hard Times*, for example, wants to rise above its own historical moment through the opposition of "head" and "heart"; whereas, for us, nothing places *Hard Times* more as a novel of the 1850s than this very opposition. It is only the text's *failure* to make good its own system of oppositions that releases it from becoming an instance of the historical, so that only if we can undermine *Hard Times*'s binary pretensions may we yet rescue it from becoming an unexceptional example of Victorian bourgeois ideology—one that urges the dehumanized workers to go to the circus, rather than on strike.

Deconstruction, as philosophy, descending from both phenomenology and existentialism, extends a sort of existential freedom to the text by performing this "rescue" mission; it tries to release the text from bad faith. Indeed, by refusing, via *différance*, to allow the text to become a stable thing, it bestows upon it the seemingly unique attribute of consciousness: being-for-itself. Whether this is possible, or worth the effort, with a text as ideologically saturated as *Hard Times*, I hardly know. I suspect that a deconstructive reading could find that the novel is less about "head" versus "heart" than about two different kinds of language—literal and figurative—and that it shows how these cannot finally be kept separate.

I think that we will see clearly that a renewed version of close reading *is* worth the effort if we take another, more sophisticated example. I have in mind a book that is almost uniquely poised: between, on the one hand, trying to negotiate an ideology of correct behavior, and on the other pondering the very processes by which ideologies are formed. This text will yield something to a style of questioning that *any* group of students is competent to undertake, provided they have a place to begin.

With *Persuasion*, the obvious place to begin is with the title. While it is true that we cannot be sure that *Persuasion* is the title Jane Austen would have given the novel had she lived to see it through to publication, well, it just *sounds* right, and it is very difficult now to imagine the story of Anne Elliot and Captain Frederick Wentworth being published under any other title—as *Anne Elliot*, say, or *Kellynch-Hall*, or *Coma on the Cobb*. The title is in any case only one result of the fact that persuasion is *everywhere* in *Persuasion*. Indeed persuasion, in this novel, is one of the most notable examples English literature offers of an over-determined sign: more is invested in it than it can possibly hold and still mean anything.

Persuasion ("by suasion") is an odd thing, and, natural as it has come to seem here, an odd title to give a novel. Where *is* persuasion? It is not entirely in anyone; it is a relational word that describes something happening *between* people. In Austen's book, persuasion is primarily the process by which society urges—rather than forcefully requires—its members to act according to certain precepts; it is the process of instilling social values. That is why I am of the belief that, were Jane Austen writing the novel today, she would call it *Ideology*.

The main instance of persuasion discussed time and again in the book is a good example of how the process operates between society and the individual. Eight years before the story begins, Lady Russell has persuaded Anne not to marry Frederick, specifically for social reasons: he is good enough for her in personal, but not in class terms. Austen is careful to give Lady Russell the authority of the mother, minus the emotional and blood tie that might have moderated a natural mother's judgment; freed from these restraints, Lady Russell is allowed to express the distilled prejudices of the landed gentry. In the present time of the narrative, and in what is the second most important instance of persuasion in the book, the same pressures are now being applied to Anne in order that she *should* marry Mr. Elliot.

Anne Elliot and Frederick Wentworth, in the course of their reconciliation, discuss persuasion at length, and each of them discusses it with other characters in the book as well. But it is precisely whenever they try to say what they really mean by persuasion that they begin to talk in random, nearly nonsensical ways. In a movement of *différance*, the novel misses its mark precisely when it attempts most earnestly to hit the nail on the head—precisely when it attempts to ground the rules and categories that would govern persuasion.

These attempts inevitably take the form of binary oppositions. In explaining herself and her persuadability to Wentworth, Anne uses two oppositions designed to distinguish good persuasion from bad. First, she dismisses Wentworth's fears that, just as she once allowed herself to be persuaded out of marrying him, so might she more recently have been persuaded into marrying Mr. Elliot:

> "You should have distinguished," replied Anne. "You should not have suspected me now; the case so different, and my age so different. If I was wrong in yielding to persuasion once, remember that it was to persuasion exerted on the side of safety, not of risk. When I yielded, I thought it was to duty; but no duty could be called in aid here. In marrying a man indifferent to me, all risk would have been incurred, and all duty violated."[7]

"You should have distinguished," insists Anne, and yet that is what she notably fails to do here. The only duty to which Anne submitted eight years ago was her filial duty to her father and her surrogate mother; *that* duty surely still stands, whatever the nature of the claims made on its behalf, and whatever Anne's response to them. As for persuasion exerted on the side of safety versus persuasion exerted on the side of risk, it is a similarly empty distinction. By persuading her away from Wentworth, Lady Russell not only denied Anne her twenties with Wentworth, but exposed her to the terrible risk of *never* regaining love and happiness: a risk that only extraordinary circumstances have prevented from becoming actual. Viewed as something that is yet to happen—which is how persuasion necessarily views everything—*any* act contains both potential risk and potential safety.

The only thing Anne says here with any real force is, effectively: "That was then, and this is now." ("My age so different," is how she puts it. "Yes, alas," we could forgive Wentworth for thinking.) Wentworth replies, unconvincingly, "Perhaps I ought to have reasoned thus."

That evening, Anne makes another attempt at distinguishing—understandably, considering her first attempt. Regarding Lady Russell, she says to Wentworth: "I am not saying that she did not err in her advice. It was, perhaps, one of those cases in which advice is good or bad only as the event decides" (p. 248).

Perhaps. But again and again, in discussions of *Persuasion*, I have asked students: "When *isn't* advice either good or bad 'only as the event decides'?" This rule doesn't ground any distinction between good and bad persuasion, any more than the safety/risk rule, since the test of *any* advice must surely be the future effects of following or not following it.

This can be focussed through an analogy. Let's say that it is early 1987, and I am considering investing all of my savings in a bullish stock-market. I ask my neighbor, Peter, for his advice. He tosses a coin in the air and says: "Forget it." I then approach my other neighbor, Paul, who happens to be the most recent Nobel laureate in Economics. Paul spends an entire semester investigating every dimension of the question I have put to him, and at the end of all this his advice is to invest. I follow his advice—and lose everything.

Surely I am entitled to call Peter's advice good, Paul's bad. *So has the event decided.* What possible criterion *could* there be for judging such advice except whether my money grows or shrinks, given that *that is precisely what I wanted to know*? Peter's advice was arrived at randomly, but it was correct, and that is all I asked it to be. A shamefaced Paul might argue that, although the result was bad, his advice was good, because of all of the time and expertise that went into framing it. My reply would have to be that the *point* of all that time and expertise was to produce a happy outcome; the result confirms the expertise, not vice versa. And if Paul then argued that his methods would *in a majority of cases* produce a better result than Peter's, I would have to tell him that what I asked him had nothing to do with a majority of cases, but everything to do with my own present case. Likewise, Lady Russell's advice had only to do with Anne's case, and like all advice it was *always* going to be judged good or bad by its future effects on her life.

Anne Elliot's two instanced speeches are not the only places where she talks inscrutably about persuasion. In her conversation with Captain Harville regarding the temperaments of men and women, Anne cites absolute loyalty and firmness as the qualities in women which make separation harder for them to bear than for men: "We certainly do not forget you, so soon as you forget us" (p.

236). And yet the moral Anne draws from Louisa Musgrove's accident on the Cobb is that this feminine firmness should have a limit: a persuadable temper, too, is a feminine asset.

Wentworth's certitude on the subject is likewise marked by contradiction. Early in the book, he is bitter about Anne's weakness, her vulnerability to what he calls "over-persuasion." Later, he is discussing with Louisa Musgrove the qualities to be sought in a woman. Louisa contrasts herself with her sister Henrietta: "I have no idea of being so easily persuaded. When I have made up my mind, I have made it." "Happy for her, to have a mind such as yours at hand!" says Wentworth. He then proceeds to describe the quality he most admires in a woman—firmness, like a nut: "My first wish for all, whom I am interested in, is that they should be firm." But Wentworth's main point against the opposite condition, weakness, is the strange point that it *renders one immune to real persuasion:* "It is the worst evil of too yielding and indecisive a character, that no influence over it can be depended on.—You are never sure of a good impression being durable" (pp. 109–10). (This common inscriptive metaphor, "impression," shows us how much language already knows about the contents of consciousness as a written text.)

So Anne Elliot thinks that women are, in their very nature, persuadable and non-persuadable—happily so, because these turn out to be precisely the mutually exclusive qualities that Frederick Wentworth is looking for in a woman. *He* is seeking a nut-like resistance to persuasion in a woman—because it makes her so much more persuadable.

This kind of close reading is bound to have effects on whatever "message" one is able to take away from the novel, and will perhaps make one more skeptical about accepting what is, after all, *Persuasion*'s central fiction: which is that there *is* a second chance; that eight lost, lonely years can be recuperated; that life goes on forever. The kind of knowledge about *Persuasion* expressed by D.W. Harding, introducing the novel a quarter-century ago, when he describes its triumph as "the harmonizing of several attitudes, which could have been distinct and even discordant, into a complex whole" (p. 20), no longer seems the final word at all. Something non-harmonizing and quite discordant lurks here; some warning about the way social values get hold of our lives; some protest against the sacrifice of desire to "higher" ends; some force disruptive and disquieting enough to exculpate Jane Austen from her brother Henry's claim that "her opinions accorded strictly with those of our Established Church" (p. 33).

In summary, this is a novel that centers thematically on a few instances of persuasion, and in which simultaneously the characters are endlessly going on about persuasion, persuadability, influence, firmness, impressionability, weakness, advice, and so on. As a result, persuasion persistently deconstructs the categories that have been erected to contain it, disrupts the oppositions that have been designed to govern its correct application. It is everywhere in the book, and finally nowhere to be found. You end up with a strange logic in a novel where the characters are being persuaded in and out of marrying each other, when at the same time their main criterion in the marriage choice seems to be how they judge each other's persuadability. I take this to be a signal instance of the logic of *différance*.

There have been two different questions involved here. First, I have argued that there *are* connections between deconstruction and New Criticism, but that these by no means detract from deconstruction's claims as a teaching method. Second, I have distinguished deconstruction from both New Criticism and New Moralism by arguing that it refuses to reconcile differences in the text, and through this refuses to give the text over completely to history, however sophisticated one's version of history. This second argument addresses what I take to be the central issue in current literary criticism—the issue of textual ideology.

I suggested at one point that deconstruction has a special affinity with the tutorial, while the more ideologically focused theories seem more suited to the lecture hall. If this suggests a dialectical story about undergraduate education—a continual process of demystification and remystification—then that is fine, because in these matters it pays to be a pluralist.

Finally, I am well aware that my view of what deconstruction is about is heterodox, but I am also aware that there are only heterodox views of what deconstruction is about. It may horrify most of those who work within deconstruction when I say that, for me, deconstruction is a variety of liberal skeptical thought, and that it is working a similar patch to that once occupied by logical positivism. Like logical positivism, it is anti-metaphysical, though much more aware than the positivists of its own complicity in metaphysics.

Above all, deconstruction is anti-apocalyptic. It inclines us towards the pause-button whenever we are being urged, from within language, to go somewhere that is outside language, "outside" either in the sense of some direct contact with reality, or in the sense of some complete transcendence of reality. It pulls us back into language whenever we are being offered something that is supposedly "beyond" the mediations, contingencies and pragmatics of language. It is neither a particularly noble, nor a morally improving project. It is more a kind of fossicking: indeed, like the New Criticism, it is a variety of modern philology, always turning its gaze back onto the history of words.

We are constantly told that criticism is being swept along on a tide of social marginalization. Some have responded by forming alliances with other disciplines, others by redirecting criticism towards social and religious prophecy. In my view, it may yet turn out to be in philology, its launching-place, that criticism finds safe-harbor—like the speaker in John Ashbery's "Soonest Mended": "always coming back/ To the mooring of starting out, that day so long ago."[8]

Notes

1. Frank Lentricchia, *After the New Criticism* (London: Athlone Press, 1980).

2. William Empson, *Seven Types of Ambiguity* (London: Penguin, 1961).

3. Jacques Derrida, *Of Grammatology* (Baltimore: Johns Hopkins University Press, 1976).

4. Northrop Frye, *Anatomy of Criticism: Four Essays* (Princeton: Princeton University Press, 1957), p. 52.

5. Harold Bloom, *The Anxiety of Influence* (New York: Oxford University Press, 1973), pp. 49–73.

6. Cleanth Brooks, *The Well-Wrought Urn* (London: Dennis Dobson, 1949), p. 4.

7. Jane Austen, *Persuasion*, ed. D.W. Harding (London: Penguin, 1965), p. 246.

8. John Ashbery, *Selected Poems* (New York: Viking, 1985), p. 89.

The Beggar's Opera and Literary Historiography: Critical Pluralism as Strategy for Teaching a Canonical Text

Robert J. Merrett

In the past two decades, I have taught John Gay's *The Beggar's Opera* fifteen times to first-year, senior undergraduate, and post-graduate students. Not only has the play always been a hit, but the social and literary issues to which it gives rise have endowed each course in which it was featured with a coherence this essay seeks to explain. The play's topical variety—its depiction of the criminal underworld, prison life, the bourgeois family, the political system, and the new capitalism—together with its mixed form and confla-tion of high art and popular culture resist critical paradigms and dissuade students from single-minded interpretations. Its polyva-lence invites them to confront the dialectic between traditional lit-erary history and newer historical stances.

To the mutual benefit of teachers and students, Gay's text refers to and prescribes its own reception, as do other major Au-gustan texts such as *A Tale of a Tub* and *The Dunciad*: all establish formal and ideological contexts for themselves plurally, this plu-rality defying historical exposition that treats seamless works over against unitary backgrounds. Yet Gay's diffuse functional reflexiv-ity celebrates his play's textual primacy, forestalling much of the recursive metacriticism practiced by contemporary theoretical methods. Since pedagogy does well to adopt the dialectical rela-tions between practical and theoretical criticism, courses are best planned around texts like *The Beggar's Opera*: it justifies literary theory to the degree it resists unselfconscious, extrinsic historical accounts of its plural functions but, inasmuch as it is not reducible to a systematic, ideological transcript of its times, it upholds traditional historicism. In showing that traditional and contemporary methods may be interdependent, Gay's text reveals how historical dialectic can provide effective methods and significant goals in the classroom.[1]

Among teachers it is a truism that the more problems a text creates, the greater is its cultural and pedagogical value. Readers of *The Beggar's Opera* cannot avoid contrary observations about the play and its history. Unique in 1728, it retains an inimitable freshness: it may have founded "ballad opera," but theater history suggests that it had no true imitator. Its uniqueness is yet more paradoxical since it alludes to many theatrical and cultural forms, bringing its action into being over against a range of social practices and memories and by raising questions about generic identity. The play borrows modes from many forms: opera, heroic tragedy, comedy of wit, the masque, the ballad, comedy of sensibility, farce, criminal biography, etc., satirizing these modes less to undermine specific forms and generic hierarchy than to unsettle audiences. Through ironical analogies, the play defamiliarizes the habits and perspectives of experienced theatergoers.

One way to introduce students to the play while allaying fears about its complexity and about critical paradoxes is to present them with the music, for the music makes accessible, through illustration and analogy, the play's mixed genres and dialectical effects. Thanks to the historiography of Max Goberman, his Everest recording of the complete songs with original instrumentation is a fine teaching resource. The *maestoso* and *allegro* styles in Pepusch's overture alert students to the coexistence of pathetic and comic modes. This generic interplay is confirmed by the way compositions of Purcell, Handel, and other court musicians resonate against the words entuned by pickpockets, fences, and prostitutes. The musical allusions show there is no disjunction between grand and popular songs: tunes with vulgar, bawdy associations do detract from the aristocratic pretensions of crooks who abuse grand music, but other ballads offer pathos and cultural history that deflate middle-class antagonism to both high and popular art, an antagonism constantly enacted by Gay's criminals.[2]

Readily conceding the worth of pop and folk music because they recognize how it defies middle-class values, most students enjoy discussing the tensions between opera and ballads in *The Beggar's Opera*.[3] They are also alert to the diverse idioms governing the adaptations of the original score. Goberman's simple scoring and reliance on original instruments validate the concept of historical recovery in the minds of students, especially when they can compare the romantic sweetness of Sir Frederic Austin's orchestrations for the 1920 Hammersmith production with the jazzy toughness of Kurt Weill's accompaniments to Berthold Brecht's 1928 version of Gay's work, *The Threepenny Opera*. The distinct musical idioms of the modern versions and their opposing ideologies defy simple claims for the progress of taste and cultural reception: that the modern versions hold high- and low-brow modes apart helps students to revisit the mixed musical styles of the original and to probe questions about how the original audience could have had such a complex sense of musical and social allusion. Introducing students to musical allusiveness in Gay's text leads to questions about dynamic tensions between aesthetics and politics and enables them to grasp the paradox that his exhibition of society's abuse of dramatic illusion restores power to the theater. Since the play's music reveals how an audience can be involved by being unsettled, it clarifies the historical issue as to whether the Augustan audience was a stable, ready-made phenomenon or whether Swift, Pope, Gay, and others structured relations between reflexive and referential meanings to create their audience.

To teach eighteenth-century texts is to invite students to see that many historical and critical methods, whether traditional or contemporary, are both stolid and inapplicable. As literary theorists, Swift, Pope, and Gay defended textual primacy by subordinating theory to social action. Not only were most critical methods developed long after the original impact of Augustan texts, but also literary history has largely ignored the extent to which texts like *The Beggar's Opera* are anti-systematic systems—works which discountenance the critical tenets they foresaw. Gay, Swift, and Pope anticipated the cultural and philosophical problems arising from narrative realism and the decline of mythopoeic vision. The musical allusions and history of Gay's text are a good place to start when it comes to deconstructing literary criticism and theory in ways suitable to post-Restoration and Augustan letters.

Of course, successful classroom presentations of *The Beggar's Opera* will not simply oppose all critical methods and their ideologies. But to make the literary and cultural dialectic of this text approachable and memorable, the instructor's task is to organize his presentation so that it will educe flaws in traditional and contemporary methods and demonstrate the need for critical pluralism.

This task is best performed by touching on theoretical issues that suggest why pluralism is germane to the historical appreciation of texts. One such issue is literary progress and the question as to whether scientific and literary progress are analogous. Thomas Kuhn's view that scientific paradigms are the necessary but limiting frameworks which must be broken if significant development is to occur may not be as germane to literary history as his claim that there is "no such thing as research without counter-instances," and that rivalry between research paradigms leads to the question, "which problems is it more significant to have solved?"[4] For instructors and students of literature the issue is: do later critical and social paradigms invalidate earlier ones?

Another issue is whether it is feasible to separate the meaning inherent in a text from the significance that accretes to it in the process of cultural reception. For E.D. Hirsch, Jr., literary works have core meanings independent of textual and social history.[5] One problem with the hermeneutic recoverability of textual meaning is thrown into relief by Michel Foucault's insistence that the evolution of social institutions like prisons and asylums is programmed by literary texts. However, Foucault's identification of textual function with political history and ideological progress is not helpful to the extent that it subsumes aesthetics to politics, without showing how much politics exploits and derives from aesthetic processes and goals.[6]

Stressing the limits of Marxism, deconstructionism, and other critical stances in course outlines is important because the relative efficacy of all methods underscores textual polyvalence. Emphasizing such relativism makes it clearer to students that pedagogical principles and methods are implicit in the ways texts function. One can present Gay as prefiguring Brecht's Marxist sense of theatrical alienation and commitment to social change. For Gay does attack decadent consumption of opera. But whether he debases the genre as does Brecht is moot. If Gay looks ahead to Brecht, he also looks back to the masque tradition which kept drama alive when the theaters were closed. Like most texts, Gay's involves plural perspectives on history and society. Hence, instructors wanting students to be lively and engaged will fully present such plurality, showing that Gay's conflation of social groups, making the poor and rich both signs of decadence, defends as much as it opposes social hierarchy, and that, even as he represents the debasement of opera in deconstructive irony and parody, his anti-form respects opera's generic ideals.[7]

While students concede *The Beggar's Opera*'s textual plurality if it is conveyed in terms of critical relativism, and can imagine themselves to be the original audience as well as contemporary actors of the play, they nonetheless ask to be presented with a sequence of topics that makes the conflicts between traditional and contemporary historical methods explicit, since taking context and background to be the first step toward textual understanding is habitual to them and to many instructors. By first addressing biographical assumptions in class, the lecturer can present what traditional literary history has to offer while showing that its certitudes, if helpful, are not certainties.

The Regents Restoration Drama edition of *The Beggar's Opera* exemplifies traditional literary history because it privileges diachronic, developmental notions. After discussing the play's bibliography, the introduction isolates theatrical conditions that favored satire and ballad opera, before subsuming the text to the Christian humanism of Pope and Swift. Professor Roberts not only unqualifiedly presents the play as the acme of Gay's *opus* and Augustan ideology, but overgeneralizes about Gay's writerly aims: allegedly, he depicted the underworld only to attack the Court and stopped Handel composing Italian opera in the 1730s.[8] The pedagogical limits of Roberts' stance are indicated partly by the fact that Gay used Italian operatic subjects in his *Achilles* of 1733 and that he worked with Handel on a production of *Acis and Galatea* in 1732.[9]

Students appreciate coming to terms with the selective evidence and the restrictive mode of traditional literary history practiced by Roberts. Eager to learn about Gay the individual, whose life was full and interesting, who was affected by major events in his times, and who knew people with political and social power, they quickly realize that Roberts' focus on contemporaries and texts influencing Gay to create his famous work, and on later authors and texts influenced by him, is not exhaustive and may be arbitrary. It is germane to his satire to discover how hard Gay sought aristocratic patronage and how much he lost in the South-Sea Bubble. It is also germane to *The Beggar's Opera*'s uniqueness to trace its urban pastoralism and generic mixtures in Gay's poetic career. For Roberts seems to avoid biographical facts that might disturb his introduction's narrative line, content instead to assert that Gay realized his intentions in his play's satirical argument. By asserting that *The Beggar's Opera* is "above all a satire" (p. xxvi), Roberts discounts its reflexive ironies as well as historical and critical issues, such as the European influence on the English stage, that arise from the text's pluralism.

If students like to assume that an author transcribes daily experience according to a unique view of life and art, their skepticism about authorial intention in texts readies them to see the limits of traditional historicism. Because Augustan satire recoils on its agents, as Swift's *Modest Proposal* shows, students will explore why biography is not *the* foundation of literary history. It is not only a new historicist tenet that writers cannot comprehend the social and political circumstances within which they compose: to Swift and Pope, writers professing superior sensibility and transcendant vision were mentally deficient and self-defeating. The framing device in *The Beggar's Opera*, with its mockery of authorship, invites students both to see the limits of biographical criticism and to realize that dramatists may be present in their plays in terms of the newer historicisms.[10]

Since the framing device presents the author as subject to actors and audience, it is fitting to hold biographical issues in abeyance while material aspects of the text are studied. Students like to be reminded that plays were written to be performed and that, as illustrated by Shakespeare's stagecraft, they are promptbooks that embody acting cues besides stories and plots. As Gay's frame stresses, plays are commodities produced by theater managers for consumers and texts crucial to the well-being of actors. Since a play-text is not primarily a mirror of its author, its textual functions require the study of its setting, characterization and genre to be mediated by material factors. Thus, in deriving topics from the materiality of *The Beggar's Opera*, one has to explore the tensions arising from its double debt to five-act dramatic and three-act operatic modes. These tensions help students to realize that Gay's play embodies distinct systems of mediation and commodification, and that their personal difficulties in reconciling these systems are linked to the theater's historical problems as a public institution.

Theater companies after the Restoration struggled for economic survival and political patronage to an extent that deeply marked all stage productions. Conflicts between the two official companies affected *The Beggar's Opera*. The rejection of the play by Colley Cibber—a rejection later regretted—and its acceptance by his rival theater manager, John Rich, who stipulated for high financial returns, affected the reception as well as production of Gay's work, and students can usefully be asked to discover why this is so. Like Pope, Gay disliked the effect of Rich's pantomimes on theatrical standards. To see why Gay's text does not simply defend drama against opera, students can relate how much he satirizes musical interference with dramatic illusion to how much he integrates music into the plot so as to resist the incursions of pantomime.[11]

To encourage students to hunt out the details which can advance their understanding of the post-Restoration theater's institutional problems it is necessary to outline the ideological forces which make political and social history inseparable from dramatic procedures. The Restoration of Charles II not only saw the reopening of public theaters in 1660, but heralded twenty-five years of counter-revolutionary dramaturgy which had an impact until Gay's time and beyond. The re-opening of the theaters was so associated with anti-republicanism that playwrighting was newly politicized: the reaction of Orrery, Dryden, Etherege, and Wycherley to the sensibility which had proscribed public theaters was profound. Yet, their intention to reject the immediate political past and to recover the tradition of Shakespeare, Jonson, and Beaumont and Fletcher was frustrated partly because, in their eyes, the social fabric torn by the Civil War was not mended by the Restoration Settlement, for the sequestrated properties of the lesser aristocracy and squirearchy were not returned to their families. Students enjoy ideological analyses of political and social conditions in place of narrative history if the former problematize learning and build on established class topics. Allusions to Shakespeare and Otway in *The Beggar's Opera* can thus be related to the unresolvable tension in the Restoration between the politicization of the theater and the collective wish of playwrights to return to drama's cultural roots, and Gay's folksongs and ballads may be linked to the carnival spirit of popular music that served as propaganda during and after the Civil War.[12]

If political factionalism after 1660 affected all dramatic codes and if playwrights, theater companies, and audiences divided along lines which grew more marked as rivalry between aristocratic, professional, and merchant classes subsequently intensified, these ideological changes had a particular effect on setting, newly making stage and social spaces extensions of each other. The arbitrariness of the Restoration Settlement gave playwrights a renewed sense of London that grew out of tensions between the desire to recover the cultural past and the awareness of its irrecoverability. The plays of Wycherley and Etherege illustrate London's demo-

graphic changes, showing how districts inside and outside the city
became socially and economically distinct. Students like mapping
the distinctions, readily seeing that dramatic settings translate the
wishes of the displaced aristocracy and transcribe the systematic
remaking of London after the return of the King, the Plague of
1665, and the Fire of 1666. One way to stress the prevalent interaction of social and dramatic settings is to ask students to determine
why Mrs. Hardcastle in Goldsmith's *She Stoops to Conquer* is laugh-
able because she cannot distinguish between Ranelagh and Tower
Wharf or the Pantheon and Southwark.[13] Gay's allusions to London accord with those in *The Country Wife* and *The Man of Mode* by
presenting the capital's life as a set of socially contrastive signs and
an extension of the theater. Gay ironically exploits the ideology of
reciprocal settings—of the displaced treating the urban landscape
as a theater to make up for lost social power.

To help students understand Gay's irony and to discourage
their viewing literary history in terms of single ideologies, it is useful to contrast *The Beggar's Opera* with plays that are not counter-
revolutionary and do not create reflexive functions from setting.
Shadwell's *The Squire of Alsatia* is a good example because it seems
to anticipate Gay by depicting London's underworld and ex-
pounding its low-life idioms. But its plot incoherently reinforces
the patriarchal ideology of benevolist Whiggism. Far from giving
drama new social functions, Shadwell's sentimental defense of the
status quo debases theatrical processes. By contrast, Gay validates
the stage by demeaning characters who belittle plays: like
Wycherley and Etherege, he creates systems of dramatic representation with ambivalent relations to social life. If Shadwell's play
helps students to recognize Gay's closeness to Restoration dramatists, it also prompts the question of whether political conservatives tried to renew, while progressives tried to erode, theatrical
traditions.

Such a question cannot be approached through Roberts' traditional view of setting. While he identifies lanes, streets, parishes,
and districts and connects these to brothels, to the dens of thieves
and gamblers, and to trade, medicine, and law as well as to the
routes between Newgate, the Old Bailey, and Tyburn, and to the
sites of theaters, he does not enable students to integrate social and
theatrical space. His elaboration of place-names does provide an
excellent geographical context, and his annotations imply the desirability of students' learning to map London's topography and to
become familiar with a historical atlas. But he ignores demography

and the plural functions of Gay's chosen sites. Students can learn much by considering the relation between the routes taken by condemned criminals and public spectacle, and by contemplating the proximity of the centres of lawlessness and legislation.

If Roberts assumes an equivalence of location and topicality, setting in Gay's text has plural functions which newer historical stances better analyze: the pluralism of Gay's setting clarifies the ideology of literary history. In mapping London, Gay's place-names debase the city in ways antagonistic to the sentimental line of plays from *The Squire of Alsatia* to *The Conscious Lovers* and *The London Merchant*, plays dignifying the capital as the moral arena of merchants. Gay's place-names signify that crime defines London and that the underworld, far from being as containable as Jeremy Collier and the reform movement—witness Farquhar's *The Beaux' Stratagem*—liked to hope, flourished, ironically, on account of reformist efforts and platitudes.

The social and dramatic contexts in which Gay's place-names challenge sentimental, mercantilist values help students to focus on the plural and systematic functions of the names, to study the gaps between social principles and contingency and between linguistic rules and arbitrariness, and to see how setting involves characterization. Gay's Newgate is not a singular place but the epitome of leading institutions: the conduct of Peachum and Lockit makes the prison stand for the Exchange, the High Court, the House of Commons, and the Cabinet Chamber. Yet their organized and criminal exploitation of money, politics, and the law means that Newgate displaces, even as it represents, the other institutions. The prison is the type of all institutions and the figure of systematic evil: the acme of social ills, Newgate shows how these ills stem from criminal practice.[14] Like the "double capacity" of Gay's characters, the prison has specific and general functions which, in illustrating his wish to heighten tensions between referential and systematic meaning, require the dialectical application of historicist and semiotic interpretations.[15]

The plural functions of Gay's setting prepare students to analyze the complex of historical topicality and literary allusiveness in terms of which his characters are both represented and displaced. If Peachum is an image of Jonathan Wild, the gangster hanged in London in 1725, Wild is also embodied by Lockit, Peachum's friend and rival. In this field of reference, Macheath is Jack Sheppard, the famous prison breaker and creature of Wild's. Yet each male part has the same referent in the political world—Robert

Walpole, the first prime minister. The plural topicality of the characters is underlined when Peachum and Lockit fight, since then they embody the feud between Walpole and his brother-in-law, Townshend.

For the purpose of designing courses and encouraging students to develop an appreciation of intertextuality, it is a help that Gay's literary allusions establish plural relations to other plays and genres. When Peachum and Lockit fight, their dialogue recalls the dispute between Brutus and Cassius in *Julius Caesar*, and when they berate their betters their words recall the discontent of Jaffeir and Pierre in *Venice Preserved*. When Macheath thinks he is about to be hanged, his speech echoes the climax of Otway's play, this following his inability to choose between Polly and Lucy, a scene resembling the one in Dryden's *All for Love* where Antony faces the opposing demands of Octavia and Cleopatra. If *The Beggar's Opera* is fairly typical of Restoration comedy in parodying and burlesquing heroic tragedy, its allusions to Handel's *Floridante* and *Alessandro* indicate to students that Gay relies somewhat uniquely on the interchangeability of roles and the *peripeteia* of motivation and agency found in heroic tragedy and Italian opera to advance his cultural and metatheatrical criticism. In the context of the enduring performances of heroic tragedies, as evidenced by Fielding's *The Tragedy of Tragedies*, which satirized more than forty of them in 1731, students can be engaged in raising questions about what light Gay's plural historical and literary references shed on the theoretical relationship of characterization to genre.[16]

But they should be warned against using the new historicist phrase, "the novelization of culture," to explain Gay's complex intertextuality and generic mixture in *The Beggar's Opera*.[17] One reason is that Gay mixed generic modes in his many literary forms. Another is that he exploits plural allusions and modes of characterization to generate themes critical of the sentimental and psychological tenets of reformers who subordinated drama to narrative. Gay's text thematizes drama's decline: scorning Polly's playbooks, her mother apes the platitudes of bourgeois comedy, and the sentimentalism of Polly, Filch, and the others is rooted in a preference for vulgarized romance. The theater and opera house are arenas for crime, while the courts are stages on which illicit parts are performed with aplomb. Macheath's reprieve is the nadir of dramatic debasement, Gay exposing the demand for generic purity as a sign of popular surrender to narrative formulae and anti-dramatic dogma.[18]

Students are engaged by discovering the limits of contemporary as well as of traditional criticism. If plural modes of allusion invite them to see that Gay's satire is socially comprehensive and collapses distinctions between popular and high art, they eagerly realize that textual reflexivity challenges generic history and truisms about literary progress. That Gay defends drama by treating the marginalization of theater ironically, and by heightening the stage's reflexive power with plural codes, warns students against equating new historicism with concepts such as the rise of the middle classes and bourgeois progress, concepts Gay personally and textually opposed. Yet traditional exposition, which moves from setting to characterization, to generic modes and on to themes, is problematic and cannot address the ancillary topics to which it gives rise—such as the relationship between representing social change and registering cultural contradictions. Yet addressing such topics integrates the study of a text into the design of the course in which it is studied.

Traditional exposition serves students well when it establishes that *The Beggar's Opera*'s themes about the growth of political parties, the role of the prime minister, the mores of court culture, and the problems of the financial revolution arise from motifs that are explicable in terms of straightforward historical description. Traditional methods apply less to the play's themes of family and married life since it defies social and literary progress: Gay does not so much fault social hierarchy as show that, in aping the aristocracy, the other ranks betray reformist concepts of companionate marriage to material and sexual vices. However, the themes that Gay creates from contradictions in the reform of the penal code wholly displace traditional exegesis. From a shrewd sense that the legislated increase in capital crimes defended property at the expense of individual rights, he assigns growth in the business of crime and thief-taking to legal reform. He realizes that such reform commodifies the media: permitting newspapers to advertise the return of stolen goods simply perpetuates robbery, and producing criminal biographies supposedly to justify penal reform only reinforces the indulgent fantasies of the ruling class, as the hero-worship attributed to the audience in the *dénouement* illustrates.

The performance history and critical reception of *The Beggar's Opera*, no less than its themes, require teachers to show that traditional topics move constantly beyond literary to cultural inquiry. The uncritical identification of audiences with the play's characters, and the opposing critical responses to its many productions in

the eighteenth century, invite students to connect its textual pluralism to cultural dialectic. Its record-breaking first season of sixty-
two performances, and more than one thousand before 1800, make
the play an acme of success. To see the play as a cultural phenomenon, students may probe how its fame grew because Lavinia
Fenton, the actress who first played Polly, left the stage to marry
the Duke of Bolton and because the other actors were depicted on
commemorative playing cards, fans and screens. They may, for the
same purpose, try to reconcile how the play was stripped of irrev-
erence during the century because of moral attacks on it by
Thomas Herring, an Archbishop of Canterbury, and Sir John
Fielding, the London magistrate, with how its festive harmlessness
was celebrated when acted by children and by adults who reversed the *dramatis personae*'s genders. Extreme reactions to *The
Beggar's Opera*—the claims it was nothing new and a dangerous
novelty—enable students to explore the literary and social dialectic
inherent in cultural phenomena. Seeing it as an entertainment with
neither serious intent nor incentives to crime, Dr. Johnson was alert
to the play's comic misrule but devalued its satire. Defoe and Sir
John Hawkins, Johnson's editor, found it a dangerous encouragement to crime and correctly thought criminals like Sheppard could
become folk heroes, but they were inadequate commentators in as-
cribing crime solely to individuals rather than to corrupt institutions as well.

The dialectical stance students must adopt in the face of the
systematic plurality of the text and of its unsteady cultural reception makes pedagogical efforts to reconcile traditional and new historicisms vital. Such efforts are rewarded when one determines the
scope the text gives to critical methods that integrate literary and
social history and that make sense of Gay's ambivalence to literary
and social conventions. Speech-act theory, semiotic analysis, and
feminist perspectives are instruments able to revise traditional
concepts of literary history in the face of Gay's simultaneous criticism and promotion of social and literary hierarchies.

The Beggar's Opera emphasizes that the meaning of spoken
words changes the world. Gay's text shows that words perform actions because language is an institution that resists the abuses of
speakers. If speech-act theory applies to his predecessors' works—
dramatic and linguistic performance being involved in one another—it is relevant to Gay because his characters depreciate
words and the linguistic conditions which make utterances significant and socially cohesive. Gay's characters accept performative

meaning but only in a negative and inverted sense. Thus, Peachum declares that all "professions be-rogue one another." Since neighbors always abuse one another, the lawyer necessarily "be-knaves the divine" (6). Macheath defines a courtier as one who "professes everything and will do nothing" (63), but neither his fellow thieves nor the gang-owners practice what they preach. All seek to undermine the social basis of meaning, posturing with words individualistically and anarchically.[19]

Students may justify the application of speech-act theory to Gay's text by exploring why he treats conversation as a mere formality and euphemism for robbery or sexual intercourse. Among the women, "spatter" and "chatter" are synonyms (55), while to the men what women "say or do goes for nothing" (67). Male abuse of performatives shows how deeply misogyny is embedded in society. Macheath believes a promise to a woman "signifies nothing" (44), yet mouths the cliché that "his word is as good as his bond" (45). As they claim to be above ceremony but subject it to their interests, so Gay's characters abuse speech as action. When Mrs. Peachum pronounces that Filch will be "a great man in history" (15), her pretended authority is personally and socially destructive. When Lockit says that he "can forgive as well as resent," his substitution of "resent" for "forget" signals a typical abuse of performatives and shows how immoral verbal action degrades communal and historical values.

While students can further trace the impact of performative meaning on Gay's social satire, they may extend their analysis of his characterization by seeing how semiotic concepts complement speech-act theory. His characters are puppets to society's codes because they speak in mixed lexical registers while abusing linguistic and moral convention. Aligning himself to other ranks and professions, Peachum also spurns these alignments. He is proud to share the "honest employment" of lawyers by acting for and against rogues (6), yet admits that lawyers are "bitter enemies to those in our way" (23). As gangster who manages his thieves' productivity, he poses both like a judge who can "soften the evidence" or declare "death without reprieve" (7), and like a rural squire whose wish to protect female partridges and breed "game" governs his view of life and death (8). In his obsession with "industry," "stock," and "credit," Peachum speaks like a money-lending merchant. But greed and self-importance inhibit him from seeing conflicts among the codes he exploits. Students enjoy uncovering the conflicts arising from professional and aesthetic pretensions. In

saying he depends on female thieves since, in prostituting themselves, they breed thieves, harden men to crime, and spread dis-
eases, Peachum falsely avers that surgeons and thief-takers are
professionally interdependent. He is also implausible in pretend-
ing to aesthetic superiority to dignify his profession. For he exposes his taste when praising one thief's "engaging presence of
mind" and "genius." The pun in "engaging" on highway robbery
and personal grace and the notion that "Crook-fingered Jack"
could be a "mighty clean-handed fellow" show that, as when he
makes aesthetic judgments or plans a "decent execution,"
Peachum's code of aesthetic sensibility unmasks his corruption
and exemplifies society's disorder (9–10).

Quick to see that there is nothing unique in Peachum's appropriation of codes, students readily detect the systematic pretension
that lies behind the common adoption of ecclesiastical, literary,
and military idioms. Thus, Mrs. Peachum thinks the Catechism
useful only as it permits a man on trial to make a good figure in
court and in the "Ordinary's paper" (16), confirming Filch's view
that "penitence" destroys a gentleman's spirit and a thief's commitment to crime (9). Filch's sense that Newgate's "favorite child-
getter" has all the "prowess of a knight errant" in rescuing so
many "ladies in distress" (63), perverts literary codes. He does so
too when, despite having been "pumped," he fears being cut off in
the "flower of [his] youth" (15). Polly's belief in the "great heroes"
of the romances lent her by Macheath perversely covers her wish
to be seduced (28), while his attempt to dignify promiscuity by alluding to Orsino's speech about love and music in *Twelfth Night* is
hollow. Despite the gang's claim to a fearless honor based on the
"law of arms" and "right of conquest" (31), Jemmy Twitcher's im-
peachment of Macheath shows that they lack honor and are destined for the noose. Since in the condemned cell Macheath's
courage is coterminous with wine, his fanciful military code signals that "the world is all alike" in pretension and depravity (80).

The Beggar's Opera offers further scope for studying what
abused codes say about discourse as society's instrument for sustaining itself. For Gay dramatizes abuses which erode systematic
relations between codes. Hence, Mrs. Trapes, the bawd, is as familiar with the world of business as Peachum and Lockit, and her
women as easily appropriate its codes, witness Mrs. Coaxer's talk
about "interlopers" and "industry" (38). When Matt of the Mint
says that Peachum is as necessary to the gang as "a bawd to a
whore" (34), the abuse of codes is shown to be as indiscriminate as

widespread: the loss of systematic differentiation vital to their operation implies that society is losing its structural sense. Yet the resistance of codes to abuse is clear when Macheath claims that the recruitment of prostitutes in Drury Lane depends on "gentlemen of the sword" (35): equating highwaymen with professional soldiers, he adopts the same implausible comparative logic that Peachum, his rival and employer, uses when he prides himself on being as indebted to the prostitutes of Drury Lane as are surgeons. The study of signs and the interaction of codes provides an objective grounding for Gay's irony, and enables students to see how much social history informs the text and validates cultural criticism.[20]

Students enjoy tracing Gay's systematic appreciation of codes when they study those signs involving his characters in the ironies of class rivalry and rejection of hierarchy. The Peachums' erratic stances to Macheath's courtship of Polly are perfect examples. Mrs. Peachum thinks Macheath a worthy husband because he is a fine gentleman, but Peachum insists Macheath lacks a genteel education because he is always worsted at gambling by lords. Mrs. Peachum would forgive Polly's affair since her daughter imitates fine ladies, but, on confirming the marriage, she chides Polly for imitating the gentry and laments that Polly has not brought a distinguished person into the family. Peachum is equally erratic: he wishes his daughter had a court lady's discretion so he could better manipulate his gang, but he blames Polly for marrying since she will be as neglected as if married to a lord, and since highwaymen abuse their wives. The Peachums' social views are systematically inconsistent: they spurn and idolize the professions, the gentry and the aristocracy. Yet their wide-ranging, reciprocal abuse of signs actualizes the drama's analytical powers. By replicating as he defies ideologies, Gay invalidates interpretations based on single historical models: his text reproduces systems of signification, yet its pluralism is not determined by them. Unlike Brecht's systematic inversions, Gay's are equally reflexive and referential. Whereas *The Threepenny Opera* presents monarchical and commercial motifs anachronistically and stridently, *The Beggar's Opera* privileges semiotic ambivalence to place itself outside and inside historical discourse, making this dialectical action a puzzling as well as polemical dramatic end.[21]

Comparing Brecht's and Gay's semiotic methods helps students see how *The Beggar's Opera*, like *A Tale of a Tub* and *The Dunciad*, turns attacks against humanism into its radical defense.

Brecht's explicit, monological reference is closer to the univocal, novelistic dialogue of Lillo's *The London Merchant* and Colman's *The Jealous Wife* than to the mixed modes by which Gay, Swift, and Pope forestalled the rise of the middle classes and Whig historians. Like the other Augustans, Gay defends humanism by eschewing an obvious program and by appropriating literary and social codes. Traditional historicism's failure to explain this radical conservatism means that current historical debate ought to revivify literary history.[22] Semiotic analysis of *The Beggar's Opera* leads students to reconceive the application of religious ideology, the growth of the aristocracy, increased differentiation in social hierarchy, the diminution of female power, and the decline of drama to Gay and the other Augustans.

Although Gay's satire is dramatic as well as social, *The Beggar's Opera* responds well to feminist viewpoints since it tackles patriarchy and misogyny. While motifs of prostitution and widowhood qualify themes of forced marriage that had dominated comic plots after the Restoration, Gay satirizes more than dramatic and social formulae. Aware that textual and sexual forms of gender may be reciprocal, he objects to social imitation of drama as much as to its self-perpetuating closedness to reality, the evidence appearing in the way his female characters objectify themselves while cultivating obsessions with death and sexual climax.

Since Gay's women lay claim to affection and conscience while they are aggressive and mercenary, their mixed motives shed light on the harm done to them by society as well as on feminism's limits. While Mrs. Peachum claims to possess an "overscrupulous conscience" that objects to murder (11), she urges Peachum to murder Macheath on account of "necessity" (26). Holding that "the sex is frail," she yet believes the first time a woman is frail she can choose to be "somewhat nice" (21). Students do not find it hard to relate her moral confusion to what William Empson calls an "eerie insistence on the sex war."[23] To Mrs. Peachum, men become handsome in the face of death: the gallows rope creates a "charming zone" (10). Polly sustains the image of her "bleeding heart" by picturing Macheath's ride in the "cart" to Tyburn (26). Her wish to save his neck undoes itself, since she wants to "throttle" him with love (52). Declining to think of marriage in terms of widowhood, Polly enjoys the very prospect when she asks to stay with Macheath "till death" (53)—a nice twist to the marriage liturgy. The view that female desire depends on men's death is stressed by

Mrs. Trapes, the bawd, who announces, when trading for stolen clothes, that her girls are "very fond of mourning" (68).

While Gay undermines the sentimental postures his women like to assume, he is as critical of male sexual attitudes, showing up by his intersection of codes the hollowness of libertinism and the reciprocal structuring of society and gender. Claiming to be a "lover of the sex" (35), Macheath categorically defames women by calling them "decoy ducks" (41). The humor of this exposure resides in the fact that, though betrayed by favorite prostitutes, he pretends to be a gentleman hunter. His misogyny is stressed when he refers to woman as "basilisk"—the fatal mythical creature—and as "treacle" in which flies drown (44), the clash in registers undoing his dissociated, self-entrapping images. To Gay, misogyny derives from sentimental wishes to pose as heroic victim, a posture undone by untrustworthiness and prevarication. Peachum voices these wishes when he consoles Macheath by declaring that the "greatest heroes" have been ruined by women—a "pretty sort of creature if we could trust them" (41).

While Gay's text contains more motifs appropriate to feminist analysis, his delineation of female perversity brings classroom debate back constantly to his trust in literary and social hierarchies. The application of speech-act theory, semiotics and feminism is self-limiting, achieving pedagogical integrity only by establishing the reciprocity of traditional and historicist methods. The newer methods, in my experience, make students keen to return to biographical criticism but ready to challenge traditional overgeneralizations, such as appear, for instance, in Patricia Spacks's introduction to Gay.

Spacks emphasizes Gay's temperamental weakness and personal ambivalence, claiming that he unwittingly inscribed these features into all his texts, and that his "ambiguities are valuable" only in *The Beggar's Opera,* which she calls the "logical culmination" of his dramatic works.[24] This sweeping claim must be qualified. Locke's and Berkeley's epistemologies problematized identity in the eighteenth century. Their concepts of plural, discontinuous selves remind students that writers cannot simply inscribe themselves into their works. It is useful to learn that Gay was cheerful yet subject to despair, that he was careless about money though needy, and that he was an aesthete who cultivated plebian tastes.[25] But such ambivalences owe something to cultural ethos and to the procedures of life-writing: Gay was probably no more ambivalent than his fellows, and biographies fittingly stress curious and problematic traits.

Far from being written singlehandedly, *The Beggar's Opera* was composed by a member of a coterie: Gay was friend to Swift and Arbuthnot, a translator for Pope, and Secretary to the Scriblerus Club. Students like exploring the extent to which Gay's personal, authorial, and social histories are involved. That he appropriated well-known songs, that friends provided him with words and songs, and that he relied on sub-literary texts which have not all been determined or analyzed gives students areas of indeterminacy within the field of biographical criticism that makes research excitingly vital to learning.

Tensions between traditional literary history and new historicism are keys to classroom debate and course design because they show that teaching cannot be confined to received opinion, that literary knowledge is a matter of probability and hypothesis, and that critical pluralism is always involved in canon formation. Teaching *The Beggar's Opera* means that its representative status must be addressed from diverse historical stances, so that it may shape courses in which it appears. Thus, its mixed genres typify the literary era as well as Gay's *opus*. Depending on Gay's earlier successes, the play also embodies theatrical ideas that stem from the seventeenth century as well as from post-Restoration drama. Since its place in the canon depends on famous actors, influential patrons, and the ethos of political opposition to Walpole and the Whigs, teachers and students should undertake to revise literary history as a result of seeing the play as a work in its own right and as a text inseparable from its plural contexts.

While traditional literary history has documented audience response and political retaliation, as well as detailing Gay's reliance on his associates, on theatrical idioms, on the affinities between comedy and heroic tragedy, and on his cultivation of high art and popular culture, it has not combined these topics. Rather it has treated the discrepancies emerging from such inquiries unsystematically. New historicisms suggest that literary studies advance by exploiting indeterminateness, textual inquiries being best pursued relatively but systematically, with critical questions leading to metacritical concepts.[26] New historicisms do not replace one paradigm by another so much as expand the paradigm of literary study, showing why plural historical stances (diachronic, synchronic, and cyclical) are crucial to literary knowledge and the processes of learning. Texts generate a dialectic of social and literary signs more accessible to plural, interdisciplinary stances to history than to traditional categories. Yet, if they convert the problems of traditional literary history into a classroom resource, new historicisms fulfill this potential only when teachers and students realize that questions about texts in their times and about textual systems are best integrated, and that answers to traditional and historicist inquiries are equally necessary to pedagogical efforts to show that literature and literary study perpetuate concepts of the past capable of vitalizing society and culture.

Notes

1. See Hans Robert Jauss, "Literary History as a Challenge to Literary Theory," and Robert Weimann, "Past Significance and Present Meaning in Literary History," *New Directions in Literary History*, ed. Ralph Cohen (London: Routledge & Kegan Paul, 1974), pp. 11–41, 43–61. My pedagogical stance has been renewed by Gerald Graff, *Professing Literature: An Institutional History* (Chicago: University of Chicago Press, 1987) and *Beyond the Culture Wars: How Teaching the Conflicts Can Revitalize American Education* (New York: Norton, 1992).

2. Goberman's recording was produced by Everest (3127/2) in 1962. For Gay's allusions to popular songs and Italian opera, see Bertrand H. Bronson, *"The Beggar's Opera"* in *Restoration Drama: Modern Essays in Criticism*, ed. John Loftis (New York: Oxford University Press, 1966), pp. 298–327. See Eric Kurtz, "The Shepherd as Gamester: Musical Mock-Pastoral in *The Beggar's Opera*," in *Twentieth Century Interpretations of the Beggar's Opera*, ed. Yvonne Noble (Englewood Cliffs: Prentice-Hall, 1975), pp. 52–55.

3. On the affective as distinct from ideological aspect of popular culture and pedagogy, see Lawrence Grossberg, "Teaching the Popular," in *Theory in the Classroom*, ed. Cary Nelson (Urbana: University of Illinois Press, 1986), pp. 177–200.

4. *The Structure of Scientific Revolutions*, 2nd ed. (Chicago: University of Chicago Press, 1970), pp. 79 and 110.

5. *Validity in Interpretation* (New Haven: Yale University Press, 1967), pp. 6–10.

6. While his view that eighteenth-century prisons bred crime applies to Gay's satire, Foucault's historical sense ignores mixed cultural phenomena: see J.G. Merquior, *Foucault* (London: Collins, 1985), pp. 101–7.

7. Recent studies promoting critical pluralism and the difference between literary and critical texts include Harold Fromm, *Academic Capital-*

ism & Literary Value (Athens: University of Georgia Press, 1991), and David H. Hirsch, *The Deconstruction of Literature: Criticism After Auschwitz* (Hanover: Brown University Press, 1991).

8. John Gay, *The Beggar's Opera*, ed. Edgar V. Roberts (Lincoln: University of Nebraska Press, 1969), pp. xii–xxix.

9. For Gay's collaboration with Handel, see William Henry Irving, *John Gay: Favorite of the Wits* (Durham: Duke University Press, 1940), pp. 283–85.

10. For definitions of new historicism, see David Buchbinder, *Contemporary Literary Theory and the Reading of Poetry* (South Melbourne: Macmillan, 1991), pp. 98–119, and H. Aram Veeser, ed., *The New Historicism* (London: Routledge, 1989), pp. ix–xvi.

11. See Alexander Pope, *The Rape of the Lock and Other Poems*, ed. Geoffrey Tillotson (The Twickenham Edition) (London: Methuen, 1940), pp. 183–84.

12. See John Loftis, *The Politics of Drama in Augustan England* (Oxford: Clarendon, 1963), pp. 63–93, and Margaret Anne Doody, *The Augustan Muse: Augustan Poetry Reconsidered* (Cambridge: Cambridge University Press, 1985), pp. 30–56 and 119–58.

13. Oliver Goldsmith, *She Stoops to Conquer*, ed. Katharine C. Balderston (Arlington Heights: AHM, 1951), p. 27.

14. See John Bender, *Imagining the Penitentiary: Fiction and the Architecture of Mind in Eighteenth-Century England* (Chicago: University of Chicago Press, 1987), pp. 87–103.

15. On Gay's sets of ambivalence, see Ian Donaldson, "'A Double Capacity': *The Beggar's Opera*," in *Twentieth-Century Interpretations*, pp. 65–80.

16. On the performance history of heroic tragedy, see Arthur H. Scouten and Robert D. Hume, "'Restoration Comedy' and Its Audiences, 1660–1776," in Robert D. Hume, *The Rakish Stage: Studies in English Drama, 1660–1800* (Carbondale: Southern Illinois University Press, 1983), pp. 46–81.

17. Bender uses Bakhtin's term positively: *Imagining the Penitentiary*, p. 87.

18. For the impact of reformers on dramatic decline, see Laura Brown, *English Dramatic Form, 1660–1760: An Essay in Generic History* (New Haven: Yale University Press, 1981), pp. 145–84.

19. See J.L. Austin, *How to Do Things with Words*, ed., J.O. Urmson (New York: Oxford University Press, 1965), and Mary Louise Pratt, *Toward a Speech Act Theory of Literary Discourse* (Bloomington: Indiana University Press, 1977).

20. Roger Fowler, *Literature as Social Discourse: The Practice of Linguistic Criticism* (Bloomington: Indiana University Press, 1981), explains the objective aspects of discourse and semiotics.

21. Brecht often refers to "the Coronation" to link Macheath's reprieve to the monarchy. Whereas Gay satirizes social networks, Brecht attacks institutions such as the crown, the church, and the middle class from a specifically economic viewpoint. Cf. Elizabeth Wright, *Postmodern Brecht: A Re-Presentation* (London: Routledge, 1989), pp. 28–30.

22. See J.C.D. Clark, *English Society 1688–1832* (Cambridge: Cambridge University Press, 1985), and *Revolution and Rebellion: State and Society in England in the Seventeenth and Eighteenth Centuries* (Cambridge: Cambridge University Press, 1986).

23. William Empson, *Some Versions of Pastoral* (Harmondsworth: Penguin, 1966), p. 182. Empson also points out that Gay's women make "betrayal itself a lascivious act" and confuse love with death (pp. 182–83).

24. Patricia Meyer Spacks, *John Gay.* Twayne's English Authors Series. (New York: Twayne, 1965), p. 129.

25. *John Gay: Favorite Of The Wits*, pp. 32, 151, 186–87, 209–13, and 289.

26. See Kevin LaGrandeur, "Aporia and the Emptied Teacher: Deconstruction and the Unraveling of (Con)'Texts,'" *College Literature* 18.2 (June 1991): pp. 69–79.

Paradise Lost and the Theory Survey

J.M.Q. Davies

There are undoubtedly drawbacks to the kind of theory course that uses, say, the two excellent anthologies edited by David Lodge as the basis for a whistle-stop tour through the "-isms" of contemporary literary theory.[1] But for logistical reasons they are fairly common, particularly in more traditionalist English departments, and even where the curriculum has been extensively theorized they are often used to provide an orientational overview. Moreover for political skeptics who nonetheless believe that literature addresses the serious as well as the ludic side of life, or for liberal humanists who still believe in the possibility of disinterested critical enquiry, the *smorgasbord* approach has considerable appeal. The obvious objection of course is that it makes for superficiality, limiting appreciation of theory as systematic discourse and increasing dependence on second-order theorists for simplified accounts and background information. Even when lucidly presented, arguments and implications are hard to follow through from week to week, and paradigms seem not to apply beyond the special case.

Not all these problems are resolved by using a single more complex literary paradigm as the recurrent focus for discussion in such courses, but from a pedagogic point of view this strategy has its advantages. For one thing, it implicitly announces literature as the ultimate object of study, even as it explores the diversity of ways and contexts in which it may be appreciated. It also helps sustain a sense of being intellectually in control in undergraduates, who sometimes feel awed and in a sense disenfranchised by the interdisciplinary nature of much theory, and by the extent of what they are obliged to take on trust. Assessing the usefulness each week of a particular essay or approach in understanding an important work, by contrast, is a finite task, and it allows students to bring their previous literary experience to bear in judging. The emphasis thus falls on developing reflective, critical, and imaginatively versatile thought habits, rather than grappling with extrinsic systems.

Using *Paradise Lost* as the principal paradigm in an undergraduate course on literary theory might nonetheless seem like the high road from Babel to Bedlam, and it is clearly only feasible with students who have done substantial work in the earlier periods already; Milton, of course, is liable to be one of the casualties in the add-on approach to the curriculum, the erosion of belief in period coverage, and the emphasis on the contemporary, the more so perhaps in Australian universities, where even before the advent of theory Milton tended to be marginalized by the lingering influence of A.J.A. Waldock and F.R. Leavis. Yet it continues to seem important that English majors at least should graduate with some deeper diachronic sense of the shape of English literature from which other literatures in English stem. And from this point of view it is hard to think of another work that has quite the vortical position of *Paradise Lost*—at once a *summa* of earlier cultural traditions and an imaginative point of departure for poetry from Pope to Blake and fiction from *Frankenstein* to *Perelandra*. Moreover its uneasy affirmation of the cardinal points of Christian doctrine, despite Milton's implication in the political, religious, and scientific paradigm shifts of his time, makes it a uniquely fascinating cultural document from a theoretical perspective too, as the diversity of theoretically-minded critics to have focused on it testifies. So that there would seem good reason for choosing it over other strong contenders with more popular appeal such as Eco's *The Name of the Rose*, a work tailor-made to function as a centralizing paradigm in the theory survey course.

It is true that focusing on a canonical text like *Paradise Lost* goes against the trend in current theory to erode the distinction between high and popular, literary and non-literary texts. But as an encyclopedic poem which assimilates a myth or folk tale to a complex theological argument, *Paradise Lost* provides ample opportunity to make this point. As William Kerrigan observes, "in the magic folds of [Milton's] epic container we find political, legal, military, and pedagogical oration, drama, hymn, panegyric, love lyric, elegy, allegory, dream allegory, Ovidian metamorphosis, pastoral, prayer, sermon, exegesis, philosophical symposium, and the education of a prince—all of these kinds of speech act, and more, fitted to the narrative of mythical events."[2] More importantly, though, from a pedagogic standpoint *Paradise Lost* provides clear illustration of many of the concepts that constitute the point of departure for current theoretical discourse—metaphysical certainty, hierarchy, teleology, patriarchy, otherness, intertextuality, closure, and so on. And from the ideological point of view, as the crowning achievement of an "acrimonious and surly republican" who was nonetheless a "bold enquirer into morals and religion," it should in principle be acceptable to theorists angelic and diabolical alike.[3] It does, however, tend to impose criteria for selecting theoretical material other than what might make for optimal presentation of the development of recent theory more abstractly conceived. Exploring *Paradise Lost* in terms of the language of Christian paradox (Lodge, I.291–304), rather than of metonymy and metaphor (Lodge, II.31–61), might for instance be more revealing textually, but less relevant to understanding the linguistic basis of much current theorizing.

In the Milton/theory course I have developed to fill specific curriculum *lacunae*, the general contours (though rather more than the actual content) of which are outlined in what follows, I adopt the obvious, though only partially historical strategy of moving from what J. Hillis Miller terms "canny" or empirical to "uncanny" or subversive modes of criticism (see Lodge, II.270), because this factors in the need for explanation in an ascending scale of difficulty for students.[4] I spend the first four weeks substantially on *Paradise Lost* itself, highlighting theoretical issues which will recur as the text gives rise to them, and introducing such orientational essentials as intentionalism (Lodge, I.333–45), Hirsch's distinction between "meaning" and "significance," and Abrams' "Orientation of critical theories" (Lodge, I.1–26) as a sort of *vade mecum* for the course.[5] But because the spontaneous imaginative response to literature is arguably quite vulnerable to theoretical self-consciousness, I encourage a rapid common-readerly first reading of the poem—a Pouletesque surrender to the marvels (rather than the difficulties) of the text, making use of professional readings and Blake's splendid watercolors as advance-organizers.[6] A measure of this strategy's success or failure is the degree of animation and perceptiveness it kindles in discussions of some of the great questions the poem has given rise to in the past—whether Milton knew human nature "only in the gross," whether this bold republican was indeed "of the Devils party without knowing it," whether the Lady of Christ's was "the first masculinist" whose disparagement of woman really "arises from his own ill luck" in marriage, and so forth.[7] Appreciation of *Paradise Lost* as a historically distinct and alien cultural document is of course a more gradualistic process. In phasing it in I tend to present a conservative initial reading, emphasizing the parallels between Milton's dualistic world of providence, free will and fate, reason and passion, charity and idolatry, angelic and infernal dreams and so on, and, say, Chaucer's as interpreted by D.W. Robertson, Jr., and his colleagues.[8] This prepares the ground for a more genuine appreciation of later readings in Macherey, Hill, or Belsey. It also makes a point about the limitations of conventional periodization.

Though narratology is generally regarded as structuralism's most substantive legacy to canny criticism, in the hands of a Bal or a Genette it can, from an undergraduate perspective, appear a dauntingly technical affair. Reading *Paradise Lost* in the light of Tomashevsky's earlier, brilliantly concise essay "Thematics," by contrast, is a manageable undertaking more likely to make a permanent impression.[9] Virtually all Tomashevsky's in-the-main binary distinctions—between ordered plot and chronological story (the epic starts *in medias res*), free as against bound motifs which change the situation (Satan's invasion of Eden), immediate and transposed or reported exposition (the War in Heaven), omniscient (Miltonic) and limited narration (Adam recollecting Eve's creation), realistic and artistic motivation (epic conventions), defamiliarization (most immediately, the epic similes)—are exemplified in the poem with remarkable clarity. The embedded narratives of the War in Heaven and the Creation also illustrate the device of framing which has often interested more recent narratologists.[10] Such exercises induce a respect for Milton's sense of form that to students unfamiliar with Homer and Virgil is not otherwise readily accessible.

A more challenging, less mechanical, but still on balance canny question which opens up the poem for students further, is whether *Paradise Lost* should be described as "monologic," in Bakhtinian terms, or "dialogic" (Lodge, II.124–56). To a degree Bakhtin tends to think of epic as typically monologic, the purveyor of a "unitary and totalizing national myth" (p. 142) from a single perspective, whereas the novel is dialogic in that it tends to counterpoint several competing viewpoints without prioritizing them—"not a dialogue in the narrative sense, nor in the abstract sense; rather ... a dialogue between points of view, each with its own concrete language that cannot be translated into the other" (p. 151). There is clearly scope for arguing that *Paradise Lost* is in essence monological. The discussions of free will and the doctrine of atonement, Satan's carefully ironized soliloquies, the warning dreams and messengers, and the strong authorial voice never leave the reader in a moment's doubt as to how events should be construed. Yet Bakhtin also concedes that "monoglossia is always in essence relative" (p. 143), and many of the strategies he regards as dialogic in tendency, such as parody, "appropriating another's discourse" (p. 146), or challenging the "absolute dogma" (p. 140) of monoglossic works are pertinent to *Paradise Lost*. A pedagogically productive question that naturally arises is whether Milton's presentation of Satan, Sin, and Death as a parodic Trinity, his appropriation of the Genesis narrative, his ongoing dialogue with the culture of Antiquity, and his speculative disquisitions on the stars and the sexuality of angels are sufficient to qualify his epic as a dialogic work. In the context of Milton's Latin syntax and his (compared to Shakespeare) strict adherence to classical notions of decorum, a more difficult question one might also ask is whether, like "the novel since the seventeenth century" as Bakhtin sees it, *Paradise Lost* does not, too, reflect "in its stylistic structure, the struggle between two tendencies in the languages of European peoples: one a centralizing (unifying) tendency, the other a decentralizing tendency (that is, one that stratifies languages)" (p. 144).

Switching attention from text and context to the reader and the act of reading, though often a novelty, is not something media-manipulated students have much difficulty with conceptually, but I find that the response to Stanley Fish's unique modulation of traditional rhetorical criticism in *Surprised by Sin* rarely seems to come up to expectations.[11] Typically, students will acknowledge responsiveness to Satan's suasive powers and their sympathy with Eve, but remain unconvinced by Fish's line-by-line entrapment theory on the common-readerly grounds that one does not take in texts in such small units. A frequent reaction is that if anything one feels over-protected and over-directed by Milton's authorial voice and narrative controls. The usual verdict is apt to concur with that of Frederick Crews, who remarks that

> though Fish's theory was clever to a fault, the reader it invoked was a dunce—a Charlie Brown who, having had the syntactic football yanked away a hundred times, would keep right on charging it with perfect innocence, never learning to suspend judgment until he arrived at the poet's verb.[12]

Norman Holland's theory that "each reader, in effect, re-creates the work in terms of his own identity theme," on the other hand, which revives questions of intentionality and opens the door to feminist responses, tends to restore students' confidence in the human interest of *Paradise Lost*.[13] Undoubtedly the poem's historical and cultural distance from us makes it easier to see that "differences in age, sex, nationality, class, or reading experience will contribute to differences in interpretation" (p. 123). And even though students might not go the whole way with Holland's claim that *"interpretation is a function of identity"* (p. 123), in the right ambience they may well acknowledge a connection between, for instance, their subliminal disposition to share Shelley's view of Satan as morally superior to God and an insubordinate streak in their own character; or between their admiration for Adam's decision to follow Eve into exile and their romantic amatory expectations. A sobering antidote to this whole approach is provided by C.S. Lewis's remarks on "egoistic castle-building" in his *An Experiment in Criticism*.[14]

With hermeneutically more suspicious modes it is easier to establish subversion of essentialism as the common factor and to anticipate areas of overlap, than to help students negotiate their way through condensed summaries of generations of Marxist or psychoanlytic thought, which sometimes put one in mind of Byron's wish that Coleridge "would explain his Explanation."[15] Using *Paradise Lost* as a test case forces one to focus on the insights or wisdom yielded rather than the system. I also find Foucault's "What is an author" (Lodge, II.198–210) strategic at about this point, because students are in a position to appreciate that *Paradise Lost* is the product not simply of Milton's conscious intentions but of the complex nexus of cultural ideas and ideals he is giving voice to.

Freud is of course made relatively accessible by the pervasiveness of his ideas and terminology in the culture. *Paradise Lost* in this context is not as neat a paradigm as that old standby "The Sandman," where Freud's interpretation of Nathaniel's fear of blindness—evidently intended by Hoffmann as a symbol of his loss of reason—in terms of the castration complex, illustrates the disparity between historicist and psychoanalytic hermeneutics with unusual clarity.[16] But it provides scope for reflecting on the usefulness of Freudian ideas as critical tools at different levels of sophistication, even on the basis of quite modest primary reading. In the context of Freud's chapters on dream symbolism, the phallic and vaginal symbolism of the "wooded Theatre" (IV.141) of Eden, and of Satan's seduction of Eve "erect / Amidst his circling spires" (IX.501–2), which Blake responded to pictorially, might seem impressive evidence of the creative role of the unconscious until the analogues in Spenser and elsewhere are noted.[17] An Oedipal reading *à la* Barthes of Satan's revolt and seduction of Eve could be used to demonstrate the strategies of condensation and displacement on which psychoanalytic criticism relies so heavily.[18] While the congruence-in-difference between Milton's moralizing presentation of narcissistic Eve and Freud's comments on feminine narcissism—ending with the disclaimer of "any tendentious desire on my part to depreciate women"—might confidently be expected to raise a few feminist hackles *cum* phallocentric chuckles.[19] Such exercises are perhaps no substitute for Kerrigan's sophisticated Oedipal interpretation of Milton's entire career, but they do put students in a position to appreciate it.[20]

The fact that all these concepts—phallus, castration, Oedipus complex, unconscious, narcissism and so on—are redefined in Lacan's linguistically based system, the aesthetic implications of which require over sixty pages even in so lucid an exposition as that of James M. Mellard, epitomizes a recurrent perplex in undergraduate theory teaching.[21] On the face of it *Paradise Lost*, with its ego-based characters and Protestant emphasis on free will, might seem less auspicious than a paradigm by, say, Virginia Woolf to illustrate Lacan's vision of a protean self, constituted or defined by its interaction with various manifestations of the Other throughout life. Yet one of the most memorable features of *Paradise Lost* is the way Eve is seduced into violating God's law by the ideal self that Satan promises her, and in doing so introjects his attitudes and outlook. As Milton's entire action, moreover, is played out between the Freudian and Lacanian poles of desire and law, it is interesting to notice subversive Romantic attitudes resurfacing at the heart of Lacan's psychoanalytic epistemology. According to Mellard,

> the paradox of Lacan's theory of the subject thus becomes this: one can be a subject-as-subject only by submitting to the greater power of the Symbolic, to the Oedipal law of alienation into language (Lacan's version of Freud's castration). But, alas, that Law exists on the side of Thanatos, not Eros. The drive toward subjectivity, therefore, is always toward death and the Symbolic; the contrary drive—toward loss of subjectivity—is always toward love and the Imaginary. (p. 32)

No less thought-provoking pedagogically is Mellard's confidence in the value of psychoanalytic criticism "because its agency of authority—language, what Lacan calls the 'agency of the letter'—potentializes almost equally all four [of Abrams's possible analytic objects]—work, world, author, audience," since language is the one agency that "contains" them all (pp. 35–36). The question Lacanian neophytes are bound to ask at some stage, though, is whether the yield justifies investment in the theory —whether on Mellard's own showing insights available to the attentive common reader are not simply being translated into an alien set of terms and concepts.

Technical terms are of course more useful in some contexts than in others: the tropes of classical rhetoric or Tomashevsky's narratology would seem less easily dispensable than Harold Bloom's exotic coinages in his Oedipal (or Blakean) theory of poetic influence.[22] But the uncomplicated core of his intertextual theory is eminently debatable in relation to Milton at the undergraduate level. If one focuses on Milton's protracted preparations for his task as poet, and agrees with Kerrigan that "the plot of his life makes better sense if we assume ... that *he did not want to begin*" (p. 133), he might indeed be seen as a chronic case of the anxiety of influence. But how useful is it to describe Milton's relation either to the classics or the Bible in terms of Bloom's strong poet wrestling with his strong precursor?

Jung's influence has not been conspicuous in recent theory—perhaps because Freud's libidinized and Lacan's decentered ego seem more plausible in a secular culture than a system of archetypes drawn from the entire corpus of the world's religions; perhaps because Frye's great experiment, in which Milton features so importantly, has proved *sui generis* and unrepeatable.[23] But whatever its scientific status, archetypalism has entered popular culture, most notably through the work of Joseph Campbell, and both its cult status and its global point of view appeal to students, who may collectively be well informed about dying and reviving gods or fall myths blaming woman and the serpent. James P. Driscoll's *The Unfolding God of Jung and Milton* is useful pedagogically because the argument, lucidly summarized in the opening chapter, is explicitly counterpointed against what are regarded as the limitations of Stanley Fish and orthodox historicism, allowing students to take stock.[24] For Driscoll, historicism is mere "nostalgia," a text a "dead artefact" (p. 3) unless related to contemporary beliefs and values: if *Paradise Lost* continues to appeal it is because "Milton the artist subverts Milton the apologist" (p. 14) for Christian orthodoxy, and intermittently provides epiphanic glimpses of the truth. Building on the Jungian premise that gods are projections of psychic forces energized through dynamic opposition, and that individuation entails a "uniquaternal" integration of the four psychic functions, Driscoll draws a correlation between them and Milton's Trinity, with Satan as the reintegrated fourth term. Thus the Holy Spirit is associated with intuition, the Son with thinking, Satan with feeling, and the Father with sensation. The defensiveness of the Father in *Paradise Lost* on the subject of free will, to exonerate himself from responsibility for creating evil, seems to Driscoll to reflect Milton's own uneasiness about a Godhead who is wholly good, while Milton's dynamic portrayal of Satan shows that the artist in him recognized his power as an energizing psychic force. Blake is mentioned only briefly in all this, but both the insights and the method are quite Blakean—another glimpse of how seminal Romantic thought has proved. Aside from its value as initiation into Jungian criticism, Driscoll's interpretation might be turned to advantage critically by asking students whether it is any less dependent on unprovable assumptions than Milton's doctrine of free will.

Unlike feminism which is now part of Western educated consciousness, Marxism, despite its topicality and the continued presence of many of the social evils it has sought to redress, is not easy to make meaningful in two weeks of a theory survey to undergraduates, for many of whom the *Communist Manifesto* may be virgin territory. Trotsky's chapter on "The Formalist School" and Edmund Wilson's humanist objections to "Marxism and Literature" (Lodge, I.240–52) are both user-friendly, but they assume familiarity with the system.[25] Morover, *Paradise Lost* is not in this context an ideal paradigm, since the nature and extent of Milton's radicalism cannot be gauged from the poem alone. A way into the critical issues entailed which I find students actively respond to because the texts are so familiar, is via Franco Moretti's brief, amusing interpretation of *Frankenstein* and *Dracula*. Frankenstein's creature and Dracula, Moretti suggests, "lead parallel lives. They are two indivisible, because complementary, figures; the two horrible faces of a single society, its extremes: the disfigured wretch and the ruthless proprietor."[26] From this vantage it is not hard for even the politically uninvolved to see the Father in *Paradise Lost* as the archetypal ruthless proprietor, and Satan and his minions as the politically repressed or other, and to perceive that this in effect was what Blake and Shelley were proposing. And since Milton classifies all pagan deities as fiends, the point can be extended to colonial oppression of the heathen and social exclusion of the ethnic other. The exercise might not qualify as serious Marxist criticism, but it alerts students to the essential congruence between the allegoresis such criticism frequently entails and the hermeneutic maneuvers of psychoanalytic criticism.

More useful perhaps because more widely applicable, especially in feminist readings, is Macherey's notion of taking cognizance of what is marginalized or left unstated in a text—a principle which, as Catherine Belsey has demonstrated in her deft analysis of tales by Conan Doyle, can be effectively adapted to the classroom.[27] I use it in conjunction with select readings from Christopher Hill's *The World Turned Upside Down*, which contains a balanced summary of his views on Milton's radicalism in an appendix. The approach leaves students a little in doubt as to whether to regard Milton as a "leisure-class intellectual" whose "contempt for the common people is explicit," or as a republican "living in a state of permanent dialogue with radical views," but it does bring home how much his ostensibly encyclopedic epic leaves unstated.[28] It also raises doubts about the adequacy of conservative historicist readings and helps make the point that, in Frederic Jameson's terms, "a new hermeneutic model enlarges or refocuses corners of reality which the older terminology had left obscured."[29] From this vantage students are then better placed to appreciate Foucauldian arguments about the relationship between power and what is accepted at a given point in time as knowledge (see Lodge II.403–4). From another perspective, Edmund Wilson (Lodge, I.252) draws attention to the resemblance between Marxism and Dante's vision: the same parallel might be drawn with Milton's teleology, perhaps noting, too, the serene confidence (Blake termed it self-righteousness) the two faiths have so frequently engendered.

If the fortunes of Marxist-based literary theory appear for the moment to be waning, feminist literary theory emanates from a revolution at least in Western thinking that shows every sign of continuing success, and in this context, too, the versatility of *Paradise Lost* as paradigm is manifest. It might also be hard to find a more dramatic instance of how notions of what is radical shift over time than in the contrast between Milton as champion of the "Rites/Mysterious of connubial Love" (IV.742–43) between Adam and Eve before the Fall, and his current status as feminism's bogey. Here, encoded in the most eloquent and prestigious poem in the language, is the myth of woman's frailty, irrationality, and innate inferiority: "Hee for God only, Shee for God in him" (IV.299). Psychologically, this fall myth hinging on woman's disobedience is a clear projection of the male need to control and dominate, which women in turn then introject: "Being as I am, why didst not thou the Head / Command me absolutely not to go" (IX.1155–56). If, as Adrienne Rich suggests, "the very act of naming has been till now a male prerogative" (Lodge, II.333), here we have Adam caught in the act of the original patriarchal linguistic sin: "My tongue obey'd and readily could name/ Whate'er I saw. Thou Sun, said I, fair Light" (VIII. 272–73). Indeed, virtually all the binary associations Helen Cixous lists as tending to perpetuate male/female stereotypes—activity/passivity, sun/moon, culture/nature, day/night, head/heart, form/matter (Lodge, II.287)—are deeply ingrained in Milton's thought and imagery. But whatever Milton meant, or thought he meant, the extrahistorical significance of Eve's disobedience is that it constitutes the archetypal act of revolt against, and bid for freedom from male oppression conducted in the name of the Father. In following her impulses and seeking equality with Adam, she is the first female existentialist taking responsibility for her own destiny. And Milton spoke truer than he knew when he had Adam make a bid for psychic wholeness in following his anima, or Blakean emanation, and so find a "paradise within" him "happier far" (XII.587). Male students disposed to murmur about Milton's deep appreciation of Eve's feminine beauty, which leaves both the devil and Raphael abashed, might be reminded that Satan is the archetypal peeping Tom, and Eve in giving in to him the archetypal Bunny. And those who assume there can be at least no complaints about the division of labor in Eden should take note that during Raphael's symposial visit it is Eve who is left to prepare "fruit of all kinds, in coat/ Rough, or smooth rin'd, or bearded husk, or shell" (V.341–42)—think of the pealing! If doubts are raised about the phallogocentric course of fallen history one need only turn to the catalogue woes foreseen by Michael—exceeded only, as Gilbert and Gubar have shown, by the blight of Milton's bogey on women's literary aspirations.[30]

Having had their common readerly responses to *Paradise Lost* thus uncannily subverted from several points of view, students should by this stage be in a position to appreciate the main thrust, if not the philosophic niceties of deconstruction. If, in the debates between Abrams, Wayne Booth, and J. Hillis Miller as to whether texts have a core of determinate meaning, deconstruction arguably comes off second best (see Lodge, II.264–85), this is not the case with Catherine Belsey's *John Milton: Language, Gender, Power*—which illustrates the notion of linguistic indeterminacy simply and effectively and shows how various subversive strategies can be combined in a critical practice which is both exacting and common-sensical.[31] Belsey explores a series of tensions or conflicts in Milton's work—"between heaven and earth, authority and freedom, man and woman" (p. 9)—which reflect tensions at a point in history when "the flight of (imaginary) presence from textuality and the emergence of language as the instrument of meaning took place" (p. 14). *Paradise Lost* "cannot inscribe the Logos, because the inscription is always also a reinscription ... not the presence of God but the triumphant presence of the signifier" (pp. 41–43). The poem is at once an absolutist theodicy and a humanist narrative; Christ is both God and Man; the androgyny of angels entertains the idea of sexual undecidability, and "the Fall is a liberation as well as a catastrophe" (p. 60). Adam and Eve's choice

> deconstructs the binary opposition between truth and falsehood, good and evil. They choose humanity, not God, but God is not finally repudiated (identified as a knave or a fool, banished). On the contrary, in the final image of the poem Adam and Eve have each other *and* Providence. The choice releases difference in place of antithesis: it demonstrates that alternatives need not be exclusive. (p. 84)

Belsey emphasizes that her reading "is not necessarily one that John Milton would have recognized or acknowledged" (p. 6), her point being that an understanding of these conflicts is important because they are still with us, even though we may disagree with the way Milton and his age resolved them. But such passages can be used to recapitulate the historicist position by asking what Milton's likely response might have been. Students are apt to be impressed by the discrepancy between Milton's faith in the presence of a God (a transcendental signified) behind the Word, and their own secularized awareness (shared with Goethe's Faust) of the semantic difficulties; but as a plea for the general indeterminacy of language, is this not a special case? Also challenging is whether Belsey's study bears out Abrams' charge (Lodge, II.267) that deconstruction, too, once its premises have been accepted, tends to be self-validating—and if so, whether this matters. Psychologically the advantage of rounding out the course with Belsey's elegant synthesis is that it provides students with a confidence-boosting index of how much they have assimilated.

It goes without saying that all this is not being proposed as a model course, since educational contexts vary enormously and with graduate students one might explore Milton in terms of no more that two or three of these approaches at a much higher level of sophistication. My main point is that, even though theory may be inherently—and often excitingly—interdisciplinary, at the undergraduate level it seems important to counter its centrifugal tendencies by anchoring discussion in textual actualities. If taking on *Paradise Lost* and half a dozen theoretical approaches, each with its own complex etiology and technical vocabulary, seems like a tall order, this exemplifies in miniature the problem English as a discipline currently is faced with. It also underlines the need for a cooperative approach to finding solutions: the effectiveness of my Milton/theory experiment is contingent on the solid grounding in seventeenth-century literature provided by my colleagues. There is clearly room for a great variety of English programs which phase in theory in a gradualistic manner, and take advantage of what it has to offer without diminishing the value of more traditional methods. The danger with programs in which *literary* organizational principles are displaced, it seems to me, is that one orthodoxy may simply be replaced by another and the development of our literary heritage obscured. I would not claim that this is the best way to teach either Milton or theory, but I believe the exercise can be both imaginatively and critically extending in a way which exemplifies the advantages of theorizing. It is also an effective way of countering the drift away from the earlier periods that the pluralized curriculum has brought about: in some academic contexts students who would not voluntarily go near a traditional course on Milton will line up for one dubbed "Deconstructing Paradise." What my more ambitious students —those who voluntarily read beyond the course and try to integrate their reading—tend to find surprising is how many strands the Milton/theory combination helps to bring together.

Notes

1. David Lodge, ed., *Twentieth Century Literary Criticism* (London: Longman, 1972); and *Modern Criticism and Theory* (London: Longman, 1988), referenced internally as Lodge I and II respectively.

2. William Kerrigan, *The Sacred Complex: On the Psycho-genesis of Paradise Lost* (Cambridge: Harvard University Press, 1983), p. 195.

3. Johnson, "John Milton," in Mona Wilson, ed., *Johnson: Prose and Poetry* (London: Rupert Hart-Davis, 1957), p. 828; and Shelley, "Preface" to *Prometheus Unbound* in *Shelley's Poetry and Prose*, ed. Donald H. Reiman and Sharon B. Powers (New York: Norton, 1977), p. 134.

4. J. Hillis Miller, "Stevens' Rock and Criticism as Care, II," *Georgia Review* (1976), pp. 330–48.

5. E.D. Hirsch, Jr., *Validity in Interpretation* (New Haven: Yale University Press, 1967), pp. 6–10.

6. Georges Poulet, "Criticism and the Experience of Interiority," in Jane P. Tompkins, ed., *Reader-Response Criticism: From Formalism to Post-Structuralism* (Baltimore: Johns Hopkins University Press, 1980), pp. 41–49; J.M.Q. Davies, *Blake's Milton Designs: The Dynamics of Meaning* (W. Cornwall, CT: Locust Hill Press, 1993), pp. 51–85 and figs. 19–42.

7. Johnson, p. 840; Blake, *The Marriage of Heaven and Hell*, pl. 6, in David V. Erdman, ed., *The Complete Poetry and Prose of William Blake* (New York: Doubleday Anchor, 1982), p. 35; and Virginia Woolf, *A Writer's Diary* (New York: Harcourt, 1954), pp. 5–6, quoted in Sandra M. Gilbert and Susan Gubar, *The Madwoman in the Attic* (New Haven: Yale University Press, 1979), p. 190.

8. See D.W. Robertson, Jr., *A Preface to Chaucer* (Princeton: Princeton University Press, 1962).

9. Boris Tomashevsky, "Thematics," in Lee T. Lemon and Marion J. Reis, eds., *Russian Formalist Criticism: Four Essays* (Lincoln: University of Nebraska Press, 1965), pp. 61–95.

10. For details of the different ways the term "framing" has been employed recently, see Jeremy Hawthorn, *A Concise Glossary of Contemporary Literary Theory* (London: Arnold, 1992), pp. 68–69.

11. Stanley E. Fish, *Surprised by Sin: The Reader in Paradise Lost* (New York: St. Martin's Press, 1967), pp. 1–56.

12. Frederick Crews, *Skeptical Engagements* (New York: Oxford University Press, 1986), p. 124.

13. Norman N. Holland, "Unity Identity Text Self," in Tompkins, p. 126.

14. C.S. Lewis, *An Experiment in Criticism* (Cambridge: Cambridge University Press, 1961), pp. 50–56.

15. Byron, "Dedication" to *Don Juan* in *Byron's Poetry*, ed. Frank D. McConnell (New York: Norton, 1978), p. 183.

16. See Freud, "The Uncanny," in *The Complete Psychological Works of Sigmund Freud*, ed. James Strachey (London: Hogarth Press, 1955), XVII.219–52.

17. See Freud, *Introductory Lectures on Psychoanalysis*, ed. James Strachey and Angela Richards (Harmondsworth: Penguin, 1973), pp. 182–203; Wolfgang E.H. Rudat, "Milton, Freud, St. Augustine: Paradise Lost and the History of Human Sexuality," *Mosaic*, 15.2 (1982), pp. 109–21; and Davies, figs. 25–26 and 35–36.

18. Freud, *Introductory Lectures*, pp. 243–49. See Roland Barthes, *On Racine* (New York: Performing Arts, 1983).

19. Freud, "On Narcissism," in *The Complete Psychological Works*, XIV.89.

20. Kerrigan, pp. 6–8, 49–54, 177–78, 295–96.

21. James M. Mellard, *Using Lacan Reading Fiction* (Urbana: University of Illinois Press, 1991), pp. 1–68.

22. Harold Bloom, *The Anxiety of Influence: A Theory of Poetry* (Oxford: Oxford University Press, 1973).

23. See especially Northrop Frye, *The Return of Eden: Five Essays on Milton's Epics* (Toronto: University of Toronto Press, 1965).

24. James P. Driscoll, *The Unfolding God of Jung and Milton* (Lexington: University Press of Kentucky, 1993), pp. 1–37.

25. Leon Trotsky, *Literature and Revolution*, trans. Rose Strunsky (Ann Arbor: University of Michigan Press, 1960), pp. 162–83.

26. Franco Moretti, *Signs Taken for Wonders* (London: Verso, 1983), p. 82.

27. Catherine Belsey, *Critical Practice* (London: Methuen, 1980), pp. 103–17.

28. Christopher Hill, *The World Turned Upside Down: Radical Ideas During the English Revolution* (Harmondsworth: Penguin, 1975), pp. 400; 395–404.

29. Frederic Jameson, *The Prison-House of Language* (Princeton: Princeton University Press, 1972), p. 132.

30. Gilbert and Gubar, pp. 187–212.

31. Belsey, *John Milton: Language, Gender, Power* (Oxford: Blackwell, 1988).

"But You Must Learn to Know Such Slanders of the Age": Literary Theory in the Study of Shakespeare

Simon Barker

There is a tantalizing reference in the opening pages of Donald G. Watson's recent book on Shakespeare's early history plays to the Arden edition of *King Henry III*, and although one member of the group of final-year students to which I brought this remarkable discovery claimed to have been reading the play in bed the night before, an interesting discussion arose concerning the kinds of cultural assumption that would help define the reception of a new Shakespeare play.[1] The group's speculation was informed by its general reading in literary theory, as well as that "applied" specifically to the Shakespeare canon, and I shall return to this towards the end of this essay leaving the ghost-play *Henry III* for the moment to haunt, as it were, the endless work of Shakespeare criticism and the previously delimited canon itself. One of the group's conclusions is, however, worth noting from the outset.

Basing their opinion partly on reactions to the occasional attribution of fragments of verse to Shakespeare, the students agreed that the authentication of a new play by Shakespeare would clearly be an issue of *public* concern, guaranteed to claim the attention of the mass media as something of a *national* moment at the very least.[2] If the group was right, then this sense of Shakespeare extending somehow so overtly beyond those educational institutions which, some of its number claimed, were in the business of keeping canonized writers on a kind of life support machine (to the detriment of other writers' work), makes Shakespeare a singular case in terms of the relationship between the study of his plays and the study of literary theory.

In this essay I wish to examine this relationship by paying special attention to this central idea of the Shakespearean canon as belonging somehow to a *public* domain, and although I hope this does not imply capitulation with the "greatness of Shakespeare" school of thought, it certainly acknowledges it as an influence which has a currency in all our practices as teachers and scholars involved with the study of early-modern culture.[3] Unfashionable as it sometimes may seem, I feel that every study needs to associate itself with a text, or rather, to *issue* a text, and for those of you as yet unacquainted with Shakespeare's *Henry III*, I shall argue my case around the set of writings that constitutes the more familiar *Henry V*.

It is no more than a commonplace to state that students encountering Shakespeare at degree level are faced with a bewildering set of problems and procedures, whatever kind of theory informs their study. The primary reading is often sufficiently daunting, even if focussed by generic sampling or in a survey-type course, but to this is added such an abundance of secondary critical material that in some cases it can have what amounts to a paralyzing effect on students, resulting in a kind of retreat towards the safer and more familiar territory of their pre-degree work, which of course *seems* theory-free and therefore "innocent." Many a college or university lecturer reading this will deny such a retreat, or complain that it simply proceeds from the poor teaching of theoretical issues, or perhaps that it is a result of a phenomenon which I recall being acknowledged at conferences in the early days of theory, that of lecturers teaching Leavis by day and writing heavily theorized journal papers by night. But it is certainly the case that more recently, participants at conferences committed to the examination of the relationship between literature, theory and teaching have signalled exactly this kind of retreat, and while observable in students' approach to other authors or genres, it seems particularly acute in Shakespeare studies.

I would argue that a range of pressures can persuade some students that the "plot and character" approach is still convincing (and can convince their examiners), and by no means the least of these is the fact that most of us live in a political and social climate which reinforces such easy interpretation of the world. In concert with this is a financial and doctrinal assault upon education at all levels in Britain which has resulted in a demoralized faculty forced to manage overstretched resources in an atmosphere dictated by a replica of "the market" and the illusion of *sustained* expansion.[4] Literary theory is difficult (as well as exciting and challenging and potentially subversive) but all the more so due to the spectacular success of the ideological program which has helped reshape the institutions in which it is taught. What was sometimes overlooked is now apparent, both that the generation teaching theory is probably more sympathetic to the claims it makes for social change than the generation which studies it, and that the "traditional" critical approach has not gone away.

For teachers committed to modern literary theory this may seem a pessimistic view which fails to acknowledge the clear *advances* made in certain areas, most notably in feminist studies, but it does explain in part the recourse to "tradition" by students, particularly when faced with examinations, or even simply caught in the absorbing atmosphere of institutional crisis which seems to prevail in British education of late.[5]

The educational institutions which reproduce Shakespeare's plays by means of critical study are far from insulated against an influential and determined cultural agenda set out by a government committed to the production of a singular national history in schools and to a public celebration of history as "national heritage," thus erasing the international history and, dare I say, the *tradition* of resistance and alternative from which literary theory itself evolved.[6] As far as Shakespeare is concerned, the forces which accompany a retreat from theory are notably *available* due to Shakespeare's place in the wider context of a national culture, and because, after some recent hesitation over the issue, Shakespeare in one form or another remains a compulsory part of the secondary examined curriculum as well as of the various "access" type courses designed to qualify non-traditional students for entry into degree-awarding establishments.[7] It is depressing to note that while much (although not all) of the recent work on Shakespeare I shall want to discuss is of a radical and productive nature, the Shakespeare taught in schools in Britain remains characterized by a reductive and conservative approach.

Having said this it would be wrong to overstate this tendency. It is evident that the teaching of Shakespeare in schools has been influenced just as much by the broadly radical agenda of recent literary theory as have other areas of literature, as well as by a laudable movement towards cultural studies and a diversification in terms of canon; those of us working in degree-level education should beware of patronizing colleagues employed at institutions in which it is far more difficult to set the agenda in the first place, especially in the framework of national curricula and examinations. It would be a self-defeating assumption of the worst kind to regard the school system as isolated from the developments in literary theory of the last two decades, and not simply because our students themselves become teachers. What should be acknowledged is the *constraint* placed upon radical teachers, having, for example, to satisfy the ideological closure of examination questions while actually believing in a radically alternative set of questions concerning the text, the canon, and the curriculum itself.[8]

In this essay I want to outline some *strategies* for the teaching of literary theory in relation to Shakespeare. Keeping in focus the potential Shakespeare offers for the kind of relapse I have described (into a *seemingly* apolitical and therefore an attractive and powerful "traditional" approach), the emphasis will be upon overtly *political* forms of study, by which I mean those which hold to the political and mostly Marxist aspirations of those writers who first organized against the critical program (and its legacy) that had come to dominate literary and cultural studies between the First and Second World Wars.[9] The emphasis is upon the British scene, since I know this best, but examining theory in relation to Shakespeare for its political *discontinuities* requires an exploration of theory elsewhere and particularly that produced in America which has been termed, rather inadequately in my opinion, a New Historicism. A set of readings, rather than a "school," New Historicism is a product of theory's rather stormy Atlantic crossing, but it is also informed by theory's collision with American New Criticism, and its growing influence in Britain and elsewhere is notable.[10]

Shaping a Critical Context

Students encountering literary theory for the first time are best served, both in their formal encounters with tutors and through their guided reading, by being provided with a *topography* of the material. This is not the same as a taxonomy which can take them through an exercise which often means an exhausting encounter with an "ism" every week or so. It is also not the same as simply "doing theory" in the sense of practicing it, since engaging in the reading and understanding of the implications of theory is a practice in itself, and relatively devalued once it is viewed as a toolkit or a set of skeleton keys with which to unlock a meaning which was somehow there in the text, but perhaps disguised as something else. The problem is that the power relations in the classroom and the coercive nature of examinations or other forms of assessment tend towards historically given absolutes rather than processes.[11]

In two senses the idea of a topography implies that students encountering modern literary theory in relation to Shakespeare are given an idea of what has gone before. First, some account needs to be taken of the sort of critical approach which informed their school studies or other pre-degree work. This may seem a weakly liberal view, yet building upon what is known is a central tenet of most educational theory and one with an enhanced imperative given the material conditions under which teaching has to take place. Since a sense of the political power of the meanings produced for Shakespeare, both within educational institutions and in the wider (and national) cultural formation, is very much to hand in the assumptions which still dictate pre-degree work, it seems neglectful to waste students' recent experiences, and not to proceed from what is known to what is knowable. And if questions of power are at stake in the meanings we produce for Shakespeare, then the paradigm of pedagogic practice itself is worth referencing in the context of an author who, if I understand the traditional summaries of his worth correctly, is constantly *teaching* us something.

Classroom practice would proceed from distribution of two kinds of written material, both almost guaranteed to be familiar to students: examination questions (and/or coursework questions from non-traditional students' access courses) and examples from a selection of the sets of students' notes which enjoy wide consumption by students. Working in groups, the students would be asked to search for the assumptions in these two sets of material and for the relationship between them. The objective is to establish with the students the discursive framework within which a set of values and an aesthetic are established, and from this point it is easy to define areas which are *not* addressed in the questions or the students' notes. Much of this material clearly depends upon students viewing the characters of a Shakespeare play as though they were real, and the student as a *reader* of plays first produced for the theatre. For this reason students will have experienced questions

asking for character judgments concerning "behavior," "personality," "quality and strength of feelings," and "state of mind." Questions on language include examination of "imagery and tone,"
"movement" of speeches and verse. The nature of this critical inquiry is linked to the wider ideological positioning of a play like
Henry V in the answers provided in the *York Notes* series:

> One of the things the play does, then is to arouse and focus feel-
> ings of patriotism. National feeling is linked to war, and the
> patriotism is military.[12]

Students might profitably be asked whether in their search for the
kind of aesthetic judgment suggested by the examination questions, they are *necessarily* to finish with such an unproblematic and
univocal reading of *Henry V* as part of a nationalist symbolic order.
On whose behalf does such a reading work, and is there anything
in the text that works against such a reading?

Second, it seems clear that students need to be introduced to
something of the history of Shakespeare criticism. No doubt this
kind of work is undertaken in most institutions, but the *degree* to
which it is emphasized varies. Some universities and colleges run
courses which attempt to show how meanings have been produced
for Shakespeare, from the early praise and parody of his
contemporaries, through Johnson, Romanticism, and the later nineteenth century (with a little theatre history thrown in for good
measure), until the plays eventually emerge into the cross-fire of
the critical discourse of the present century. There is, of course,
something rather too comfortable in an approach such as this, especially if it tends towards the proposition that somewhere back
before the early commentaries were written, there existed a "pure"
Shakespeare somehow uncluttered by such discursive analysis and
"processing."[13] Better this though, than the rather greater danger
of creating a new orthodoxy out of post-structuralist literary theory by banishing from the classroom all critical texts which pre-
date May 1968.[14] The success of presenting Shakespeare in such an
extended historical landscape is, of course, to recognize that due to
the developments in a variety of fields, this is itself an uneven and
shifting terrain: an effort is worth making on behalf of the idea that
"literary theory" existed before "Literary Theory" just as there was
"literature" before "Literature."[15]

Working with the increased numbers of students now evident
on the British tertiary scene, a practical approach to teaching this
history is to reinforce lectures which attempt to survey the princi-

pal waves of critical thought (and also to determine for the students the rationale behind the selection of material as it is presented) by asking them to undertake a similar exercise with reference to a particular play. The point is to trace the lines of thought which substantiate the assumptions in the examination questions and students' notes by recognizing their inscription in the larger body of material which might be thought of as more "scholarly." Groups of students can research and select extracts for distribution to the larger seminar, explaining the choice and outlining (or even underlining) the key-words, values, and assumptions which have produced a reading for the play in the past. Casebook and Critical Heritage-style volumes are good source material, and the study might be limited (by teaching time as much as anything) to criticism of the twentieth century.

These two locating strategies are helpful since they reveal Shakespeare criticism in general as something produced dialectically rather than as a continuum, or at least as the product of a developing and highly charged debate (in which students' contributions become an influential component), rather than a body of thought arrested by the received truths of recent literary theory. The educational merit in the production of a critical topography early in a course should be that it specifically challenges students tempted to take refuge in a simple reproduction of a number of theoretical positions, or worse still, to retreat to a seemingly subjective interpretative approach lying *beyond* the paralysis I mentioned before, which determines a specifically conservative material practice.

The strength of this approach lies in its potential for defamiliarizing the critical discourse that has shaped their views on Shakespeare at school, or on access courses, and in preparation for secondary examinations. The spectre that haunts all engagements with theory, that of the "innocent" interpretation based on plot, character, and a normative judgment is not so much exorcised in this classroom approach as given a material presence and a contribution to the positioning of the student in the overall contest for the meanings of Shakespeare. It is no longer a safe refuge on the end of the field of study to which to retreat when the theoretical going gets tough.

Turning to *Henry V*, I shall want further to emphasize these ways in which students should be able to *locate* themselves in their studies, as *implicated* in the theory that is related to the production of meaning for the play, and therefore in a politics which extends

beyond the discrete zone of cultural activity implied by the notion
of "institution" itself, and especially at the moment when the institution turns its attention to the examination of an author as privileged as Shakespeare. At one level this is simply a call for theory to
be shown to be *about* something (and to reclaim it from a *belle
monde* tendency which is always at hand, ready to reduce all theory to the proverbial tale of sound and fury), but also to help students discriminate *between* theories and, given the political implications of some of the theory they are likely to discover in relation to
Shakespeare, generally to interrogate the ideas that shape their
study.

Three Ways with a "Text"

I want to support this position by reference to three related areas of critical concern, each of which enables it to be demonstrated
to students that beyond the tendency to see "theory," or even
"Theory," as a singular critical mode suggesting in itself a sense of
solution and therefore *closure*, lies an *open* contest in which are focused explanations and models of social organization and power.
In the short term, these may simply shape students' commitment
to these kinds of issue in the classroom; but in the world beyond
the institution they may also find another role, even a sinister one,
in legitimizing a diet of political belief and action. Given this,
Henry V is an easy choice, but I hope some of what is said can be
seen as relevant to other plays, just as it should be seen that my
selection of three critical "approaches" from the theoretical positions available from the work of the last twenty years or so is not
an exhaustive one.[16]

The three areas to be dealt with are those which, like others,
foreground issues of the relationship between the subject and the
state. This is a loose formulation, but one which captures the brief
outlined above, by *implicating* students in the critical discourse and
by revealing theory's *relevance* to the material world which conditions the experiences of students as they work.[17] It is my contention that however unwelcome has been the rightward march of
the state (in Britain and elsewhere), it has "politicized" students to
a degree which significantly outweighs the political commitment
to the left which is usually associated with the more encouraging
years of the sixties and seventies. In terms of the classroom, for example, while it is sadly no longer possible to assume even a liberal

setting for teaching and study, or even a liberal response to these activities, it is possible to elicit judgments on a range of issues (and from a wider range of students) concerning aspects of politics which might not have been on the agenda in those heady days. And however unpromising initial judgments may be, in the actual circumstances experienced by students (poverty, packed classes, the need for "transferable skills"), they are arrived at in an environment in which state policy is "lived" in an immediate way.[18]

In a sense, then, students have passively "done the reading" on matters that are recorded in some of the theoretical approaches to Shakespeare long before the plays themselves were addressed through the critical discourse. Taking wide definitions, the areas ripe for a strategic exploitation of this environment include first the "political criticism," which examines in an overt way the relationship between subjects and the state.[19] Second, on the basis that there have been advances here in literary theory and in the wider sense of the social formation, "gender studies" represent a critical area where students have long been reading the implications for their own subjectivity.[20] Third, since it operates in the public domain, and shows what is at stake in terms of national culture, the whole business of what is loosely described as "the Shakespeare industry" or "Bardolotry" can provide a productive and practical approach.[21]

Political Criticism

To say that all criticism is political, given the distinctive elements I want to emphasize here, is saying no more than can be said of all forms of writing. Students undertaking courses in general theory will already know this, and so it falls to the teacher to survey the *policy* at work in Shakespeare criticism. In fact it is worth noting that the innovations of literary theory were applied rather later to Shakespeare than to other canonized authors. For example, the kinds of Marxism which might be identified with the redefinition of the relationship between ideology and the base/superstructure model were seen first at work on texts produced in the period of mature capitalism and since. The move towards examination of early-modern culture in terms of a materialist critical discourse is significantly a product of the 1980s and as such is marked, for better or worse, by the increasing influence of a sophisticated form of deconstruction blended with aspects of Foucauldian discourse theory.

In order to develop an argument around the actual classroom practice which would follow an initial situating of students within the history of criticism and in relation to their own previous practices, it is necessary to examine some of the implications of recent critical debate for all these concerns. This is by no means a straightforward area, especially for a critic set against the reductive tendency inherent in the labelling of critical schools or influences. Yet if students are to engage with theory, then their teachers should be aware of a critical schism, notably with respect to early-modern scholarship, that has finally upset the comforting notion that despite eclectic sources and a range of methodologies, "theory" was cohesive enough to be considered a unitary body of thought, implying a political practice (or "policy") that was univocal.

Students will be aware in Shakespeare criticism of the familiar preoccupations of post-structuralist thinking in terms of its anti-humanist, anti-normative and anti-interpretative basis. A survey of the history of recent developments in Shakespeare criticism would further suggest that a focus has been the examination of the *historicist* nature of some of the most influential criticism which helped define the teaching of Shakespeare in the period of modernism and into the post-war years, and if we can speak of a concerted policy, then it is one which inevitably produced a Shakespeare *politicized* for the educative purposes for which the canon was designed. Although it would be a mistake to overlook the further post-war preoccupation with genre and aesthetics, which marked the proliferation of Shakespeare criticism during the sixties and early seventies (which is best read in the New Critical introductions to the Arden editions), or Northrop Fyre's Myth-Criticism and other anthropological approaches, I would argue that there is an unbroken line of historicist thinking at work in twentieth-century Shakespeare criticism.[22] Shakespeare criticism is therefore distinctive in the field of literary theory (old and new), and if we include that which post-structuralists would read as political in the work of that New Criticism, as well the special place Shakespeare has been allotted in wider *cultural histories*, it is easy to see that students will respond to being situated in a contest for the meaning of Shakespeare in terms of this unusually overt sense of "policy."

For many commentators on the contemporary Shakespeare critical scene, this is a contest which is being fought out between

British and American scholars. There is a certain symmetry in this alignment which endangers students' awareness of the issues at stake. The temptation to provide a neat conceptualization of literary theory by recourse to new sets of "isms" is almost overwhelming, yet the overly cultivated critical landscape which this produces tends to obscure the *discontinuities* inherent in each of the "schools" which are "established" for students' inspection. It remains unclear what exactly is embraced by the terms New Historicism and Cultural Materialism, though they enjoy a certain ascendancy in critical terminology at present.

Clearly there is a common antipathy towards the humanist Shakespearean œuvre established by critics such as E.M.W. Tillyard, F.R. Leavis, and others, which offered a specific *historical* image of the Elizabethan era as one of organic cohesion, rendered through a hierarchical apprehension of the world by participating subjects in a kind of "Golden Age" of history and literary production, although opposition to this view of the Renaissance was well under way before the publication of the major studies which have been associated with the labels New Historicism and Cultural Materialism.[23] And as Hugh Grady has recently shown, some of the theoretical basis which underpins the work of these critics has a mutual source.[24] Yet what is most clear is that critics who have volunteered an identity indicated by these terms (or have been unwillingly included in the paradigms which they suggest) share a sense of political engagement which is of *consequence* for students alerted to the ramifications of the work undertaken, in the much wider terms of social organization and power. Attempts to define these terms simply by distinguishing an "Atlantic divide" tend to smooth over the discontinuities in each "school" by offering short-hand analyses which sometimes come close to parody. In *Towards the Postmodern Shakespeare*, New Historicism and Cultural Materialism are clearly distinctive. The former, an American phenomenon, started in 1980 with Greenblatt's *Renaissance Self-Fashioning: From More to Shakespeare*.[25]

Although some problems are identified in Greenblatt's approach, and Greenblatt's writing so dominates discussions of New Historicist theory in Grady's volume and elsewhere that you wonder just how many writers are needed to form a recognizable school, Cultural Materialism (the British "family relation") is defined *against* this given American model. And Cultural Materialism clearly holds overtly political credentials that the "family" may take exception to:

There is a sense of passion and commitment quite different from, say, Greenblatt's personal but unpolitical accents.

British cultural materialism has roots in an activist British Left that give it different qualities, different strengths and weaknesses, from the much more academically orientated American new historicism.

The connections to a political Left bring with them, along with passion and commitment, occasional suggestions of the familiar Left vices of dogmatism and sectarianism.[26]

There is much to comment on in this summary. For one thing, although it is certainly possible to speak in *very general terms* of particular characteristics which distinguish some of the kind of historicist work recently undertaken in Britain from that produced in the United States, this sort of taxonomy *defines* the terms upon which each work of scholarship (or which author) is to be included, and is thus self-fulfilling and misleading. Many an American work of Shakespearian criticism evokes a politics and a sense of "passion" which would puzzle students faced with such indices in their reading.[27] Similarly, there is a certain kind of British work of criticism, inevitably labelled Cultural Materialism, that seems to be produced according to a crude formula which involves patronizing the memory of the late Marxist critic Raymond Williams, a pat on the head for Terry Eagleton (followed by a general rubbishing of his approach), and some crude assertions concerning Shakespeare's revolutionary zeal. Such writing as this leaves the larger socialist project which engaged Williams and Eagleton somewhat embattled.[28]

The great danger in reading criticism *through* a taxonomy is that the terms upon which it is framed are exactly those which used to distinguish "literary theory" (with its interdisciplinary sources, Continental "otherness" and alien style) from the homely common-sense and Anglo-Saxon innocence of what had gone before. Old battles are being refought (with students as a kind of traumatized civilian population) *within* literary theory, and typically in surveys which can describe Greenblatt's work as "personal but unpolitical," but that of the passionate Marxists as part of a "Manichean class-struggle ... projected onto disputes which can ill support such political moralization."[29]

It is not just that students with an eye on recent developments might respond to political criticism by noting that issues of class (and race and gender) have certainly not gone away in Britain or the U.S., but that the classification of "approaches" into the "political" and "unpolitical" overturns the one judgment that can be made about post-structuralist literary theory, that it operated on the assumption that there was no such thing as the "unpolitical." Restoring this assumption to the classroom allows students to read theory in relation to Shakespeare, by encouraging them to judge readings for their *ideological* implications and thus their implications for a material practice.

There is a sense here of empowering students, within the compass of "political criticism," to look beyond simple taxonomies (and especially those worked out geographically) for what is *at stake* in the criticism which produces readings of the play at hand. In such a scheme, criticism of early modern culture becomes a site for a contest over paradigms of power and authority. Recent critiques of the politics of Greenblatt's work, for example, have suggested that there is a marked incompatibility between his analysis of power and that of other forms of historicist thought. The subversive or oppositional voices which Greenblatt engages, previously regarded by critics and historians as striking at the core of the Elizabethan church-state (and thus dispelling the twentieth-century "Golden Age" myth of the Renaissance) turn out, in fact, to be a *product* of power in the first place. As a critical practice, this implies an aesthetics in which we marvel at the intricate seamlessness of this power structure. In terms of contemporary political paradigms and those subject to them, the result is one of paralysis and pessimism, since if opposition is the product of power, simply a necessary "other," then political opposition is itself capitulation.[30]

Having established that a very powerful dimension exists in such work, teaching based upon a move away from labelling "approaches" might at the same time, however, investigate the attractions of gathering such work together in artificial "schools," and with regard to the contemporary political scene, leading students to consider the critical views *marginalized* by such schemes. In fact the diversity of critical opinion on *Henry V* suggests a teaching strategy which would encourage students to range across the body of critical work looking for the way that its components *resist* classification. A model for this kind of strategy is to be found in the work of critics who investigate the political implications of the meanings they produce for *Henry V* by examination of Shakespeare's place at the center of Elizabethan revisionist historiography.[31]

Working to produce a *Henry V* in the classroom which would accord with marginalized views of what was going on in Elizabethan historiography might well depend upon students having at least a nodding acquaintance with the work of Tillyard on this subject as "background," together with a view of the way that Shakespeare processed the chronicle sources in order to arrive at the "text" we call *Henry V*, though at some point, for the sake of bibliographical accuracy, it is only fair to students to point out the instability of this seemingly fixed artifact, given the disparities between the Folio and the Quarto.

Working with source and interpretation (chronicle and Tillyard) unfixes the relationship between "text" and "meaning," and invites speculation on the relationship between modern reader and early-modern spectator as subjects. In terms of classroom practice, such work is profitably undertaken in groups, each rehearsing a particular component of the diverse "sources" (ancient and modern) which necessarily constitute the "text" for the "reader." With this work done it is easier to investigate extracts from the play in terms of readings which address the ideology through which meaning is produced. There is space in this essay for three examples of how work might proceed.

> But pardon, gentles all,
> The flat unraised spirits that hath dar'd
> On this unworthy scaffold to bring forth
> So great an object: can this cockpit hold
> The vasty fields of France? Or may we cram
> Within this wooden O the very casques
> That did affright the air at Agincourt?
> O, pardon! Since a crooked figure may
> Attest in little place a million;
> And let us, ciphers to this great account,
> On your imaginary forces work.
>
> (Prologue, 8–18)

Examination of the function of the Chorus in the play leads students back to the kind of assumptions that have been made about the relationship between the early-modern spectator and the theatre as a place of artifice. The commonly-held view of the Chorus' lines is that they operate in defense of the paucity of the Elizabethan stage in terms of illusion, and in support of the capacity of the human imagination fired by Shakespeare's inspirational poetry. As a framework for the play, however, the part of the Chorus can be said to have a role which is suggestive of the treatment of *history* itself in a play which is hard *at work* in terms of historiography. Thus the audience member is *invited* to work hard at the construction of an imagined real, while at the same time being invited to consider exactly the way in which that "reality" is made. The "unity" of the play, in Tillyard's terms, is put into question by a reading which emphasizes how that unity is structured. It is worth speculating with students that it is Shakespeare's most "patriotic" play (or at least the one which features most overtly a molding of the past for specific contemporary resonance), that demands the presence of a chorus to help the process along, and a chorus, at that, which alludes to this process not through the conventions of Elizabethan poetics, but through the materiality of *work* itself, forging for the audience the link between a "made" history and the construction of a place for Essex in the contemporary *Realpolitik* of the Elizabethan state.

> But now behold,
> In the quick forge and working house of thought,
> How London doth pour out her citizens,
> The mayor and all his brethren in the best sort,
> Like to the senators of th'antique Rome,
> With the plebeians swarming at their heels,
> Go forth and fetch their conqu'ring Caesar in;
> As, by a lower but by loving likelihood,
> Were now the general of our gracious empress,
> As in good time he may, from Ireland coming,
> Bringing rebellion broached on his sword,
> How many would the peaceful city quit
> To welcome him! Much more, and much more cause,
> Did they this Harry.
>
> (Act V, scene 1, 22–35)

The formal device of the Chorus turns out to have a function well beyond the business of trying to encourage an audience to see an army where there is only a small knot of spear-carrying actors. The unity of the play, in terms of the message of patriotism and the meaning for the Elizabethans in terms of the policy in Ireland especially, actually *depend* upon the Chorus. Addressing with students the assumed unity of the play's representation of an unproblematic organic history can proceed from this observation using this sense of device almost metaphorically: the contradiction evident in a play which resorts to higher degrees of artifice in order to present a "natural" truth of patriotism, has its equivalent in the other organizing devices which produce the traditional notion of

the play as smoothly narrating the Tudor Myth. The play realizes
in Henry's triumph the *hope* expressed for Elizabeth's state, though
not without having to cite the layers of Roman society which
Shakespeare so graphically described as detrimental to "national
unity" in the later play, *Coriolanus*. Pushing the parallel, and without the capacity to produce a complete (and tragedy-free) re-writ-
ing of history, Shakespeare's Chorus has to end the play by admit-
ting what the Olivier film had to omit, that Henry V's heroic adventure in France and triumph at home were in fact quickly over-
turned by history itself:

> Henry the Sixth, in infant bans crown'd King
> Of France and England, did this king succeed;
> Whose state so many had the managing,
> That they lost France and made his England bleed.
>
> (Epilogue, 9–12)

Second, for students working with the text in the classroom
(and reading sources and criticism in the library), the search for
contradiction and discontinuity continues when they are directed
to some of the further commonplaces of the orthodox interpretations of *Henry V*. A second case-study might be the presentation of
Henry himself. Throughout the play, Henry's right to rule and to
wage war against France is continually reinforced. Students might
be asked to select and discuss exactly how the image of Henry is
presented by contrasting scenes which construct him in terms of
the "naturalness" of his position in terms of his God-given lineage
and hierarchy (Act I, scene 2), and the much-discussed "democracy" of his relationship to the common people of his country, and
in particular, the scene in which the disguised Henry discusses the
war with the three soldiers (Act IV, scene 1):

K. Henry:	By my troth, I will speak my conscience of the king: I think he would not wish himself anywhere but where he is.
Bates:	Then I would he were here alone; so should he be sure to be ransomed, and a many poor men's lives saved.
K. Henry:	I dare say you love him not so ill to wish him here alone, howsoever you speak this to feel other men's minds: methinks I could not die any where so contented as in the king's company, his cause being just and his quarrel honourable.

Will: That's more than we know.

Bates: Ay, or more than we should seek after; for we
            know enough if we know we are the king's
            subjects. If his cause be wrong, our obedience
            to the king wipes the crime of it out of us.

                        (Act IV, scene 1, 119–34)

In scenes such as this the nature of the relationship between
Henry's "democratic" relationship to his subjects and the military
expression of the power structure which separates him from them
begins to be interrogated. It is possible to read the scene as foregrounding a contradiction between the ethic of war and the matter
of Christian conscience, responsibility, and the whole notion of
what constitutes the "nation" that is shaped through the action of
the war.

Third, it seems to me that further discussion of warfare and
contradiction in *Henry V* can proceed along a number of lines. Students may benefit from an inquiry which contrasts the scenes dealing with the common soldiers (often reduced or even cut from
productions) with extracts from contemporary documents which
theorized the whole business of the necessity of foreign wars to the
stability of the state. These suggest that Shakespeare was keying
his play into a substantial body of contemporary thought, the focus
of which was to idealize militarism in a state which, according to
many writers, had neglected a tradition of arms viewed as having
reached a high point in the battles undertaken by the real Henry V.
The business of militarism was never far from that of national
identity (as is the case with Act III, scene 2) or from the threat of
internal insurrection and subversion.

Alternatively, students brought up on the sets of students'
notes which describe the play as unproblematically supportive of
the just war, might be asked to re-examine Shakespeare's juxtaposition of Henry's heroism with the scenes which offer the audience
glimpses of the reality of that heroism-in-effect. Henry's attitude to
the citizens of Harfleur is revisited in Michael Williams' critique of
the king's position, "when all those legs and arms and heads,
chopped off in a battle, shall join together at the latter day." Students can be encouraged to gather other pairs of scenes which,
taken together, undermine the "unity" of the play in the terms set
out by traditional criticism, while at the same time fashioning a
Shakespearean hermeneutic of contradiction and plurality which is
a long way from the pessimism of the New Historicism. The histo-

riography of the play proceeds towards the comfortable model of patriotism, allowing oppositional views as bulwarks to a dominant power structure, only through a careful policing of these alterna- tives and a determined sense of closure in the face of contradiction.

Gender Studies

At first reading *Henry V* does not seem an obvious choice of text for study in relation to a criticism which develops the relation- ship between the Shakespeare text and issues of gender. Yet it is in gender studies that students will discover an application of literary theory to Shakespeare which best serves a classroom approach in which they locate their own intellectual and social position. This is not just a case of "having done the reading" due to the prominence of matters of gender in the world beyond the classroom, but also that gender studies represent the most highly developed theoreti- cal area in terms of their relation to issues of historiography, sub- jectivity, representation, and theatre practice.[32] In terms of the slide towards easy reductive classification of "approaches," gender and sexuality have, so far, been refreshingly free of the kind of consoli- dation into "schools" which characterizes other forms of overtly political criticism. Moreover, debates concerning gender are fre- quently characterized by an announcement of theoretical source and the political implications of the approach which is being es- tablished.[33]

Students reading *Henry V* will be familiar from the meanings produced for the play by critics labelled New Historicist or Cul- tural Materialist with matters of nationalism, myth, class and mili- tarism. Questions of gender can interrogate these issues, defamil- iarizing what are becoming, in some historicist accounts, danger- ously narrow positions, simply rehearsing the more traditional re- sponses which Graham Holderness has described as "either wholly positive or wholly negative ... either celebratory (patriotic, nationalistic, ringing with "England's glory"); or denunciatory (pacifistic, anti-imperialist, hostile to the "political" character of the Lancastrian kings)."[34] In fact there is a further investigation to be made of the ideological imperative of the militarism which read- ings of *Henry V* have produced, as well as the metaphorical rela- tionship between the act of marriage and territorial ambition, which certainly seems to have been of sufficient interest to Shake- speare's audience for him to extend the business of the play (into what we call the fifth act), in a manner which at one time disturbed more traditional critics who occupied themselves with an aesthetic pursuit of dramatic symmetry. In terms of militarism, contemporary critiques of Elizabethan foreign policy and the lack of a standing army were bound up with fears that Englishmen were becoming effeminate and too unwarlike.[35] *Henry V* can be read as mediating a position for the warlike male in relation to courtship and love: Henry's dealing with Princess Katharine, his "plain" approach and graduation of types of language appropriate to the occasion can be read as a kind of corrective, in terms of contemporary debate, for the "mincing" of the courtiers. That the marriage is fully tied in with territorial ambition and control needs no emphasis for, as Westmoreland says,

> The king hath granted every article:
> His daughter first, and then in sequel all,
> According to their firm proposed natures.

> (Act V, scene 2, 350–52)

The Shakespeare Myth

If it is the case that the treatment of literary theory in the classroom should proceed from what is familiar to the students, then a principal concern should be with the close attention that has been paid to Shakespeare's plays in the public domain. In this respect *Henry V* has a particular role, and has been for some time a subject of close inquiry, not least because of its association with a sense of "national spirit" in times of crisis (most notably due to Laurence Olivier's film version), and as an enduring endorsement of Shakespeare's commitment to sovereignty. In fact, it is likely that students unused to visiting the theatre will have encountered either the Olivier film or Kenneth Branagh's much-discussed attempt to reconcile a "classic work" to a popular audience, while at the same time endorsing the "market values" of the 1980s. The ideological project of Olivier's film is well documented, while the considerable dogma which attended the funding and promotion of the Branagh film may be neglected until the passage of years gives it new significance.[36]

As a classroom approach, attention to Shakespeare in terms of what we might call the sociology of his cultural status is well established, and students can read of this in accounts of anything from the significance of the Royal Shakespeare Company and its relations to state subsidy to the reasons why the Bard's face appears on British banknotes and credit cards. British students encountering Shakespeare's plays at Stratford may take pleasure from the fact that in recent years the bookstalls at the RSC's theatres in Stratford and London have been graced by the very demythologizing works of critical theory that would have been banished, had the "myth" of Shakespeare found itself beginning to be undermined by the attention of critics determined to deconstruct his special place in the official national culture. Yet the kind of approach which investigates Shakespeare's cultural status is a compelling and important one for three principal reasons.

First, it is closely aligned to the notion that literary theory in the classroom should develop from what the students know, and it is difficult for British students, at least, to have avoided some contact with Shakespeare in their studies at school. Second, a study of the "institution of Shakespeare" leads inevitably to a pressing concern with the world beyond education, due to its focus upon matters of nationality and, by implication, race and class. What occasionally surfaces in discussions of national curricula in Britain is the relationship between culture and the ethnic diversity of an ex-colonial power, though, as Michael Bristol has demonstrated, this is not an inquiry restricted to the British experience.[37]

Third, it is a critical agenda which firmly establishes for students a recognition that what underpins questions of patriotism and nation, militarism and patronage of the arts, is a concern with the overall value of Shakespeare "for himself" and encourages judgments to be made in terms of what *essentially* maintains his historical endurance. There are problems for students who too readily translate the myths which certainly reinforce the cultural significance of Shakespeare into an easy dismissal of his work. If literary theory has a commitment to social change then it is endangered, for example, if it engenders a *passivity* among students which would dismiss, say, the politically motivated representations of the plays in the theatre.[38] Yet rather this than a recourse by students to "traditional" evaluations of Shakespeare by means of a discourse which assumes Shakespeare's value as an embodiment of received notions of "human nature."[39]

Again, the most vital approach to these wider issues of Shakespeare's work (and biography) as an emblematic force in a cultural history, leads students back to some of the fundamental philosophical questions which can be associated with the advent of post-structuralist literary theory. A key might be the way that Shakespeare is represented as displaying these essential characteristics of a timeless causal human nature. Students might be asked to investigate the implications of the specific notions of human nature that are offered by agents responsible for those media which guarantee the survival of Shakespeare's plays in the public domain of film, theatre, and radio. An interesting text to use in this context might be, for example, a recent radio interview with Peter Hall, whose claims for Shakespeare include an extraordinarily negative summary of human existence.[40]

A practical approach to this area of study can involve students bringing to the classroom examples of material which uses image or references to Shakespeare in the construction of a variety of modern iconographies. At one time it was possible to determine a kind of semiotic table which would distribute the material according to categories such as parody and humor, advertising, or political discourse. Kenneth Branagh's 1992 production of *Hamlet* in London, sponsored extravagantly by Persil, seems to fit all three.

Conclusion: Shakespeare's *Henry III*

At stake in these approaches to a single Shakespeare play is history: the critical history in which the students find themselves; the way in which Shakespeare's plays have been framed in order to represent the historical moment in which they were written; the twentieth-century history which has shaped the students responsible for the representation of Shakespeare in their own work as scholars.

What is also at stake is a notion of aesthetics, and for a re-definition of this critics of the left might want to start to think along the lines advanced by Terry Eagleton in his recovery of an anterior meaning for the term as a critique of the state.[41] There seems to me a danger with Shakespeare, after all the valuable work done in deconstructing this powerful cultural signifier, of throwing away the political baby with the mythologizing bathwater and leaving the plays forever operating in the public sphere as agents of "right thinking," while the academic left simply opens a space for students to despise what they always found difficult. There is a sense in recent accounts of the teaching of Shakespeare in Britain that it begins to address a kind of vacuum, best summarized in Isobel Armstrong's positive and optimistic account of some recent stage productions in which she writes:

> It is not really necessary to ditch the category of literature and
> abandon Shakespeare just because they are fetishized by liberal
> humanists and manipulated by an elitist ideology. It is a question
> of redefinition and reconstruction. The category of aesthetics, so
> long despised by the left, requires a radical rethinking, along
> with the idea of literature.[42]

This was the view of the group of students which pondered the
discovery of Shakespeare's new play, *Henry III*. Even at the level of
the imagination the play already seemed to be moving towards the
set of assumptions that would claim it for the right, and in the
present political climate in Britain the discovery was almost
guaranteed to restore a sense of nationhood and patriotism akin to
that generated by the Falklands adventure. The last thing the
editors of the tabloids would do, the group suggested, was to
actually read the thing, so some suggestions were made as to how
the new play should be considered. These included the idea that
the left should steal the new play to save it from falling into the
hands of the right—a crude piece of scholarly intervention
perhaps, but a necessary one in the current atmosphere of
insecurity and intolerance which has turned Britain into a land of
cultural and material impoverishment.

Yet since the play did not actually need to be read to justify all
manner of jingoistic claptrap, and despite the crude nature of the
times, the students finally decided that the arrival of Shakespeare's
Henry III was an event worthy of celebration by literary theorists.
Here was a chance, the students thought, to re-examine what theory was actually about, and given the kind of criticism they had
been reading in relation to *Henry V*, a chance also to rehearse and
thus strengthen a socialist tradition that stretched further than a
tabloid editor's expense account—that of never being afraid of the
opposition.

Notes

1. Donald G. Watson, *Shakespeare's Early History Plays* (London:
Macmillan, 1990), p. ix. The reference is a misprint for Anthony Hammond's Arden edition of *King Richard III* (London: Methuen, 1981).

2. Apart from the occasional discovery of new fragments of verse to
enhance the canon, challenges to the authorship of Shakespeare's plays are
also considered noteworthy. Debates over Shakespeare's place in the na-

tional curriculum have featured regularly over recent years, especially in such quintessentially Conservative newspapers as the *Daily Mail*. In addition to these features, it is worth noting the more casual references to Shakespeare that pepper political rhetoric, especially in times of "national crisis." See my essay "Images of the Sixteenth and Seventeenth Centuries as a History of the Present," in F.A. Barker *et al.*, eds., *Literature, Politics, Theory* (London: Methuen, 1986), pp. 173–89.

3. I should admit that opposed as I am to the near deification of Shakespeare within the framework of an orthodox cultural hegemony, I do not share the pessimistic opinion held by some critics that his work is so saturated with conservative values that it is beyond reappropriation by the left.

4. The expansion of tertiary education in Britain has been a significant political exercise and one accompanied by some of the more dishonest of Conservative rhetoric. There is no equation between expanding numbers and financial support. Like high-school teachers, tutors in higher education have faced deteriorating staff/student ratios and standards are likely to fall. In the face of these material circumstances the challenge set for teachers by theory-related issues is the more difficult, while the political ramifications of theory, at the same time, become necessarily more apparent.

5. The British National Union of Students, itself under attack from government for its supposed "closed shop" policy, bears witness to students' responses to the crisis in its surveys of members' experiences.

6. This gathering of history into heritage has been the subject of a number of conferences and publications in Britain of late, developing the ideas set out in such work from the last decade as Patrick Wright's *On Living in an Old Country* (London: 1985). The link between this phenomenon and formal education is traced in my own "The Armada Year: Literature, Popular Histories and the Question of Heritage," in Daniela Corona, ed., *Communicazione Sociale e Testo Letterario*, Annali dalla Facolta dell' Universita di Palermo (Palermo, 1990). The most recent development in Britain is the privatization of sites of historic interest formerly in the care of the government agency English Heritage.

7. See Lesley Aers and Nigel Wheale, *Shakespeare in the Changing Curriculum* (London: Routledge, 1991).

8. A continuing area of concern for critics of the left in England has been the ideological weighting of school curricula, especially since the publication of Peter Widdowson, ed., *Re-Reading English* (London: Methuen, 1982).

9. For an account of this, see Antony Easthope, *British Post-Structuralism* (London: Routledge, 1988).

10. The formal links between New Historicism and earlier American critical schools is remarked upon by Hugh Grady in his *The Modernist Shakespeare* (Oxford: Clarendon Press, 1991), pp. 113–57.

11. The result of such a mediation of theory for students is the reductive reflex which gives taxonomic singularity to areas of thought which, in fact, are the sites of considerable contest: *the* Marxist approach, *the* feminist reading. Still more damaging, if theory is taught without an acknowledgment of its pre-history, is the assumption of simple equations, such as Marxism + historical reading = Marxism.

12. See Derek Longhurst, "'Not for All Time for an Age': An Approach to Shakespeare Studies," in Peter Widdowson, ed., *Re-Reading English* (London: Methuen, 1982), pp. 150–63; and Charles Barber, *Henry V*, York Notes (London: Longman, 1980), p. 50.

13. This comes close, of course, to legitimizing the allegations still made by students that critical analysis is simply parasitic and, by implication, hostile to a given notion of an aesthetic.

14. Parallels between the advent of critical theory and the events of 1968 are made in a number of volumes seeking to rehearse the impact of theory. See especially Barker's introduction to *Literature, Politics, Theory*, pp. ix–xvi.

15. The remapping of the critical discourse attached to Shakespeare over the centuries is a continuing process. Grady, for example, has recently re-examined the much-cited work of E.M.W. Tillyard in his *The Modernist Shakespeare*, pp. 158–89.

16. Other approaches would include, for example, that derived from psychoanalysis, or the radicalizing of Shakespeare achieved by reading the plays within the context of Brecht's dramatic theory.

17. In many ways my approach here would coincide with that outlined in this volume by D.G. Myers.

18. A symptom of the success of the last decade and a half of the right's triumph has been a slow decline in political activity by students (itself only ever a reflection of activity in the world beyond the institution), at the very time when matters of grants and funding would seem to call for most response.

19. An initial example would be Catherine Belsey's *The Subject of Tragedy* (London: Methuen, 1985), which takes a broad view of this relationship.

20. Lisa Jardine's *Still Harping on Daughters* (Brighton: Harvester Press, 1983) is a good example of this kind of criticism.

21. See, for example, Graham Holderness, ed., *The Shakespeare Myth* (Manchester: Manchester University Press, 1988).

22. See Francis Mulhern, *The Moment of Scrutiny* (London: Verso, 1981), and John Drakakis's introduction to *Alternative Shakespeares* (London: Methuen, 1985), pp. 1–25.

23. An example would be the early work of Terence Hawkes, such as *Shakespeare's Talking Animals* (London: Edward Arnold, 1973). See also the work gathered in his volume of essays, *The Shakespearian Rag* (London: Methuen, 1986).

24. Grady, p. 230.

25. Stephen Greenblatt, *Renaissance Self-Fashioning: From More to Shakespeare* (Chicago: University of Chicago Press, 1980). In *The Modernist Shakespeare* Hugh Grady writes, "Greenblatt's work broke the long, unspoken taboo within Renaissance studies of interrogating the relation between the canonical masterpieces of Renaissance literature with the horrifying colonialist policies pursued by all the major European powers of the era, including Elizabethan and Jacobean England. And he undertook his enquiry by means of a sophisticated notion of the subject partially borrowed from Lacan, combined with a sensitivity to the epistemological pervasiveness of culture learned equally from Foucault and the American anthropologist Clifford Geertz" (p. 228).

26. Grady, p. 228.

27. A good example would be Annabel Patterson's *Shakespeare and the Popular Voice* (Oxford: Blackwell, 1989).

28. This is ironic, of course, since it was Raymond Williams who coined the expression "cultural materialism."

29. Grady, p. 232.

30. For an analysis of the politics of New Historicism see M.D. Jardine, "New Historicism for Old: New Conservatism for Old? The Politics of Patronage in the Renaissance," in Andrew Curr, ed., *The Yearbook of English Studies* (London: Modern Humanities Research Association, 1991), vol. 21, pp. 286–304.

31. Examples of this kind of approach would include Jonathan Dollimore and Alan Sinfield, "History and Ideology: The Instance of *Henry V*" in Graham Holderness Drakakis, Nick Potter, and John Turner, *Shakespeare: The Play of History* (Basingstoke: Macmillan, 1988); and Annabel Patterson, *Shakespeare and the Popular Voice* (Oxford: Blackwell, 1989).

32. A seminal example of work which brings these aspects together in an examination of Shakespeare's comedies is Catherine Belsey's "Disrupting Sexual Difference: Meaning and Gender in the Comedies" in Drakakis, pp. 166-90.

33. An example would be the introductory remarks in Lisa Jardine's *Still Harping on Daughters*.

34. Holderness, p. 62.

35. See Simon Barker, "'The Double-Armed Man': Images of the Medieval in Early Modern Military Idealism" in John Simons, ed., *From Medieval to Medievalism* (London: Macmillan, 1992).

36. See Holderness, "'What Is My Nation': Shakespeare and National Identity," *Textual Practice*, 5.1 (Spring 1991), pp. 74–93.

37. Michael D. Bristol, *Shakespeare's America, America's Shakespeare* (London: Routledge, 1990).

38. An interesting contrast for students of *Henry V* is between the Olivier version and the play's treatment by the English Shakespeare Company in *The War of the Roses* (Itel Videos).

39. For a discussion of assertions concerning "human nature," see Alan Sinfield, *Literature, Politics and Culture in Postwar Britain* (Oxford: Blackwell, 1989), pp. 139–51.

40. See Hall's conversation with Paul Allen on *Kaleidoscope* (BBC Radio 4, September 19, 1992).

41. Terry Eagleton, *The Ideology of the Aesthetic* ((Oxford: Blackwell, 1990).

42. Isobel Armstrong, "Thatcher's Shakespeare?" in *Textual Practice*, 3.1 (Spring 1989), p. 1–14.

Part Four
Re-Viewing the Subject

Problems in Search of Solutions: Teaching Theory in the Classroom

Alan R. Roughley

The importance of teaching theory today cannot be underestimated. Students of literature must also be students of theory. From a practical perspective, even the most basic kinds of research activities are going to produce articles and books which require students to have some familiarity with theoretical approaches to the authors whom they study and on whom they write their essays. Of course all students and teachers have theoretical paradigms with which they work, even if they are not conscious of these paradigms as theoretical. Perhaps the most obvious of these paradigms are those which the literary discipline frequently took as self-evident "truths" that required little or no intellectual reflection: the name of the author as an author-itative signifier of the literary work; the role of the author as the originator and guarantor of literary meaning; the unity of literary form and content; and the representative or mimetic function of literature as an art form. These and other fundamental principles of literary interpretation were intrinsic to the naïve empiricism of the ideologies with which English Literature was developed as a university discipline during the first half of the century. While it is now possible to see such paradigms as theoretical positions determined by particular ideologies, it is also important to recognize that many students are still taught by teachers who continue to employ them as self-evident truths of the discipline. Such teachers may be opposed to theory or they may simply see little purpose in questioning what they perceive as non-theoretical issues. Some of them may actively fear and distrust theory; others may see theory as an acceptable part of the discipline (even if they prefer that others teach it). There is probably no one, single motivation uniting such teachers who, for whatever reasons, are not active proponents of theory. Such teachers still make up a large part of the staff in many literature departments today, and their influence has a significant effect upon the ways in which students learn about literature and the extent to which theory can be incorporated within a department's courses.

The effective teaching and study of theory is of course very much affected by the size and nature of the department in which one teaches or studies. In a small department staffed by teachers committed to concepts like the canon or the central importance of the author's position within the mainstream traditions of English literature, theory will often be viewed with skepticism or hostility. Teachers and students of theory in such a department are going to find approaching literature from a theoretical perspective very difficult even if their colleagues and peers are not openly hostile to such an approach. The situation where such hostility does exist is summarized in Cary Nelson's account of teaching in a department where a "large percentage of undergraduate courses is taught by faculty members antagonistic to theory":

> Many undergraduates ... never have any contact with recent theory, and those who do encounter the politics of the discipline rather directly. Undergraduates who become interested in feminism, for example, are guaranteed punishment for that interest if they try to pursue it in a variety of other courses. Undergraduates will even sometimes be prohibited from writing about women and minority writers because instructors consider these insufficiently important subjects for term papers.[1]

A student in my own department recently experienced a punishment similar to that which Nelson describes and was penalized by the instructor for submitting a paper on Shakespeare which contained more footnotes referring to Derrida than to Shakespeare. The ideology at work is a familiar one: Shakespeare is the great English writer and his canon is the primary focus of attention. Derrida is only a critic, and his ideas should not be given more attention than Shakespeare's text. Criticism should clearly mind its place and continue to operate as the "handmaiden" of Literature. That the student actually learned something about the ways in which Shakespeare's texts operate was less important than the fact that certain authorial and canon-determined rules had been broken.

Many students whose primary experience of literature is gained in such classes where emphasis is placed on the author, the canon and what frequently (if not misleadingly) might be called a "common sense" approach to understanding the meaning of a text, are going to ask why they should bother themselves with theoretical perspectives in a course when they can do equally well, and sometimes even better, without them. Assuring undergraduates who ask such questions that they are already theorizing, or that theoretical perspectives on texts are quite commonplace in departments elsewhere, is not usually a convincing enough answer to assuage them; nor is the argument that learning to theorize is an intellectual process that is an intrinsic part of learning to think. For theorists unfortunate enough to find themselves in departments like the one described by Nelson, where the majority of staff members openly express their dislike of theory, teaching can seem like a Sisyphean task. Even the few students who are willing to develop a theoretical perspective on the texts that they study are going to set aside such a perspective if it affects their chances of attaining good grades in other classes.

Theorists in larger departments are going to fare much better even if such departments do not emphasize theory as an important part of the curriculum. Large departments tend to have a much wider range of approaches to literature than their smaller counterparts, and as a result they are much more likely to allow and even encourage a pluralistic approach to the ways in which literature is studied and taught. The drawback with larger departments is that they can offer a variety of critical approaches to the subject which not all students are capable of comprehending. Unless there is a willingness among staff members to explain their own ideological approaches in relationship to those of their colleagues, students can become confused about the sort of approach that they should take in their own work. This in turn can lead to a sometimes counterproductive series of trial-and-error experiments which students must perform, as they learn that what helps them to achieve good grades in one course will not necessarily have a similar effect in others.

I have been fortunate enough to have had the experience of studying and teaching literature and theory in England, Canada, the United States, and Australia. There are many differences and similarities in the ways that literature courses are structured and taught in these countries at both the undergraduate and graduate (or postgraduate) levels, but one of the most striking similarities that I have discovered is the persistence of negative attitudes towards theory held by students and their teachers. While theory is more or less an accepted part of the curriculum in many depart-

ments in North America and the United Kingdom (this is particularly true at the graduate level in the United States and Canada),
there is still a considerable number of departments in both places
where theory is still viewed with skepticism or fear or a mixture of
both. During the first part of this decade in Australia, the country
in which I am currently teaching, the debate about the use and effectiveness of theory in the teaching of literature has only recently
begun to emerge in many places.

To attempt to teach theory without giving some serious consideration to current debates about theory would leave one in a
naïve, if not completely untenable, position. Expecting students to
come to terms with the complexities of these debates would be
equally naïve and would probably discourage many students from
studying theory. Consider, for example, the kind of response that
Nelson's introductory summary to theoretical developments over
the last twenty years might produce in an average, first- or second-
year undergraduate:

> One conclusion we can draw from the last 20 volatile years is that
> theory is not a transcendent, unchanging category of thought but
> rather a socially and politically constituted domain of discursive,
> institutional and interpersonal practices. It is not merely, there-
> fore, that the content of theory courses changes over time, but
> also that the cultural space occupied by theory, the cultural func-
> tion that it serves, and the very nature of the activities encom-
> passed by the notion of theorizing are continually open to ·
> change.[2]

Setting aside the important question of the relationships between
theory and politics (and theory clearly has significant political implications), this introduction demonstrates the level of rhetorical
sophistication that is required in order to comprehend writing on
theory that is intended for an audience with some knowledge of
theory. For a student with little knowledge of theory and its developments over the past twenty years, the passage would make little
sense. While Nelson's passage attempts to define what theory is
not, it says nothing of what it *is*. The level at which one approaches
the introduction of theory to students is something that needs careful consideration in the construction of any course with a theoretical component. While this is obvious, the discouraged and frustrated complaints that I have heard from many students suggest a
common situation in which the obvious is *not* being stated.

Many students faced with a passage like Nelson's are going to
view it as they view theory for the first time: they perceive it as a

complex, confusing, and bewildering mixture of ideas and terms with little or no relevance to the literary texts that they are studying. Teachers with a limited amount of theoretical experience may share this view and unconsciously reinforce it in their students. Faced with the challenges of coming to terms with literary texts— and particularly the figurative and "difficult" language of poetry or other texts which rely heavily on metaphor, metonymy and other figurative techniques—students can perceive the reading of theoretical texts as an undesirable and unnecessary chore that must be performed in addition to the reading of literature and writing of essays that must be done to complete course requirements. The traditional distinction between theory and literature does little to alter such perceptions. The problems are many. One must find a way of introducing students to theory without alienating them; of helping them to understand that theory is not simply an adjunct to Literature but an intrinsic part of both Literature and their own intellectual development; and of making them aware of the anti-theoretical, and sometimes anti-intellectual, ideologies that they will probably encounter in some of their teachers and fellow students.

The range of texts devoted to theory is very wide and growing more so at the present time. The range of texts which focus on introducing students to theoretical issues is more limited, but still offers a choice that ranges from dictionaries of literary and critical terms through basic introductions to various critical approaches (New Criticism, Marxism, Structuralism, Semiotics, Feminism, Poststructuralism, and Cultural Theory, etc.), to more challenging collections of samples from theorists of various schools. While these texts have their obvious uses, it is difficult to find one text suitable for the wide range of interests and abilities that one often encounters in a typical undergraduate class (if there is such a thing). Students who have difficulties in understanding fundamental literary terms and techniques often find any theoretical text difficult to deal with. Then there are students who may find the comprehension of theoretical terms and issues a little easier, but who sometimes have problems in applying the theory to the literature that they read, or indeed in understanding why theoretical approaches are necessary at all. As a student once asked me, "I can understand what the characters are doing in this story, so why do we need to bother with all this theory stuff?" More advanced students may have fewer difficulties, but they still need guidelines in understanding how to read texts from various critical frameworks and in bridging the traditionally perceived gap between the literary text and the theoretical method.

In introducing first-year students (or senior students who have had a limited theoretical experience) to theory, I find it helpful to use introductory theoretical texts, and to augment readings from these texts with some fundamental theoretical information which gives them the opportunity to become familiar with a few comparatively simple concepts. The importance of the choice of the text cannot be stressed too much. A text like Philip Rice and Patricia Waugh's *Modern Literary Theory: A Reader*, for example, offers an excellent selection of theoretical essays for senior undergraduates, but my experience has been that first-year students find the complexities of the material intimidating.[3] A text like Wilfred Guerin's *A Handbook of Critical Approaches to Literature* is much more accessible for students who are being introduced to theory.[4] It provides models of exegeses from various critical positions that focus on four target texts which can be easily incorporated into an introductory or junior undergraduate course.

Such a text should be augmented with material that the students can use to help them understand their theoretical readings, and to follow theoretical developments that have influenced historical attitudes to literature and language in general. I begin by introducing them to the original Greek concept of theory and encouraging them to investigate the historical changes in the semantic values attached to the term "subject" that have occurred since the eighteenth century. The former enables them to understand how theorizing can itself be a method that is not necessarily separate from other concepts of method or practice; the latter can help them to come to terms with polysemy in relation to both their own writing and the texts that they study. The differing semantic values attached to "subject" can also offer a useful pedagogic framework for enabling students to grasp the distinctions between the metaphoric and metonymic axes of meaning. They can also be used to help students to come to terms with the related distinction between the synchronic and diachronic aspects of linguistic operations. Of course this sort of material has to be presented over time. The material that I am suggesting as a useful introduction to theory should probably be offered over a one-semester period.

A considerable amount of resistance to theory seems to arise from students' notions of theory as a set of abstractions couched in an esoteric language that is difficult to comprehend. Explaining that theory is something which they already do in their reading and writing can help to overcome this resistance. The etymological derivation of theory from *theorein*, or "to behold," is a useful starting point. Asking students how they have already looked at, and made sense of, texts with which they have some familiarity usually brings a useful set of responses that can provide the basis for a discussion in which the students can understand their own reading strategies as theoretical endeavors. Helping students to understand the distinctions between physical and intellectual "sight" also provides the opportunity for investigating the nature of metaphor. Once they grasp how the physical process of seeing is carried across to the process of intellectual apprehension, they can grasp the fundamental metaphoric process with ease. At this point one can lead students into an exploration of traditional literary metaphors as well as the philosophical use of metaphor that theorists like Derrida find so important in theory and philosophy.[5]

Few students find it difficult to describe what a particular novel or story is about. Many of them will answer such a question with a simple character and/or plot summary, but such summaries can be used to show students how they are already using some sort of theory in order to explain their understanding of fictional structures. Because of the widespread influence of Aristotle's *Poetics* in Western literary theory, many students work with simple variations of notions of plot and character that are similar to those in Aristotle's text. Helping them to compare their own distinctions with those of Aristotle is a valuable pedagogical exercise. It gives an historical context for the basis of theory; it provides the opportunity for comparing a classical theory with a modern adaptation of it (Northrop Frye's "Theory of Symbols" is useful for this purpose); and it helps students to understand that in distinguishing between plot and character they are already theorizing along lines similar to those followed by a major, classical philosophical theorist.[6] While teaching Aristotle's *Poetics* to students is no different to what many teachers of literature have done since literature became acceptable as a university discipline, teaching it as a method of theorizing that is similar to the ways in which students already read can help students to overcome some of their fears and doubts about theory as a difficult and unnecessary way of approaching literature.

Once students realize that their own understanding of plot and character comes from a theoretical perspective similar to that offered in the *Poetics*, they are usually more receptive to considering the other four elements of tragedy (thought, spectacle, diction, and

music) identified by Aristotle as useful tools for their own readings
of fictional narratives. Their own understanding of plot structure
can also be theoretically formalized using Aristotle's criteria for the
tripartite construction of a well-made tragedy. Using Frye's adaptation of these terms for non-dramatic genres provides students
with a useful taxonomy for their own interpretations. Frye's translations of Aristotle's terms and his arrangement of these terms into
the two tripartite groups of *mythos, ethos, dianoia,* and *lexis, opsis,
melos,* provide the students with the following taxonomic system
for textual analysis:

Heading	*Aspect of the Text*
(1) Mythos	Plot, Syntax, and Grammar
(2) Ethos	Character, Moral Positions, and Authors' Positions in relation to the reader (classical genres of lyric, narrative, and drama)
(3) Dianoia	Thought, Theme, and Content
(4) Opsis	Images and Visual Aspects of Theatre, Film, etc.
(5) Lexis	Diction, Semantics, Denotation, and Connotation
(6) Melos	Phonetics, Rhyme, Rhythm, and Metre

Frye's complex, circular and hierarchical taxonomic system is
rarely given much attention in contemporary theoretical studies,
yet his adaptation and use of Aristotle's terms remains a valuable
pedagogical tool. It provides students with a more traditional,
"literary" context for theory and offers a useful introduction to the
principle of polysemy which Frye foregrounds in establishing the
various levels on which he sees symbols operating. Because Frye's
system is organized according to a linear, hierarchical model, it can
also be used to familiarize students with the concept of the "model
of the line" that poststructuralist critics like Derrida see operating
in phallogocentrism's "repression of pluri-dimensional symbolic
thought." From a Derridean perspective, the "linear model" is the
"epic model."[7] It is of course in both biblical and classical epic
forms that Frye locates many of the archetypes for subsequent literature.

At this point there is the opportunity to introduce students to some of the fundamental ideological differences between a more traditional, literary critic like Frye and the poststructuralist, analytic methods of Derrida. From a poststructuralist perspective, Frye's hierarchical taxonomy operates on a linear model as it divides and categorizes Literature into its component genres and polysemic levels of operation. It participates in a repression of the very polysemy that it seeks to explain by separating the various elements of polysemy into single units that can be isolated for critical examination. At the same time, Frye's humanist perspective views literature as an organically constructed and developing body of words giving expression to humanity's desires, hopes and aspirations. It sees Literature offering us unattainable ideals that we nevertheless continue to hold in order to educate ourselves. Frye affirms the humanistic values of literature; Derrida questions the use of literature as a term that can be applied to writing which questions the very ideals that Frye sees as important. This necessarily simplistic introduction to the differences in the two positions can also be used to outline some of the basic distinctions between structuralist and poststructuralist theories in a way that opens up paths for future investigation as the students develop in their critical thinking.

Because of the number of semantic values available for the term "subject" (the *OED* lists over twenty semantic and grammatical senses of the term), it can be used as an introduction to polysemy and a variety of grammatical functions that students can explore in their own analyses. Students already have some sense of the subject that they are studying and of the subjects on which they write. They also have various notions of the functions of grammatical subjects, and these concepts of the subject can be used in helping students to practice their own theoretical interpretations. They can also be used to prepare students for more difficult, poststructuralist ideas on the operations of the subject that they will encounter as they continue with their study of theory.

The poststructuralist concept of the instability of the subject can be approached gradually through the various functions of the subject in poetry. Donne's Sonnet 10, "Death Be Not Proud," provides a useful if arbitrary example. Students should be directed to the various operations of the subject in the poem. Even the first two lines are sufficient to allow students to become familiar with several notions of the subject working simultaneously: "Death, be not proud, though some have called thee/ Mighty and dreadful, for thou art not so." Students have little difficulty grasping the function of death as the subject of this poem or of "some" as the subject of the subordinate clause, "though some have called thee." They can be made aware of more complex operations of the subject through a consideration of Death's dual role as the subject of the poem and the object of the persona's address: it is at once the subject of the persona's speech, and, as the personified receiver of the persona's words, the object, or addressee, of the discourse. The poem's multiple subjects can also be used to prepare students for such complex ideas on the subject as Julia Kristeva's theory of the splitting of the subject of the self in language.

In Kristeva's theory, the subject becomes split as it enters language, and this splitting is part of the "psychic aspect of writing as trace of a dialogue with oneself (with another) ... as a splitting of the writer into subject of enunciation and subject of utterance."[8] Students can gain some insight into this splitting by considering how their own writing requires them to occupy at least two positions: that of the subject who writes or enunciates and that of the subject that they articulate in their writing. They could also be encouraged to explore the Donne poem in terms of the similar distinction between the fictional persona as the subject who enunciates the address to death and the subject of death as the subject of the poem as an utterance, or articulation, of death's attributes and functions. At this point there is also the possibility of introducing students to the related, psychoanalytic theory of the splitting of the subject that occurs at the mirror stage of development described by Lacan.[9] This is a complex theory, but with some simplification, students can approach it through the concept of the split subject that we have examined. Some awareness of Lacan's theory provides the basis for a later investigation of psychoanalytic theory in more detail.

The historical developments that have occurred since the eighteenth century in concepts of the subject and the self can also be fruitfully explored through the idea of language itself as a subject. A valuable, historical context for these developments are the two major shifts, or "discontinuities" in the development of language from the Renaissance to the modern period that are defined by Michel Foulcault. Prior to its subjection to principles of reason in the eighteenth century (and this subjection can be drawn to the attention of students as another example of the polysemy of "subject"), language had an ontological quality which it lost as it came to be dominated by reason and function primarily as a means of representation subjected to the scientific and logical principles that result in the production of dictionaries. These dictionaries can be considered as the ordering of language according to a scientific, logical taxonomy not unlike that employed by Frye in his *Anatomy of Criticism*.

Following the eighteenth century, language slowly started to regain some of the qualities that it lost as it became subjected to reason and logic. As Foucault suggests, the border between language as Neoclassical and Modernist subject,

> had been definitely crossed when words ceased to intersect with representations and to provide a spontaneous grid for the knowledge of things. At the beginning of the nineteenth century, they rediscovered their ancient, enigmatic density.... Once detached from representation, language has existed right up to our own day, only in a dispersed way: ... for those who wish to achieve a formalisation, language must strip itself of its concrete content ... language may sometimes arise for its own sake in an act of writing that designates nothing other than itself.[10]

These changes in the ideas of language as a subject are something that can be used to help students comprehend mimetic theory and representation in language, as well as the self-reflective or self-referential aspect of language that is so important in modernist and post-modernist writing and structuralist and poststructuralist theories about writing and language.

These two shifts in language as a subject are also closely related to the linking of language and the structure of the self that one finds in Freudian and post-Freudian psychoanalysis. Jacques Lacan's investigation of "The Freudian Unconscious and Ours" explains how the "combinatory operation" of linguistics produces a linguistic structure "that gives its status to the unconscious."[11] The developments in language and ideas of the self can also be drawn together for students with the concept of the subject in a way that can provide the students with further examples of the multi-symbolic, or polysemous, semantic values of "subject" and an awareness of diachronic shifts that occur in the meanings of the term.

These areas that I have mapped out as adjuncts to the text chosen to introduce students to theory are offered as guidelines which one might follow over a fairly extended period of time. I have found that they can be taught over a semester, but a longer period of time would be necessary for the students to explore these areas in depth. The advantage to the areas that I have sketched out is that they can be related to each other in a number of ways, and this makes them more readily accessible to the students. They are also areas that can be explored quite quickly or over a longer period of time depending on the time available. Each of the areas can be used as a central, focal point to which the other areas can be related. The historical developments in language identified by Foucault can be used to explore changing developments in the mimetic or representational function language and literature, as well as the polysemous operations of the subject that allow developments in the subject of language to be related to developments in, for instance, the subject as the self; the subject of literature; and the various subjects represented by language according to theories of mimesis.

Representations of the subject can also be used to direct students towards psychological concepts of the self and poststructuralist notions of the self and the subject in writing. Alternatively, the idea of the subject can be explored through Frye's humanist ideas on the role of literature, and Frye's taxonomy can be used as a practical tool for interpretation or as a means for investigating the classical, historical influences on traditional literary interpretation. Of course, one could also direct students from Frye's use of Aristotle into the more philosophical investigations of language and metaphor found in Derrida. The advantage of using such radically different approaches as those provided by critics like Frye and Derrida is that they allow for a comparative investigation of the different kinds of ideological approaches to language and literature that students are likely to experience in classes taught by teachers with different attitudes towards theory.

Notes

1. Cary Nelson, "Introduction: Teaching Theory Today," *College Literature*, 18.2 (1991), pp. 1–4.

2. Nelson, p. 1.

3. Philip Rice and Patricia Waugh, eds., *Modern Literary Theory: A Reader* (London: Edward Arnold, 1989).

4. Wilfred L. Guerin *et al.*, eds., *A Handbook of Critical Approaches to Literature*, 3rd ed. (New York: Oxford University Press, 1992).

5. See, for example, Derrida's discussion of metaphor and the "heliotrope" in "White Mythology: Metaphor in the Text of Philosophy," *Margins of Philosophy*, trans. Alan Bass (Chicago: University of Chicago Press, 1982), pp. 207–71—especially pp. 245–57, "The Flowers of Rhetoric: The Heliotrope."

6. Northrop Frye, "Ethical Criticism: Theory of Symbols," in *Anatomy of Criticism: Four Essays* (Princeton: Princeton University Press, 1957), pp. 71–128.

7. Jacques Derrida, *Of Grammatology*, trans. Gayatri Chakravorti Spivak (Baltimore: Johns Hopkins University Press, 1976), p. 86.

8. Julia Kristeva, *Desire in Language: A Semiotic Approach to Literature and Art*, trans. Leon S. Roudiez (New York: Columbia University Press, 1980), p. 74.

9. Jacques Lacan, "The Mirror Stage as Formative of the Function of the I as Revealed in Psychoanalytic Experience," in *Écrits: A Selection*, trans. Alan Sheridan (New York: W.W. Norton, 1977), pp. 1–7.

10. Michel Foucault, *The Order of Things: An Archaeology of the Human Sciences* (New York: Random House, 1970).

11. Jacques Lacan, "The Freudian Unconscious and Ours," *The Four Fundamental Concepts of Psycho-Analysis*, ed. Jacques-Alain Miller, trans. Alan Sheridan (New York: W.W. Norton, 1977), p. 21.

"Yung and Easily Freudened": Psychoanalytic Theory in the Literary Classroom[1]

M.E. Roughley

As strange as it seems (to me at least), I am often called upon to defend the use of psychoanalytic theory in the analysis of so-called literature, especially when that literature is not ostensibly or "consciously" predicated upon Freudian concepts. The calls usually come from students, most often those who have taken enough university psychology to *know* that Freud-is-Dead or have gotten along perfectly well in their study of literature to this point without trespassing upon that-which-is-not-proper-to-literature. Although I do find these calls "strange," I welcome them because they serve beautifully as pretexts for questioning the illusion (so useful to pedagogy) of a perfectly logical rationale to literary analysis. I consider these calls invitations to reconsider the very grounds upon which we perform literary analysis, or analyses of literature, rather than demands for justification of yet another sort of theoretical "game." The ensuing pedagogical exercise, then, is less to instruct students in the finer points of Freudian or Lacanian psychoanalytic hypotheses than to use certain of these hypotheses or concepts as levers to pry open and investigate the presuppositions, held by many students, about the distinctions and relationships between literature, theory, psychology, philosophy, theology, and so on, according to which the specific field of literature is constituted. A primary assumption of this exercise is that so-called literature does not exist as an isolated disciplinary category but is a "special case" of human significatory practices. Consequently, we are less interested in *what* literature means within a closed "literate" system than with *how* it means or how its meaning is generated in relation to general systems of signification.

The "Freud" and "Lacan" that I will be acknowledging in this essay are not the theorist/therapist figures of a stringently demarcated field of psychology: rather, they are the signatures of specific articulations, informed as much by the articulations of other discursive fields and of the signifying systems that underlie all human communication as by the history of psychology. Certainly, neither Freud nor Lacan limited their work to one field of study, and both frequently cited poets, dramatists, novelists, philosophers, anthropologists, and linguists in developing the proofs of their arguments. Paying attention to Freud and Lacan quite often means assuming permeable borders between the different disciplines, borders that will readily permit, say, the transfer of a conceptual structure from Hegel's *Phenomenology* or Goethe's *Faust* to Freud's *Beyond the Pleasure Principle* with a minimum of interference. Of course, there will always be interference of sorts—a permeable border is still a border and both permeation and translation will have their effects on the reading of the transferred material—and we should remain alert to the differences arising from the interference; however, we should also continue to recognize that psychoanalytic theory *is* to a large degree predicated on that-which-is-not-proper-to-psychology (from an academic point of view), on the analogous and the transferred from other discourses.

What all of these discourses have in common is a focus on the constitution of the human subject (*qua* subject) and/in its communications with others (whatever the "other" might be). At the level of the subject and its significant exchanges, the normally insuperable borders between discursive or disciplinary fields become most permeable. After all, it is a bit difficult to adhere to rigid or exclusive categorical distinctions when working at a level logically prior to such distinction. The project of this essay is to provide a (necessarily reductive) introduction to the sort of "poststructuralist" psychoanalytic theory practiced (on "patients" and on "texts") by writers like Jacques Lacan, Julia Kristeva, and Luce Irigaray, and, to a certain extent, like Jacques Derrida. To facilitate this simple introduction, I will be concentrating on the general "theme" of the subject and its constitution and will leave many relatively peripheral topics untouched. This follows my own pedagogical practice: the notions of the "subject" and "identity" as viable areas of investigation are already familiar, in some guise, to most second-year English students at least, and I have found that this is the surest ground on which to set basic introductions to psychoanalytic theory.

What follows has been synthesized from various lecture and seminar notes and is, in many ways, paradigmatic of my "general introductions" to psychoanalytic theory as literary theory. I have chosen the pseudo-lecture format because it allows me to demonstrate the "delivery" of the material while describing and justifying that material. I should point out that much of what follows is usually directed to students at honors level and above. It assumes developed communication and research skills, some basic familiarity with psychology, philosophy, and linguistics, and a degree of intellectual independence. There is no reason why competent undergraduate students cannot be introduced to some of this material (if their native tendency toward the dogmatic can be circumvented), and I have certainly been presented with some sophisticated Freudian and Lacanian textual analyses by third-year students. However, most undergraduates, in my experience, lack the necessary background or the motivation to follow "the Freudian thing" very far.[2]

According to Sigmund Freud then,

> creative writers are valuable allies and their evidence is to be prized highly, for they are apt to know a whole host of things between heaven and earth of which our philosophy has not yet let us dream. In their knowledge of the mind they are far in advance of us everyday people, for they draw upon sources which we have not yet opened up for science.

> We probably draw from the same source and work upon the same object, each of us by another method.[3]

In 1927, Freud was awarded the Goethe Prize by the City of Frankfurt. This prize was awarded annually "to a personality of established achievement whose creative work is worthy of an honor dedicated to Goethe's memory,"[4] and its presentation to Freud seems particularly apropos for at least three reasons. First of all, Freud, throughout his works, consistently and persistently cites Goethe's work as illustrative and/or authoritative, and he is known to have credited Goethe's essay *Die Natur* with influencing his decision to enter medical school. Goethe is, in many ways, a "father figure" to Freud. Secondly, like Goethe's, Freud's practices encompass both the artistic and the scientific: despite Freud's constant attempts to render psychoanalysis perfectly "scientific," his work is also always dependent upon an "artistic apprehension" (whether conscious or unconscious) of both the object and the perceiving subject that precludes the ideal objectivity assumed by the dominant concept of the "scientific." Thirdly, like Goethe, Freud had an interest in the repressed or "dark side" of human subjectivity, and a willingness to address that which is usually shunned. As W.H. Auden puts it,

> he went his way,
> Down among the Lost People like Dante, down
> To the stinking fosse where the injured
> Lead the ugly life of the rejected.

> And showed us what evil is: not as we thought
> Deeds that must be punished, but our lack of faith,
> Our dishonest mood of denial,
> The concupiscence of the oppressor.[5]

There is something of the *literato* about Freud. He was extremely well read, and as a writer he was a skillful, sophisticated rhetorician. (Students are often surprised to find that they actually *like* "reading Freud.") It is worth reading Freud's literary criticism, if only to see how a considerate and generally unimposing "Freudian" analysis is performed. However, I am less concerned, from a poststructuralist perspective, with the performance of Freud-as-critic than with the underlying structures that permit the hybridization of literature, philosophy, and psychoanalysis.

Certainly, one of the most crucial structural concepts is that of analysis as "reading." This semiotic notion seems to underpin all of the Freudian project: the obsessive patient, under analysis, produces "oracular" successions of "key-words" which she and the analyst must "work into sentences" in order to re-call the traumatic event; the hysteric produces symptoms that function as physical "signs" (metaphors, metonyms) for psychical disturbances; the dream produces narratives with "latent" as well as "manifest" contents through which the motivating "wish" may be read, and so on.[6]

That which is "read," the wish motivating the dream, arises from the "unconscious." Freud's discovery of the unconscious is perhaps his single greatest contribution to Western thought and is, in the conceptual history of the human "subject," a "Copernican revolution" to match Einstein's in physics, Marx's in politics, and Darwin's in biological history. After the discovery of the unconscious, the human subject could no longer be defined in terms of consciousness and perception: conscious perception, or perception of consciousness, could no longer be taken as the "proof" of existence. The full effects of this radical alteration of the subject have yet to be realized—we still allow "reason" a certain privilege over "unreason," for example—but few in the so-called Western world would now dispute the existence of the unconscious or deny its operations in our day-to-day experiences. We are all familiar with the significance of "Freudian slips" and the motivations of dreams, even while we cling to holistic notions of the unified or definitive self.

There has been a great deal of "gossip" about the unconscious, and most people unfamiliar with Freud's work have a rather fuzzy perspective on the concept. This perspective needs to be refined, especially if one intends to go on to a study of Lacan's work which is predicated precisely upon the *Freudian* unconscious and not upon subsequent readings, or misreadings, of that concept. For Freud, the unconscious is constituted for the most part by "repressed" material, or material that cannot be admitted to consciousness because that admission, for some reason or other, would prove disastrous to the existent (or "organism," as Freud frequently chose to call the human being). The unconscious does not, for Freud, come into being *before* the institution of the ego: "the unconscious" is not another term for the id, and it is not simply another word for the libido either.[7] Moreover, the Freudian unconscious is *not* a *sub*conscious:

> We must also steer clear of the distinction between the *super-conscious* and the *subconscious*, which has found such favour in the more recent literature on the psychoneuroses, for just such a distinction seems to emphasise the equivalence of what is psychic and what is conscious.[8]

Freud is anxious to avoid assuming an orthodox, Cartesian equivalence between psychic activity and consciousness, "once so all-powerful and overshadowing all else." In the Freudian articulation, the unconscious is the primary site of all psychic activity and "consciousness" is rendered as no more than "a sense-organ" which is "excitable by qualities, and incapable of retaining the trace of changes: i.e. devoid of memory."[9] A consciousness that is merely an "organ" of perception and "devoid of memory"? This is quite a comeuppance for the *cogito*.

> [T]he unconscious must be accepted as the general basis of the psychic life. The unconscious is the larger circle which includes the smaller circle of the conscious; everything conscious has a

preliminary unconscious stage, whereas the unconscious can stop
at this stage, and yet claim to be considered a true psychic function. The unconscious is the true psychic reality.... [10]

At various stages throughout his work, Freud attempted topo-
graphical diagrams of, or metaphors for the functioning of what he
called the "psychic apparatus," "the instrument which serves the
psychic activities."[11] One of the simplest diagrams (or "theoretical
fictions") of this apparatus is offered as Fig. 3 in Chapter VII of *The
Interpretation of Dreams*, and a brief consideration of this diagram
will help to illustrate the basic relationships between the unconscious, conscious and preconscious systems constituting the apparatus. We must, though, heed Freud's warning that we "keep our
heads and do not mistake the scaffolding for the building."[12]

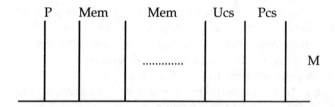

At the level of primary processes, this sequence of systems (like
"the different and successive systems of lenses of a telescope") is
traversed by "excitations," or quantities of stimulation from external or internal influences—say, a smack from a sibling (external) or
the arousal of an instinct (internal). These excitations first strike the
P-system, sensory perception, which retains no traces of the excitations, and then run through the systems to the "motor end," M or
motility in reaction to the stimuli. The excitations, once admitted
by the P-system, move through the psychic apparatus causing disturbances to and changes in that apparatus. These disturbances
leave lasting traces, "memory-traces," and "the function relat[ing]
to [the] memory-trace we call 'the memory.'" The constitution of
the memory occurs in the Mem-systems "lying behind" the P-system, as it were. These Mem-systems, of which there are many, organize the memory-traces according to various forms of combination (association, similarity, though rarely chronology) which will
facilitate the transmission of subsequent excitations. (It might help
to think of the memory-traces as series of related grooves or canals
engraved in the psychic "substance" [the "neurones"] which, once
established, permit a freer flow of similar excitations through the
apparatus so that the apparatus is not being continually disturbed

anew by the same stimuli.) The Mem-systems are unconscious. "Our memories ... are unconscious in themselves. They can be made conscious, but there is no doubt that they unfold all of their activities in the unconscious state."

The subsequent systems through which the excitations must move are what are here known as "the criticizing system": the Pcs (preconscious) and the Ucs (unconscious) systems. If the excitations haven't been exhausted by resistances in the "substance" in the Mem and Ucs systems and have enough force left to enter the Pcs, they may "reach consciousness without any further detentions" and become voluntary motility. However, "lying behind" the Pcs-system, much as the Mem lies behind the P, is the Ucs-system which is a rigorous censor of exciting processes and their traces. The Ucs-system, abetted by the Pcs-system, will not permit anything into the Pcs that would threaten the integrity of the apparatus by, say, encouraging dangerous or inappropriate actions. The only time when this censoring and "repressive" system is weakened is, to all intents and purposes, during sleep, when the dream enables the figurative release of unconscious material.

This diagram and my brief explication of it do not, by any means, constitute a comprehensive account of Freud's "psychic apparatus," but they should prove a useful "scaffolding" to the apprehension of the functioning of the apparatus. Two Freudian additions to this illustration should also be noted. First of all, there is Freud's speculative footnote to the diagram: "The further elaboration of this linear diagram will have to reckon with the assumption that the system following the Pcs represents the one to which we must attribute consciousness (Cs) so that P = Cs." In other words, the consciousness that succeeds the Pcs is also the sensory perception that retains no traces. Sensory perception is, then, already a result of generally unconscious processes: "everything conscious has a preliminary unconscious stage."

Secondly, we should note Freud's addition in *Beyond the Pleasure Principle* of an "outer layer" or "shield" to the P-Cs system. This layer, which has been "toughened" by the constant bombardment of external excitation, protects the "living organism" against excessive stimulation. "*Protection against* stimuli is an almost more important function for the living organism than *reception* of stimuli."[13] (One can almost hear Virginia Woolf's Miss La-Trobe muttering, "reality too strong for 'em."[14]) Freud then goes on to develop the metaphor of sense-organs making "tentative advances towards the external world" with "feelers." We will come across a related metaphor for "perception" when we consider the narcissistic ego.

What I hope will have become clear by now is that what the analyst and analysand attempt to "read" in the dream and the hysterical or neurotic symptom is "the general basis of the psychic life," rather than specific material locked away in some small recess of an otherwise "conscious" subject.

The concept attendant to that of "reading," though it is not a concept *consciously* developed throughout the Freudian text, is the notion of psychical activity, especially the constitution of memory, as a form of "writing." I place the term "writing" in quotes to emphasize the metaphor's extension: "writing," in this consideration, is a process of marking, engraving, tracing on any receptive surface. The emphasis is on the mechanics of the process rather than on conventional production or a "product." In his attempts to articulate what he calls his "theoretical fictions" on psychic functioning, Freud frequently has recourse to "writing" metaphors.[15] He writes of "memory traces" on the "neurones," of "scars" (especially narcissistic scars) that "mark" an imagined wound or castration, of "breaches" or grooves in the psychic "substance."[16]

These "writing" metaphors reach their apogee in his 1925 essay "A Note Upon the 'Mystic Writing Pad.'"[17] In this short essay—which is a supplement to *Beyond the Pleasure Principle*—Freud offers a specific articulation of the constitution of memory as a process akin to writing on a child's toy, the "magic" writing pad with a celluloid sheet that can be lifted to erase the etchings on its surface. For Freud, the Mystic Pad has the two essential prerequisites for any would-be analogue for the mnemic apparatus: it has "an unlimited receptive capacity and a retention of permanent traces."[18] It has an unlimited receptive capacity because the upper layer, upon which one writes, can be erased and cleared for the subsequent writing without retaining past marks that would distort that writing. The "permanent traces" of previous writings, however, are retained in the wax slab underlying the entire apparatus. The relationship between the covering sheet (composed of the celluloid and a piece of wax paper) and the wax slab is roughly analogous to the relationship between the "protective shield against stimuli" and the receptive surface behind it which compose the system *P-Cs*. In other words, the Mystic Pad is not only a metaphor for mnemic processes; it can also work as a partial metaphor for the perceptual functions.[19]

The concept of an essential metaphorical "writing," if we take it on board, revolutionizes "literary" orthodoxies of/about writing. "Writing" is no longer significant of this or that book, the given *opus* of this or that author, or even the specific process of crafting or creating distinct literary products. At the very least, "writing," as a functionary metaphor, is responsible for and enables our apprehension of otherwise "unseen" psychic processes: if we follow Lacan, which we will presently, "writing" can be seen as a seminal metaphor actually complicit in the constitution of these processes.

You likely will have noticed that I have managed to write several pages on Freud without dwelling upon the id, the ego, the superego, or the Oedipal and castration complexes. This is because I have attempted to avoid complicity with certain problematic (from a poststructuralist perspective) descendants of the Freudian text as much as it is because of the exigencies of space. Any student interested in pursuing psychoanalytic theory will of necessity become familiar with the psychic agents and complexes: the "trick" is to prevent these delineations from becoming prescriptive (which they are not in the Freudian text). Certain Freudian literary criticisms of the 1950s and 1960s (and even the 1970s), particularly in the Anglophone West, erected themselves precisely on these fundamental agents and complexes as though they were immutable principles, which is perhaps why the "general public" has come to associate Freudian criticism with an almost ludicrous rigidity. The psychic agents and the complexes seem to have been "applied" to literary texts as fixed grids, and the ambiguous and deferring processes of "writing" have been ignored. Consequently, a fictional character could have an Id, Ego and Superego (though where "he" might have kept them doesn't seem to have been considered), and could be seen as suffering an unresolved Oedipus complex, for example. More subtle critics would refer to the psychic agents and complexes of an "author," a reference that some twentieth-century writers have wilfully subverted by parodying the "yung and easily freudened."

Part of the problem with this "Freudian criticism" is that it was predicated on what could only be called the "methodologized" Freudianism of certain practices such as "ego psychology." This Freudianism is purposive: its sole aim is to render functional or to improve the dysfunctional or inadequate Self as defined by the status quo. This "purpose" puts it at odds with both the avant garde or experimental arts/literature (which tend to see the status quo itself as dysfunctional) and an "investigative" Freudianism for which the goal of therapy is redefined in the recognition of the unified Self as a necessary fiction or a delusion.

The Freudianism that we now are concerned with is that predicated not on the notion of the ego as the axis of "reality" inhibiting the "unrealistic" demands of the id and the superego, but on the concept of the ego as a "narcissistic" economy of libidinal forces.[20] While the first model of the ego—as an axis of "reality"—is a bona fide Freudian model, and most useful to a therapeutic practice that would abet the ego in maintaining its illusion of a unified self, its post-Freud developments have tended to ignore the eruptive and destabilizing effects of the unconscious in the determination of that "reality." The second model, on the other hand, recognizes the activity of the unconscious in the constitution of psychic realities and acknowledges an essential instability of the "subject." Another way of putting it is that the first model is complicit with dominant Humanist notions of the "subject" as the Cartesian *cogito*, while the second is complicit with post-Enlightenment notions of the subject as also "subject to" relativity, indeterminacy, alterity, and so on.

The Freudianism predicated on the second model of the ego is the one most pertinent to contemporary literary and philosophical concerns and is the one which leads us to, prepares us for, not only the work of Lacan but the works of Derrida, Kristeva, and Irigaray as well. Freud's "narcissistic ego" is repeatedly a focal point of these subsequent theoretical projects: we do need to have some comprehension of its constitution before moving on to the Lacanian text.

The notion of the ego as "narcissistic" is developed through Freud's "middle period," between the positing of his theories on infantile sexuality and the Oedipus and castration complexes and the development of his final definitive theories of the id, ego, and superego. This period produced a great number of publications, many of which are marked by a notably "speculative" style, as if Freud were moving out into areas previously unsuspected, let alone uncharted (although Freud is quick [perhaps too quick] to note that his "speculations" are attempts to describe "facts of daily observation" and should not be read as the manifestation of any "philosophical system" that *might* have been adopted).[21] Some of these essays are among his better known works: *Beyond the Pleasure Principle*; "Instincts and Their Vicissitudes"; "Repression"; "The Unconscious"; "On Narcissism: An Introduction"; and "Mourning and Melancholia."[22]

The narcissistic ego is, virtually, a reservoir of libido, of specifically sexual energies that need to be "contained" unless directed onto "objects":

> The ego is a great reservoir from which the libido that is destined for objects flows out and into which it flows back from those objects.... As an illustration of this state of things we may think of an amoeba, whose viscous substance puts out a pseudopodia.

> Psychoanalysis ... came to the conclusion that the ego is the true and original reservoir of libido, and that it is only from that reservoir that libido is extended onto objects.[23]

Without going into the complicating areas of primary and secondary narcissism, which are peripheral to our focus here, although not to the theory itself, we can summarize this ego and its functions as follows. The "ego" is a reservoir of libido awaiting an object or objects. When an object is identified (when the ego "identifies with" an object-choice), the libido flows "out of" the ego, as it were, and onto the "object" which, if it is an agreeable "object," the ego will want to "introject" or, amoeba-like, incorporate within itself. This ego is quite capable of identifying with part of itself and introjecting that as "object": actually, it is only by objectifying and introjecting its "self" that the narcissistic ego can "know" itself. By incorporating the "object," the ego replenishes its store of libido, and could be said to be contentedly "in love." Of course, these operations are fraught with peril (any number of mishaps can occur to an amoeba), and I will turn to some of the potential problems in a moment. First, though, we should stop here to consider the lineaments of the ego and the object presented thus far.

Obviously, this "ego" is dependent upon neither "consciousness," "rationality," nor "reality." It *wants* to be *satisfied*, filled up again, in the most essential, "primitive," way. And what it tries to satisfy itself with is an "object" or the idea of an object that is *right* because the ego *identifies* with it, because it has primary narcissistic value, because it refers the ego to or reminds the ego of the stage of its primary narcissism before there were any other "objects" at all.

> The development of the ego consists in a departure from primary narcissism and gives rise to a rigorous attempt to recover that state.[24]

To a certain degree, the ego (with its "object[s]") is its own account. However, the ego is also modified both by the objects for which it forms ideas and by "real" events or by what Freud calls "material reality." When the ego identifies with an "object," it may model itself on perceived characteristics of that object and thus alter its own constitution. The ego can also be radically altered should the object die or be withheld or withhold itself, in which case the ego can find its store of libido seriously depleted. The ego's only perspective is itself, but that perspective is nonetheless contingent upon the ego's relationships with others. Such a concept of the ego is complicit with neither a sense of a reality universally perceptible (for every ego has its own "reality," as it were), nor a holistic notion of the self (for every ego is mutable and partial according to its social relations).

The picture that we end up with is that of a conscious/unconscious ego that is simultaneously self-contained *and* dependent upon others for its (always changing) shape, that is always desiring and reaching out for objects (including its "self") from which it is necessarily alienated, that is subject to fantasy (its introjected "objects") rather than to reality, and that is inherently split, being both subject and "object." Is it any wonder that, at the end of *Tales of Love*, Julia Kristeva identifies the twentieth-century subject as ET?[25]

If I seem to be spending a disproportionate amount of time on Freud and not nearly enough on Lacan, who is the more "difficult" theorist "without a doubt," I would like to counter any disquiet by offering two "facts." First of all, my decision to focus primarily upon the unconscious and the narcissistic ego was determined by this essay's trajectory towards Lacan. In other words, Lacan has been on board since the beginning. Secondly, Lacan's work is *always* the work of reading Freud: that is what Lacan does. The Freudian text is the only access to the Lacanian text, and I have found that the students who spend most of their time with Freud's work are those who have the least difficulty with Lacan in the final analysis.

Lacan's battles with Freudians, especially those of his own *école freudienne* and with the authorities at the École Normale Supérieure, are legendary. His insistence on "going back to Freud," and on maintaining the concept of the unconscious as *the* seminal concept of psychoanalysis, was seen as rather provocative by many professional analysts who had gone on to construct new orthodoxies as "corrections" of Freud. Moreover, Lacan frequently set out deliberately to provoke the "professionals":

> A technique is being handed on in a cheerless manner, reticent to
> the point of opacity, a manner that seems terrified of any attempt .

to let in the fresh air of criticism. It has in fact assumed the air of a formalism pushed to such ceremonial lengths that one might well wonder whether it does not bear the same similarity to obsessional neurosis that Freud so convincingly defined in the observance, if not in the genesis, of religious rites.[26]

According to Lacan, psychoanalysis had erred in turning away from the "daylight" of Freud's discovery:

Such is the fright that seizes man when he unveils the face of his power that he turns away from it even in the very act of laying its features bare. So it has been with psychoanalysis. Freud's truly Promethean discovery was such an act, as his works bear witness.[27]

Freud's "truly Promethean discovery" was, of course, the unconscious: among the essential "features laid bare" in that frightful moment, according to Lacan, is the relationship of the unconscious to language. This relationship, which is the most significant to psychoanalysis in Lacan's view, has failed to sustain the interest of practicing psychoanalysts, and even Freud himself, again according to Lacan, did not venture as far into the study of the functions of speech as he could have. Freud's "talking cure" certainly established the field, and the field is sustained, if only at times latently, throughout the Freudian text itself; Freud simply may not have realized the potential significance of the unconscious's relationship to language.

To a large extent, Lacan's reading of Freud is an articulation of the latent field in Freud's writings. His reading is facilitated by the science of linguistics which although contemporary to Freud's project, was not available to him. This incorporation of structural linguistics in psychoanalytic theory, leading to the development of "psycholinguistics" as well as to radical changes in some branches of psychoanalysis, may prove to be Lacan's greatest contribution to contemporary Western thought. It is certainly worth considering the effect of this contribution on the concepts of both the unconscious and language.

The Lacanian unconscious is essentially Freud's read from a different angle. In this reading, what "the psychoanalytic experience" discovered "in the unconscious is the whole structure of language."

This simple definition assumes that language is not to be confused with the various psychical and somatic functions that serve it in the speaking subject—primarily because language and its structure exist prior to the moment at which each subject at a certain point in his mental development makes his entry into it.[28]

In other words, the unconscious of any given subject is already structured by language, specifically by the language into which the subject is born. For example, the "memory-traces" laid down in the Mem-systems of Freud's diagram are laid in accordance with the associative structures determined by the structure of language. The "structure of language" that Lacan assumes is that delineated by de Saussure in his *Cours de linguistique générale*: that is, language *per se* is a self-regulating system of signs, and "meaning" depends upon the differential relationships between these signs rather than on any sort of correspondence between a specific word and a specific concept.[29]

If you recall the concept of the amoeba-like narcissistic ego and consider it as determined by the structure of language, you may recognize the extent of Lacan's "revolution." In a sense, Lacan's theory elides the determinations of what Freud called "material reality" in its articulation of the development of the subject, or of the subject as "identity." An example of this elision is Lacan's notion that genital organization does not determine sexual identity, which remains an indeterminate "result" of the organized unconscious. In other words, the sexed subject is made, not born.

At the risk of disfiguring Lacanian concepts by gross reduction, I shall attempt to give a brief account of Lacan's concept of the development of the (narcissistic) ego in relation to the three orders: the "imaginary," the "symbolic," and the "real." In Note 7 of this essay, I give a short summary of the Freudian account of the development of the ego from a part of the id, and the simultaneous splitting into conscious and unconscious, in response to the exigencies of the environment. According to Freud, the child is first made aware of itself, as a distinct being, when it meets the resistance of the environment to its demands. Lacan's addition to Freudian theory is the insertion of a mirror, a specular image, in the moment of splitting. The "mirror stage" marks the ego's recognition of itself *as a distinct image* (its reflection in a mirror, literally and figuratively): for the ego, the *moi* or "me" is always an objectified image of its body that it mistakenly identifies as its self. As Lacan frequently points out, our identities are basically mistaken identities.

The mirror stage corresponds with the order that Lacan calls the "imaginary." The imaginary is the realm of images "collected" or introjected by the ego in its initial attempts to posit itself in its environment or to apprehend its environment in relation to itself (the image of "mother" in relation to the image of "baby," for example). As Elizabeth Grosz puts it, the "imaginary is ... the narcissistic structure of investment which transforms the image of otherness into a representation of the self."[30] This "pre-oedipal" order, although structured by "language" or social order ("environment") that determines the images and their organizations, is not, however, a realm of linguistic significance. Such significance belongs to the order of the "symbolic," which the child enters as it begins to speak. The post-oedipal symbolic is the realm of rule-based social and linguistic systems in which the subject *je* or "I" (as signifier) takes its place. (We should remember that this order is an internalized order and not society *per se*.) The relation of the symbolic to the imaginary is repressive: from the moment of the ego's entry into the ("father"-dominated) symbolic, the ("mother"-dominated) imaginary is seen to be disorderly and dangerous—except in the instances of "divine madness" or "artistic inspiration."[31]

These orders are preceded and persistently underlain by the order of the "real." The "real" is sort of a non-concept "standing for what is neither symbolic nor imaginary and remains foreclosed from the analytic experience, which is an experience of speech," according to Alan Sheridan. "What is prior to the assumption of the symbolic, the real in its 'raw' state (in the case of the subject, the organism and its biological needs), may only be supposed...."[32] The "real," then, is "impossible" to the speaking subject: it remains untouchable, as it were. This "real" should not be confused with "reality" which is a psychic fantasy and therefore quite knowable. The real we are born with; reality we dream up.

The developments of the imaginary and the symbolic (and their alienation from the real) depend upon the agency of the "other" (Lacan's derivation of Freud's "object") and the "Other," a problematic concept that Lacan never defines precisely, probably because it is finally indefinable. As Anthony Wilden has noted:

> It is not possible, for instance, to define the Other in any definite way, since for Lacan it has a functional value, representing both the "significant other" to whom the neurotic's demands are addressed (the appeal of the Other), as well as the internalisation of this Other (we desire what the Other desires) and the unconscious subject itself or himself (the unconscious is the discourse of—or from—the Other). In another context, it will simply mean the category of "Otherness," a translation Lacan himself has employed. Sometimes "the Other" refers to the parents: to the

> mother as the "real Other" (in the dual relationship of mother and child), to the father as the "Symbolic Other," yet it is never a *person*.[33]

Whatever im-personal form it takes, the Other is essential to the development of the narcissistic ego as a desiring, speaking subject. As Lacan consistently points out, the development of the subject takes place in a dialectical structure—in its simplest form between "me" and the Other—rather than a linear and positive process. The subject comes into being in the recognition of and in response to the Other, which is always itself inaccessible. The function of the "other" ("*objet petit a*," "*autre*") or "object" is to cover the apparent "gap" in the ego left by the "absence" of the desired Other. This ego *is* an ET, an extraterrestrial (extrareal) always calling "home" (the Other).

Now, what does all of the above contribute to the concept of "language"? Language, it would seem, is all about us (in both senses of the phrase) as speaking subjects, constituting our psychic lives and our desires as it is constantly being "deformed" in our singular calls to the Other. It forms "us" as "we" deform/reform it in a relationship of mutual interdependence: there is no language without subject, and no subject without language. This concept of language gives a certain urgency and seriousness to our endeavor as "analysts" of literature. As Julia Kristeva writes, in her *Desire in Language*:

> there remains the necessity to pay attention to the ability to deal with desire for language, and by this I mean paying attention to art and literature, and, in even more poignant fashion, to the art and literature of our time, which remain alone, in our world of technological rationality, to impel us not toward the absolute but toward a quest for a little more truth, an impossible truth, concerning the meaning of speech, concerning our condition as speaking beings.[34]

Reading, from this poststructuralist, psychoanalytic perspective, is investigative and performative. The reader does not set out methodically (because there is no set method) to analyze the artefact text (because there is no artefact) according to the precepts of critical authority (because, like subjectivity, authority is not immutable). The reader, like all readers everywhere, assumes a certain perspective in reading, but the perspective assumed is neither authoritative nor prescriptive. Students often find the apparent "amorphousness" of this approach alarming, if not downright threatening: they may grasp the "theory" quickly enough, but the "practice" proves much more elusive, too "limitless." This is usually because they do not yet have the reading background to recognize the theoretical concepts involved in the practice, and because they still cling to the notion that an analysis or analytic practice must have an end (in both senses of the word). However, this doesn't mean that some students, particularly at third-year level and above, should not be encouraged to try their hands at this sort of analysis. They should—with caveats against citing Freud or Lacan or Kristeva, say, as absolute, systematic authorities. This analytic practice is not a practice of imposition: it is more the use of psychoanalytic concepts to "tease" out the "repressed" of the text, its essentially "written" condition.

The following is a very brief consideration of Herman Melville's short story "Bartleby" which is intended only as a simple demonstration of how this teasing out might work.[35] This is the sort of "initial analysis" that I might introduce to an honors seminar group with the notion that the seminar members would then jointly take the analysis a bit further. The seminar would follow a one-hour lecture along the lines of the material presented above and be predicated on set readings from Freud's "On Narcissism," "Mourning and Melancholia," *The Interpretation of Dreams, Beyond the Pleasure Principle,* and Lacan's *Écrits.*

"Imprimis": I don't think that anyone would disagree with an initial statement that "Bartleby" is the first-person narrative of a failed exchange between two agents, the nameless narrator and his unaccountable scrivener, or copyist. The agents are, of course, important to our analysis, and my initial comments will be directed to them; however, the principal focus of this psychoanalytic reading must be the exchange and its failure, for it is the *failed* exchange of language upon which the entire narrative, itself an exchange between a posited reader and writer, is hinged. From this perspective, it could be said that "Bartleby" is the narrative of an unrequited desire.

One of the interesting things about this narrative of desire is that it is so dominated by the narrator, the "I." "I am," "I mean," "I pleased," "I waive," "I believe," "I know," "I belong," "I make some mention of myself," "I am a man" (p. 57): these clauses are all from the first two paragraphs of the story (and they are not the sum of such clauses in these paragraphs). These clauses indicate both essential and intentional qualities of the subject in the "symbolic": the subject *is,* it *means,* it refers to its *self,* it defines, categorizes, demarcates, and proclaims itself eminently reasonable.

Moreover, "I" is a lawyer, the conveyancer of deeds and distributor of the "original" scripts of law to its "law-copyists." An essential quality of the "I" is that, beyond its self-reflective designation, it is nameless: our narrator has no name. It is not, then, *this* I or *that* I, but the paradigmatic lawful "I" of the symbolic that claims this discourse, this "biography" of Bartleby. The title "Bartleby" is a bit of a ruse, for this isn't the story of Bartleby at all. It is the story of the "Other's" refusal of "my" gift, of the subject's unrequited love for an untouchable, repulsively attractive, Other on the far side of the symbolic.

That our subject narrator "desires" Bartleby is evident in his inability to shake off his fascination with the copyist. The more repulsive and peculiar Bartleby becomes, the more attracted the narrator is to him. In the course of their relationship, the narrator finds himself being "ignominiously repulsed," "disarmed," "unmanned," seized by an "over-powering stinging melancholy" (pp. 73, 76–77), and driven to uncharacteristic acts, yet he cannot leave Bartleby alone. He must always offer things to him.

It is tempting to see Bartleby as significant of the "imaginary," a disorderly and dangerous possibility of revolution, but this is not a sight that the text affords. Bartleby seems to be on the far side of the symbolic, at some sort of "end" of the symbolic, where it might border on the "real." After all, Bartleby comes from "the Dead Letter Office," the graveyard of the signifying letter, rather than from the generative realm of the imaginary. Like the image of Narcissus that entices from the other side of the watery border between life and death, and in enticing refuses to give or receive "love," the ghostly Bartleby offers only the negative preference, nothing or death, to the entreaties and offers of the desiring subject.

Bartleby is the significant Other to the narrating "I." This is not to say that he necessarily *is* the narrator's "unconscious" or "real" or alter ego or death (Bartleby + Narrator ≠ One Whole Being), although he certainly bears the marks of all four. It would be more to the point to say that Bartleby is the constitution of the Other by and for the speaking subject. He is a necessity both to the narrating "I" and the narrative itself. He is the always remote object of desire necessary to the dialectical development of both subject and discourse.

To this point, I have proceeded on the assumption that "Bartleby," as the story of a failed exchange of language, is also about the operations of desire *in* language. This assumption, more than any other, requires explication as it is the lynch-pin of this abbreviated

"Lacanian" analysis. The text offers us the hinge of the failed exchange, and that hinge is sustained by a particular tropic nexus, copy ~ letter ~ food. This nexus constitutes that which would be exchanged between the narrator and Bartleby. And, if we have any doubt that what is to be exchanged is essential and substantial by nature, the text provides a number of connections between eating and "character" or "soul" or existence and a number of equations of eating, or its negative of hunger, with copying and writing. The narrator's descriptions of his three scriveners are underpinned by an assumed relationship between character and what one eats or drinks. Moreover, "self-approval" can be "delicious" and a good deed can be "a sweet morsel for [the] conscience," so what one "eats" may be of a "metaphysical" substance (p. 72). Work, specifically the work of law-copying, is also analogous to eating:

As if long famishing for something to copy, he seemed to gorge himself on my documents. There was no pause for digestion. (p. 67)

What the lawyer offers, then, in employing his scriveners is not only work, but both physical and spiritual sustenance and the Law that may be graven again in its own image. What he offers is the sustenance of significance. Bartleby's "sin" is to refuse this significance: he goes against "nature" (although he "lives on gingernuts," he is not "hot and spicy" [p. 72]); he gradually comes to refuse the sustenance of work and food which is tantamount to refusing the letter of the Law "offered" to him by his employer; and he eventually prefers not to live, refusing to send that letter that his would-be "saviour" has promised, three times, would be answered. This "unaccountable" behaviour of the Other brings the narrator face-to-face with the abject realization of the impossibility of significant "communion" or "salvation." The letter, the call, the signifier that one offers to and attempts to exchange with the Other—the signifier of "love," "hope," or "good tidings"—never reaches its destination, which seems to be on the far side of the symbolic, or signification, "moulder[ing] in the grave" (p. 99).

This truncated consideration of Melville's "Bartleby" will, I hope, give some idea of how a reading of a text from a psychoanalytic perspective might proceed. From this point, I would expect students to consider and discuss in greater detail the constitutions of the symbolic and the Other in this story. I would particularly encourage them to investigate the relationship between the letter, the Law, and the act of copying. The grub-man's mistaken identification of the law-copyist as "a gentleman forger," for example, might be targeted as a "place" to begin "teasing out" the significatory underpinnings of the Law in "Bartleby"—the copying of Law as, possibly, forgery.

As I have suggested more than once, poststructuralist psychoanalytic theory is not for the "faint-hearted" or "under-fed" student, or teacher. The work of Freud, Lacan, Kristeva, et al. is very challenging, and engaging in this work is not a simple process of mastering a set of critical techniques. I often tell students that if they are going to broach this area, they should be aware that they will be taking on a lifetime's venture. Many students are intimidated by both the material and its apparent "unendingness"; almost as many become fascinated by the analytic possibilities opened up by this theoretical field; and a substantial number go on to realize those possibilities in graduate research programs. However, whether or not they will go on to work in this field, all students of literature can benefit from an introduction to the Freudian subject and its descendants. After all, the Freudian subject is the twentieth-century subject *par excellence*. "We are all ET's."

Notes

1. James Joyce, *Finnegans Wake* (New York: Viking, 1982), 115.22–23.

2. Having somewhat disparaged undergraduate students, I should in all fairness point out that first-year students seem to have little trouble coping with the basic outlines of the Freudian subject if it is discussed in relation to texts at hand. Texts like Conrad's *Heart of Darkness*, Kafka's *Metamorphosis*, Plath's *Winter Trees*, Joyce's *Dubliners*, and Beckett's *Endgame* are all very productive in this context.

3. Sigmund Freud, "Delusions and Dreams in Jensen's *Gradiva*," in *The Pelican Freud Library* (Harmondsworth: Penguin, 1974), Vol. 14, pp. 34 and 114. *The Pelican Freud Library* offers the same translations (with occasional editions) by James and Alix Strachey offered by *The Standard Edition*.

4. See "The Goethe Prize" in *The Pelican Freud Library*, Vol. 14, pp. 461–72.

5. W.H. Auden, "In Memory of Sigmund Freud," in *W.H. Auden: Selected Poems*, ed. Edward Mendelson (London: Faber, 1979), pp. 91–95.

6. As noted, this semiotic notion does underpin all of the Freudian, and the Lacanian, project. The particular instances exampled here, though, may be found in Freud's and Breuer's *Studies on Hysteria (The Pelican Freud*

Library, Vol. 3, and *The Standard Edition*, Vol. 2) and in *The Interpretation of Dreams* (*The Pelican Freud Library*, Vol. 4, and *The Standard Edition*, Vols. 4-5). The particular translation of *The Interpretation of Dreams* that I will be referring to in this essay is that of A.A. Brill in *The Basic Writings of Sigmund Freud*, ed. A.A. Brill (New York: Modern Library, 1966), pp. 181–552.

7. The "id" is the primary state characterized by a chaotic mentality and an aim which is simply the gratification of all essential needs. When the id comes up against the intransigence of its environment in relation to some of its "demands," part of it is modified into the "ego" which begins to "control" or inhibit the incompatible or inappropriate demands for the sake of the safety and integrity of the organism itself. The point at which the ego is developed from part of the id is the point at which the splitting of conscious and unconscious is instituted in the subject. The "libido" is purely sexual energy. There are three types of libido, corresponding to three stages of development in the ego: ego-libido, which is a pure egotism without an external object; narcissistic libido, which is ego-libido erotically tinged; and object-libido, which is properly directed to an external object. Obviously the id and the libido function unconsciously, but neither could be said to be the unconscious *per se*.

8. Freud, *The Interpretation of Dreams*, p. 544.

9. *Ibid*., pp. 544–45.

10. *Ibid*., p. 542.

11. Of course, such an "instrument" has no anatomical site, as such: it is a psychological concept that, at this stage in the development of psychoanalytic discourse, is dependent upon familiar anatomical or mechanical metaphors for its articulation. I will be considering the illustrative function of the metaphoric below.

12. Freud's diagram and the text which I am offering a synopsis of here can be found in Chapter VII of *The Interpretation of Dreams*, pp. 468–549.

13. Freud, *Beyond the Pleasure Principle*, in *The Pelican Freud Library*, Vol. 11, p. 299. *Beyond the Pleasure Principle* can also be found in *The Standard Edition*, Vol. 18.

14. Virginia Woolf, *Between the Acts* (London: Grafton Books, 1978), p. 130: "She wanted to expose [the audience], as it were, to douche them, with present-time reality. But something was going wrong with the experiment. 'Reality too strong,' she muttered. 'Curse 'em!'"

15. Freud continually stressed the metaphoric and/or figurative status of his writing. For Freud, as for the Romantics, the figurative enables the "description" of the unseen or previously unknown. In *Beyond the Pleasure Principle*, for example, he refers to "our being obliged to operate with the scientific terms, that is to say with the figurative language, peculiar to psychology.... We could not otherwise describe the processes in question

at all, and indeed we could not have become aware of them." (*The Pelican Freud Library*, Vol. 14, p. 334.)

16. For those who are interested in the "deconstructive" Freud, I would suggest reading Jacques Derrida's reconsideration of Freud's notion of "breaching" (the translation of *bahnung* is problematic) in "Freud and the Scene of Writing," in *Writing and Difference*, trans. Alan Bass (Chicago: University of Chicago Press, 1978), pp. 196–231.

17. Freud, "A Note Upon the 'Mystic Writing Pad,'" in *The Pelican Freud Library*, Vol. 14, pp. 427–34. (Also in *The Standard Edition*, Vol. 19, pp. 225–32.)

18. *Ibid.*, p. 432.

19. One of Freud's rhetorical "gifts" is his ability to "milk" a metaphor for all it's worth, and in this essay, the Mystic Pad is well and truly milked. Having established its validity as representative of mnemic and perceptual functions, Freud goes on to use it as an opening into a new area of investigation:

> But I must admit that I am inclined to press the comparison still further. On the Mystic Pad the writing vanishes every time the close contact is broken between the paper which receives the stimulus and the wax slab which preserves the impression. This agrees with a notion which I have long had about the method by which the perceptual apparatus of our mind functions but which I have hitherto kept to myself.

The apprehension of discontinuity in the functioning of the Mystic Pad leads Freud to *reveal* the (long suppressed) possibility of a discontinuity in the functioning of the system *P-Cs*, which, he *further suspects*, "lies at the bottom of the origin of the concept of time." Our recognition of "time" and its passing, rather than being dependent upon a consciousness of continual progression, it seems, is dependent upon the "gaps" in consciousness itself. The concept "time" is the result of staggered bouts of consciousness. Thus, the Mystic Pad not only represents the functioning of mnemic processes, but offers access to a possible anti-humanist articulation of an originary concept of a so-called "universal," *time*. And underlying all these representations of memory, perception and time is an "essential" metaphor, the metaphor of "writing."

20. In Freud's work itself, there is no clear distinction between types of ego such as is posited here. Any distinction arises as much out of subsequent Freudian practices as out of any hints or tendencies in the Freudian text. For a very useful account to the two sorts of "ego" see Elizabeth Grosz, *Jacques Lacan: A Feminist Introduction* (Sydney: Allen & Unwin, 1990).

21. Freud's debts to and intriguing denials of the philosophical are examined in Jacques Derrida's *The Post Card: From Socrates to Freud and Beyond*, trans. Alan Bass (Chicago: University of Chicago Press, 1987). And Anthony Wilden, in "Lacan and the Discourse of the Other" (Jacques La-

can, *Speech and Language in Psychoanalysis*, trans. A. Wilden [Baltimore: Johns Hopkins University Press, 1968], pp. 159–311), in considering Lacan's philosophical heritage also offers some comment on Freud's debt to philosophical systems.

22. These are the essays that I primarily direct students to when they are investigating the concept of the narcissistic subject. The last two, "On Narcissism: An Introduction" and "Mourning and Melancholia," appear to be particularly accessible to students—and the latter seems to be especially appealing to students of literature, perhaps because its ostensible theme is the coincidence of love and death. Conveniently, all of these essays can be found in Vol. 14 of *The Pelican Freud Library*.

23. Freud, "On Narcissism: An Introduction," pp. 67–68, and *Beyond the Pleasure Principle*, p. 324.

24. "On Narcissism: An Introduction," p. 95

25. Julia Kristeva, *Tales of Love*, trans. Leon S. Roudiez (New York: Columbia University Press, 1987), pp. 382–83: "Today Narcissus is an exile, deprived of his psychic space, an extraterrestrial with a prehistory bearing, wanting for love. An uneasy child, all scratched up, somewhat disgusting, without a precise body or image, having lost his specificity, an alien in a world of desire and power, he longs only to reinvent love. The ET's are more and more numerous. We are all ET's."

26. Jacques Lacan, *Écrits*, trans. Alan Sheridan (New York: Norton, 1977), p. 37.

27. *Ibid.*, p. 34.

28. *Ibid.*, pp. 147–48.

29. See "The Agency of the Letter in the Unconscious," in *Écrits*, pp. 146–78.

30. Elizabeth Grosz, *Sexual Subversions* (Sydney: Allen & Unwin, 1989), p. xviii.

31. Julia Kristeva offers fascinating studies of the eruptions of the "imaginary" (or "semiotic") as productive of ecstatic religious states and/or of art in *Tales of Love* and *Powers of Horror*, trans. Leon S. Roudiez (New York: Columbia University Press, 1982).

32. *Écrits*, pp. ix–x.

33. Wilden, pp. 263–64.

34. Julia Kristeva, *Desire in Language*, trans. Thomas Gora, Alice Jardine, and Leon S. Roudiez (New York: Columbia University Press, 1980), p. ix.

35. Herman Melville, "Bartleby," in *Billy Budd, Sailor and Other Stories*, ed. Harold Beaver (Harmondsworth: Penguin, 1985), pp. 57–100.

36. *Ibid.*, pp. 73, 76, and 77.

On Site:
If On a Winter's Night a Traveller and Creative Pedagogy

Darren J. Tofts

"Focus for now on the concrete experience of this story, as a simulation of a more abstract practice to be tested at another time."

(Gregory L. Ulmer)[1]

Teaching literary theory is quite different from introducing students to a way of thinking theoretically about literature. The teaching of what have come to be conventional literary theory courses will continue to have an importance for the human sciences, particularly with respect to the historical development of theory, its discontents, and its breakdown of the boundaries of specialization which had traditionally compartmentalized discourse. However, the institutionalization of theory over the past decade is a sign that what was once unsettling has become domesticated. No longer prompting questions about the academic study of literature, literary theory has itself become an object of academic study, subsumed into the system and the ideological disinterestedness of scholarly meta-languages which it initially had the potential to subvert. What is now required to revitalize the critical force of theory is not, I believe, a new way of teaching it, but a modification of traditional pedagogical practices capable of regenerating the interrogative impulse of theory through dramatic use: a practical application of the implications of theory, not an academic reiteration of them.

Pedagogy, that is, should be envisaged as a dramatic practice—as the production of theoretical knowledge by students through reading literary texts. A creative pedagogy should avoid offering theory as something to be consumed, and instead aim to focus and appropriate the prominent cultural questions which have increasingly been at the forefront of contemporary thought. Attention in the classroom situation to what Linda Hutcheon terms the "process of meaning-making in the production and reception of art" can not only activate the reflexivity of postmodern culture, but also generalize its epistemological underpinnings—"how our sign systems grant meaning to our experience."[2] Foregrounding the processes through which we strive to know a literary text deconstructs the traditional hierarchical paradigm of teachers instructing students. At the same time it empowers students by altering their relationship to knowledge as something to be produced through doing—through encounter.[3] Patricia Parker has noted in this respect that a deconstructive pedagogy which is concerned with how, as opposed to what something means, "enables students to respond to what is there before them on the page" and prompts them "to work out the logic of a reading on their own rather than passively deferring to the authority of superior learning."[4]

As a focus of exploratory activity, the metafictional text can be used to creatively foster the kind of creative self-resourcefulness referred to by Parker. Metafiction is defined in terms of the exploration of theories of fiction through the writing of fiction. As a practice in dialogue with its own theory, metafiction has been recognized as a highly didactic form. John Barth noted in 1967 that the reflexivity of the contemporary avant-garde as a whole offered "a way of discussing aesthetics ... illustrating 'dramatically' more or less valid and interesting points about the nature of art and the definition of its terms and genres."[5] Barth's assessment of the instructive potential of the reflexive tendency in art is useful in pointing out the ability of metafiction to overtly prompt theoretical consideration of the text. It is, however, suggestive of the polite discourse of the drawing-room, which has the effect of defusing the performative impact of metafiction. In the same essay Barth noted Borges' famous reflection on the metaphysical ramifications of the "play-within-a-play" strategy in *Hamlet*. The citation is significant, for more succinctly than Barth, or any other commentator on metafiction, Borges' observations on the "inversions" in *Hamlet*, *Don Quixote*, and the *Thousand and One Nights* highlight the fact that metafiction operates by confrontation, by upsetting the reader's ontological and epistemological space. For Borges, the disruption of conceptual certainties is cathartic, a "portal of discovery," for the reader is drawn out of his/her world *into* a realm of discourse; or to put this another way, the reader is made aware of the discursive nature of his/her own representations of self:

> ... these inversions suggest that if the characters of a fictional work can be readers or spectators, we, its readers or spectators, can be fictitious. In 1833, Carlyle observed that the history of the universe is an infinite sacred book that all men write and read and try to understand, and in which they are also written.[6]

Prior to the coining of the term metafiction in 1970 by William H. Gass, and well before Derrida and *Of Grammatology*, Borges' attention to the reflexive tendency in art indicated that with reading, there are no outside/inside oppositions.

As a meta-discourse this genre would appear to provide a ready-made pedagogy *à la mode*. However, teaching metafictional texts exclusively would inhibit rather than liberate a creative pedagogy, for as with using theoretical texts alone, the emphasis on one kind of writing does not produce the disruptive sense of difference. Metafiction is conspicuous as a genre because it is different from more conventional, deceptively unselfconscious forms of writing. The perception of difference can be produced by contextualizing the metafictional text within a sequence of texts that are recognizable as fictions, which can stimulate investigation of the ways different kinds of writing operate according to specific codes and depend upon the reader's implicit knowledge of these codes. I participate with students in an undergraduate course on twentieth-century literature and literary culture, which is part of the Bachelor of Arts degree at the Swinburne University of Technology in Melbourne. While I do not introduce the students to theoretical texts as such, the choice of unfamiliar or marginalized texts alongside twentieth-century repertory "classics" immediately defamiliarizes the notion of the institutionalized study of literature by confronting their expectations about what such a course might or should involve. This initial challenge to the naturalism of the traditional literary curriculum situates the set texts in a dialectical rather than rhetorical perspective.

With respect to the departure from teaching within an established canon, the choice of texts has been important in orienting students toward a different way of thinking about what literature is. In choosing texts which the students are unlikely to have encountered before in formal literary studies (such as Flann O'Brien's *At Swim-Two-Birds*), it is possible to generate an uninhibited nego-

tiation of ideas about literary representation, for they have no preconceived notions about the texts, and do not approach them
armed with a barrage of ready-made interpretations. While this
may be initially confrontational, it is constructively so. Being dramatically forced to consider the possibility that the study of literature may involve more than routine reading of the work of classic
authors equips them with one of the most important strategies required to understand and articulate the current state of literary
culture: that literary theory involves a fundamental shift in attitude
to the subject. Such a shift in attitude addresses questions which,
for many students, are not customarily thought to be germane to
literary studies, such as what is literature, how, as a practice of
writing, does it stand in relation to empirical reality, what texts
should be studied as literature, and what are the assumptions
which underlie the privileging of certain texts over others.

This process of defamiliarization and reorientation is furthered
by studying a sequence of progressively less realistic, more self-
conscious texts—for instance, Jean Bedford's *Sister Kate*, Tennessee
Williams' *A Streetcar Named Desire*, Marguerite Duras' *The Lover*,
Samuel Beckett's *Waiting for Godot*. Situated as the end result of a
process by which the literary text becomes less familiar as representation of social realities and increasingly concerned with its
own materiality as writing, the metafictional text is contextualized
in such a way that it can be profitably used to consolidate emergent questions about what makes the previous texts in the course
either possible or impossible as representation. The *use of the process* by which the metafictional text is contextualized is important
in this respect, because it incorporates into the discussion the students' own experience of working through a textual progression
which reciprocates, then violates, their intuitive expectations of
how literary representation should operate. The emotional and
epistemological dynamic of disruption/critical investigation which
I have noted in relation to Borges is generated as an effect of an encounter with the textual development.

Student reaction to this approach is variable, and the degree to
which they either accept or reject it depends upon a range of criteria which are never the same from year to year, such as age, motivation for tertiary study, the kind of subjects taken concurrently
with literature, and the expectations they have of what literary
studies may involve. The last point is very important within the
overall process of a creative pedagogy which is fundamentally dia-
critical and depends upon the confrontation and uncovering of the

students' intuitive literary beliefs (what the structuralists would call "competence"). Although English departments within many Australian universities have been transformed by theory, and more recently cultural studies, students coming into tertiary programs still have fairly entrenched, traditional notions about what literature is and how it should be studied. Subsequently, confusion, uncertainty, even impatience are often common initial reactions to my course, particularly as the texts become less realistic. But since their own responses are critically monitored and discussed (that is, are as much an object of study as the literary works themselves), generally they soon become intrigued. What seems to interest them most is the manifest difference in the nature of their response that the different kinds of writing produce. As a consequence, the latter part of the course usually involves the students' pursuit of more critical explanations of their assumptions about literature, language, and reality which representational conventions encapsulate (ideally, this reflexivity takes place when the students are encountering metafiction).

While I change the syllabus as a matter of course, to maintain the spontaneity of the textual encounter and avoid the repetition of already formulated discovery, the metafictional text which has been by far the most effective in the overall project is Italo Calvino's *If On a Winter's Night a Traveller*.[7] The fictional readers' quest for the missing book takes them on a journey in which every aspect of book culture is encountered: they visit universities, attend seminars, interview professors, explore publishing houses and the processes of book production, and are put into contact with authors and translators. The problem of the "continuation of the novel" (p. 59) inevitably involves consideration of ideas *about* novels, and the reading of them:

> You are impatient, you and Ludmilla, to see this lost book rise from its ashes, but you must wait until the girls and the young men of the study group have been handed out their assignments: during the reading there must be some who underline the reflections of production methods, others the processes of reification, others the sublimation of repression, others the sexual semantic codes, others the metalanguages of the body, others the transgression of roles, in politics and in private life. (p. 62)

This reportage of the proceedings of the seminar room is metonymic of the way the book reflects the situation of actual readers attempting to bring their own critical meta-languages to bear on *If On a Winter's Night a Traveller* itself. Students frequently note how reading *If On a Winter's Night a Traveller* is an unsettling experience, because it blurs the distinction between their own world and the world of the book, and thereby complicates the task of objectifying it—of gaining critical purchase on it.

In dramatizing the situation of readers, and every facet of the reading process, the text foregrounds the proposition that ideas about reading (and writing) unavoidably inform and condition our reading practices. A focal element in the movement of texts away from realistic representation is the awareness *of* reading as a cognitive activity of production, rather than passive consumption. A plot showing readers struggling to continue an act of reading is in this sense an apt metaphor for the pursuit of meaning, and in particular it dramatizes the concept that fictional representation is dependent upon the collaboration of the reader—indeed that reading is a condition of representation. The most pertinent enunciation of this idea in the book is proffered by Irnerio, the "Nonreader":

> I've become so accustomed to not reading that I don't even read what appears before my eyes. It's not easy: they teach us to read as children, and for the rest of our lives we remain the slaves of all the written stuff they fling in front of us. I may have had to make some effort myself, at first, to learn not to read, but now it comes quite naturally to me. The secret is not refusing to look at the written words. On the contrary, you must look at them, intensely, until they disappear. (p. 43)

In order for the phenomenal world to exist, and for a realistic world to be represented in writing, perception and reading must appear natural (that is, invisible) as cognitive activities. The expectation of "innocent reading" (p. 93), so longed for by the "Reader," for example, is only possible when readers are unconscious of being readers.

The text's critical narcissism signifies a "pedagogical motive" implicit in the statement "I am writing," which for Calvino invokes the "field of problems" connected with the meta-discursive processes of the last thirty years, and its reflexivity discloses an opposition to

> the illusoriness of art, to the claim made by realism to lead the spectator to forget that what he has before his eyes is an operation performed by means of language, a fiction worked out with an eye toward a strategy of effects.[8]

When in this highly interrupted text a fictional diegesis gets going, it is illustrative of Derrida's grammatological notion of writing: an ostensible fictional text is infiltrated by another effaced writing, such that two writings are legible simultaneously:

> The novel begins in a railway station, a locomotive huffs, steam from a piston covers the opening of the chapter, a cloud of smoke hides part of the first paragraph.... The pages of the book are clouded like the windows of an old train, the cloud of smoke rests on the sentences. (p. 14)

In *Of Grammatology* Derrida refers to writing as "all that gives rise to an inscription in general, whether it is literal or not and even if what it distributes in space is alien to the order of the voice: cinematography, choreography, of course, but pictorial, musical, sculptural 'writing.'"[9] In any act of fictional representation, writing begins before enunciation, before alphabetic inscription, in the theory of the text—the "totality of what makes it possible" (p. 9). *If On a Winter's Night a Traveller* is conscious of itself as a palimpsest, and it foregrounds a meta-discourse to declare the duplicity of all writing. Writing is a textualization of experience, and textuality is itself the performance of a writing *"sous rasure."* Writing begins before "the book" in the form of a discourse which stands, apparently, outside the material fact of the text ("You are about to begin reading Italo Calvino's new novel, *If On a Winter's Night a Traveller*"), but which is, in fact, the narrative discourse itself, reflecting on its function as the story's producer. In the passage quoted above, the infiltration of this "writing before the letter" discloses the theoretical precept that the reality effect being produced is a construct of the mobilization of conventions which allow language to appear transparent, but at the same time, through various strategies of disguise, conceal the fact of language use, and of various codes of production, in the interests of verisimilitude and social contract. The manufactured illusoriness of fictional, not to mention linguistic referentiality, is frequently declared throughout the text in an equally overt way:

> It is only through the confining act of writing that the immensity of the non-written becomes legible, that is, through the uncertainties of spelling, the occasional lapses, oversights, unchecked leaps of the word and the pen. Otherwise what is outside of us should not insist on communicating through the word, spoken or written: let it send its messages by other paths. (p. 144)

It dramatically enacts these theoretical insights, then, through a dual strategy of monitoring the actual/fictional reader's activity ("You have now read about thirty pages and you're becoming caught up in the story" [p. 25]), and reflecting critically on the assumptions behind fictional discourse, and the mechanics of narrative ("The novel you are reading wants to present to you a corporeal world, thick, detailed" [p. 39]). It is this dual strategy of self-inspection which gradually prompts students, after their initial frustration, to consider the heuristic possibilites of the text. Indeed, a common response from students is that it uncannily "reviews" and articulates the theoretical ideas elicited by the previous textual sequence from realism to metafiction.

For Calvino, the activity of writing is an interdiscursive process which transgresses different kinds of writing, and collapses oppositions such as novelist/theorist. Multiple writings alternate and interact, drawing the reader into the exploration of pressing cultural questions. Informed by the "process of theorization" initiated by structural linguistics, *If On a Winter's Night a Traveller* represents a new metafictional trope, for it is permeated by a discourse which goes by the name of "literary theory."[10] Self-consciously drawing on a "library of multiple specializations" which breaks down and questions what literature is and how it works, the text admits its reader into a scene of writing which is creatively pedagogical.[11] As a written artifact, its modest two hundred pages potentiate the kind of creative dynamic which Gregory Ulmer prescribes for the teaching of the human sciences in the postmodern classroom, whereby the orientation of learning is performative rather than simply reproductive, writerly rather than readerly. Working on *If On a Winter's Night a Traveller* with students in the classroom is an example of what Ulmer calls "post(e)pedagogy," "the exploration by means of art and autography of the relation between the student and knowledge."[12] Imaginatively rethinking Barthes' text/ work opposition in terms of the teaching process, Ulmer's neologism "textshop" registers a concept of learning which subversively undermines paradigms of instruction/appropriation, repetition/acquisition. The classroom situation should operate like an avant-garde text, where reflexive attention to the conventions of representation, to the role of the reading subject, and to interpretive strategies is as much an effect as an object of encounter with it. Within the exploratory scene of the writerly classroom, encounter with *If On a Winter's Night a Traveller* produces "simultaneously theory, critical combat, and pleasure; we subject the objects of knowledge and discussion—as in any art—no longer to an instance of truth, but to a consideration of *effects*."[13]

With its inscribed discourse of literary theory, *If On a Winter's Night a Traveller* not only invokes a library of multiple specializations, but it imagines (as well as creates) a new kind of reading subject for whom reading a novel involves (will demand) more than discrete consideration of a literary text. Calvino, like Borges, wrote literature "while thinking of a shelf of books that are not all literary," and for an audience well read in different kinds of writing. The "hypothetical bookshelf" of which *If On a Winter's Night a Traveller* is a part, and by which it has been informed, is the library of postmodernism, and the reader who walks its corridors not only has literary expectations, but "epistemological, semantic, practical, and methodological requirements."[14]

Like Borges' "multiform library," *If On a Winter's Night a Traveller* produces an "unprecedented language" which is better suited to the cultural needs of the postmodern reader, for it exposes the illusoriness of perceiving theory and practice as separate discourses. Through a strategy of textual ventriloquism, *If On a Winter's Night a Traveller* prompts the reader to participate in the performace of, and as consequence come to terms with, some of the most important theoretical concepts of postmodernism—the differential play of meaning, the suspension of closure, and so on—concepts which are indexed in such recurrent meta-statements as:

> I would like to be able to write a book that is only an incipit, that maintains for its whole duration the potentiality of the beginning, the expectation still not focussed on an object. (p. 140)

And as each story breaks off on the verge of a *dénouement*, its conclusion activates the potential of a new beginning in terms of the fictional readers' pursuit of the continuation of the text, which is supposedly located elsewhere, but is forever dispersed. The titled beginnings of novels are traces of fundamental narrative statements (surveillance and pursuit, unknown menace and evasion, resolution of a mystery) operating in a process of differentiation, as each story re-works not only other stories, but the predicament (the story) of the readers as well. The speaker in the opening story makes sense of the fictional world in which he finds himself by treating the phenomena around him as signs to be read:

> The cat arches its back, the cashier closes her cash register and it goes pling. All these signs converge to inform us that this is a little provincial station, where anyone is immediately noticed. (p. 14)

He gradually orients himself into his world (and therefore constructs it *as* a world) through this semiotic activity, and the genre
with which he conceptualizes (and contextualizes) his own situation, the detective story, mirrors the actual reader's reflexive
awareness of his/her own fictional status as a reader of signs, and
the need to make *If On a Winter's Night a Traveller* meaningful
through a sleuth-like pursuit of a narrative code which will explain
and give coherence to the heterogeneous narrative fragments of
which the novel is made:

> Only the ability to be read by a given individual proves that what
> is written shares in the power of writing, a power based on some-
> thing that goes beyond the individual. The universe will express
> itself as long as somebody will be able to say, "I read, therefore it
> writes." (p. 138)

The focus on readers and the activity of reading is thus thematized
in the text's principal diegesis, that of two readers in search of a
book to read, which will enable them to complete an act of reading.
But it is also actualized in terms of the text's self-conscious situation of a reader beyond its own materiality who will be required to
perform as a reader.[15] As is the case with the fictional readers and
their desire to possess the complete text, *If On a Winter's Night a
Traveller* will only become a book when it is produced through the
activity of reading. Constructed as a function of the text's own becoming, the reader who holds *If On a Winter's Night a Traveller* in
his/her hands is caught in its sequence of readers reading; encounter with *If On a Winter's Night a Traveller* processes readers *en
abyme* ("I have had the idea of writing a novel composed only of
beginnings of novels" [p. 156]), confronting them with metaphysical problems of identity and subjectivity (do I, does writing, exist
outside reading?).

The possession of a complete text is metaphorically imaged in
terms of desire:

> The pleasures derived from the use of a paper knife are tactile,
> auditory, visual, and especially mental. Progress in reading is
> preceded by an act that traverses the material solidity of the book
> to allow you access to its incorporeal substance. Penetrating
> among the pages from below, the succession of slashes that one
> by one strike the fibers and mow them down—with a friendly
> and cheery crackling the good paper receives that first visitor,
> who announces countless turns of the pages stirred by the wind
> or by a gaze.... (p. 38)

The fictional readers' collaboration with Ludmilla is as much concupiscent as it is bookish (texstatic), and for them the pleasure of the text and the satisfaction of coitus produces a complete reading. Paralleling the textual bliss of the fictional readers, the reading subject of *If On a Winter's Night a Traveller* is gendered as male, the text female, and the reading of it is fetishized sexually in terms of foreplay (holding it), penetration and rupturing (the cutting of the pages), and finally possession (the completion of an act of reading). Apart from parodying the unquestioned assumption of a universal "he" outside the text, the gendering of the reader as male and the text as the female Other dramatizes the sexual politics of reading in scopophillic (patriarchal) terms, for we are never allowed to forget in this text that reading is ultimately an activity of looking. As the Other, *If On a Winter's Night a Traveller* is something to be controlled through being known. Its discontinuous surface, its indeterminacies, are resolvable through the strategy of interpretation; meta-language is master-language.

The most characteristic motif of postmodernist fiction is dialogue between books:

> Today I will begin by copying the first sentences of a famous novel, to see if the charge of energy contained in that start is communicated to my hand, which, once it has received the right push, should run on its own. (p.140).

The theoretical precept which dialogism involves (there is nothing outside the text but other texts) is put into practice in the writing/reading of *If On a Winter's Night a Traveller* through a range of intertexts, the principal and most frequently cited being *The Thousand and One Nights*. Silas Flannery's project for a novel on the model of *The Thousand and One Nights* is an instance of the text's strategy of embedding stories *en abyme,* and Flannery himself, suffering from writer's block, only writes beginnings of novels. The unfinished novels within *If On a Winter's Night a Traveller* mirror and duplicate aspects of the intercalated story of the readers' search for the missing, complete book. Some of them, alternatively, retell classic stories, such as the Oedipus myth in *Around an Empty Grave*. Such is the degree of infinite regress in the text that intertexts within intertexts are also absorbed. The translator Ermes Marana emulates the predicament of Scheherazade, deferring revolution in Saudia Arabia by prolonging the Sultana's reading pleasure in the suspension of the beginning of the story. The import of Marana's design recalls the "magical" "602nd" night (so beloved of

Borges) when Scheherazade tells her own story and initiates "the possibility of continuing indefinitely" which, for Stephen Albert in Borges' "The Garden of Forking Paths," provides an example of how a book can be infinite.[16] In terms of textual repetition Borges' "Pierre Menard, Author of the *Quixote*" is traced in Silas Flannery's temptation "to copy out all of *Crime and Punishment.*"[17] Flannery's fascination with the practice of the copyist emulates Borges' interest in quoting other texts—Pierre Menard himself being the invention of an invention, Valery's M. Teste.

If On a Winter's Night a Traveller invites an act of reading which is euretic rather than hermeneutic, for it does not so much demand to be known as to elicit a process of knowing.[18] Its inscribed discourse of literary theory focusses performatively the kinds of questions that can be asked of an act of fictional representation. Treating knowledge of itself as process rather than product, and reorienting the reading subject's relationship to knowledge in terms of the asking of questions, it assumes the status of an "event." *If On a Winter's Night a Traveller* constructs its readers as philosophers, engaged in the process not of reading according to established rules, but of formulating the "rules of what *will have been done.*"[19]

While it is generically promoted as a novel, it persistently deconstructs its status as fiction. Despite the frequency of references to it in critical works on metafiction, it has not as yet been recognized as a work site for the production of literary and cultural theory. Critics, publishers and pedagogical institutions persist in compartmentalizing it according to preconceived disciplinary boundaries, yet fail to acknowledge its subversion of such demarcations. The ideological stumbling block is, of course, the perception that Calvino is a writer of fiction first and a theorist second, and that if we want to read his theoretical work we should confine ourselves to *The Literature Machine*. This divisive, binary approach to Calvino has been used to account for the thematic and stylistic development of his writing. Martin McLaughlin traces Calvino's fiction from the 1940s to the 1980s in terms of a gradual movement away from neorealism and fantasy to reflexive engagement with the "problems of being a writer in the post-modernist age."[20]

A more profitable way of thinking of this development is to recognize in it the retracing of an *œuvre*, a gradual uncovering of the conditions of fiction, and a recognition that any story requires only to be interrogated in a particular way, asked the right questions, to wax theoretical about its means of production, its writing before the letter. The way in which I have utilized *If On a Winter's*

Night a Traveller in my seminars in some way appropriates the manner in which it prompts consideration of the silenced discourses of Calvino's previous fiction.

Metafictional writers such as Calvino problematize the culturally installed opposition of writer/theorist, but they also require of culture a new means of coming to terms with metafiction. When it is recognized that distinctions between theory and practice are illusory (ideological), then texts such as *If On a Winter's Night a Traveller* will no longer be the objects of theory, but the initiators of it.

The changing role and subject position of the critic has anticipated the theoretical and ideological shift required to see *If On a Winter's Night a Traveller* as an important cultural praxis. Critical discourse within Anglo-American scholarship has in recent years shown signs of modification in the light of the pedagogical implications of theory in the postmodern age. Peter Gidal's *Understanding Beckett*, for example, treats critical discourse as an intertextual space, as an entrance into the writing of Beckett through other writings.[21] The work is a complex bricol(l)age of the inscriptions of Beckett, Gidal, and an array of critical, political and theoretical writings. The reader encounters a freeze-frame image of Billie Whitelaw in *Footfalls* through a quotation of Lenin's "On Dialectics," or explores memory, speech, and artifice in *A Piece of Monologue* in terms of Wittgenstein's *Remarks on Colour*. *Understanding Beckett* is as much a meta-critical text as it is a reading of Beckett, for it dramatizes the possibilites of criticism in the light of the diverse agendas of postmodernism.

The shortcoming of a critical text such as this is that it perpetrates a meta-language in order to account for a method by which the student participating in the dynamics of the classroom can become creatively involved with the theory and practice of *If On a Winter's Night a Traveller* through a performative activity of writerly reading. Even to attempt to imitate through the form of this essay the experience of encounter with the text would be fallacious, for it would still involve a textualization of an activity of production whose temporal and spatial scene is the writerly classroom. To "teach" the text is an irrelevant and inappropriate concept (convention perhaps would require me to put the term under erasure). As a site of the production of knowledge, the dynamics of the classroom condition a collaborative engagement between tutor and students in a process of encounter and discovery. *A priori* engagement with *If On a Winter's Night a Traveller* as the climax of a process of textual encounter testifies to a new pedagogy in the con-

text of a larger cultural critique which Gayatri Spivak has anticipated for the future of teaching in and of the humanitites: an
"arena of cultural explanations that question the explanations of
culture."[22] This text, then, must itself be recognized as a supplement standing in for something that can only be traced after the
event. Perhaps this recognition of the limitation (and falsehood) of
this kind of critical discourse is the most convincing testimony to
the need for a new attitude to pedagogical practice. An account of
how students may encounter *If On a Winter's Night a Traveller* in
the writerly classroom is only useful in corroborating the heuristic
process of activity, of dramatic involvement, of performance.

Creative pedagogy will certainly necessitate greater reflexivity
in the discursive practices which surround it, greater awareness of
their anteriority:

> The first sensation this book should convey is what I feel when I
> hear the telephone ring; I say "should" because I doubt that writ-
> ten words can give even a partial idea of it. (p. 106)

Notes

1. Gregory L. Ulmer, "Theory Hobby: 'How-To Theory,'" *Art & Text*,
37 (1990), p. 96.

2. Linda Hutcheon, *A Poetics of Postmodernism* (London: Routledge,
1988), p. x.

3. For a discussion of this notion in relation to the concept of literacy,
as developed by Paulo Freire, see L.S. Finlay and N. Smith, "Literacy and
Literature: Making or Consuming Culture?" *College Literature*, 18.2 (1991),
p. 60.

4. Patricia Parker, "Teaching Deconstructively," in G. Atkins and M.
Johnson, eds., *Writing and Reading Differently: Deconstruction and the
Teaching of Composition and Literature* (Lawrence: Kansas University Press,
1985), p. 141.

5. John Barth, "The Literature of Exhaustion," *The Atlantic*, 220.2
(1967), p. 29.

6. Jorge Louis Borges, "Partial Magic in the *Quixote*," in *Labyrinths*
(Harmondsworth: Penguin, 1983), p. 231.

7. Italo Calvino, *If On a Winter's Night a Traveller* (London: Picador,
1982).

8. Calvino, "Levels of Reality in Literature," in *The Literature Machine* (London: Picador, 1989), p. 109. The essays collected in this volume were previously published in America as *The Uses of Literature* (Orlando: Harcourt, 1986).

9. Jacques Derrida, *Of Grammatology*, trans. Gayatri Spivak (Baltimore: Johns Hopkins University Press, 1976), p. 9.

10. Calvino, "Levels of Reality," p. 110.

11. Calvino, "Whom Do We Write For? or The Hypothetical Bookshelf," in *The Literature Machine*, p. 84.

12. Ulmer, "Textshop for Post(e)pedagogy," in Atkins and Johnson, pp. 61–62). Ulmer explains post(e)pedagogy in terms of education's response to the information overload entailed by the electronic paradigm, in which the teacher must redefine his/her function, as well as acknowledge the necessity of new technologies within the classroom. The French "e" is included to indicate that his approach is not only "beyond" the old pedagogy but that it is also a pedagogy for the age of video and computers (*poste* as "set").

13. Roland Barthes, *Roland Barthes*, trans. Richard Howard (New York: Hill & Wang, 1970), p. 90.

14. Calvino, "Whom Do We Write For?" p. 84.

15. The distinction between thematized and actualized narrative strategies is developed by Linda Hutcheon in *Narcissistic Narrative: The Metafictional Paradox* (London: Methuen, 1984), Chapters 3 and 5, respectively.

16. Borges, p. 51.

17. Borges, p. 141.

18. Gregory Ulmer has been the most energetic proponent in recent years of an approach to pedagogy which perceives knowledge as the product of euretics, whereby art is not interpreted, but is used "for the making of theory" (*Teletheory: Grammatology in the Age of Video*, London: Routledge, 1989, p. 20). The importance of Ulmer's work has yet to be fully recognized; however, it is more than likely that it will be as vital to the human sciences in the 1990s as Derrida's has been for the 1980s, especially as it is applied to the transformation of pedagogical discursive practices in the light of poststructuralist theory.

19. Jean-François Lyotard, *The Postmodern Condition: A Report On Knowledge* (Manchester: Manchester University Press, 1991), p. 81.

20. Martin McLaughlin, "Calvino's Library: Labyrinth or Laboratory?" in E. Haywood & C. O'Cuilleanáin, eds., *Italian Storytellers: Essays on Italian Narrative Literature* (Dublin: Irish Academic Press, 1989), p. 263.

21. Peter Gidal, *Understanding Beckett: A Study of Monologue and Gesture in the Works of Samuel Beckett* (London: Macmillan, 1988). For an account of the ideological implications of Gidal's critical practice for Beckettian critical discourse, see Darren J. Tofts, "Beyond the Fatuous Clamour? New Beckett Criticism," *Meridian*, 10.1 (1991), pp. 45–51.

22. Spivak, "Explanation and Culture: Marginalia," in *In Other Worlds: Essays in Cultural Politics* (New York: Routledge, 1988), p. 117.

Rhetoric, Reader-Response Theory, and Teaching Literature

Larry Anderson

I was recently reminded of the continuing tension that exists between theory and pedagogy. Our office of Academic Affairs sponsored a series of Faculty Development Seminars, one of which was on teaching techniques. I paraphrase a colleague who was speaking against putting a lot of time and effort into pedagogical methodologies: we are, after all, professors, not teachers. His way of enunciating the words "professors" and "teachers" made clear his disdain for teachers, and thus, I suppose, teaching. Certainly much silliness—as well as true harm—has occurred in the name of teaching, but teaching goes on in our classrooms, even my colleague's. A subtle deception is perpetrated by those who do not, or choose not to, realize that teaching takes place, even when they deny that they are teaching.

So I do not debate whether we teach or profess; in professing we are always already teaching. The more useful debate centers on how and to what extent we "expose" our teaching. In my own wrestling with this debate, I have begun to develop an approach that seems to enable students to become better readers of literature, which I assume to be the ultimate goal of introductory literature courses. This approach combines one of the oldest arts of discourse—rhetoric—with one of the more recent theories of literary criticism—reader-response theory. In what follows I propose to outline this approach, quoting from a number of student papers. While I use this approach with all genres, my examples and illustrations will come from discussions of fiction.

The following remark comes from a student in an "Introduction to Fiction" class: "The only reason I try to create themes is because I 'suffered' through twelve years of being taught to 'search

for the theme.' I would much rather ignore it and enjoy the story—
no subliminal imbeds please!"

I am fascinated by her negative view of her previous instruction ("suffered"), and the fact that she sees something subliminal
in the teaching of literature. I take the comment, which I see as a
version of the Pygmalion-in-the-classroom syndrome, at face
value, because it describes a situation I see every semester. Students see "reading literature" as a theme hunt, and for all practical
purposes are generally unable to talk about plot, setting, and the
other elements out of which themes emerge. This lack of familiarity with literary concepts is due to training, of course, training that
seems to get in the way of students' developing an appreciation for
literature.

Much of the teaching I do involves undoing this earlier training. It makes little sense in this type of course to lecture on the history of critical approaches to literature. Rather, I assume that the
content of such a course is the literature itself, the work of the students to read it, and the work of the professor to help the students
gain some appreciation for it. These assumptions may be challenged by those who see a difference between theory in the research mode and theory in the classroom. However, I question that
any real difference exists. The tension between these two modes of
theory is the result of circular reasoning. If we do not recognize the
classroom, and what happens in it, as significant to our professions, then we would certainly not find it worthwhile to develop
and explore theories of what transpires there. So, with no theoretical perspectives having been developed, the circle completes itself:
the lack of theoretical perspectives is taken as an indication that the
classroom holds nothing that is theoretically interesting.

Training—to return to my earlier point—can influence us in
ways we are not even aware of; I find this to be the case with students' literary training. Let me quote from one of any number of
students:

> Humbert is so twisted he can find passion and lust in anything
> Lolita says or does. This is not my idea of a hero, and Nabokov's
> attempts at making me feel sorry for Humbert are useless.

I have the feeling that whatever sympathetic qualities in Humbert I
might point out, this student at this time would not accept them, a
refusal that goes beyond the level of simple understanding. Later

in the same essay, this student indicates a development in her appreciation of literature:

> Throughout my schooling, I was always taught that everything had symbolism and a hidden meaning. Though at first I did not agree with that, it slowly stuck with me and now I expect symbolism everywhere. Nabokov's attitude toward symbolism was a welcome change, though I was disappointed that all the references to guns had no symbolism at all.

I am beginning to believe that timing makes a difference; perhaps appreciating literature is developmental. We admit as much when we require the study of literature from the primary grades through college. We talk about the desire to make readers of our students (what does that mean, anyway?—I'm not so sure that teachers and schools "make" anything), to introduce them to classics of literature, to our heritage, to our culture, to our values. This is a heavy burden to place on literary studies, bringing us to the canon debate: whose heritage, whose culture, whose values, are being privileged? This is not the place to engage this debate; rather, I raise it to make the point that the use of a reader-response approach deflects (avoids? dodges?) this important question of privileging by privileging each student's response. A reader must first come to an egocentric understanding of a work before being able to construct and appreciate exocentric understandings.

My first goal is to get students thinking about the expectations they bring to their reading of literature, which is not easy for them to do. When they do recognize expectations, they often apologize for them:

> It is hard to say what my expectations of literature are. I expect to be able to relate to the characters in the novel. I definitely expect literature to have a theme or a meaning, even if it's hidden deep within the story. I try not to look for certain things while reading literature, but I always find myself drifting back to characterization.

Note first the apparent contradiction: she admits to having expectations (to relate to characters, to find a theme) but then claims to not look for certain things. I would say that an expectation implies a looking-for. In addition, this student apparently sees little connection between characterization and theme; she almost apologizes for her drifting back to characterization.

Unfortunately, students often understandably have little success in their hunts for meaning (probably because it's hidden deep within the story!), and so end up frustrated:

> My reading strategies influenced my attitude towards *Lolita*. One very important factor in this is that I always try to find some point that the author is trying to make. Search as you may in this novel, no main point is made besides the fact that the author wants to poke fun at any conventional point.... I felt that there is no reason for writing a story if it has no point, which lowered even more my opinion of *Lolita*.

This student is grappling with what I call the paradox of the point—if you go looking for a "point" you will probably not find one, because in looking for the point you overlook those elements that combine to create "the point." This student can be made to see that her idea of a "point" comes from her training and her expectations, and is an idea that can be expanded to include the concept of satire.

Unlike my colleague, I find the classroom quite theoretically interesting, full of continual reminders of why I eventually majored in English—a love of reading. If asked to explain further, I would say I was *moved* by stories, with "moved" suggesting a personal, emotional response. Furthermore, as I suggested above, it may be that this personal response is a necessary stage in developing literary appreciation. And maybe it is susceptible to instruction, can be hastened by teaching to it instead of teaching away from it.

Taking an approach that makes the students' responses the focal point does not automatically require that we either ignore "primary interpretation," as E.D. Hirsch calls it, or renounce out of hand any other methods of "secondary interpretation."[1] The one constant that must always exist in a discussion of literature is the transaction between the text and its reader, and one's pedagogy cannot help but be based on some understanding of this transaction. Acknowledging this transaction does not necessitate denying the presence of the text in order to validate the importance of the reader. My attempts to articulate an understanding of this transaction led me to use rhetoric as a framework within which to approach literature, an idea certainly not original to me.[2]

Rhetoric stands on two fundamental beliefs—that all discourse is contextual, and that no discourse is random. The first implies that to appreciate a text, one needs to understand its context. With literature students I explain context by referring to the forces of human interaction—historical, sociopolitical, cultural, etc.—and to how these must certainly influence the creation of texts. We talk about ideology, and how a literary work can echo its context and circumstances, or stand contrary to them. Granted, this conversation is rather simplistic, but it does have its effect, if the following quote is any indication:

> Perhaps, the acceptance or rejection of a piece of literature like *Lolita* is based solely on ideology. The reader will not accept an · ideology that goes too far out from his own. Perhaps that says something about all of us who enjoyed *Lolita*.

This remark does not reflect a sophisticated understanding of the interplay of ideological forces and literature within a culture, but for my purposes it serves very well. If nothing else, the comment indicates a level of awareness about a reader's interaction with a text that many beginning students do not have.

The second fundamental belief underlying rhetoric, that no discourse is random, implies an intentionality on the part of writers. This concept of intentionality lives a schizophrenic existence within most English departments. Authorial intentionality is usually never far from the central concerns of writing classes, whereas it often becomes peripheral in literature classes, especially those taught from a New Critical perspective. Also implied by this second fundamental rhetorical belief is the assumption that discourse is received by an interested reader, and a third implication follows: that discourse is "about" something. The combination of intentional writer and interested reader results in a text that concerns some identifiable subject(s) or topic(s). My goal here with students is simply to invite them back to the literal level of the text, to get them to feel comfortable with talking "only" about such things as setting, character, and plot.

My ulterior motive in this retreat to the literal is to help students understand that we all read with bias. We all employ reading strategies, whether we are aware of them or not, and what we take away from a text ultimately is determined by the reading strategies we use. As one student put it:

> Chapter 29 struck me more than any other in the novel, as Lolita is described as basically a pregnant slob in an unkempt house. The overwhelming feeling that occurred to me at that moment

was what a waste of potential Lolita had become. Suddenly the story aligned with a personal reading strategy, as I feel one of life's greatest tragedies is the waste of your personal potential. As this was the only part of the novel that I could relate personal thoughts to, this idea of wasted potential will be what I remember from *Lolita*.

The phrase "aligned with a personal reading strategy," may raise some eyebrows, but it is misleading because the student is not talking about a reading strategy but rather a set of beliefs or values, and this is the level at which readers are moved. The student needed to synthesize some understanding of plot, setting, and characterization by this point in the novel in order to arrive at the thematic understanding of "wasted potential." My goal here is to help students see how their expectations—articulated or not—lead them to make judgments; before discussing our judgments we must first examine the expectations that fostered them.

The techniques I use to get students thinking about their reading strategies are those devised by Kathleen McCormick.[3] The students are continually asked to reflect on their immediate reactions to texts and to analyze what their reactions say about themselves as readers. Many students are successful:

I think my willingness to finally let go of some of my conventional reading strategies helped me enjoy the novel *Lolita*. I also think I was able to overcome my personal ideas of immoral sexual acts in order to enjoy the novel.

Only after articulating her own reading strategies was she able to move beyond a merely personal reaction to one aspect of the novel and come to appreciate the work over all. Another student comes to a similar understanding of her reading process, and this enables her to appreciate *Lolita* in a way many students cannot:

I find that I enjoy a story or novel much more if it relates to me in some way. I feel this is why I loved *Pride and Prejudice* and enjoyed *Lolita* a great deal. To me *Pride and Prejudice* was like a typical soap opera; it happens in everyday life. *Lolita* had the same effect.... At least once in our lives, even if it was at a young age, we have fallen for someone and things just never worked out.... This is basically what happened in *Lolita*. Poor Humbert never really got what he wanted.

Notice the sympathy for Humbert; most students are unable to respond to him in this way. This response was made possible by the student first relating to the novel in a personal way and then recognizing her own reading strategies.

I first began using this approach out of a sense of frustration with the results I had been getting with the students in these introductory literature courses, and I was not certain what to expect. But I am continually amazed by students' ability to eventually understand their own reading strategies, and then use that understanding to further their own appreciation of literature. Let me share just a few examples:

> I think that because of our having to read *Lolita*, my expectations of what literature should be have changed. Before, I wanted a piece of literature to follow a clear-cut path. I guess I am used to reading conventional literature. I wanted a story to have a set plot, setting, point of view, etc., but things have changed. It is nice to read a story where you do not know what to expect.

His reference to "reading conventional literature" is a recognition of his own "conventional" reading style. In order to consciously read in an unconventional way, one must first recognize the conventionality of one's initial reading style. I would say this student has become a better reader.

Another student registered a similar response in commenting on Kurt Vonnegut's *Slapstick*:

> I enjoyed the novel because of the fact that it did not have to make sense. I looked at all the conventional elements from a different perspective and thoroughly enjoyed the novel. I could look at some of the different stories read in this class unconventionally, and appreciate quite a few that I might not have at the semester's beginning.

This student would now seem in a better position not only to do well in the formal study of literature, but also to become a life-long reader.

I would have to say that I am more concerned with teaching a *reading process* than I am with teaching a particular selection of texts. It is *reading* that I teach:

> Before this class I had to force myself to read something because I thought I hated to read. But now that I have come to realize what I like to read, and the styles I like to read, I find reading more an enjoyment than a chore.

How can it be that this student *thought* he hated to read? He indicates that reading had always been a chore for him, which probably means that he could never find that deeply-hidden meaning. But somehow he has discovered what he likes to read and—most importantly—finds reading enjoyable. Isn't this what it's all about?

No, of course not; that is not what it's all about. A criticism sometimes made of the kind of subjective approach advocated here is that it does not make for—and may actually prevent—any real insight into literary works. My experience, however, suggests that this is not the case. For instance, in writing about *Slapstick*, a student notices the repetition that Vonnegut uses in Wilbur's responses ("I had to laugh. Hi Ho.") and points out that similar repetition is not used when Wilbur is crying. She accounts for this by saying that "perhaps Vonnegut wanted to lend more sincerity to Wilbur's crying than to his laughing." I would call this a genuine critical insight. The same student continues:

> One section that combines several elements discussed above is when Wilbur talks about a song that Melody and Isadore should learn for "when they set out for new adventures on the Island of Death." It goes like this:
>
> > Oh, we're off to see the Wizard
> > The wonderful Wizard of Oz
> >
> > *   *   *
> >
> > If ever a whiz of a Wiz there was,
> > It was the Wizard of Oz.
> >
> > *   *   *
> >
> > And so on.
> >
> > *   *   *
> >
> > Hi Ho.   (202)
>
> I'm not sure what Vonnegut wants us to feel from this emphasized section. My feeling was a sense of irony, comparing the junk-heap of NYC to the Land of Oz and comparing Wilbur to the Wizard. Everyone believed that Wilbur and the Wizard were great men, but the Wizard turned out to be a cheap magician and Wilbur has no grandiose opinions of himself.

Working away from her initial response and articulating her strategies for dealing with unconventional literature, this student has "made sense" of this novel. Or here is another student trying to come to grips with the same novel:

> As for the ultimate effect of Vonnegut's unconventional use of the elements upon me as a reader, the most I can possibly say is that there can not be a more appropriate title than *Slapstick* for this novel. It epitomizes my reaction: full of lively characters to whom I could relate, but had little sympathy for, in outrageous but possible situations, being ultimately victimized by life's events and tests, and proving that some of us are "not very good at life." Just as I react to Laurel and Hardy, I react with laughter rising from a broken heart, and a "Hi Ho."

The idea of victimization is a profound one; taking a personal, subjective approach—to begin with—did not prevent this student from reaching this insight.

One more example will illustrate that a reader-response approach is not incompatible with students' achieving some insight into a literary work. The following excerpt is from a student's essay discussing the concept of rebellion in Ken Kesey's *One Flew Over the Cuckoo's Nest*. Notice that her understanding of the novel has its roots in a personal connection to the novel that the student had earlier been encouraged to make:

> McMurphy humanized that sanitarium and everyone in it.... In the end I saw hope for those Acutes who found their courage. I guess I just have a weak spot for a rebel and that certainly describes McMurphy.... He would stand up to anyone and as a shy person I find that an admirable trait. His fire spread to the other men and I enjoyed watching them learn to live.

This student, in recognizing the source of her admiration for the protagonist, is able to reach an appreciation of the novel on her own terms, which just happen to be terms that most other readers would find acceptable.

The case that I have been trying to make amounts to a recommendation that introductory literature courses become courses in reading as much as they are courses in interpretation. I have suggested that a developmental component exists as students move from "reading" to "interpretation," and that an effective way to begin this reading instruction is by incorporating reader-response criticism into one's course design. The student illustrations I have used, naturally, are the strongest ones I have collected over the past few years, and represent a minority of the students in any single class. The majority of students, however, do make progress; I see most of them increasing their level of awareness of their own reading strategies and, as a result, their appreciation of literature. I would like to close with a few comments about the planning that goes into this approach.

Obviously, I must consider the individual texts the students will read; I make my own personal response to each text and anticipate how students may respond, looking for ways to avoid the ever-popular and least effective reaction: "I was confused" (or, "I didn't understand it"). For example, with Katherine Anne Porter's "The Jilting of Granny Weatherall," I will ask students to consider a reader who has recently had a relative, especially an elderly one, become ill or pass away. It is no great feat to get them to see that that reader will respond more intensely to the story than a reader without that recent experience. This is understandable. Inevitably, someone in the class is in a similar situation and willing to talk about it. Rather than have students acknowledge-and-disregard the experience, I tell them this is exactly where they want to begin their interaction with the story.

I have used Susan Glaspell's play *Trifles* (1916) with good results—students generally don't have trouble responding to this play.[4] The action takes place in a single scene, a farmhouse kitchen shortly after the turn of the century. The farm belongs to Mr. and Mrs. Wright; Mr. Wright was found lying in his bed the day before strangled with a piece of rope, and Mrs. Wright, though she denies it, is being held on suspicion of murder. The play contains five characters: the County Attorney and the Sheriff, who have come to search for clues, the Sheriff's wife, who is collecting some things to bring to Mrs. Wright in jail, and a neighboring couple, Mr. and Mrs. Hale. It was Mr. Hale who discovered the murder when he stopped by to talk with Mr. Wright.

The action quickly divides along gender lines. The three men, as they look for evidence, criticize Mrs. Wright for being a poor housekeeper. They also make fun of Mrs. Hale and the Sheriff's wife, Mrs. Peters, for concerning themselves with trifles—jars of fruit Mrs. Wright had recently put up and an unfinished quilt—while a *murder* investigation is going on. Mrs. Hale bristles at the criticism of Mrs. Wright, but both she and Mrs. Peters remain in their place at the kitchen table, out of the way (though the table is center-stage). As the investigation proceeds, these "trifles" lead the women, and the audience, to an understanding of what must have taken place. As a result, the two women decide to keep the evidence from the men. The play ends with the men having discovered absolutely nothing that would prove Mrs. Wright's guilt.

Students typically react strongly to the decision of the two women to hide evidence. Let me share the responses of two students in particular, Melissa and Justin.

The essays students eventually wrote are what Kathleen McCormick terms interactive response statements.[5] The students' thinking about a text begins with the Reading Journals, in which I ask for brief responses under four headings: Questions, Associations, Comments, and Gist. For the last of these I ask students to state whether they find the work optimistic or pessimistic; they *must* choose one or the other, and then indicate reasons for their choice. In this case, Melissa found the text optimistic while Justin found it pessimistic. Melissa's response was based on characterization, while Justin's was based primarily on plot.

Both began with an emotional response, as I encouraged them to; in fact, both began with the *same* reaction: anger. Melissa was angry at the men for the way they treat the women. She accused them of being insensitive and arrogant, and because of this treatment she felt they deserved to come up empty-handed. Justin was angry about not being told, finally, who killed Mr. Wright and why. He acknowledges the clues the women find, but seems to look for the authority of the author: "However, the author never explains who actually killed the bird.... the author has just left me hanging...."

Melissa did not display this same lack of certainty; it was provided by the evidence uncovered by the two women: "Without the dead canary, the men should have a hard time proving that Mrs. Wright murdered her husband." She was not, however, completely satisfied with the play's ending. She wanted to see the trial, to see Mrs. Wright's acquittal. "Most of all," she says, "I would like to know the ladies' help had not been in vain." In a sense, Melissa ended up being as focused on plot as Justin was, a tendency I find prevalent among the students I teach.

Both of these essays I found successful, for two reasons. First, both students referred to specific scenes and dialogue within the play in order to support their theses. Second, both students—Justin more so than Melissa—took the opportunity to think about their reading strategies. Melissa confessed to guessing what a story is about based on its title; she thought this play fitted its title perfectly. Justin explained that he realized he always looks for "negative evidence," by which he seems to mean incriminating evidence. This dovetails with his need-to-know: "I like to be given all the facts followed with a good polished ending." *Trifles* does not meet these expectations, and so he was disappointed. But this is something I can explain to him, that the act of reading literature is always situated. We can improve students' reading by helping them understand first their own situatedness.

The course does have a long-term plan. We begin with conventional texts and talk about them in conventional ways. The students are comfortable with this since it is in line with their expectations. During this time, though, I focus on raising their awareness of their own reading processes, the expectations they bring to reading, and why they have those expectations. Late in the semester we get to unconventional works, texts like "Lost in the Funhouse," "Cortez and Montezuma," *Lolita, Slapstick*. These less conventional works can be viewed as simply being less compatible with the students' general expectations and reading strategies, but not less readable or, ultimately, understandable. Students still find themselves responding to one or more aspects of the works, as seen above in some of my student illustrations. And if they have a response, they have a way to talk about the text.

My approach asks students to figuratively watch themselves as they read a text and observe the effects that text has on them. Once at this point—and it takes some doing—they are ready to write, and it is easy to demand support: you say this story made you angry? Okay, show me where and explain why. This can only be done satisfactorily by a close reading and analysis of the text. This rhetorical approach, in combination with reader-response theory, gives students a beginning point. It gives them something concrete to write about and, more importantly, makes better readers of them.

Notes

1. E.D. Hirsch, Jr., "Back to History," *Criticism in the University*, eds. Gerald Graff and Reginald Gibbons (Evanston: Northwestern University Press, 1985), pp. 189–97.

2. See Terry Eagleton, *Literary Theory: An Introduction* (Minneapolis: University of Minnesota Press, 1983).

3. Kathleen McCormick, "Theory in the Reader: Bleich, Holland, and Beyond," *College English*, 47 (December 1985), pp. 836–50; see also Gary Waller McCormick and Linda Flower, eds., *Reading Texts: Reading, Responding, Writing* (Lexington: Heath, 1987).

4. Susan Glaspell, *Trifles Literature: The Human Experience*, eds. Richard Abcarian and Marvin Klots (New York: St. Martin's, Press, 1990), pp. 616–28.

5. McCormick, pp. 836–50.

Part Five

Two First-Year Courses

Malory and Macherey,
Ballads and Belsey:
Teaching Theory and the Medieval Text

Stephen Knight

Medievalists are a contradictory group. Some seem devotedly con-
servationist, the sort of people who, as Malcolm Bradbury once
wrote, weave their own clothes and bake their own bread, yet it
looks as if they bake the curtains and weave the bread. Other medievalists, however, are extremely high tech and in many departments are the computer evangelists. Equally paradoxically, many
scholars devoted to the Middle Ages seem to be radically empiricist and anti-theory, and yet they deal confidently with Aquinas,
Abelard, polysemantic allegory, and other scholastic niceties that
make Lacan read like Asterix.

In terms of theory, these contradictions are becoming dynamic.
If the medieval end of departments of English has been in the past
theoretically quiet, that silence has certainly been broken. Authors
like Eugene Vance and Lee Patterson have served notice of a theorizing intent; feminist medievalists like Carolyn Dinshaw and Judith Ferster have made a particular impact very recently.[1]

That is in research, though. There would still be very many
medievalists who feel that undergraduate teaching requires careful
familiarization with language, contexts, genres, concepts, the full
armory of annotation and explication that both detains and en-
riches the process of teaching medieval texts. For students with an
interest in medieval studies, theory therefore often only begins at
the graduate level.

There are problems with such a late encounter, since it requires
students to make a readjustment of a major kind, and it also involves some quite elementary labor before harvesting these new
fields of blossoming theory. It is an unusual student who can pick

up, say, feminist theory and in a relatively short time produce a solidly original thesis drawing on that material.

Pedagogically speaking, it would be much better for medieval students if they could engage with aspects of theory as they first encounter the texts and their language, as is a normal experience these days for students of literature that is modern, postmodern, and whatever comes next. Then by graduation time young medievalists would have a good knowledge of what theories might be of value to their own work, a fair amount of practice in such methods, and so be more likely to produce innovative and professionally valuable graduate work by projecting a secure methodology through material and contexts that are themselves the prime object of research.

The interest in putting this notion into practice was in part a personal one, because of my belief in its value, but also institutional, since the English Department at the University of Melbourne already had three full-year courses in first year, at a fairly high level of theorization. The decision to add one with a major medieval component implied that to attract the best students and to be on even terms with the other courses, it must have some standing in terms of theory. No choice is a good choice, as the old proverb has it.

But strategy is sometimes simpler than tactics. The question was just how to do this without short-cutting the necessary elements of "translation," both linguistic and contextual. In part the solution was to choose texts carefully, and that came largely from long experience, selecting material where students would be inclined to read for interest and so undertake linguistic work themselves. Malory's Arthuriad, in the Oxford Standard Authors edition (still quite cheap), a non-normalized text with adequate glossary, had proved valuable in this role before.[2] Added to that, a Chaucer tale seemed correct; again experience showed that *The Franklin's Tale* was one where the issues of importance, in the simple "teaching medievalism" sense, were raised by the narrative in process and so could be read into the text. The opposite is true of, say, *The Merchant's Tale* or *The Nun's Priest's Tale*, where in order to explain ironies the teacher must undertake a long detour through medieval "normalcy," and progress is slow or non-existent.

But there were other darker purposes in mind, namely that those particular texts would lend themselves very well to a theorized reading, as will be revealed in what follows.

To give the conclusion first (a classical rhetorical structure), there was a good deal of success in this venture of theorized medievalism. Among our graduates this year who took the course in first year will be students who have studied Chaucer and modern feminist theory, Malory and post-modern fiction, late medieval ballads and Australian narrative, all on an equal footing and with evident profit.

It is clear that transference across periods can exist and can have a positive effect. The medieval material can operate as an illuminating contrast, a kind of pre-modernism that sets the period of classic realism in an interrogating frame. Good students can see the historical and the analytic value of comprehending theoretically the patterns of alterity that the medieval texts provide.

At the initial planning stage of the course, a basic strategy was "estrangement" in the Brechtian sense. In fact it was decided to exploit a long-standing feature of the Australian academy. Traditionally, following a British model, each department had a "language" section, which taught Old and Middle English and also the History of the English Language and some rudimentary semantics or stylistics. The development of linguistics in the 1960s tended to change that, and in some locations the "language" element dwindled to one or two underemployed medievalists. But in the larger departments there has remained a sense that medievalists are also linguists, and some of them have pursued that interest into semiotics.

So this year-long, first-year course was shaped as half medieval and half modern/semiotic, to build in a deliberate structure of estrangement; the medieval component was used to de-naturalize students' normal concepts of the text, the character, the narrator, and so on. On that basis, in the second semester, contemporary Australian literature could be read, also in terms of theory, for a semiotic reading of its own constructions and as a cultural formation relative to a place and time. The medieval material, that is, was not only presented as valid and open to theory in its own terms, but also as itself a theoretical instrument of inquiry. Alterity as a pedagogical instrument is a definite potential strength of medieval literary work.

Within that overarching strategy, it was a matter of reflection just what types of theoretical approach would be most suitable both for the handling of the medieval material and for the intention to instrumentalize in a modern direction what was learned through the medieval texts.

Here I have some firm opinions that all might not share. It seems to me that the obsession in modern theoretical discourse with the construction and deconstruction of the subject and her/his authority and body is itself a subjective compulsion grounded in classic realism and its context. However, the subject is not a "given" in medieval texts, and externality, not privacy, is the notionally "normal" ontology. This is especially the case with Malory, and though Chaucer does in some areas present the question of a marginal subjectivity, especially in *The House of Fame,* this does not emerge as a "normal" construct. As a result it seemed that in the medieval part of the course subject-oriented theory from the Lacanian context was not immediately appropriate—but might become so in the second part of the course as attention turned to the modern period.

In a similar way the Derridean analysis of meaning relies heavily on the literary tradition and its developed apparent imperatives. Accordingly, those analyses of the relativity of signification would not engage well with texts where the impersonal was asserted consistently as a norm; where an instrumental theory of discourse was, through rhetoric, the basic concept of language; where verification rested on a theory of divine immanence, and where the impersonal was asserted consistently and the underlining notion of a superhuman given was present in both an epistemology external to the human function and, through the patterns of "Gothic" or "vertical" structure, in the form itself.

It remains a project to read medieval texts against Lacan and Derrida, and potentially a valuable one: Lacan especially for the late medieval period of emergent subjectivity, and Derrida for the high medieval classics of apparently marmoreal language. But that project needs to be presaged by a lengthy understanding of the ideologies of form and implied context in those texts—a postgraduate project indeed.

Foucault appeared more directly interesting for medieval theory, but his work also seems a more senior concern, though also a positive one. Medievalists can find Foucault oversimplistic, because in some ways he continues the humanist project of marginalizing the Middle Ages and using them as a dark age against which his own illumination can shine more clearly. Like most aspects of the enlightenment, the Foucauldian insights can be projected back several centuries in at least incipient form.

Yet Foucault's method, especially as realized through neo-historicism, has many possibilities for reading medieval institutions through their surviving discourses; I have myself ventured into analyses of medieval gardens and food in this direction. There are larger quasi-Foucauldian projects which seem full of possibilities, such as a reading of Kent as a sub-text both literal and metonymic for *The Canterbury Tales.* Some of these notions could be and were used in passing in the first-year course, though there is a great danger with such material. The experienced researcher who uses some of her/his pointed ideas as a teacher may tend to inspire callow jargonesque imitations—the Leavisite phenomenon was one example. Nevertheless, it did seem legitimate to touch on some neo-historicism and sub-Foucauldian ways in which, if read properly so that text and context become each other's co-text, the Middle Ages might for a comprehension of Western practices become the Central Ages.

But if all those were in some way illusions to be alluded to, there were still some theorists, or at least theories, directly appropriate for first year. Perhaps swayed by the antique Australian model of language and medieval literature as potent combination, but also with a view to the inherent value of semiotics, the course planners decided that this subject needed to be in there, because it had a basic value of penetrating the husk of language to the kernel of discursive practice, to use a good medieval image. And unlike the traditional practices of *explication du texte*, semiotics presses, particularly in the Hallidayan inflection resident at Sydney University for a decade, towards a social reading of texts, a theoretical position related to Raymond Williams' cultural materialism, which is close to the center of my own interests, and was also a mainstream approach in the department.

But semiotics was to be handled with a difference. Because there were other theoretical matters that seemed of primary importance in the first, medievally-oriented semester, semiotics as such was never raised in that early sequence of the course; rather, attention was held at the level of traditional stylistics in the context of both Malory and Chaucer. The texts were read, especially in tutorial classes, for formations of syntax (especially Malory) and vocabulary (especially Chaucer). Jakobson's notions were used to clarify matters of combination and of selection, and students were asked to write fairly short expositions of passages in an overtly stylistic mode to indicate their understanding of the ways in which the significance of the text was linguistically assembled.

This had a dual role. Partly it lifted language study above the level of mere linguistic mechanics (underlining *hem* as it used to be called down in the trenches of English 1 at Sydney). And partly by foregrounding language as the medium of meaning, textual and social, it prepared a position for a full development of semiotics early in the second semester, where this topic was addressed fully, relying on Kaja Silverman's guide, *The Subject of Semiotics*.[3] From there on students were encouraged to apply those insights to their own reading; they collected dossiers of decodable material, and also focussed on modern Australian novels in a discourse-aware frame of mind, with some highly interesting results: the tendency to value and comprehend newly the special power of Elizabeth Jolley was striking.[4]

That movement—from stylistics into semiotics—worked well, but it was a rather simple relation between the medieval and the modern, in which the theoretical weight was modern. But the medieval and its theorized possibilities had more part than that to play in this course. The concepts that seemed most possible and most useful to explore with first-year students, who were mostly encountering a medieval text for the first time, lay in the areas of narration, structure, characterization—or genre and mimesis, to theorize a little. First of all, the course tackled the issue of expectation; it confronted "normal" ideas of what made a text "good" and asserted that "common sense" ideas of structure, nature, and value in literature are in fact relative to a particular culture.

The classes began with selections from Malory, each sequence read in company with a chapter from Catherine Belsey's book *Critical Practice*.[5] The purpose was to foreground the special and constructed nature of narrative in the classic novel tradition, and to speculate on the social meaning of such constructions by adducing the nature of different kinds of construction.

I asked students first to read *The Tale of Sir Launcelot*, Book 3, as it is sometimes called (Book 6 in Caxton's edition). A guide to Malory's English was provided, with special attention being paid to "false friends" which students would know but misinterpret, such as "large" meaning generous or "small" meaning slim.

The immediate purpose was to show a fully episodic narrative in function; brief enough, based on short "takes," all about Sir Launcelot, yet resisting any sense of rational or cumulative order. This was contrasted with the shape of the classic novel, and the class read and were lectured on the thoughts in Belsey's first chapter about "common sense."[6] Students were brought to recognize that episodic structure has its own para-sequential logic, not unlike a video clip. This perception was then contextualized, as classes were urged to think about the implications for epistemology and ontology of this difference in fictional structures. Belsey provided an account of the nature of "expressive realism" and Malory's episodic text provided a contrast, with a deducible ideology behind it in feudal, impersonal, honor-centred ideas of value and being.

Associated with this argument was an analysis of the narrational style and the representation of character. A chronicle style, a narrator without diegesis, who cannot internalize any knowledge, characters who are "two dimensional"—all this material was read not only for surprise and dismay, but also for confirmation of Belsey's exposition of the nature and meaning of the novel.

This analysis proceeded through reading the grail story, where "character" remains two-dimensional in a striking way, and the development towards the climax is not made through humanist moralizing but by means of an overarching Christian design—evidently "vertical" structure, and more sophisticated than the honor-linked serial coherence of the Launcelot Tale. Shlomith Rimmon-Kenan's book *Narrative Fictions* was valuable at this stage to specify the various patterns of narrative and their precise denomination.[7]

Belsey's chapters on character and on context were read during these weeks; on the basis of her argument that the novel is a specifically bourgeois form, a projection was made from the different structural forms observed in Malory. It was argued that the medieval model of narrative and character was authentic to a particular social and economic structure, a pattern which was outlined and supported with secondary sources from medieval scholarship such as Postan and Hatcher.[8] As well as supporting the Belseyan argument about the relation of the novel to a period, an economy, this analysis extended into identifying gender appropriation in Malory through the treatment of female characters, especially Guinevere.

As the last two Books of Malory were read, further theoretical issues were encountered as they come up in *Critical Practice*. One was Pierre Macherey's argument about strain and absence.[9] It was readily apparent that the earlier Books showed an absence of "character" in the modern sense. What was stressed in Machereyan terms was the "strain" element in the development of Launcelot and Guinevere towards "three dimensional" characters, and the way in which the text finally forecloses that development in a Christian resolution which, through the device of "confession," partly humanizes the formerly two-dimensional form. Religion can be read as the medium for personalization of the formerly de-personalized text, and cultural materialist points could be made in passing about the role of the church and its partial production of proto-humanism in the period, via mysticism, *devotio moderna* and so on.

In this way, Macherey's notion of the contextually "unspeakable" was developed. So was Belsey's argument about the "interrogative text," and in the final stages of this sequence it was argued that Malory's text is finally dialogic in voice: in part a classically feudal and gothic narrative, focussed on the multiple causation of the collapse of the Round Table; in part a more personalized narrative focussed on Launcelot and Guinevere and resolving in what looks very close to being their moralized tragedy.[10] These two narratives interrogated each other, and (here emerged an important thread to be pursued later) the style of what P.J.C. Field calls "romance" and "chronicle" were the dominants of these conflicting modes.[11]

That is, without naming it as such, a semiotic dialogism was identified between two historical forces in the text, between the two mutually interrogating elements of the final sequence. A crucial epitome of that dynamic conflict was seen in the contrast between Sir Ector's paratactic eulogy and elegy (honorific/feudal) for his dead brother Launcelot, and the hypotactic, internally evaluating speeches (moral/protobourgeois) made by Launcelot, Guinevere, and Gawain about their personal roles in the catastrophe. The shades of the moralistic prison house are seen closing around the medieval externalized narrative. So in the context, and in the language of theory, the "memorable" parts of the Arthuriad are estranged for students and shown as part of a history of discourse— the shadow of Foucault again touching the program.

This sequence of six lectures and supporting classes had, in theory at least, taken students from ignorance of any medieval texts to a fair grasp of relatively easy Middle English, and had provided some knowledge in the structures of the medieval culture. But students also had learned about: different ways of structuring a narrative; modes of the narrator's voice; alternative ways of conceiving character; the socioeconomic determinants and connections of those variant modalities; the possibility of a dialogic structure in a text; style and its variations as a producer of social meaning; genre as a discursive social form; the constraints in discourse within a given context; and the capacity of a text to interrogate its constraints. They had also learned to recognize some of the initiating gestures towards the classic novel and also the cultural formation of the subject, which were both data for this course and matters that had value in other, later areas of their work.

Not all of the fifty students mastered all this material—though quite a lot did. But all of them were made aware of the department's view that this kind of theoretical positioning was important and would help them understand better not only how texts are made but how we, our culture, and so our society, are constructed in part at least through textualities.

With that unit acting as a primer in both theory and medieval texts, the course turned to Chaucer. Taking the texts out of historical context was itself polemical, to show that history need not be sequential.

Another staff member planned and taught the Chaucer material, and I will merely paraphrase its structure here. She developed several strands from what had gone before and added considerable amounts of material to it. The fairly simple features of Malorian style are mostly syntactic, but in the case of *The Franklin's Tale* a range of lexical issues emerge to develop a new level of complexity along the Jakobsonian axis of selection. As was planned, students were in fact being prepared for the semiotic analysis to come, though at this stage that kind of discourse analysis was held at the level of denotation and connotation.

The previous introduction of gender-linked representation, made through the character of Guinevere, was developed at considerable length through Dorigen and her treatment in the text, and at this stage feminist critics, especially Carolyn Dinshaw, became appropriate. Notions of patriarchal voice, stereotypical containment, secondary roles, the male gaze, and so on were thus brought into the students' conceptual vocabulary.

The tale also affords the possibility to speak more fully about genre. Romance and chronicle had been mentioned in the case of Malory, but at this point the possibilities, appurtenances and underlying structures of romance become available for analysis, and could be used as an estranging introduction to the forms of the novel that either deal with or repress gender issues. In addition the notion of genre as a socially related voicing could be presented, a Hallidayan position, and an issue to be taken up in the second part of the course.

The more difficult language of Chaucer and the more complex interrelationship of elements in the text made it much more appropriate to teach him after Malory. Previous experience had shown that Chaucer was a difficult introductory text if anything more than simple language study was envisaged. It is hard to bring enough theorized material into lucid use on Chaucer as a first text, because so many of his references are oblique; a great deal of exposition is necessary before the point of his reference can be made out. Theory of the kind intended is difficult to introduce in a situation where one of the elements is silent and the mode is primarily ironical, as is so often the case with Chaucer. Malory's text, on the other hand, acts out the socially basic forms, thematic and formal, from knightly violence to courtly love. It proved right to take the authors "out of order": ahistoricity produces a better historical method. In general, selecting both the mode and the sequence of handling texts is a crucial part of successful teaching, especially when it has aspirations to handle theory.

The Chaucer sequence developed much and confirmed much, but the last section of this one-semester course paid attention to something that had not been fully developed through the two major texts, namely the formation of the subjective voice as narrator. The narrator in Malory is stubbornly impersonal, except for a few intrusive controlling moments (as when he refuses to say whether Launcelot and Guinevere were actually in bed or not when they are caught); the voice of the Chaucerian narrator does not raise this point to visibility, not even in *The Pardoner's Tale*, where the apparent humanism of the text hardly stands up to a searching analysis, either medieval or theoretical.

It seemed important to contextualize and provide some theoretical vocabulary for the discussion of the subjective narrator, and so this was dealt with in two final weeks where shorter and later texts were employed. The ballad "Clerk Saunders" (Child, no. 69) was read, to show how both in narrative and in mimesis it is impersonal, fragmented, unsentimental.[12] The whole affective structure of "expressive realism," as Belsey describes it, is absent, yet the text expresses real enough issues in a specific social context— like other ballads from this maior theme-group, it represents the constraint of a daughter's sexuality by the men in her family.

With the "theme" and the impersonal mode of this ballad established, its tone was then contrasted with the "addition" which often appears at the end of it, namely "Sweet William's Ghost" (Child, no. 77).[13] This completion or "return" episode (some narratological discussion with the class framed the presentation of this phenomenon) acts as a patriarchal foreclosure, itself expressed in fully sentimentalized and empirical terms—here, still with Belsey, we have expressive realism to the life, even in death.

Against that double text were contrasted several "renaissance" sonnets, in which the subjective narrator as sentient construct is in full unproblematized flow. This is the sort of poem that most of the students would have recognized in unestranged comfort when they started the course, expecting as they did to resume their school essays on Keats and Yeats; but that kind of poem, and its ideologies of consciousness and form, had by the end of the semester been located and relativized in its constructed context, by means of a reasonable amount of theorized understanding.

In these ways, it has seemed possible to teach medieval literature for itself in a theorized context; to introduce students to theory; and to prepare them for a full analysis of their own literary world in a mood which eschews the naïve dangers of "common sense."

To theorize one's own practice is a part of any proper course, and in some ways this semester evidently hewed fairly close to the long-established process of teaching first-year students how to read. This was not a text-free theory course, such as some advocate and some enjoy. It used the students' interest in texts as a way of asserting the value of theory, by giving them texts which were strange and using theory as the explicatory key. At present, I believe that is by far the best way to introduce theory. I also firmly believe that theory itself is much the best introduced, even if in a preliminary and dilatory way, in first year. Then it becomes a normative tool, just part of the way you do things at "uni"—to use the uniquely Australian slang term.

Different contexts will have different discourses: that is one of the issues this and any decently theorized course should communicate. There is a whole range of special conjunctures upon which the Melbourne course I have been describing was based. It attracted quite good quality students, fairly well-trained formally, and with quite a high opinion of themselves and their abilities. You could challenge them to keep up with you and not get brickbats in return. Staff and resources are also part of the transaction: with other colleagues, in other years, in other places, with other texts available, this process no doubt could, or would have to, look quite different.

There were also things left out. The grail story, for example, was used in this process as a back-up text, through which to reinforce issues like the absence of "character," the nondiegetic narrator, the lack of moralized tension and revelation (especially when Launcelot just can't beat his perfect son Galahad). Elsewhere, in fact, in a more senior "Arthurian Legend" course, the same text is opened up to Jungian analysis, with its avatars in the grail legend.

A greater dissatisfaction to a determined cultural materialist like myself is the amount of rich material that had to be omitted, such as the origins of romance (in the change of inheritance practices in twelfth-century France, crossed with the advent of the Crusades); or the context of *The Canterbury Tales*, including thoughts about the pilgrimage as the Peasant's Revolt in fictional reverse (discussed in my book *Geoffrey Chaucer*).[14]

But you must leave things out to have a workable structure, and you must thoughtfully repeat what you have chosen to privilege as the key issues of theory, and you must in all modes of practice remember your aims. The principles at work in this medieval course were to introduce students to a reasonable range of the language of narrative analysis, and to set those unusual texts, as discovered, against the allegedly "normal" novel, with the impact of denaturalizing the novel and revealing the social context which speaks through the medieval and, by implication, the modern text.

Between Macherey and Belsey, with their attendant sources and theoretical providers, the course zigzags repeatedly across the texts, and as a result produces some fairly clear-minded readers aware of the meaningful difference that can exist in texts and their contexts. And so on, or back, to their own culture, estranged and critical, as Brecht would have had it.

If you want to teach theory in a medieval context (or indeed in any first-year context), the first maneuver, in my view, is to select carefully the elements of theory appropriate for such distanced texts and for these students at this stage of their career. Those theories must have reasonably good handbooks readily available. There must be a full feedback process in seminars or tutorials. The course should be team-taught, with a good interchange of staff opinion and responsibility, lest theory become dogma, or worse, eccentricity.

Those things provided, there are special opportunities in using medieval literature as a framework for theoretical analysis. It makes for well-founded theorists, in whatever period they work. And it makes for good medievalists, too. They might still weave their own curtains and bake their own bread, but the curtains are not tightly drawn against the modern world, and the bread they eat is that of intellectual nourishment.

Notes

1. See Eugene Vance, *From Topic to Tale: Logic and Narrativity in the Middle Ages* (Minneapolis: University of Minnesota Press, 1989), and *Mervelous Signals: Poetics and Sign Theory in the Middle Ages* (Lincoln: University of Nebraska Press, 1986); Lee Patterson, *Negotiating the Past: The Historical Understanding of Medieval Literature* (Madison: University of Wisconsin Press, 1987); Carolyn Dinshaw, *Chaucer's Sexual Poetics* (Madison: University of Wisconsin Press, 1989); and Judith Ferster, *Chaucer on Interpretation* (New York: Cambridge University Press, 1985).

2. Malory, *Works*, ed. Eugene Vinaver (Oxford: Oxford University Press, 1971).

3. Kaja Silverman, *The Subject of Semiotics* (Oxford: Oxford University Press, 1983).

4. The text used was Elizabeth Jolley's *Foxybaby* (St. Lucia: University of Queensland Press, 1985).

5. Catherine Belsey, *Critical Practice* (London: Methuen, 1986).

6. Belsey, pp. 1–36.

7. Shlomith Rimmon-Kenan, *Narrative Fictions: Contemporary Poetics* (London: Methuen, 1983).

8. See M. Postan, *The Medieval Economy and Society: An Economic History of Britain in the Middle Ages* (Harmondsworth: Penguin, 1975); and E. Miller and J. Hatcher, *Medieval England: Rural Society and Economic Change, 1086–1348* (London: Longman, 1978).

9. Belsey, pp. 103–24.

10. Belsey, pp. 85–102.

11. See P.J.C. Field, *Romance and Chronicle: A Study of Malory's Prose Style* (Bloomington: Indiana University Press, 1971).

12. Francis J. Child, ed., *English and Scottish Popular Ballads* (1882–98; rpt. New York: Dover, 1965), II. 156–58.

13. Child, II. 226–29.

14. Stephen Knight, *Geoffrey Chaucer* (Oxford: Blackwell, 1986).

Humanism and the Teaching of Theory

Richard Freadman

I

Though literary theory has held a prominent place in North American and Commonwealth literature department syllabuses for over a decade, fundamental questions about the nature and teaching of such theory persist, at least for some. Two such questions are particularly pertinent for a volume on theory and the classroom. How is theory to be defined? How might particular construals of the term influence the way in which it is taught?

But why do the questions arise at all? In part they arise because within literary studies the term "theory" has been used with bemusing variability. Consider the following six familiar construals of the term in literary studies. One, theory is often used to designate a range of analytic and interpretive practices which operate in a mode of negative critique—critique directed at established literary-intellectual protocols, assumptions, practices, and at various ideological aspects of the social formation. Two, theory is often characterized exclusionistically: on this account it signifies any intellectual practice that is not empiricist, positivistic, liberalistic, humanistic, pluralistic, analytic (in the sense of analytic philosophy), and so on. Three, theory is frequently employed as a global descriptive term for a range of political/intellectual movements, the majority anti-humanist in orientation: Marxism, (Post)structuralism, Feminism, Postcolonial studies, (Post)Freudian psychoanalytic discourses, Reception theory, and others. Four, theory is sometimes taken to be the typical activity of cultural moments in which settled understandings of the world are persistently and radically put in question. Five, a less political usage construes theory as a meta-discourse which describes, and perhaps prescribes, the activity of critical interpretation (much postmodern theory, of course, refuses the distinction between theory and practice). A sixth and more general deployment of the term theory equates it with self-reflexive conceptualization pertaining to some form of rational inquiry.

For the prospective teacher of theory, at whatever level, this is an imposing list. But there are further complications that need to be negotiated before long-deferred decisions about pedagogic method can be taken. One such complication has to do with assumptions about theory and its connections with critique. Though I have singled out a particular construal of theory that emphasizes its function as critique, the fact is that the first four of the six conceptions noted above all equate theory, either implicitly or explicitly, with radical critique—with what is often termed *oppositional practice*. Exclusionistic definitions exclude what are seen as *status quo* discourses, as do most of the anti-humanist theory movements; and the fourth construal, what I shall term theory-as-radical-interrogation, is of course inherently predisposed to radical critique. A further and related complication is that each of the oppositional practice conceptions holds, again either implicitly or explicitly, that oppositional practice necessarily entails an opposition to humanism. Humanism is the allegedly sovereign "Other" of avant-garde literary theory—that which is to be opposed, to be excluded from the universe of theory, to be put in question when questioning becomes radical and persistent. And there is an additional and again related factor, one which compounds this anti-humanist tendency. It is widely assumed that the sixth of these conceptions—theory as conceptual self-reflexivity—does not accommodate humanism. As readers of introductions to literary theory will know, the "othering" of humanism extends to a denial that it can be theoretical; that it can operate in the light of a consciously articulated, self-reflexive systematicity. It is not of course denied that humanists possess theories; but such theories are said to exist at a level of loose and unscrutinized ideological predisposition.[1] As such, they are considered poor candidates for high order meta-critical discourse of the kind denoted by the fifth of these conceptions.

In the light of the above, consider now two hypothetical theory teachers, each of whom represents a distinctive and significant disposition towards theory. The first is a committed postmodern, oppositional political critic. She subscribes to various emancipationist projects—class, gender, and racial emancipation—and tends to associate the ethos of rational inquiry with the ideological sources of oppression. She may have difficult decisions to make within the field that oppositional theory presents—she may for example find it hard to endorse a poststructuralist refusal of referentiality because it threatens the historical tenets of her Marxism—but in general she can occupy with relative comfort the intellectual universe of oppositional possibility. As a teacher she is likely to presuppose and promulgate the social-political commitments that inform her oppositional stance, and to deny that humanistic options have political and therefore educational validity. For her, literary theory and humanism are antithetical terms.

The position of my second hypothetical theory teacher is somewhat more problematic. She shares some of the first's emancipationist commitments: to class, gender, and racial emancipation. She also shares particular conceptual commitments—say to certain Marxist accounts of class—together with an impatience with some prominent precursor modes of criticism. She considers much Leavisite and New Critical discourse to be politically and theoretically inadequate. However, she cannot accept all aspects of the oppositional mode. She wants to maintain (or to develop) a more substantial account of individual human subjects than anti-humanist theory will countenance. She also believes that, notwithstanding the anti-humanist rhetoric of such theory, certain of its forms—especially some of the neo-Marxist and neo-Freudian variants—are rooted in and to some extent reflect traditions that have strong humanistic elements. This may particularly be the case with respect to the human subject. Just as importantly, she does not concede that the extremely various intellectual currents that constitute the history of humanism demonstrate that it is congenitally incapable of systematic conceptual self-reflexivity. Nor does she wish to relinquish the descriptive and even prescriptive function of theory as a meta-discourse; a discourse which is conceptually distinct from its object: in this case literature (or other forms of text). For her, then, humanism can lay claim to theoretical status, and she characterizes herself as a member of an intellectual species rare in the present climate: she thinks of herself as a humanist theorist.[2]

The predicament of this second teacher and theorist sets the context for this paper. Because her position on theory combines elements that would nowadays be considered antithetical, she cannot when designing a theory course merely follow the pedagogic precedents of oppositional theory, nor the structure of the textbooks that reflect the assumptions of such theory. Instead, she needs a format that will permit unfashionable combinations and that will reflect her humanist commitments. In constructing such a format she will need to consider how her course can accommodate the often exclusionistic commitments of others, and the anti-humanism that runs deep in contemporary theory.

Perhaps her first step will be to ask how and how far the sort of humanism she espouses might predispose her to a particular kind of syllabus design. Let us assume that, given her commitment to substantive conceptions of the individual subject, hers is the kind of humanism that will accord particular emphasis to intellectual freedom of choice—to students' entitlement to encounter and choose, in a suitably self-reflexive way, from a representative range of intra-disciplinary discourses. Such an orientation apparently entails some form of pluralism; but as recent debates have shown, pluralism remains a deeply problematic notion. Thus, if my humanist teacher were to consult the version of pluralism that Wayne C. Booth identifies and advocates as "limited pluralism" in *Critical Understanding: The Powers and Limits of Pluralism*, she might well find it uncongenial because it effectively sees pluralism as the exclusive province of humanism, and apparently construes certain anti-humanist discourses as unamenable to pluralistic dialogue.[3] This will not do for her, partly because much of the contemporary theory that excludes humanism is nevertheless pluralistic in its accommodation of other anti-humanisms (thus Marxism, psychoanalysis and deconstruction, say, are often combined in synthetic theoretical discourses). But more importantly it won't do because it is her wish precisely to make as many options as practicable available to students, including options that are hostile to her humanism. Does this then mean that she should aspire to some peculiarly pure form of "modal" or "methodological" pluralism, a form that presupposes nothing but the desirability of putting all possibilities on view?[4]

Here again, my second teacher might consult recent discussions, for instance Ellen Rooney's account of pluralism in *Seductive Reasoning: Pluralism as the Problematic in Contemporary Literary Theory*. Rooney sees pluralism as a hegemonic practice which traverses humanist and anti-humanist discourses alike, and which is marked by a seductive aspiration to dialogue, persuasion, and inclusiveness—values which compel it to conceal or rationalize inevitable acts of exclusion.[5] Similarly, Bruce Erlich, in an article entitled "Amphibolies: On the Critical Self-Contradictions of 'Pluralism,'" argues that pluralism is always someone's pluralism and, as such, that it always reflects an embedded power relation. For

Erlich, the entire "self-contradictory" project of pluralism should now give way to discourses that chart and change power relations, for it is these relations that shape dialogic possibilities.[6] Even Booth seems to acknowledge that there can be no Archimedian release from monism; no space in which options may be displayed with complete dispassion. Pluralism, he fears, may be a "disguised monism."[7]

My humanist teacher might well concede this point, and might even agree with another commentator on pluralism, W.J.T. Mitchell, that "we are all dogmatists in some way or other."[8] Certainly, insofar as her pluralism appropriates in order to fashion a position that must ultimately exclude some alternative projections, her humanism is a monism—even a dogmatism—of a kind. But both theoretically and procedurally it is a monism that accords central importance to the ideal of diversity; a diversity, moreover, which is committed to fair and detailed representation of positions that are radically opposed to its own values and assumptions. However elusive that ideal may be, it gives educational expression to an aspiration that runs deep in the culture and which claims her allegiance. She may worry about the threat of what Marcuse calls "repressive tolerance"—the claim that the ethos of toleration in pluralistic liberal democracy defuses the power of oppositional discourses.[9] But better this than a repressive intolerance, especially at a time when viable alternative political models seem unavailable. Her preference, then, is for a pluralist pedagogy that will reflect a social-democratic politics, that will highlight the discursive positions of various theories and their relations to social power, and which may in practice achieve some of pluralism's educational aims, notwithstanding its conceptual and political shortcomings. Reassuringly, she finds that such a position is not without support among prominent literary theorists. Thus in an article "The Future of Theory in the Teaching of Literature," she finds Gerald Graff arguing from what appears to be a left liberal stance not unlike her own.[10] Graff proposes a pedagogy which makes the staging of disciplinary conflicts the organizing principle of literary studies education. He advocates what he terms a "functional pluralism" which, like conception four above, construes theory as the moment of radical self-reflexivity. Thus we have

> "theory" conceived not as a specialised idiolect (though it will and should remain that at some level), but as the generalized language for staging conflicts in ways that increase rather than lessen institutional viability. Theory is potentially the medium in

which the literary, cultural and educational conflicts which
underlie professional differences can be worked through and
made part of the informing context of literary education.[11]

This proposal is of particular interest to humanist teachers like the
one I have postulated because Graff sees such a humanist-pluralist
staging of disciplinary conflict as an inherently theoretical enterprise. Indeed, his extensive researches into the institutional history
of literary studies have led him to conclude that "the history of
academic professionalization of literary studies" belies the notion
that "'theory' and 'humanism' are naturally at odds."[12] So conceived, then, theoretical humanism seems not just a viable, but an
historically validated project.

My second teacher's humanist commitments may thus dispose
her to a course organized around the staging of disciplinary conflicts, but such "functional pluralism" would neither entail nor li-
cense a denial of the monistic character of her humanism. On the
contrary, it would be imperative that she make humanism itself a
subject of the self-reflexivity that informs a theory course of this
kind. This would entail an open declaration of the humanist-pluralist perspective that underlies the course, and open acknowledgment of pluralism's ultimately monistic character. Further, her
postulation *qua* theorist of a distinction between theory and its object will also have an important pragmatic consequence: literary
texts will be accorded prominence in the course; a prominence
which grants them a presumed margin of independence from theory and its associated critical practices. Here my teacher may find
herself at least partially in sympathy with Booth who, in an article
entitled "Pluralism in the Classroom," argues that humanistic discourse is "precisely the kind that places the richness of particular
achievements at the center: it is the particularity of particulars that
we find most valuable in the human works that come our way."[13]
Such a formulation may help to secure the text against a reduction-
ism that merely transposes its discourse into that of a sovereign
theoretical "idiolect." It will also permit particular theories to be
assessed, at least in part, with reference to the complexity and
comprehensiveness of the account they yield of particular instances of the class of objects to which such theories refer: texts.
However, my humanist teacher might wish to qualify Booth's
strictures by noting that just as no theory can exhaust the particularity of a text, so no text can wholly elude the explanatory and interpretive strategies of theory; nor can the text be conceived as existing in some state of aesthetically inviolate isolation from social-

ideological forces. Her course will need, therefore, to foster an active sense of dialectical exchange between text and theory.

As the reader will no doubt have surmised, the position I have sketched through the figure of the second theory teacher is very much my own position. In what follows I shall describe a first year English course titled *Literature, Criticism, Theory,* which I designed with the assistance of colleagues (particular thanks and acknowledgment are due here to Ann Blake, Graham Burns, Keryn Carter, and Chris Palmer) at La Trobe University in Melbourne, Australia. It is a course that tries to embody the theoretical humanist, functional pluralist, position outlined above.

II

But before describing the unit it may be useful to sketch in the institutional context in which it came into being.

Established in 1966, the La Trobe English Department had been characterized by a deep commitment to undergraduate teaching and an intellectual orientation that combined elements of traditional humanist scholarship with Leavisite moral and canonical emphases. The first-year courses that were offered during the period up to 1992 tended closely to reflect these commitments. A great deal of time was spent—and very effectively so—in introducing literature and literary critical techniques and terms to large groups, many of which contained a significant proportion of poorly prepared students. Introductions tended to focus on the canon and on a combination of contextual and evaluative discourse. Such an intellectual profile was typical of many—indeed most—Australian English departments up to the time of the advent of contemporary literary theory. However, as the impact of theory began to register, departments responded in varying ways and degrees to the new developments.

Like many, the La Trobe English Department incorporated elements of theory, often in a piecemeal way, during the 1980s. In 1990 it sought formally to articulate the disciplinary philosophy underlying such incremental change through an agreed commitment to pluralism. Where practicable, the department was to represent the full range of options available in contemporary criticism and theory; but humanist courses and approaches were also to retain a strong presence.

Theory was already well established at honors and M.A. levels, and an increasing number of courses either centering on or incorporating elements of theory were being established at second- and third-year levels. Trends in the discipline, and in particular the needs of prospective honors and postgraduate students, dictated that theory now also be systematically represented (it had been addressed selectively in some existing courses) at first-year level. The eventual configuration of first-year courses reflected the department's pluralist credo. Two of the existing courses were to remain: one a comparative introduction which focuses on modernism in first semester and Shakespeare in the second; the other an introduction to mainstream literature, with particular emphasis on poetry.

The two new first-year courses represent theory in different ways. The *Literature, Criticism, Theory* course endorses and is structured by a "functional pluralism." The other course—*Reading Culture*—is advocative in orientation: focusing largely on Australian literature, it offers introductions to various modes of oppositional theory and practice in respect to race, gender, and other cultural-ideological thematizations.

The title of *Literature, Criticism, Theory* reflects the somewhat unorthodox and composite conception of theory that informs it. "Literature" comes first, partly because the course is intended at one level as an introduction to literature, but also because we wanted to promote a perception that theory is in some sense answerable or responsible to the literary text—that theory cannot operate or be assessed in isolation. In placing "criticism" next, we hoped to discourage unduly *a prioristic* conceptions of criticism. While wishing to emphasize criticism's inevitable "theory-ladenness," we did not want to prompt the impression that theory is wholly determinative of critical practice. The text and the particularities of the practitioner will also inevitably help shape critical practice. The course tries to demonstrate the necessary reciprocity between theory and practice.

Having in a preliminary way established these relations among key terms, the course embarks on its central pedagogic strategy: to rotate a set of texts through various critical/theoretical perspectives, and to encourage students to assess evaluatively and comparatively the powers and possible limitations of the perspectives in question. How appropriate and how satisfactory is this approach to this particular text? What about the competing claims and strategies of *that* approach? Might there in fact be some areas of commonality as well as opposition between these perspectives?

Such are the kinds of recurrent question the course hopes to pose. It would, however, be inaccurate to say that the environment provided for such questions was politically wholly self-effacing. Like my imaginary humanist teacher, we began with the premise that certain emancipationist commitments had undeniable claims to prominence in literary studies and, as will become apparent, these constitute key concerns in the course. *Literature, Criticism, Theory,* then, is far from apolitical; however, it attempts among its various introductions to reflect some of the different weightings of the political that mark various critical/theoretical discourses, and even to air some positions in which political advocations play little explicit part.

Choices of texts were governed principally by three criteria. First, texts should be reasonably complex and (in some sense) significant *qua* text. We wanted the course to acquaint students with the experience of involvement with works of challenging power and sophistication. Secondly, texts should in a fairly self-evident way lend themselves to particular modes of theorizing and interpretation—preferably to a number of such modes. We wanted students to be able to compare, say, humanist, Marxist, and feminist readings of a given short story. Thirdly, the selection should be predominantly, though not exclusively, modern and contemporary in order to permit an initial sense of experiential access, particularly for those who have read little literature hitherto. (The presence of Chaucer is in part intended to confront students with cultural alterity.) Our intention was that this initial ease of engagement, of experiential identification with the text, would itself later become the subject of discussion as we moved on to ideology, reader response, and other issues pertaining to the formation of attitudes and interpretive responses. Course texts in order of appearance are: Alice Walker, *You Can't Keep a Good Woman Down*; D.H. Lawrence, *The Prussian Officer and Other Stories*; John Fowles, *The French Lieutenant's Woman*; Roland Barthes, *Mythologies*; *The Norton Anthology of Poetry* (Donne, Blake, Dickinson, Frost, Brooks, Lorde, Lowell, Rich); Geoffrey Chaucer, "General Prologue" to *The Canterbury Tales*; William Shakespeare, *Hamlet*; and Joseph Conrad, *Heart of Darkness*. Prescribed texts also include an introduction to literary theory, an anthology of contemporary theory and criticism, and a handbook of critical and theoretical terms: Raman Selden, *A Reader's Guide to Contemporary Literary Theory*; Dennis Walder, *Lit-*

erature in the Modern World; and M.H. Abrams, *A Glossary of Literary Terms.*[14] The selection of critical/theoretical perspectives was in part governed by the need for reasonably comprehensive and representative coverage, but also by the imperatives of accessibility. Accessibility here meant three things: that positions presented were susceptible to introduction at a conceptual level that would be manageable (with effort) for first-year students; that perspectives be readily referenced by students to familiar aspects of social and cultural experience (gender, class, etc.); and, finally, that the predominantly humanist orientation students had acquired at school be represented, identified as one among a range of approaches, and evaluated comparatively. The presence of familiar humanist discourse was also to be used as an occasion for consolidation of basic generic and critical concepts.

Perspectives represented are: humanism, feminism, Marxism, psychoanalysis, structuralism, postcolonial, race-oriented approaches, and reader response. Poststructuralism is given only passing attention. The course is taught in a sequence of modules based around a particular text, with each text bracketed, on the one hand, with a social/conceptual marker, and on the other, a critical/theoretical perspective. Thus, Gender: *The French Lieutenant's Woman:* Feminism. Each module centers on a particular approach. So the Fowles module is preceded by Marxism seen in relation to some Lawrence short stories. Approaches are sequenced as follows: humanism, race-oriented criticism/theory, Marxism, feminism, structuralism, reader response, psychoanalysis, postcolonial.

Even after decisions had been made about basic matters like the sequencing of approaches and texts, logistical problems remained. After all, the course aimed to do many things: in addition to introducing works of literature and a range of critical/theoretical approaches, it needed to introduce some of the founding concepts of contemporary theory, to raise general issues, and to make room for comparative discussion—something that one weekly lecture could not adequately accommodate. This meant planning lecture schedules and tutorials in considerable detail.

It seemed desirable for lecture sequences to move from the familiar to the unfamiliar, and from concepts to their "application" in critical practice. To accommodate these needs, lecture modules were divided into three: an initial genre-based lecture would help to consolidate knowledge of familiar humanist conceptions and terms; this would be followed by a lecture which introduced a central concept or set of concepts from contemporary theory. The third lecture in the sequence would then read a text or texts in the light of issues covered in the previous two lectures, particularly in the second. Thus, for example, the module on feminism and *The French Lieutenant's Woman* begins with a genre-based introductory lecture on the novel, concentrating on realist and metafictional traditions and possibilities. This is followed by a lecture on the concepts of gender and patriarchy and their applications in literary and cultural studies. The final lecture in the sequence concentrates on a feminist reading of Fowles's text, identifying the implications that the concepts in question have for critical practice.

In terms of abstract design such sequencing reflects course priorities. However, we felt that it would mean proceeding at a pace that would test all but the most accomplished of our first-year students. Clearly, lectures needed to be highly succinct; there would also have to be a degree of co-ordination between lectures that had often not been necessary or common in more traditional genre-gap or period-based first-year courses (many of which had enjoyed the luxury of two weekly lectures in early resource-rich days). There was no place in a course such as this for the discrete "one-off" lecture on a given text, delivered with little reference to what had gone before or was to come after it. For this reason we devised a booklet of lecture abstracts that outlines the scope of each lecture and indicates its connection to other lectures and its place both in the module sequence and the course as a whole. Lecturers were asked to confer in the preparation of lectures and, where possible, either to attend or to read the scripts of colleagues' presentations.

Course objectives that could not be achieved in lectures needed to be taken up in tutorials. Despite resource pressures to move to a seminar-based teaching format, the department had decided to retain the traditional two-hour, first-year tutorial (with greater concessions to the seminar format in second and third years). Given the range of objectives that needed to be accomplished in tutorials, the two-hour format seemed less a luxury than a necessity. It was to be used principally for four purposes: first, to reinforce and (as would often be necessary) clarify lecture material; second, to facilitate detailed discussion of course texts; third, to raise general course issues such as the competing claims of pluralism and political commitment, the nature and relationship of theory and criticism, canonicity and evaluation, and so on; finally—and importantly—tutorials would focus on comparative text-oriented discussion of course works. Here we would consider (among other things) the adequacy of approaches, both in general and in respect to given texts; areas of conflict and possible commonality between approaches; and characteristic rhetorical and conceptual strategies in various critical and theoretical discourses. Here again, however, pragmatic problems presented themselves.

We were concerned that it might be asking too much of the average La Trobe first-year student, particularly in the early stages, to read significant amounts of literary theory and criticism in addition to the reading of course texts. Lectures would provide exemplification of various approaches, but it would be useful if further brief examples could be used in tutorial discussion. To meet this need we opted for the compromise solution of a book of illustrative excerpts, which would juxtapose examples (or composite examples) of different kinds of readings of course texts—for instance, excerpts of feminist, Marxist, and humanist readings of *The French Lieutenant's Woman*. Such excerpts could readily be prepared and discussed in tutorials and would be supplemented by articles from the Walder collection and course bibliographies. The plan, then, was to "workshop" approaches comparatively in tutorials.

To further assist discussion and assimilation of unfamiliar concepts and movements, we prepared additional handouts. One contains a comprehensive list of terms and concepts that are necessary for literary and cultural studies in the 1990s. The list includes familiar humanist terms—versification, narrative analysis, genre definitions, and much else—together with the vocabulary of the "new theory": critical/theoretical movements, terms deriving from these (gender, discourse, ideology, the unconscious, etc.). Terms generally associated with contemporary theory are asterisked, and students are made aware that literary studies now virtually require two vocabularies (albeit vocabularies that overlap in places). We chose Abrams' *A Glossary of Literary Terms* as a prescribed text for the course because recent editions include both contemporary and more traditional terms. Students are advised to familiarize themselves with Abrams' accounts of the listed terms and concepts. In addition, we prepared definitions of the theoretical terms which are most prominent in the course: literary criticism, literary theory, canon, gender, patriarchy, race, colonialism, humanist and constructivist conceptions of self, ideology, stereotyping, discourse class, sign, signifier, discourse, the unconscious, id, super-ego and repression, race. Definitions are prefaced by commentary drawing attention to the variable ways in which many of these terms are used in critical and theoretical discourse; in some instances definitions incorporate variant usages or construals of terms. So, for example, the entry on ideology distinguishes between a "neutral" or "anthropological" definition—ideology as a systematically connected set of beliefs, assumptions, values, etc., characteristic of a given culture or cultural group—and a "false consciousness" notion of ideology which builds into the first definition notions of exigent hegemonic motivation and alleged processes of naturalization and concealment. Course definitions were circulated to all staff members who were to lecture in the unit (there are five course tutors, all of whom lecture in the course, but other staff members also give lectures). They were asked to alert students to any divergent terminological usages that might occur in their lectures, and to explain to students their reasons for using terms as they do. It was hoped that these measures would help overcome one of the principal difficulties of teaching theory: the bemusing variability of usage, not least, as I have argued, in respect to the term "theory" itself.

A further addition to course support materials that seemed desirable was the provision of model topics and questions (the course was to be assessed on the basis of 50% for the year's work and 50% for the final examination). Since the department had not hitherto attempted to teach theory in any systematic way at first-year level, there would be no earlier examination questions or topic lists from which students could gauge the kinds of skills the course would be likely to reward. We ourselves spent some considerable time trying to decide what forms of competence the course would aim principally to promote. We decided on the following: one, the ability to make an initial and reasonably sophisticated code-cognizant reading of a literary text; two, to grasp and compare methodological options, both in abstraction and in respect of texts; three, to be able to comprehend and, within reasonable limits, to write conceptual and polemical prose; four, to be aware of salient aesthetic, philosophical, and political debates pertaining to literary and cultural studies; five, the capacity for self-reflective examination of one's own training, assumptions, and reading practices; six, the ability— and of course inclination—to make and to argue for assessments among methodological and political options. These priorities in turn suggested a range of assessment modes and tasks: comparison of competing readings of course texts; invitations to self-reflexivity in respect to critical assumptions and reading habits; opportunities to analyze and comment on passages of discursive prose; chances to discuss the treatment of course issues—gender, race, the self—in various texts; encouragement to consider and discuss general course and disciplinary issues; and so on. To give a tangible sense of expectation we prepared a set of sample topics. The list given to students (with accompanying reassurances about incremental increases in the difficulty of assessment tasks) was as follows:

Sample Topics

(i)   Discuss the representation of race relations in Alice Walker's story "Advancing Luna—and Ida B.Wells."

(ii)   What sort of reader are you? Try to reconstruct your reading of a particular text, focusing on the ways in which your background, assumptions, values, and training influenced this reading and the choices you made as you read.

(iii) Passages A and B represent two contrasting ways of reading a Lawrence short story. Compare and contrast the interpretation offered in each of these passages, saying which you consider the most valid and why.

(iv)   Analyze and discuss the arguments presented in the following passage. [Here a short passage of discursive critical/theoretical prose would be provided.]

(v)   Marxists tend to emphasize class struggle and class consciousness in reading texts, and feminists gender ideology and the struggle against patriarchy. But even if you take a relatively simple story, for example Lawrence's "Second Best," it will emerge that each of these approaches overlooks a lot. Do you agree?

(vi)   Bruce Woodcock argues that John Fowles, his character Charles, and ultimately *The French Lieutenant's Woman* as a whole, are in the grip of male anxiety, and that such anxiety generates restrictive forms of fantasy. By contrast, Victoria Tarbox sees Fowles as presenting a free and open narrative. Which view of the author and of the book do you find more convincing?

(vii) If you have a favorite form or school of literary theory/criticism, explain the reasons for your preference. You may wish—but are not required—to refer to a particular literary (or non-literary) text or group of texts during your discussion.

No doubt further kinds of topics will suggest themselves, particularly in respect to literature and other media (film adaptations of course texts and/or other texts by course authors are to be screened throughout the year).

Distilled and expressed in a couple of pages, the course outline for our twenty-six-week, first-year English course looks like this:

FIRST SEMESTER

Week	Lecture	Topic
1	I	**Introduction**
	II	**Three Ways of Reading**
2		Reading for humanist concerns: what is literary humanism?
3		Reading for gender: Alice Walker: "The Abortion"
4		Reading for race and class: Alice Walker: "A Sudden Trip Home in the Spring"
	III	**Class: D.H. Lawrence:** *The Prussian Officer and Other Stories*: **Marxism**
5		Introduction to narrative: A: the short story: Lawrence: "Odour of Chrysanthemums"
6		Ideology, class and literature: Marxism
7		D.H. Lawrence stories: class: "The Daughters of the Vicar," "The White Stocking," "Odour of Chrysanthemums"
	IV	**Gender: John Fowles,** *The French Lieutenant's Woman*: **Feminism**
8		Introduction to narrative: B: the novel (using *The French Lieutenant's Woman*)
9		Gender, patriarchy and literature: Feminism
10		*The French Lieutenant's Woman*: Gender
	V	**Race: Alice Walker,** *You Can't Keep a Good Woman Down*: **Race Criticism and Theory**
11		Race, ideology and literature

In conclusion, I shall give a slightly more detailed account of how a section of the course works in practice—in the classroom—and of initial student response.

III

The module devoted to *The French Lieutenant's Woman* will illustrate conveniently the course's *modus operandi*. As described above, this text is bracketed with the topic gender and the "movement" feminism. The first lecture offers a (necessarily extremely selective) introduction to the novel. After brief reference to definitional preliminaries—the novel's diversity and resistance to stable definition—two interrelated issues are singled out for particular attention. The first is historical and focuses on the existence of competing traditions and conceptions of the novel: realist and metafictive. Discussion of the metaphysical and epistemological trajectories of these traditions/conceptions leads into the second issue: an introduction to salient narratological terms and considerations. Discussion here begins with familiar rhetorical designations for narrative point of view; it then connects these with the earlier account of traditions/conceptions (the roles of self-reflexive narration in realist and metafictive traditions); finally, it links self-reflexivity of the kind that appears in Fowles's novel—a self-reflexivity at once embedded and partially disbelieving in a powerful historical facticity—to the problem of reference and its ideological constraints. Detailed illustration from the novel is offered here. These points are not pursued at this stage. Rather, the problem of reference is taken up in relation to the film adaptation of the novel, which is screened early in the module week.

The second lecture concentrates on definitional matters: gender and patriarchy are explained, and a preliminary account is given of their impact on and application in literary studies. Varieties of feminism are then discussed, as are some of the possible modes of interconnection between feminism(s) and other course perspectives. The third lecture offers an extended account of the text; an account that is oriented towards gender and patriarchy. Issues here include: the novel's account of the historical embeddedness and evolution of conceptions of gender; critical charges of sexual stereotyping in the narrative; the presentation and politics of the Sarah-Charles relationship; the relationship between Sarah and the narrator; the novel's (arguably) ambivalent disposition towards patriarchy and patriarchal narrative modalities.

Tutorials begin by raising questions about areas covered in the lecture. Particular attention is paid to key concepts (sex, gender, patriarchy). Course definitions are used to clarify and consolidate these terms. We then turn to a more general discussion of the text. The aim here is to promote and reflect individual interest and engagement with the work and to elicit areas of interest that may not be accommodated by course objectives and interests. At this point, then, the discussions of the text construe it as illustrative of particular course issues, but not as exhausted by them: the text is presumed to be more complex and diverse than the interpretive strategies we have in mind for it. Suitably "open" engagement with the text will suggest other interpretive angles and perhaps modify or extend the ones with which we begin. The next stage of discussion narrows the focus to particular course discourses: in this case feminist and, to a lesser extent, Marxist. We consider in detail variant feminist readings and inquire how these might relate to interpretations that focus more on the novel's presentation of class. Finally, we use critical extracts—feminist, Marxist, humanist, psychoanalytic—to extend comparative discussion of various "perspectives" on the text. Here we might consider a concept like possessive individualism and the ways in which (say) Marxist, feminist, even humanist critics/theorists of the novel might take it up. Throughout the tutorials on this text more general issues like reference, historiographical narrative, and omniscient narrative strategies are discussed, sometimes with reference to the film adaptation.

As I write, at the conclusion of the first semester of the course's existence, indications of student response are highly favorable. The course easily filled its quota of 150, retention rates have been high, and responses to a survey form circulated in the final lecture of the semester were satisfying. Because a more detailed survey is to be done towards the end of the year, this one was brief. It asks students to indicate by ticking a box whether they found the course to date "very good," "satisfactory," or "disappointing." They were also given a section in which to record any criticisms of the unit, and another in which they could note positive features of the course. About two thirds of the group responded. Of these, 61% reckoned the course "very good," 35% "satisfactory," and 4% "disappointing." The written comments were generally very favorable. Respondents were particularly enthusiastic about the introductions offered to various critical/theoretical perspectives, and about course signposting and texts. Virtually all criticisms related not to course objectives and strategies, but to particular instances in which the execution of these objectives had seemed inadequate: lectures that were inadequately organized or too technical, or that failed sufficiently to relate critical/theoretical perspectives to particular texts, or that did not offer sufficiently clear explanations of key concepts.

The staff teaching the course have generally been pleased with its performance. Tutorial discussion is of course stronger in some groups then others, but has in most cases been lively and engaged. Most students are coping adequately or better with the course. Some are producing truly outstanding first-year work. There are two principal areas of concern: first, that it takes constant repetition of even basic concepts like gender and ideology to achieve any degree of confident understanding, and even after such repetition confusion persists among more limited students; second, this kind of course highlights what has in many instances been inadequate training in basic expository and discursive skills. Some students who are able at the outset of the unit to write a reasonably literate, if limited, essay of a more conventional text-based high school kind, have had great difficulty writing coherent text-based essays on topics requiring discussion of critical, theoretical, or political issues. The pressure of unfamiliar conceptual demands has in these cases caused a marked deterioration in the standard of written expression and organization. But in general the course to date seems to have been rewarding for staff and students alike.

Notes

1. See, for example, Terry Eagleton, *Literary Theory: An Introduction* (Oxford: Blackwell, 1983), p. 198.

2. For present purposes it is only necessary and possible to represent a position such as this, and its accompanying arguments, in brief outline. For a more detailed account see Richard Freadman and Seumas Miller, *Rethinking Theory: A Critique of Contemporary Literary Theory and an Alternative Account* (Cambridge: Cambridge University Press, 1992).

3. Wayne C. Booth, *Critical Understanding: The Powers and Limits of Pluralism* (Chicago: University of Chicago Press, 1979).

4. Booth, "Pluralism in the Classroom," *Critical Inquiry*, 12:3 (1986), p. 473.

5. Ellen Rooney, *Seductive Reasoning: Pluralism as the Problematic in Contemporary Literary Theory* (Ithaca: Cornell University Press, 1989).

6. Bruce Erlich, "Amphibolies: On the Critical Self-Contradictions of 'Pluralism,'" *Critical Inquiry*, 12:3 (1986), pp. 521–48.

7. Booth, *Critical Understanding*, p. 201.

8. W.J.T. Mitchell, "Pluralism as Dogmatism," *Critical Inquiry*, 12:3 (1986), p. 497.

9. Herbert Marcuse, *Eros and Civilization* (London: Abacus, 1972).

10. Gerald Graff, "The Future of Theory in the Teaching of Literature," in Ralph Cohen, ed., *The Future of Theory* (New York: Routledge, 1989), p. 261.

11. Graff, p. 263.

12. Graff, p. 251.

13. Booth, "Pluralism in the Classroom," p. 474.

14. Details of the secondary works cited are: Raman Selden, *A Reader's Guide to Contemporary Literary Theory* (Brighton: Harvester, 1985); Dennis Walder, ed., *Literature in the Modern World: Critical Essays and Documents* (New York: Oxford University Press, 1991); and M.H. Abrams, *A Glossary of Literary Terms*, 5th ed. (New York: Holt, Rinehart & Winston, 1988).

Select Bibliography

Abrams, M.H. *A Glossary of Literary Terms*. 5th ed. New York: Holt, Rinehart & Winston, 1988.

———. *Natural Supernaturalism: Tradition and Revolution in Romantic Literature*. New York: Norton, 1971.

Adam, Ian, and Helen Tiffin, eds. *Past the Last Post: Theorizing Post-Colonialism and Post-Modernism*. London: Harvester, 1991.

Aers, Lesley, and Nigel Wheale. *Shakespeare in the Changing Curriculum*. London: Routledge, 1991.

Alter, Robert. *The Pleasures of Reading in an Ideological Age*. New York: Simon & Schuster, 1989.

Ashcroft, Bill, Gareth Griffiths, and Helen Tiffin. *The Empire Writes Back: Theory and Practice in Post-Colonial Literatures*. New York: Routledge, 1989.

Atkins, G. Douglas, and Michael L. Johnson, eds. *Writing and Reading Differently: Deconstruction and the Teaching of Composition and Literature*. Lawrence: University of Kansas Press, 1985.

Baker, H.A. *Reading Blake: Essays in the Criticism of African, Caribbean and Black American Literature*. Ithaca: Cornell University Press, 1976.

Bakhtin, Mikhail. *The Dialogic Imagination*. Ed. Michael Holquist. Trans. Caryl Emerson and Michael Holquist. Austin: University of Texas Press, 1981.

———. *Problems in Dostoevsky's Poetics*. Trans. Caryl Emerson; intro. Wayne C. Booth. Minneapolis: University of Minnesota Press, 1984.

———. *Rabelais and His World*. Trans. Hélene Iswolsky. Cambridge: MIT Press, 1968.

———. *Speech Genres and Other Late Essays.* Trans. Vern W. McGee. Austin: University of Texas Press, 1981.

Bal, Mieke. *Lethal Love: Feminist Literary Readings of Biblical Love Stories.* Bloomington: University of Indiana Press, 1987.

———. *Narratology: Introduction to the Theory of Narrative.* Trans. C. van Boheemen. Toronto: University of Toronto Press, 1983.

———. *On Story Telling: Essays in Narratology.* Sonoma, CA: Polebridge Press, 1991.

———. *Reading Rembrandt: Beyond the Word Image Opposition.* Cambridge: Cambridge University Press, 1992.

Barker, Francis A., et al., eds. *Europe and Its Others.* Colchester: University of Essex Press, 1985.

Barthes, Roland. *Image, Music, Text.* Trans. Stephen Heath. New York: Hill & Wang, 1977.

———. *Mythologies.* Trans. Richard Miller. London: Jonathan Cape, 1972.

———. *On Racine.* Trans. Richard Howard. New York: Performing Arts Journal Publications, 1983.

———. *The Pleasures of the Text.* Trans. Richard Miller. New York: Hill & Wang, 1973.

———. *Roland Barthes.* Trans. Richard Howard. New York: Hill & Wang, 1970.

———. *S/Z.* Trans. Richard Miller. New York: Hill & Wang, 1974.

Batsleer, Janet, Tony Davies, Rebecca O'Rourke, and Chris Weedon. *Rewriting English: Cultural Politics of Gender and Class.* London: Methuen, 1985.

Bell, Roseann P. *Sturdy Black Bridge: Visions of Black Women in Literature.* New York: Anchor, 1972.

Belsey, Catherine. *Critical Practice.* London: Methuen, 1980.

———. *John Milton: Language, Gender, Power.* Oxford: Blackwell, 1988.

———. *The Subject of Tragedy.* London: Methuen, 1985.

Bennett, Tony. *Formalism and Marxism.* London: Methuen, 1979.

Berger, John. *Ways of Seeing.* Harmondsworth: Penguin, 1971.

Bhabha, Homi K. *The Location of Culture.* London: Routledge, 1994.

———, ed. *Nation and Narration.* London: Routledge, 1990

Blackburn, Robin, ed. *After the Fall: The Failure of Communism and the Future of Socialism.* New York: Verso, 1991.

Bloom, Harold. *The Anxiety of Influence: A Theory of Poetry.* New York: Oxford University Press, 1973.

——, ed. *Deconstruction and Criticism.* New York: Continuum, 1980.

——. *A Map of Misreading.* New York: Oxford University Press, 1975.

Bonnycastle, Stephen. *In Search of Authority: An Introductory Guide to Literary Theory.* Peterborough: Broadview, 1991.

Booth, Wayne C. *Critical Understanding: The Powers and Limits of Pluralism.* Chicago: University of Chicago Press, 1979.

Bourdieu, Pierre, and Jean-Claude Passeron. *Reproduction in Education, Society, and Culture.* Trans. R. Nice. London: Sage Publications, 1977.

Bowie, Malcolm. *Freud, Proust and Lacan: Theory as Fiction.* Cambridge: Cambridge University Press, 1987.

Brewster, Anne. *Towards a Semiotic of Post-Colonial Discourse.* Singapore: National University Press, 1989.

Brooks, Cleanth. *The Well Wrought Urn: Studies in the Structure of Poetry.* 1949; New York: Harcourt, 1975.

Buchbinder, David. *Contemporary Literary Theory and the Reading of Poetry.* Melbourne: Macmillan, 1991.

Budick, Sanford, and Wolfgang Iser, eds. *Languages of the Unsayable: The Play of Negativity in Literature and Literary Theory.* New York: Columbia University Press, 1989.

Butler, Johnnella E., and John C. Walter, eds. *Transforming the Curriculum: Ethnic Studies and Women's Studies.* Albany: State University of New York Press, 1991.

Carroll, David. *The Subject in Question: The Languages of Theory and the Strategies of Fiction.* Chicago: University of Chicago Press, 1982.

Carter, Paul. *The Road to Botany Bay. An Essay in Spatial History.* London: Faber & Faber, 1987.

Chatman, Seymour. *Story and Discourse: Narrative Structures in Fiction and Film.* Ithaca: Cornell University Press, 1978.

Cohen, Ralph, ed. *The Future of Literary Theory.* New York: Routledge, 1989.

Craige, Betty Jean, ed. *Literature, Language and Politics*. Athens: University of Georgia Press, 1988.

Crane, R.S. *The Idea of the Humanities and Other Essays Critical and Historical*. Chicago: University of Chicago Press, 1967.

Crews, Frederick. *Skeptical Engagements*. New York: Oxford University Press, 1986.

Culler, Jonathan. *On Deconstruction: Theory and Criticism after Structuralism*. Ithaca: Cornell University Press, 1983.

————. *The Pursuit of Signs: Semiotics, Literature, Deconstruction*. London: Routledge, 1981.

————. *Structuralist Poetics: Structuralism, Linguistics, and the Study of Literature*. Ithaca: Cornell University Press, 1975.

de Man, Paul. *Blindness and Insight: Essays in the Rhetoric of Contemporary Criticism*. 2nd ed. Minneapolis: University of Minnesota Press, 1983.

————. *The Resistance to Theory*. Minneapolis: University of Minnesota Press, 1986.

Deleuze, Gilles, and Felix Guattari. *Anti-Oedipus: Capitalism and Schizophrenia*. Trans. Robert Hurley. Minneapolis: University of Minnesota Press, 1983.

Derrida, Jacques. *Of Grammatology*. Trans. Gayatri Chakravorti Spivak. Baltimore: Johns Hopkins University Press, 1976.

————. *Writing and Difference*. Trans. Alan Bass. London: Routledge, 1978.

Doty, William G. *Mythography: The Study of Myths and Rituals*. Tuscaloosa: University of Alabama Press, 1986.

Drakakis, John, ed. *Alternative Shakespeares*. London: Methuen, 1985.

Dreyfus, Hubert L., and Paul Rebinow. *Michel Foucault: Beyond Structuralism and Hermeneutics*. Brighton: Harvester, 1982.

Driscoll, James P. *The Unfolding God of Jung and Milton*. Lexington: University Press of Kentucky, 1993.

Eagleton, Terry. *Ideology: An Introduction*. New York: Verso, 1991.

————. *Literary Theory: An Introduction*. Oxford: Blackwell, 1983.

————. *Myths of Power: A Marxist Study of the Brontës*. London: Macmillan, 1975.

————. *The Rape of Clarissa*. Oxford: Blackwell, 1982.

———. *William Shakespeare*. Oxford: Blackwell, 1986.

Easthope, Antony. *British Post-Structuralism*. London: Routledge, 1988.

Eco, Umberto, Richard Rorty, Johnathan Culler, and Christine Brooke-Rose. *Interpretation and Overinterpretation*. Ed. Stefan Collini. Cambridge: Cambridge University Press, 1992.

Ellis, John M. *Against Deconstruction*. Princeton: Princeton University Press, 1989.

Engell, James, and David Perkins, eds. *Teaching Literature: What Is Needed Now*. Cambridge: Harvard University Press, 1988.

Felski, Rita. *Beyond Feminist Aesthetics: Feminist Literature and Social Change*. Cambridge: Harvard University Press, 1989.

Fish, Stanley E. *Is There a Text in This Class? The Authority of Interpretive Communities*. Cambridge: Harvard University Press, 1980.

———. *Surprised by Sin: The Reader in Paradise Lost*. New York: St. Martin's Press, 1967.

Fisher, Dexter, and Robert B. Stepto, eds. *Afro-American Literature: The Reconstruction of Instruction*. New York: Modern Language Association, 1979.

Foucault, Michel. *Discipline and Punish: The Birth of the Prison*. Trans. Alan Sheridan. New York: Pantheon, 1977.

———. *The History of Sexuality: An Introduction*. Trans. Robert Hurley. New York: Random House, 1978.

———. *Madness and Civilization: A History of Insanity in the Age of Reason*. Trans. Richard Howard. New York: Pantheon, 1965.

———. *The Order of Things: An Archaeology of the Human Sciences*. Trans. A.M. Sheridan. London: Tavistock, 1966.

Fowler, Roger, ed. *A Dictionary of Modern Critical Terms*. London: Routledge, 1973.

———. *Literature as Social Discourse: The Practice of Linguistic Criticism*. London: Batsford, 1981.

Freud, Sigmund. *Introductory Lectures on Psychoanalysis*. Trans. James Strachey. Harmondsworth: Penguin, 1973.

———. *Jokes and Their Relation to the Unconscious*. Trans. James Strachey. Harmondsworth: Penguin, 1976.

———. *The Standard Edition of the Complete Psychological Works*. Ed. James Strachey. 24 vols. London: Hogarth Press, 1953–1975.

Fritschi, Gerhard. *Africa and Gutenberg: Exploring Oral Structures in the Modern African Novel.* New York: Peter Lang, 1983.

Frye, Northrop. *Anatomy of Criticism.* Princeton: Princeton University Press, 1957.

———. *The Great Code: The Bible and Literature.* New York: Harcourt Brace, 1983.

———. *The Return of Eden: Five Essays on Milton's Epics.* Toronto: University of Toronto Press, 1965.

Gates, Henry Louis, Jr., ed. *Black Literature and Literary Theory.* London: Methuen, 1984.

———. *"Race," Writing and Difference.* Chicago: University of Chicago Press, 1986.

———. *The Signifying Monkey: A Theory of African-American Literary Criticism.* New York: Oxford University Press, 1988.

Genette, Gérard. *Narrative Discourse: An Essay in Method.* Trans. Jane E. Lewin. Ithaca: Cornell University Press, 1980.

Gilbert, Sandra M., and Susan Gubar. *The Madwoman in the Attic: The Woman Writer and the Nineteenth-Century Literary Imagination.* New Haven: Yale University Press, 1979.

———, eds. *Shakespeare's Sisters: Feminist Essays on Women Poets.* Bloomington: Indiana University Press, 1979.

Goodheart, Eugene. *The Skeptical Disposition in Contemporary Criticism.* Princeton: Princeton University Press, 1984.

Grady, Hugh. *The Modernist Shakespeare.* Oxford: Clarendon Press, 1991.

Graff, Gerald. *Beyond the Culture Wars: How Teaching the Conflicts Can Revitalize American Education.* New York: Norton, 1992.

———. *Literature Against Itself: Literary Ideas in Modern Society.* Chicago: University of Chicago Press, 1979.

———. *Professing Literature: An Institutional History.* Chicago: University of Chicago Press, 1987.

———, and Reginal Gibbons, eds. *Criticism in the University.* Evanston: Northwestern University Press, 1985.

Greenblatt, Stephen. *Renaissance Self-Fashioning: From More to Shakespeare.* Chicago: University of Chicago Press, 1980.

Griffiths, Gareth. *A Double Exile: African and West Indian Writing Between Two Cultures.* London: Boyars, 1978.

Grosz, Elizabeth. *Jacques Lacan: A Feminist Introduction.* Sydney: Allen & Unwin, 1990.

Gugelberger, Georg M., ed. *Marxism and African Literature.* London: James Currey, 1985.

Gunn, Daniel. *Psychoanalysis and Fiction: An Exploration of Literary and Psycho-analytic Borders.* Cambridge: Cambridge University Press, 1988.

Hall, James W., and Barbara L. Kelves, eds. *Opposition to Core Curriculum: Alternative Modes of Undergraduate Education.* Westport, CT: Greenwood, 1982.

Handelman, Susan A. *Slayers of Moses: The Emergence of Rabbinic Interpretation in Modern Literary Theory.* Albany: State University of New York Press, 1982.

Harari, Josué V., ed. *Textual Strategies: Perspectives in Post-Structuralist Criticism.* Ithaca: Cornell University Press, 1979.

Harris, Wilson. *The Womb of Space: The Cross-Cultural Imagination.* Westport, CT: Greenwood, 1983.

Hart, Kevin. *The Trespass of the Sign: Deconstruction, Theology and Philosophy.* Cambridge: Cambridge University Press, 1989.

Hartman, Geoffrey H. *Criticism in the Wilderness: The Study of Literature Today.* New Haven: Yale University Press, 1980.

———, ed. *Deconstruction and Criticism.* London: Routledge, 1979.

———. *Psychoanalysis and the Question of the Text: Selected Papers from the English Institute, 1976–77.* Baltimore: Johns Hopkins University Press, 1978.

———. *Saving the Text: Literature, Derrida, Philosophy.* Baltimore: Johns Hopkins University Press, 1982.

Hawthorn, Jeremy. *A Concise Glossary of Contemporary Literary Theory.* London: Arnold, 1992.

———. *Unlocking the Text.* London: Arnold, 1987.

Henricksen, Bruce, and Thaïs E. Morgan, eds. *Reorientations: Critical Theories and Pedagogies.* Urbana: University of Illinois Press, 1990.

Hill, Christopher. *Milton and the English Revolution.* London: Faber, 1977.

———. *The World Turned Upside Down: Radical Ideas During the English Revolution.* Harmondsworth: Penguin, 1975.

Hirsch, E.D., Jr. *Cultural Literacy: What Every American Needs to Know.* Boston: Houghton Mifflin, 1987.

————. *Validity in Interpretation.* New Haven: Yale University Press, 1967.

Holderness, Graham, ed. *The Shakespeare Myth.* Manchester: Manchester University Press, 1988.

Holland, Norman N. *The Dynamics of Literary Response.* New York: Oxford University Press, 1968.

————. *5 Readers Reading.* New Haven: Yale University Press, 1975.

Holub, Robert C. *Reception Theory: A Critical Introduction.* London: Methuen, 1984.

Hull, Gloria T., Patricia Bell Scott, and Barbara Smith. *All the Women Are White, All the Blacks Are Men, But Some of Us Are Brave: Black Women's Studies.* Old Westbury: Feminist Press, 1982.

Humm, Peter, Paul Stigant, and Peter Widowson, eds. *Popular Fictions: Essays in Literature and History.* London: Methuen, 1986.

Hutcheon, Linda. *Narcissistic Narrative: The Metafictional Paradox.* London: Methuen, 1984.

————. *A Poetics of Postmodernism: History, Theory, Fiction.* New York: Routledge, 1988.

Irigaray, Luce. *The Sex Which Is Not One.* Trans. Catherine Porter. Ithaca: Cornell University Press, 1985.

Iser, Wolfgang. *The Act of Reading: A Theory of Aesthetic Response.* Baltimore: Johns Hopkins University Press, 1978.

————. *The Implied Reader: Patterns of Communication in Prose Fiction from Bunyan to Beckett.* Baltimore: Johns Hopkins University Press, 1974.

Jackson, Rosemary. *Fantasy: The Literature of Subversion.* London: Methuen, 1981.

Jameson, Frederic. *Marxism and Form: Twentienth Century Dialectical Theories of Literature.* Princeton: Princeton University Press, 1971.

————. *The Political Unconscious: Narrative as a Socially Symbolic Act.* New York: Cornell University Press, 1981.

————. *The Prison House of Language: A Critical Account of Structuralism and Russian Formalism.* Princeton: Princeton University Press, 1972.

JanMohammed, Abdul. *Manichean Aesthetics in the Politics of Literature in Colonial Africa.* Amherst: University of Massachusetts Press, 1983.

Jefferson, Ann, and David Robey, eds. *Modern Literary Theory: A Comparative Introduction.* London: Batsford, 1982.

Johnson, Barbara. *The Critical Difference: Essays in the Contemporary Rhetoric of Reading.* Baltimore: Johns Hopkins University Press, 1980.

————. *A World of Difference.* Baltimore: Johns Hopkins University Press, 1987.

Johnson, Robert A. *We: Understanding the Psychology of Romantic Love.* New York: Harper & Row, 1983.

Kandinsky, Wassily. *Concerning the Spiritual in Art.* Trans. M.T.H. Sadler. New York: Dover, 1977.

Kavanagh, Thomas M., ed. *The Limits of Theory.* Stanford: Stanford University Press, 1989.

Kermode, Frank. *The Genesis of Secrecy: On the Interpretation of Narrative.* Cambridge: Harvard University Press, 1979.

————. *The Sense of an Ending: Studies in the Theory of Fiction.* New York: Oxford University Press, 1966.

Kerrigan, William. *The Sacred Complex: On the Psycho-Genesis of Paradise Lost.* Cambridge: Harvard University Press, 1983.

Krieger, Murray. *Northrop Frye in Modern Criticism.* New York: Columbia University Press, 1961.

Kristeva, Julia. *About Chinese Women.* Trans. Anita Barrows. London: Boyars, 1986.

————. *Desire in Language: A Semiotic Approach to Literature and Art.* New York: Columbia University Press, 1981.

————. *The Kristeva Reader.* Ed. Toril Moi. New York: Columbia University Press, 1986.

Kuhn, Thomas S. *The Structure of Scientific Revolutions.* Chicago: University of Chicago Press, 1962.

Lacan, Jacques. *Écrits: A Selection.* Trans. Alan Sheridan. New York: Norton, 1977.

———— *The Four Fundamental Concepts of Psycho-Analysis.* Ed. Jacques-Alain Miller. Trans. Alan Sheridan. New York: Norton, 1978.

Leavis, F.R. *Education and the University: A Sketch for an "English School."* London: Chatto & Windus, 1943.

———. *Revaluation: Tradition and Development in English Poetry.* London: Chatto & Windus, 1936.

———, and Denys Thompson. *Culture and Environment: The Training of Critical Awareness.* London: Chatto & Windus, 1933.

Lemon, Lee T., and Marion J. Rees, eds. *Russian Formalist Criticism: Four Essays.* Lincoln: University of Nebraska Press, 1965.

Lentriccia, Frank. *After the New Criticism.* London: Methuen, 1980.

Literary Theory in the Classroom. A special issue of *College Literature,* 18.2 (1991).

Lodge, David. *After Bakhtin: Essays on Fiction and Criticism.* New York: Routledge, 1990.

———. *The Language of Fiction: Essays in Criticism and Verbal Analysis of the English Novel.* London: Routledge, 1984.

———, ed. *Modern Criticism and Theory.* London: Longman, 1988.

———. *The Modes of Modern Writing: Metaphor, Metonymy and the Typology of Modern Literature.* London: Arnold, 1977.

———, ed. *Twentieth Century Literary Criticism.* London: Longman, 1972.

———. *Working with Structuralism.* London: Ark, 1988.

Lukács, Georg. *Studies in European Realism.* Intro. Alfred Kazan. New York: Grosset & Dunlap, 1964.

Lyotard, Jean-François. *The Postmodern Condition: A Report on Knowledge.* Trans. G. Bennington and B. Massumi. Manchester: Manchester University Press, 1979.

MacCannell, Juliet F. *Figuring Lacan: Criticism and the Cultural Unconscious.* Lincoln: University of Nebraska Press, 1986.

McCormick, Kathleen, Garry Waller, and Linda Flower, eds. *Reading Texts: Reading, Responding, Writing.* Lexington: Heath, 1987.

McHale, Brian. *Postmodernist Fiction.* New York: Routledge, 1989.

Macherey, Pierre. *A Theory of Literary Production.* Trans. Geoffrey Wall. New York: Routledge, 1978.

Maclean, Marie. *Narrative as Performance: The Baudelairean Experiment.* London: Routledge, 1988.

Mahood, M.M. *The Colonial Encounter.* London: Rex Collings, 1977.

Mannoni, O. *Prospero and Caliban: The Psychology of Colonizations.* New York: Praeger, 1964.

Marshall, Brenda K. *Teaching the Postmodern: Fiction and Theory.* New York: Routledge, 1992.

Martindale, Colin. *The Clockwork Muse: The Predictability of Artistic Change.* New York: Basic Books, 1990.

———. *Romantic Progression: The Psychology of Literary History.* Washington: Hemisphere, 1975.

Matejka, Ladislav, and Krystyna Pomorska, eds. *Readings in Russian Poetics: Formalist and Structuralist Views.* Cambridge: MIT Press, 1971.

———, and Irwin R. Titunik, eds. *Semiotics of Art.* Cambridge: MIT Press, 1976.

Mellard, James M. *Using Lacan Reading Fiction.* Urbana: University of Illinois Press, 1991.

Merquior, J.G. *Foucault.* London: Fontana/Collins, 1985.

Metz, Christian. *The Imaginary Signifier: Psychoanalysis and the Cinema.* Trans. Celia Brilton, Annwyl Williams, Ben Brewster, and Alfred Guzzetti. Bloomington: Indiana University Press, 1982.

Miller, J. Hillis. *The Ethics of Reading.* New York: Columbia University Press, 1989.

———. *Fiction and Repetition.* Cambridge: Harvard University Press, 1982.

Miller, James. *The Passion of Michel Foucault.* London: Harper Collins, 1993.

Miller, Seumas. *Rethinking Theory: A Critique of Contemporary Literary Theory and an Alternative Account.* Cambridge: Cambridge University Press, 1992.

Mitchell, W.J.T. *Against Theory: Literary Studies and the New Pragmatism.* Chicago: University of Chicago Press, 1985.

———, ed. *On Narrative.* Chicago: University of Chicago Press, 1980.

Moi, Toril, ed. *Sexual/Textual Politics: Feminist Literary Theory.* London: Methuen, 1985.

Moore, Stephen D. *Literary Criticism and the Gospels: The Theoretical Challenge.* New Haven: Yale University Press, 1989.

Moretti, Franco. *Signs Taken for Wonders.* London: Verso, 1983.

Mukherjee, Meenakshi. *The Twice-Born Fiction*. New Delhi & London: Heinemann, 1971.

Mulhern, Francis. *The Moment of Scrutiny*. London: Verso, 1981.

Mulvaney, D.J., ed. *The Humanities and the Australian Environment*. Canberra: Australian Academy of the Humanities, 1991.

Narogin, Mudrooroo. *Writing from the Fringe: A Study of Modern Aboriginal Literature*. Melbourne: Hyland House, 1990.

Nazareth, Peter. *Literature and Society in Modern Africa*. Nairobi: East Africa Literature Bureau, 1972.

Nelson, Cary, ed. *Theory in the Classroom*. Urbana: University of Illinois Press, 1986.

Nelson, Emmanuel S. *Reworlding: The Literature of the Indian Diaspora*. New York: Greenwood, 1992.

Newman, Charles. *The Post-Modern Aura: The Act of Fiction in an Age of Inflation*. Evanston: Northwestern University Press, 1985.

Newton, K.M. *Interpreting the Text: A Critical Introduction to the Theory and Practice of Literary Interpretation*. New York: St. Martin's Press, 1990.

———. *Twentienth-Century Literary Theory: A Reader*. Basingstoke: Macmillan, 1988.

Ngugi wa Thiong'o. *Decolonizing the Mind: The Politics of Language in African Literature*. London: Currey, 1986.

Norris, Christopher. *The Contest of Faculties: Philosophy and Theory After Deconstruction*. New York: Methuen, 1985.

———. *Deconstruction: Theory and Practice*. London: Methuen, 1982.

———. *Derrida*. London: Harper Collins, 1987.

———. *Paul de Man: Deconstruction and the Critique of Aesthetic Ideology*. New York: Routledge, 1988.

———, and Andrew Benjamin. *What Is Deconstruction?* New York: St. Martin's Press, 1988.

Ong, Walter J. *Orality and Literacy: The Technologizing of the Word*. London: Routledge, 1982.

Parrinder, Patrick. *The Failure of Theory: Essays on Criticism and Contemporary Fiction*. Brighton: Harvester, 1987.

Passmore, John. *The Philosophy of Teaching*. Cambridge: Harvard University Press, 1980.

The Politics of Teaching Literature. A double issue of *College Literature,* 17.2/3 (1990).

Pratt, Mary Louise. *Imperial Eyes: Travel Writing and Transculturation.* New York: Routledge, 1992.

Prawer, S.S. *Karl Marx and World Literature.* Oxford: Oxford University Press, 1976.

Propp, Vladimir. *The Theory and History of Foiklore.* Ed. Anatoly Liberman. Trans. Ariadna Y. Martin and Richard P. Martin. Minneapolis: University of Minnesota Press, 1984.

Rice, Philip, and Patricia Waugh, eds. *Modern Literary Theory: A Reader.* London: Arnold, 1989.

Richards, I.A. *Principles of Literary Criticism.* London: Routledge, 1926.

————. *Practical Criticism: A Study of Literary Judgement.* London: Routledge, 1929.

Ricoeur, Paul. *Freud and Philosophy: An Essay on Interpretation.* Trans. Denis Savage. New Haven: Yale University Press, 1970.

Rimmon-Kenan, Shlomith. *Narrative Fiction: Contemporary Poetics.* London: Methuen, 1983.

Ruthven, K.K. *Feminist Literary Studies: An Introduction.* Cambridge: Cambridge University Press, 1984.

————, ed. *Beyond the Disciplines: The New Humanities.* Canberra: Australian Academy of the Humanities, 1992.

Rylance, Rick, ed. *Debating Texts: Twentienth-Century Literary Theory and Method.* Toronto: University of Toronto Press, 1987.

Said, Edward W. *Culture and Imperialism.* London: Chatto & Windus, 1993.

————. *Orientalism: Western Conceptions of the Orient.* New York: Routledge, 1978.

————. *The World, the Text and the Critic.* London: Faber, 1984.

Salusinszky, Imre. *Criticism in Society.* New York: Methuen, 1987.

Saunders, Ian. *Open Texts, Partial Maps: A Literary Theory Handbook.* Nedlands: Centre for Studies in Australian Literature, University of Western Australia, 1993.

Saussure, Ferdinand de. *Course in General Linguistics.* Trans. Roy Harris. London: Duckworth, 1983.

Scholes, Robert. *Structuralism in Literature: An Introduction.* New Haven: Yale University Press, 1974.

———. *Textual Power: Literary Theory and the Teaching of English.* New Haven: Yale University Press, 1985.

Sedgwick, Eve Kosofsky. *Epistemology of the Closet.* Berkeley: University of California Press, 1990.

Selden, Raman. *A Reader's Guide to Contemporary Literary Theory.* Lexington: University Press of Kentucky, 1985.

———. *The Theory of Criticism from Plato to the Present.* London: 1988.

Showalter, Elaine. *A Literature of Their Own: British Women Novelists from Brontë to Lessing.* London: Virago, 1978.

———, ed. *Feminist Criticism: Essays on Women, Literature and Theory.* New York: Pantheon, 1985.

Silverman, Kaja. *The Subject of Semiotics.* Oxford: Blackwell, 1983.

Simonton, Dean K. *Genius, Creativity and Leadership: Historimetric Inquiries.* Cambridge: Harvard University Press, 1984.

Sinfield, Alan. *Literature, Politics and Culture in Postwar Britain.* Oxford: Blackwell, 1989.

Slemon, Stephen, and Helen Tiffin, eds. *After Europe: Critical Theory and Post-Colonial Writing.* Sydney: Dangaroo, 1989.

Sontag, Susan. *Against Interpretation and Other Essays.* New York: Delta, 1961.

Spivak, Gayatri Chakravorty. *In Other Worlds: Essays in Cultural Politics.* New York: Routledge, 1988.

Sturrock, John, ed. *Structuralism and Since: From Lévi-Strauss to Derrida.* Oxford University Press, 1979.

Suleiman, Susan R., and Inge C. Crossman, eds. *The Reader in the Text: Essays on Audience and Interpretation.* Princeton: Princeton University Press, 1980.

Summers, Anne. *Damned Whores and God's Police: The Colonization of Women in Australia.* Harmondsworth: Penguin, 1975.

Tallack, Douglas, ed. *Literary Theory at Work: Three Texts.* London: Batsford, 1987.

Teaching Postcolonial and Commonwealth Literatures. A special double issue of *College Literature,* 19.3 (1992)/20.1 (1993).

Thornton, E.M. *The Freudian Fallacy: Freud and Cocaine.* London: Paladin, 1986.

Todorov, Tzvetan. *The Conquest of America: The Question of the Other.* Trans. Richard Howard. London: Harper & Row, 1984.

———. *The Conquest of the Other.* Trans. Richard Howard. New York: Harper, 1982.

———. *The Fantastic: A Structural Approach to a Literary Œuvre.* Trans. Richard Howard. Ithaca: Cornell University Press, 1975.

———. *Introduction to Poetics.* Trans. Richard Howard. Brighton: Harvester, 1981.

———. *The Poetics of Prose.* Trans. Richard Howard. Ithaca: Cornell University Press, 1977.

Tompkins, Jane P., ed. *Reader-Response Criticism: From Formalism to Post-Structuralism.* Baltimore: Johns Hopkins University Press, 1980.

Tong, Rosemarie. *Feminist Thought: A Comprehensive Introduction.* London: Unwin Hyman, 1989.

Trotsky, Leon. *Literature and Revolution.* Trans. Rose Strunsky. Ann Arbor: University of Michigan Press, 1960.

Ulmer, Gregory L. *Applied Grammatology: Post(e)-Pedagogy from Jacques Derrida to Joseph Beuys.* Baltimore: Johns Hopkins University Press, 1985.

Vance, Eugene. *From Topic to Tale: Logic and Narrativity in the Middle Ages.* Minneapolis: University of Minnesota Press, 1989.

———. *Mervelous Signals: Poetics and Sign Theory in the Middle Ages.* Lincoln: University of Nebraska Press, 1986.

Veeser, H. Aram, ed. *The New Historicism.* New York: Routledge, 1989.

White, Hayden. *Metahistory: The Historical Imagination in Nineteenth Century Europe.* Baltimore: Johns Hopkins University Press, 1973.

———. *Tropics of Discourse: Essays in Cultural Criticism.* Baltimore: Johns Hopkins University Press, 1973.

Whitlock, Gillian, and Helen Tiffin, eds. *Re-Siting Queen's English: Text and Tradition in Post-Colonial Literatures.* Atlanta: Rodopi, 1992.

Widdowson, Peter, ed. *Re-Reading English.* London: Methuen, 1982.

Williams, Raymond. *The Country and the City*. London: Granada, 1973.

———. *Marxism and Literature*. Oxford: Oxford University Press, 1977.

Williamson, Judith. *Decoding Advertisements: Ideology and Meaning in Advertising*. London: Boyars, 1978.

Wilson, R. Rawdon. *In Palamedes' Shadow: Explorations in Play, Game and Narrative Theory*, Boston: Northeastern University Press, 1990.

Wright, Elizabeth. *Psychoanalytic Criticism: Theory and Practice*. London: Methuen, 1984.

Young, Robert, ed. *Untying the Text: A Post-Structuralist Reader*. London: Routledge, 1981.

Index